MEDIEVAL PAINTING

A HISTORY OF EUROPEAN PAINTING

MEDIEVAL PAINTING

Text by
LUISA MARCUCCI
of the Uffizi Gallery, Florence
and
EMMA MICHELETTI
of the Accademia Gallery, Florence

A STUDIO BOOK

THE VIKING PRESS, NEW YORK

translated by

H. E. SCOTT

Original title: LA PITTURA IN EUROPA

Published in London by Studio Books (Longacre Press Ltd), 161 Fleet St
and in New York by The Viking Press, Inc., 625 Madison Avenue.
Printed in Italy by Fabbristampa

CONTENTS

FROM THE FOURTH TO THE THIRTEENTH CENTURIES

In the early centuries of Christianity there was no distinctive style of Christian art. Christianity spread through a world of ancient civilisation, steeped in Mediterranean and especially in Graeco-Roman culture, and the art forms already established in this world continued in use. The art of the new religion was in its origins pagan both in technique and in form. Content was another matter although at times, when pagan subjects could be divested of their original meaning and given a new symbolic significance, they too were adopted by Christians. So there developed a style of painting based on the use of symbols and emblems, in which Christ might be represented by a fish, and a dove became the symbol of the soul in a state of innocence. This system was widely used, not only for single subjects, but even for complex stories derived from the old myths such as the legend of Psyche, which came to mean the struggle of the human soul to reach Heaven. Until Christianity received Imperial recognition, symbols were a necessary device; they were used above all in the catacombs, and are more commonly found in the Graeco-Latin world than in the East, either because of the type of civilisation already established in the Mediterranean, or because the Western, and especially the Latin mind, prefers to express itself realistically. The forms used were always taken from real life even when their meaning was symbolic.

There was, then, no formal break in style or method of expression between pagan and Christian art in the early centuries of the new era, and we cannot speak of Christian painting, if by that we mean a style of art which truly expresses a new conception of either earthly or spiritual life. The most we can say is that there were paintings by artists who were Christians. New subjects were selected from the Testaments, but methods of expression remained unchanged, and symbolic meanings were given to new themes (for example, " Noah Emerging from the Ark " signified the soul's achievement of peace). When removed from their historical and human settings the pictorial effectiveness of these new subjects was very limited.

Yet there is no lack of poetry in the catacomb paintings. It is to be found in the freshness and ingenuousness of a newly-born sensibility. It must be remembered that the artists, many of them talented painters, had to work in difficult surroundings, in dark tunnels and archways. Many of the paintings are tomb decorations, and the artists had to smear their plaster on rough walls, which, if they were made of tufa, as in Rome, were apt to crumble. But the pagan technique which they employed called for a carefully prepared smooth surface — the kind of surface which may be seen in the remains of decorations in Roman houses, or at Herculaneum and Pompeii. Nor did the Christians attach much decorative or aesthetic importance to their paintings. They were executed for religious reasons or simply for practical purposes, and served to recall the evidence and mysteries of the Faith. This practical approach explains both the iconic and symbolic nature of the primitive paintings in burial-grounds. It was a characteristic which was to continue for a long time, and their summary treatment and direct quality have sometimes — though wrongly — been called " impressionistic ". A few essential lines sufficed to create an image which was valued not for itself, but only as a symbol. It was not the way in which the picture was painted that was important, but the idea behind it. This characteristic was to be a lasting one, and it is clear that from the outset Christian painting tended to make the human form more spiritual and at the same time more striking by reducing it to essentials.

The catacomb paintings of the first to the sixth centuries may be said to represent the final stage in the history of classical painting. Whether good or bad, they closely resemble contemporary pagan pictures, particularly those of the first three centuries A.D. The very well-known Amorino, for example, which was found in the cemetery of Domitilla and which is ascribed to the first century, might just as easily have been found in the private house of a pagan.

It is in Rome, between the fourth and fifth centuries, that we can see the beginning of a break-away, and the development of a separate trend in burial-ground paintings. There is a tendency to concentrate on the spiritual aspect of the human figure rather than on external beauty, whether in representations of the Deity, the saints, or even symbolic pictures of the Good Shepherd and the Orans Virgin (i.e. the Virgin praying with arms uplifted). It may be that a classical feeling for austere feminine beauty still persists, as in the wall-painting on the tomb of the *Matrona Veneranda* in the same cemetery, yet the artist is clearly interested in portraying an inner spiritual feeling by means of expressions and gestures. Perhaps naturalism was distorted, yet figures were composed for the purpose of expressing feelings and emotions. An example is the wall-painting in the cemetery of Domitilla, where Christ is shown among the apostles, a bold design in the way of gestures and foreshortening. Another example is the wall-painting of S. Peter and S. Paul in an archway of the same cemetery; here the heads are so vigorous that they are almost caricatures. And again there is the celebrated Orans Madonna in the Ostriano cemetery, where realism is transfigured by the artist's determination to convey a sense of spiritual detachment.

No doubt it was popular art. Yet if it is compared with contemporary classical art there is equally no doubt that it possesses more genuine feeling, and fulfils, more richly than contemporary classical art, the spiritual and moral requirements of the time. The development of expressionism was a sign of new feeling in Western art, but in Italy, at any rate in official painting, this promise of a new evolution came to nothing.

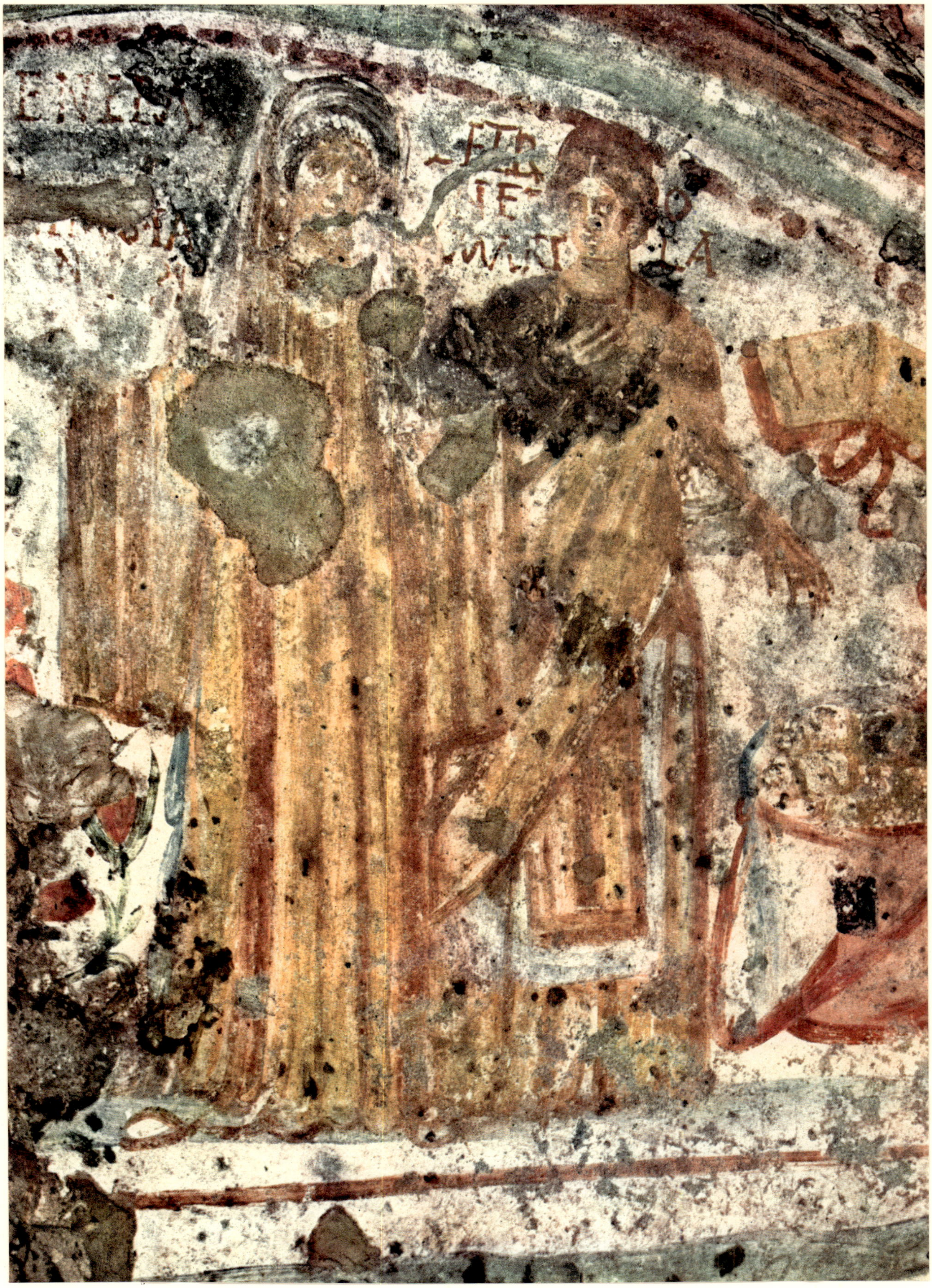

Paleo-Christian art: La Matrona Veneranda and S. Petronilla.
Cemetery of Domitilla, Rome

Official Christian painting began to take shape towards the end of the fourth century, but the source and centre was not in the West; it was in the East, at Constantinople. It was the style known as Byzantine, although the precise, unmistakeable characteristics of this style, which remained substantially unchanged for centuries, were not to be crystallised until the sixth century.

The development of Christian painting, if it is to be considered as the painting of the new civilisation, was slow and laborious; at times it hardly seemed to move at all. But when it did finally emerge in a clear, well-defined form, it was not only greeted with tremendous enthusiasm; it was supported by the united power of the Byzantine Empire and the Church.

One reason for the slow growth of Christian painting, even after the Imperial adoption of the Faith in the fourth century, was that Christians, like Jews, had a feeling of repugnance towards representational art, and the use of symbols was prolonged throughout the early centuries. Even after the triumph of Christianity in the fourth century, and the tremendous creative activity which followed, with its outcome in the building and the elaborate decoration of basilicas, baptisteries and tombs, the Church still objected to any representation of the mysteries of religion, its figures or acts, and demanded the continuance of the old pagan forms, which were to be used symbolically. The Church's commands applied especially to the symbols inspired by the naturalistic school of Alexandria.

During the fourth and fifth centuries decorative motifs of cherubs gathering grapes, of *putti* fishing in a river, or doves and peacocks, are almost universal. The most typical and splendid example in mosaic is in the tomb of S. Costanza in Rome. But similar motifs are to be found in the chapel of el Bagaouat in Egypt (fourth century); in the rotonda of S. George at Salonika (fifth century); in the Baptistery of the Orthodox and tomb of Galla Placidia at Ravenna (fifth century); and in the apses of S. John Lateran and S. Maria Maggiore in Rome.

In some of these buildings more concrete and lifelike motifs, such as figures of the saints or portraits, are to be found alongside the usual symbols. We may trace them to a change in taste in the fifth century, a change brought about by the need for an art whose purpose was the instruction of the faithful — a need which lasted throughout the Middle Ages. Its origins lay in the great building fervour of the fourth century. " Decoration " became a clarion call, and artists had drawn more from pagan themes than the permitted symbols. They had, for example, included such extraneous matter as scenes of hunting and fishing . The consequence was that the symbols themselves ultimately lost their significance and became merely part of the decoration. By the end of the fourth century, a number of Popes found this decoration childish and useless, and proclaimed the need for an art that was educational or edifying, an art to be based upon incidents from the Testaments and the lives of the martyrs. This programme of education and edification was a logical consequence of symbolism. But now a wholly new factor appears — an interest in historical realism.

Eastern influence dominated the development of Christian painting between the fourth and fifth centuries. It is to be found long before, of course, in the pagan classical world, but with Christianity, which was itself an Eastern religion, it became even stronger. The iconography of the Gospels and the portrait-figure of Christ — no longer symbolic — were finally settled in Palestine between the fourth and fifth centuries; the Virgin, apostles and other saints acquired their traditional appearances during the same period.

The Greek tradition too had great prestige throughout the whole Mediterranean area; in Rome and in Campania, as well as in Egypt and in Asia Minor. Since the State had recognised the Church, had sanctioned a particular style of Christian art, and had then helped to establish and diffuse this art, it was only natural that the Church should foster the Greek element. But both in Rome and in the East the new religion developed primarily among the common people, and local styles prevailed in figurative expression. Such local movements as had withstood the general spread of Greek culture were certainly helped in their struggle for survival by Christianity as well as by the fall of the Roman Empire. This is particularly true of the Asiatic and Egyptian hinterland, since the coastal cities where Hellenism was strongest were Alexandria, Antioch and Ephesus. A trend which had operated for centuries was now at least partially reversed. Instead of spreading their civilisation inland the rich and flourishing coastal centres began to feel the pressure of external influences which modified, without wholly rejecting, the classical tradition.

While these movements of penetration and fusion were slowly taking place between the West and the East, between two civilisations and two wholly different social and political systems, there was founded in their main area of contact the city of Constantinople. The year was 330.

Destined to become the capital of the Empire, and hence the richest, most powerful and most magnificent of cities, Constantinople was from its foundation a great artistic centre. Yet until the sixth century here was, strictly speaking, no " Byzantine " art. Up to that period centres such as Antioch and Ephesus were more important, and the dominating influence during the fifth century seems to have been Syrian. This is obvious, for example, in such important monuments as the tomb of Galla Placidia and the Baptistery of the Orthodox at Ravenna. The important fact is that from the beginning Byzantium attracted representatives of the many different artistic movements which were growing up round the Mediterranean, movements based upon Hellenism and on a variety of complex Eastern trends from Persian to Coptic, but including the fundamental spiritual element of Christianity. It was at Byzantium that the fusion of diverse civilisations and sensibilities took place, giving birth to an art that was unique and unmistakeable, and followed definite rules and plans established in the sixth century. The foundations of Byzantine art were laid in Egypt, Asia Minor and Syria, but it was only in Constantinople that it acquired an order and originality which enabled Syrian, Persian, Egyptian and classical motifs to be combined and transformed into something new. The Government at Constantinople was determined for both political and religious reasons to maintain the classical characteristics of the Greek-Roman-Eastern world.

Byzantine art was both political and clerical, an instrument of state authority as well as a means towards religious discipline for both emperors and priests. Having become the established religion, Christianity adopted the tastes of those who had given it recognition. And since the State had been proclaimed defender of the faith it also encouraged and organised the spread of Christian art, which soon, in marked contrast to its origins, acquired the same characteristics of luxury and pomp as court art.

Although no examples have survived, it can be deduced from written sources that Byzantine painting was originally secular rather than religious, and that religious art adopted the secular style. Eastern influence was strong, both aesthetically and in technique and materials. In Eastern civilisations art had always been used to glorify the sovereign, both by the use of rich materials and splendid colouring, and by a dignified and solemn portrayal of his actions. It followed that in Byzantium classical naturalism and liveliness became stiffer, and were replaced by rigidity and monotony of expressions and gestures. Naturally the same change took place in religious subjects. They too, by assimilation and imitation, were treated in a rich and abstract manner, since the sovereign and his court were to be regarded as an earthly example of the beauty and splendour of God and His heavenly court.

Nevertheless Eastern influence does not entirely account for the stiff, abstract manner which characterises Byzantine painting. The very reasons which enabled so many trends to be fused, inevitably brought into being a formula which enabled the emotional richness and technical experience of centuries to be arranged in a definite and orderly structure, and which also led to an extreme regard for stylised forms and precious materials. It was a kind of " Mannerism " founded on wisdom acquired through many centuries and drawn from every latitude and climate in the history of civilisation. Byzantine art is perhaps the most excessively mannered style that has ever been known; at once tragic, aristocratic, and popular, it flaunts an exaltation that is worldly as well as spiritual.

Nor does Eastern influence explain by itself the love of luxury, solemnity and detachment from the everyday world. These characteristics were the result of a very acute observation of the real world on the part of Byzantine artists who succeeded in isolating and using the few essentials which are necessary for a general understanding of life. Christianity was the other vital factor in the formation of Byzantine art. In spirit it was Christian. Rich materials were valued for their indestructibility; it made them suitable for pictures intended to last and for this reason mosaics were preferred to wall-paintings. The hieratical repetition of gestures, the other-worldly expressions, the contemplative immobility and the abstraction are the perfect counterparts of the spirituality of a religion whose deepest aspiration was towards another world. Gold and rich colours exalted the imagination and gave an understanding in this world of the magnificence and splendour of the next.

To sum up: Christianity, Hellenism and the East were the fundamental elements in the formation of Byzantine art.

Throughout the fifth century, when the various confluent trends in Byzantium were not yet welded together, and Christian ideology and aesthetics had not been firmly established, no firm line was drawn between symbolism and edifying narrative. The most important examples of the work of the new school are at Ravenna: in the tomb of Galla Placidia and in the Baptistery of the Orthodox, both of which date from about 450.

In these two monuments the interior mosaic decoration displays both the symbolic and narrative trends. Vivid memories of classical art are combined with a taste for colour, fantasy and richness which are all typically Eastern. Syrian influence prevails in the tomb of Galla Placidia, but in the Baptistery the Alexandrian tradition is very much to the fore, particularly in those parts which are more strictly decorative, where marble incrustations and stucco work simulate architectural surroundings, as in the well-known Greek illusionism. This style of decoration, originally Greek, is also found in the church of S. George at Salonika.

The mosaics in the tomb of Galla Placidia are among the oldest in Ravenna, and are certainly the most striking, partly on account of the narrow space which they decorate. The incredible beauty of the colouring, the high formal quality, the superb decorative arrangement, which is dignified in spite of its richness, the costly materials — all these combine to make this monument the masterpiece of fifth-century mosaic. The blue vault is interwoven with motifs of red, white and golden flowers, giving the appearance of a costly quilt. The blue cupola, on the other hand, is sprinkled with gold stars, and has a golden cross, the symbol of Christ, placed between symbols of the Evangelists In the lunettes beneath the drum of the cupola eight figures of prophets or apostles are framed in pairs by vine tendrils with lilies and roses; in the side lunettes deer drinking from the fountains of life face each other, while up above doves are also

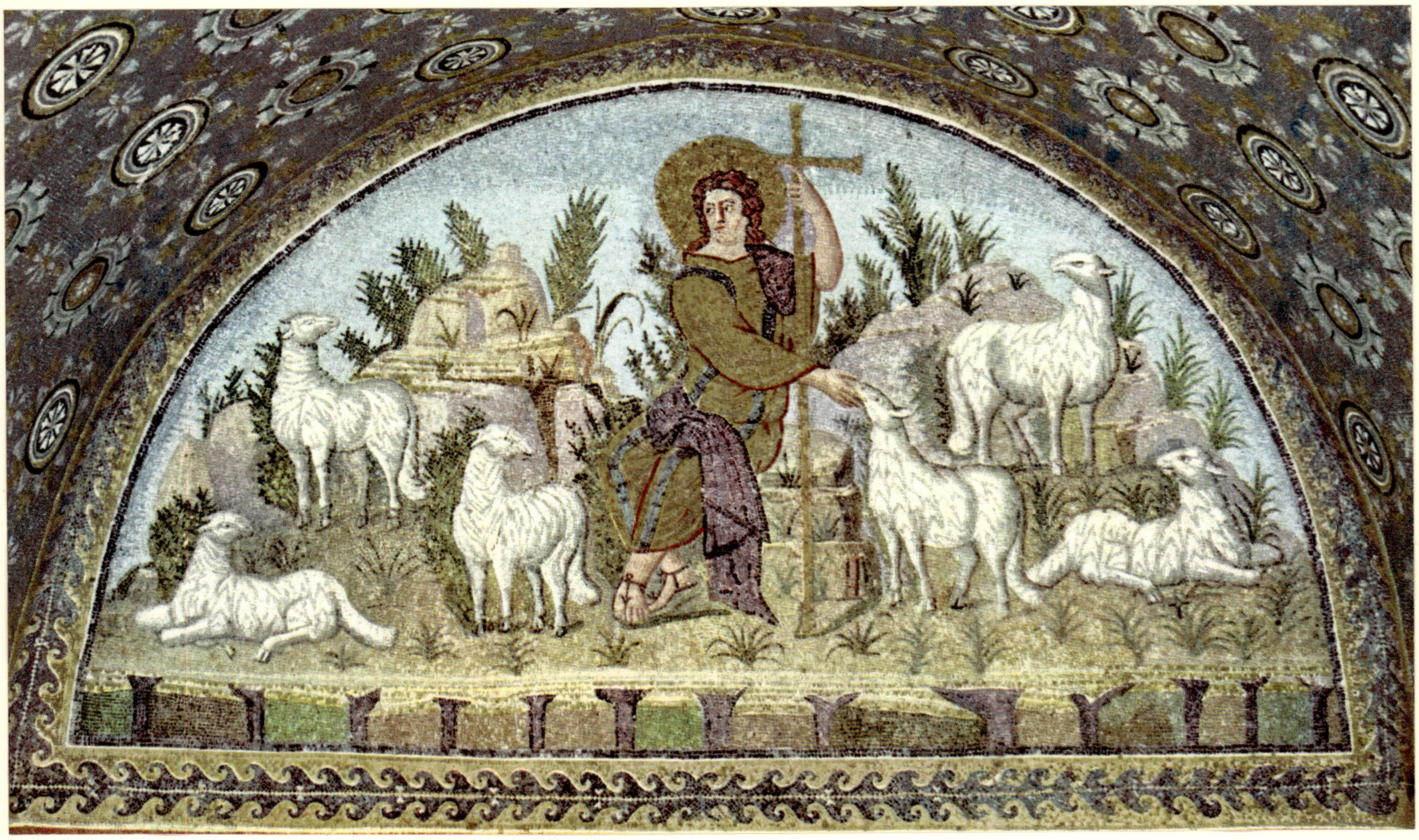

Byzantine art: The Good Shepherd. Mausoleum of Galla Placidia, Ravenna

drinking from a cup. In the lunette opposite the entrance is a martyr, possibly S. Lawrence, beside the gridiron with lighted coals and an open cupboard containing the Gospels. In the lunette at the front, above the door, is the Good Shepherd. There is perhaps no other work which expresses so clearly as do these lunettes the transformation which was then taking place in Christian iconography. On the one hand the Good Shepherd, the most cherished theme of symbolic painting, and the one which had inspired the most imaginative interpretation, is here given masterly treatment. Obviously classical, or more precisely Alexandrian, in feeling, it is presented with a new majesty in the rendering of the figure, and the symbolic meaning is hidden beneath the more concrete manifestation of royal divinity. On the other hand there is a scene of martyrdom, but although the individual images, from the form of the Saint himself to the Gospels for whose sake he endured martyrdom, are entirely naturalistic, there is no action; instead, the composition is emblematic and suggests symbolic painting. Nevertheless this picture shows the strength of a movement which was seeking to express the lives of individual Christians in more realistic terms.

Both Syrian and Alexandrian influences of about the same period are to be found in Ravenna, the one in the tomb of Galla Placidia and the other in the Baptistery of the Orthodox. This is, of course, because the artists came from Byzantium, where representatives of the different schools in the ancient world had been gathering for some time past and where their various styles were now being merged. There are classical characteristics too, probably for the same reason and not due to direct Roman influence. Rome herself at that time felt the Eastern influence, although her painting cannot be properly called Byzantine any more than can that of Ravenna. No doubt local craftsmen helped the Byzantine artists at Ravenna, but the general feeling was imposed by these artists who brought a direct reflection from the great capital to the smaller one.

Unlike other places on the outskirts of the Empire, Ravenna, because it was the capital of the Western Empire, and later of Byzantine Italy in the time of Justinian, had a court art. Although almost all examples have been lost, it must have been closely linked with the art of Constantinople. Today, although the decoration of the palaces has disappeared, and only the religious buildings remain, no city other than Ravenna can give even a limited idea of the splendour of the court art of Byzantium.

In the sixth century Byzantine painting achieved its most original expression, flourishing and expanding to its extreme limits. This was due in part to the completion of the work of organising a multiplicity of different cultures and drawing up a political, religious and social system, a work on which the Government in Constantinople had been engaged since its origins; and in part to the great personality of the Emperor Justinian. Throughout his reign there was tremendous building activity both in Byzantium and in other important cities of the Empire; now, as never before, the capital took the lead in matters of artistic taste, and in doing so reflected the will of the Emperor.

And so churches and palaces — for private citizens vied with the Emperor in their ideas of grandeur — were covered with wall-paintings and mosaics of sacred and historical scenes, mythological and decorative. Works of art in the capital were used as models for the whole of the civilised world. Procopius gives lengthy and detailed descriptions of buildings erected by Justinian; the Emperor founded churches which were copied all over the Christian world until the twelfth century, such as SS. Sergius and Baccus, the Holy Apostles, and S. Sophia, whose interior was to be the most sumptuously decorated of all. Both the architecture and the fresco or mosaic decoration of these churches must have been copied, particularly in the more important cities such as Salonika and Ravenna, which were closely connected with the central government.

Of this so-called " golden age " of Byzantine painting practically nothing remains. The conquests, first of the Arabs and then of the Turks, resulted in the destruction or obliteration of the most important examples of an art which lasted for a thousand years. The few traces which remain at Constantinople, or in other cities in Greece or Asia Minor, are not sufficient to give a complete picture of the great period of Byzantine painting in the sixth century, nor of its final phases. All we have are some written sources, which are however numerous, detailed and descriptive. In recent years excavations in many Mediterranean countries, including Palestine, have been fruitful, but Italy remains the place where the various stages in the history of Byzantine painting can best be studied. Ravenna and Parenzo in particular give the best idea of the quality and character of sixth-century painting.

In the churches and palaces of the sixth century the historical-monumental style triumphed both over the picturesque Alexandrian decoration and over the symbolic Christian style. This is true both of wall-paintings and mosaics, mosaic being the favoured medium most frequently used in the sixth century. If we remember how Justinian, with his high conception of the monarchy as an earthly image of divine power, carried his vision of magnificence and royal dignity to lengths which were almost absurd, we can understand how the technique of mosaic came to be so widely established during his long reign. Mosaic was more durable than fresco, and enabled rich materials, including precious stones, to be used, thus fulfilling a taste for the luxurious which was more prevalent than ever. The hardness of the materials also helped to convey the aesthetic idea of majestic, remote figures, and lent itself to coldly symmetrical compositions. As a medium for decoration mosaic had immense capabilities. In fact decoration has never been so important, or reached so high a level, as in Byzantine art, for although the Byzantines were able builders, they subordinated architecture to decoration. Exteriors were simple and for the most part quite plain, but interiors were completely covered by rich mosaics.

Decoration became more important than the form which produced it, because in itself it was a study, a vision, an ecstasy even, depending essentially on colour and light, two abstract indefinable entities outside form. It is true that the most costly materials were used to create this ethereal effect, but their spiritual importance lay in their intrinsic golden or coloured light, that is to say a quality produced by the materials, yet one which transcended them and was transformed into ecstatic meditation or silence and rapture. Contrasting with this profound decorative feeling the figure had become historical, possibly even a portrait instead of a symbol, and might be expected to disturb the mystery of colour and light of those surfaces and vaults. But this is not so; it is drawn into the total harmony, and by skilful composition actually adds to the effect of flashing light and colour. And yet it is not effaced, because the rapt expressions, the spiritual hands, and the hieratic gestures stand out vividly against the splendour of the backgrounds and richness of the costumes.

In order to judge (as well as we can in view of the actual state of preservation of these works) the style and quality of mosaic painting in the time of Justinian, we must turn first to the church of S. Vitale at Ravenna, consecrated in 547. The two famous mosaics facing each other in the choir, showing Justinian and Theodora and their court, were executed at this time, and were probably among the last mosaics in the church to be finished. They are the most famous surviving examples of this historical-portrait type of court art, and convey a true idea of the splendour, the luxury, and the hieratic formality of the court of Byzantium.

Against a background of gold, their heads crowned and bejewelled and encircled with golden haloes, the Emperor and Empress, followed by their respective suites of dignitaries, soldiers, eunuchs, and ladies, are proceeding towards the altar to lay upon it their offerings of gold. These scenes evidently allude to the contributions made by Justinian and Theodora towards the building of the church, and are thus linked to an historical event. At the same time they are abstract exaltations of earthly power, which, as it was considered as coming from God, was fittingly represented in a sacred place.

There is no doubt, especially as the portraits of the two rulers had to be good likenesses, that artists were summoned from Byzantium to carry out the mosaics. Heir in this respect of the Greek tradition, Byzantine art attached a great deal of importance to the likeness, even if it was transformed into idealistic terms. When the idealisation was less strict Byzantine portrait painters achieved a certain amount of expression, as is shown by the faces of the dignitaries who are accompanying Justinian — for example the lively head of Bishop Maximian who is nearest to the artist. Even the secondary figures have an individual character: the firmness of the soldiers, the shrewd expressions of the courtiers, the obsequious smiles of the priests, the beauty of the ladies-in-waiting, especially of the two nearest to Theodora, whose exquisite feminine quality is especially noticeable. Naturally, however, in both mosaics — where the taste of the age, the costumes and surroundings are more important than the personality of the artist — it is the majesty of the attitudes and the richness of the materials which stand out above all.

Many artists no doubt worked on the mosaic decoration of S. Vitale, but each part blends so well with the others that it seems as if one mind had planned and directed the whole. The various themes are cleverly arranged and chosen, and the style is directed towards the essential aim: the celebration, half ecstatic and half intellectual, of God and the men, the rulers of the Church, whom He has destined to bear witness to His glory in the past and in the present. In the golden apse is the very fine Theophany,

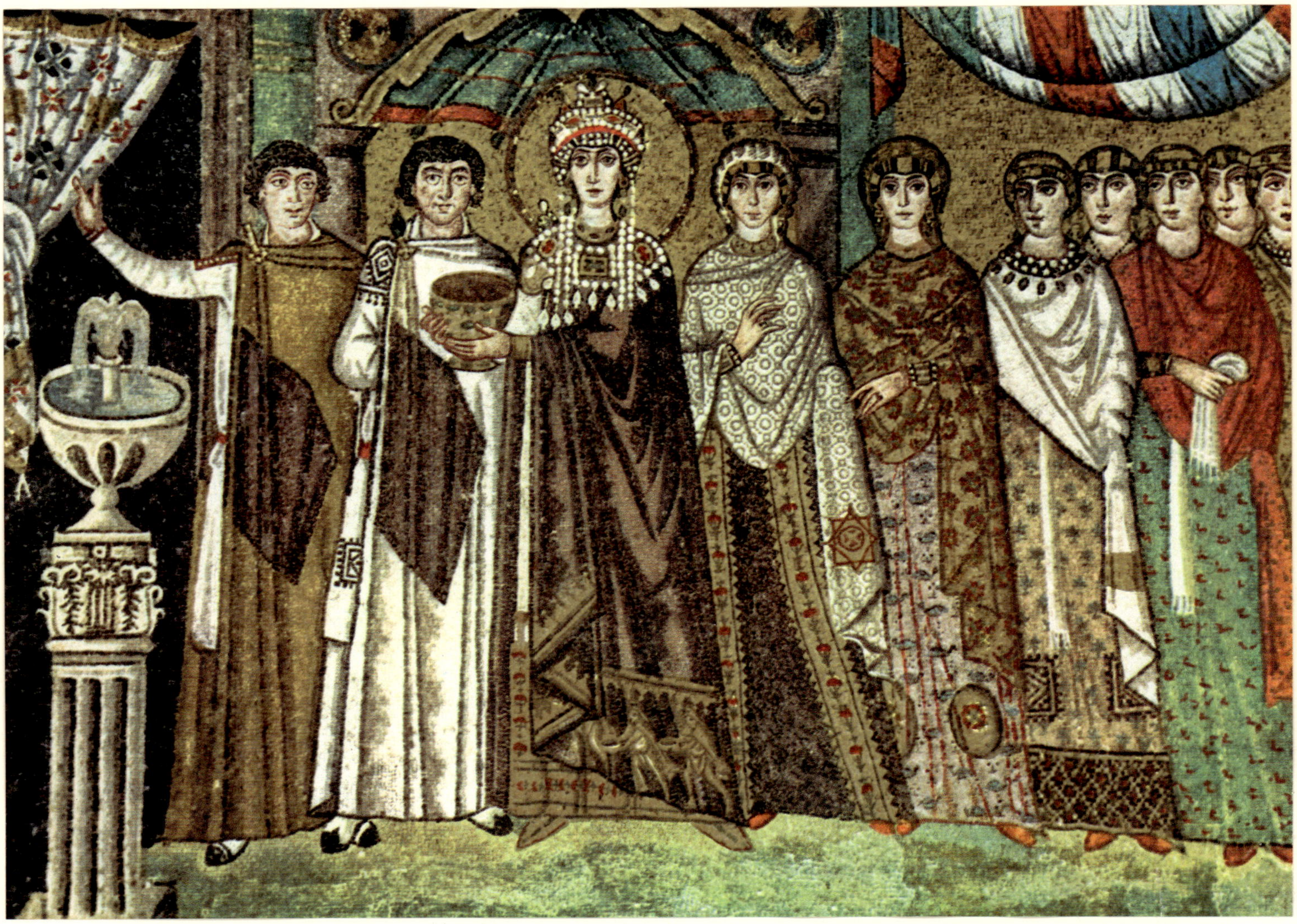

Byzantine art: Theodora and her suite. S. Vitale, Ravenna

with Christ as a young beardless philosopher seated on the blue globe of the universe between two Archangels, with S. Vitale who is receiving a crown, and Bishop Ecclesius who is offering Him a model of the Church. The vault is a masterpiece of decoration with motifs used in an original manner. The gold appears through a dense stylised pattern of branches among which are animals and birds. This rich and spring-like carpet is crossed diagonally by great garlands of flowers and fruit, while in the centre of the hangings angels support a circle with an image of the Divine Lamb. Scenes and characters from the Old and New Testaments abound, along with symbols chosen with great care to lead up to the supreme sacrifice of the Lamb which is perpetuated in the Mass; they range from prophets and apostles to Hospitality and offerings of Abraham, Melchisedech and Moses. The intellectual aspect of the work in S. Vitale is particularly interesting in its combination of realistic detail and liturgical abstraction. The old symbolism is to be found appearing once more in this new, intellectual context.

S. Vitale is not alone in Ravenna in showing the high level of Byzantine art in the sixth century. But nothing else equals its perfection, not even the apse of S. Apollinare in Classe (consecrated in 549) or the chapel of the Archbishop's Palace. The same combination of worldly and religious feeling which belongs to the mosaics of Justinian and Theodora is also found in the famous procession of the virgins towards Mary, and of the martyrs towards Christ, in S. Apollinare Nuovo. They were in fact carried out about the same time and are certainly later than the other mosaics in the Church, dating from the time of Theodoric. The same musical quality and decorative elegance is to be found here, but derived now from the repetition of a single motif on a gold background. So powerful is the suggestion that it comes from a world of legend and fantasy somewhere beyond the earth, that it seems as though the repetition could be continued indefinitely. The feeling for order and harmony in these two mosaics recalls the Phidian bas-reliefs. This is also true to some extent of the similar feeling for a calm, noble beauty based on rhythm. Byzantine art had become anti-classical, but it never lost its classical substratum.

Another mosaic which can be grouped stylistically with the sixth-century mosaics in Ravenna is that of the apse of the cathedral at Parenzo, where the Virgin and Child

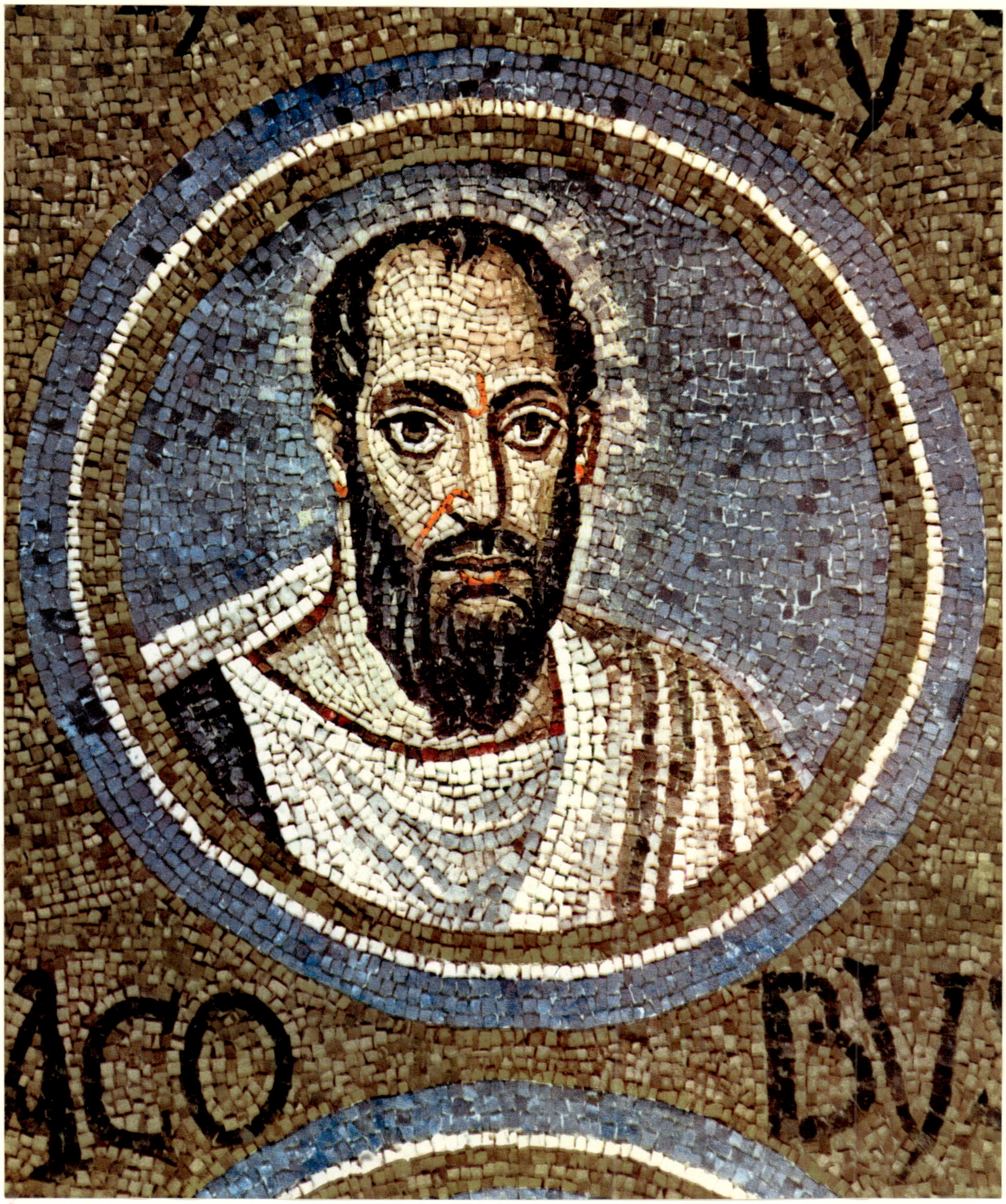

Byzantine art: S. Paul. Archepiscopal Chapel, Ravenna

are enthroned between two Angels and four Saints, Bishop Euphrasius, Archdeacon Claudius and his little son. From now on, in this historical-portrait school, sacred characters are commonly found alongside real people.

Salonika is another city of the Byzantine world where an interesting group of mosaics, similar in style to those in Ravenna and Parenzo, has been preserved. Since it was an important city closely bound up with the life of the capital, the mosaics give a fairly good idea of sixth-century mosaic painting in Constantinople. Those in the church of S. Demetrius bear a particular resemblance to those in S. Apollinare Nuovo at Ravenna and in the Cathedral of Parenzo. As a result of the fire in 1917 which destroyed the greater part, many of them are no more than fragments. Their date is by no means certain, and historians have attributed them variously to the fifth, sixth and seventh centuries.

The work was certainly not all completed in the same century, but the most important group probably dates from the time of Justinian. The interesting point about the decoration in this church is that it consisted of separate panels unconnected with each other. It seems probable therefore that they were dedicatory offerings commissioned by private citizens in gratitude for favours received. If this is so, they are the oldest known example of paintings as dedicatory offerings in a church, and are therefore more closely connected with icon painting than with architectural decoration, especially if they were commissioned by private persons. Another important point to note is the lack of symbolism in S. Demetrius. A taste for historical portraits, on the other hand, is particularly noticeable. This provides a good reason for ascribing the mosaics at least to the second half of the sixth century. While recalling very strongly the style of the works in Ravenna and Parenzo, particularly in the lifelike nature of some of the heads, and the ritual gravity of the poses, which are of a slightly earlier date, they show a decidedly more polished technique. The best examples of this are on the panels of the entrance pillars, with " S. Sergius " and " S. Demetrius, Patron Saint of Children ", and, most effective of all as a physical and psychological portrait, " S. Demetrius between the Archbishop and the Governor of Salonika ". These three pictures are strongly reminiscent of S. Vitale in Ravenna, although there the painting has a formal note. It has been said that in treating S. Demetrius as a dedicatory panel the artist has used a freer treatment, and has thus produced a more penetrating portrait, with colouring which, although fine, is less than sumptuous. Both at S. Vitale and S. Apollinare there is a more decided and memorable imaginative suggestion. At S. Demetrius there is a note of serene and calm contemplation, with a style which is less mannered and which recalls more directly the distant classical models. One technical point is of special interest: the faces are executed with very small *tesserae*, which enables the surface to be blended in such a way that the features are not altered even when seen from close to. This technique was employed for icons, and therefore leads one to suppose that icons were widely used at that time, although nothing earlier than the sixth century has survived. It has been thought that the use of icons in worship was prevalent among the upper classes, and gave rise to the production of works of high quality from that period only, since the examples dating from the fourth and fifth centuries, which have been found in excavations in Palestine and elsewhere, are very rough and popular. Yet the iconic style and the technique of certain details of the mosaics of S. Demetrius, such as the Byzantine passion for decoration of which the use of sacred images on clothes is an example (Theodora at Ravenna has an " Adoration of the Magi " on her robe), and their liking for precious objects in general, would lead us to suppose the contrary. On the other hand a tendency towards icons, with a consequent almost magical isolation of the symbol, had existed in Christian art since its origins. Naturally icons were in more general use during later centuries, and we must remember

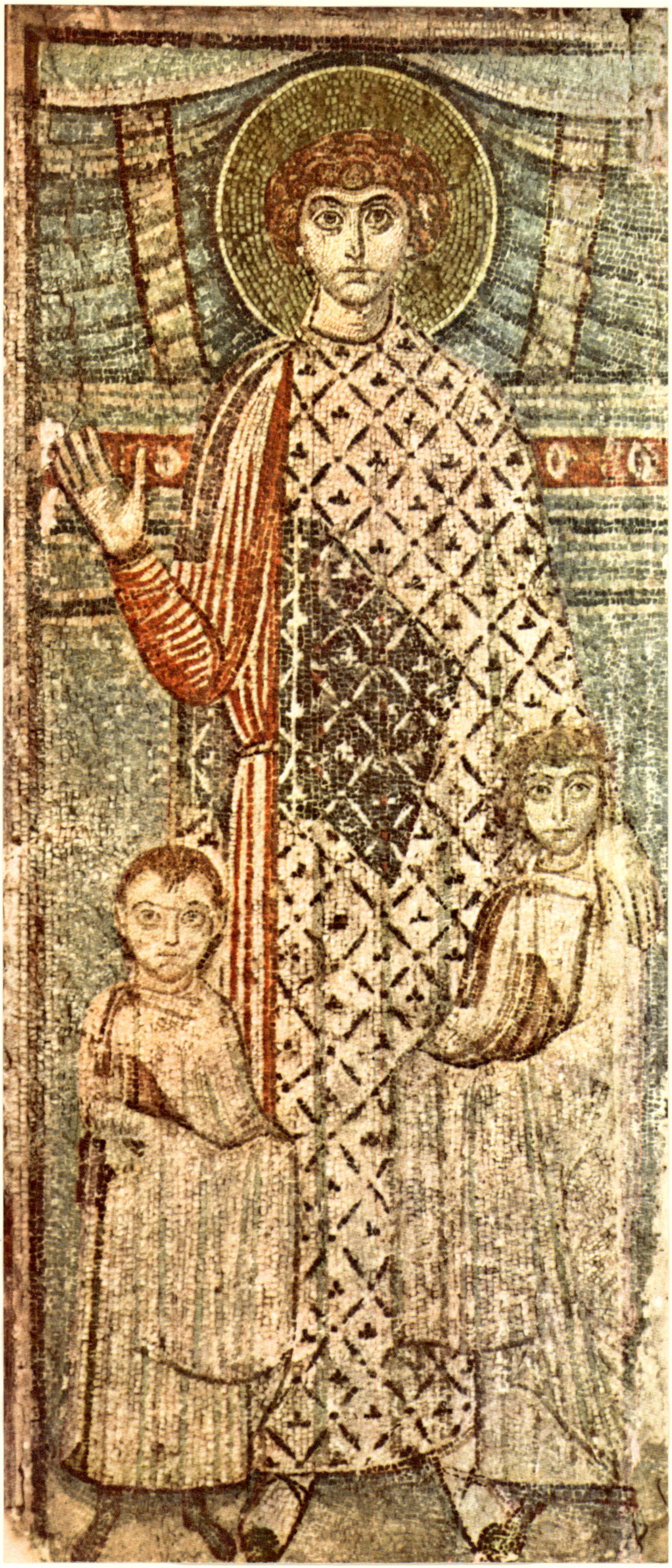

Byzantine art: S. Demetrius, Patron Saint of Children. S. Demetrius, Salonika

with regard to the scarce examples dating from earlier times that these portable pictures were, like furniture, easily damaged and dispersed, and were of course the easiest objects to destroy during the iconoclastic period.

If Ravenna is the best place to study the Byzantine art of the sixth century, then Rome is certainly so for the seventh. Rome was at this time more an Eastern than a Western city, with a large colony of Greek priests and merchants, and many Syrian and Greek popes who were loyal to Byzantium, and were regarded by the Emperors as a help in spreading the Faith and as a bulwark against Barbarian invasions. From the fifth century onwards Eastern artists were usually responsible for both wall-paintings and mosaics in Rome, while local craftsmen copied their style. The survival of a local tradition, which much later contributed to a genuine Italian Renaissance of painting more than it ever did to the Eastern school of Roman painters, was due to the existence of classical buildings and other works of art which continued to survive in great numbers despite invasion and plundering, and changes in taste and doctrine. At the beginning of the Middle Ages Rome had the richest store of classical remains in the whole of the Mediterranean area. The Byzantines, who (despite the transformation they had effected) considered themselves as the true heirs and successors of the ancient Greek and Latin tradition, treated these remains with respect.

The Roman classical tradition continued to possess a measure of vitality up to the early years of the sixth century. In the fine mosaic in the apse of SS. Cosmas and Damian which dates from the time of Felix IV (526–530), there is an obvious attempt to create plastic forms and spatial effects in the blue sky splashed with falling clouds, shaded from red to deep blue; and the calm gestures of the figures are designed not according to the Byzantine rhythm, but with a majestic amplitude which recalls statues of the Caesars and senators. Possibly even the faces, especially the very beautiful, severe face of Christ (although they obey an iconography which was now permanent), have a certain mobility when compared with the supremely idealised faces in the mosaics at Ravenna.

By the seventh century all these figurative elements seem to have disappeared. And if the decoration of the most important Roman monuments at that time is similar to those in the capital of the Empire, we must conclude that it was in the seventh century that Byzantine painting began to take on that typical mechanical and rigid appearance, which gives it the appearance of a tired, long-drawn-out exercise copied from the elegant and poetical manner of the sixth century. This cultured, intellectual art had, then, reached the highest level of its expressive and imaginative possibilities in the sixth century, the century which saw the culmination of its development.

The well-known mosaic in S. Agnes Outside-the-Walls (c. 625-638) is remarkable for an extraordinary effect of colour and gold. But it has lost that magical absorption and ecstasy which made the figures appear as one with the dream-like colour in S. Apollinare and S. Vitale. Nor has it that mysterious beauty, so rich and subtle that it seems to be wrapped in gold, almost like a jewel encased and preserved in a jewel box. S. Agnes, crowned and dressed like an empress, loaded with gold and precious stones, towers above the figures of two popes (largely restored), in the vast golden vault of the apse. The composition, as Toesca remarks, is very significant: Byzantine art was clearly becoming increasingly abstract and severe. The sacred figure in the picture would gain in effectiveness and power if she were isolated in vast spaces of pure golden light without symbols, or at least without any landscape background. Here we can see a search for greater transcendency and at the same time great decorative power. But the remote, ethereal face of S. Agnes, no longer realistic in spite of the touches of rouge on her cheeks, reaches such a point of schematic absurdity that she seems like a caricature of her forebears in Ravenna.

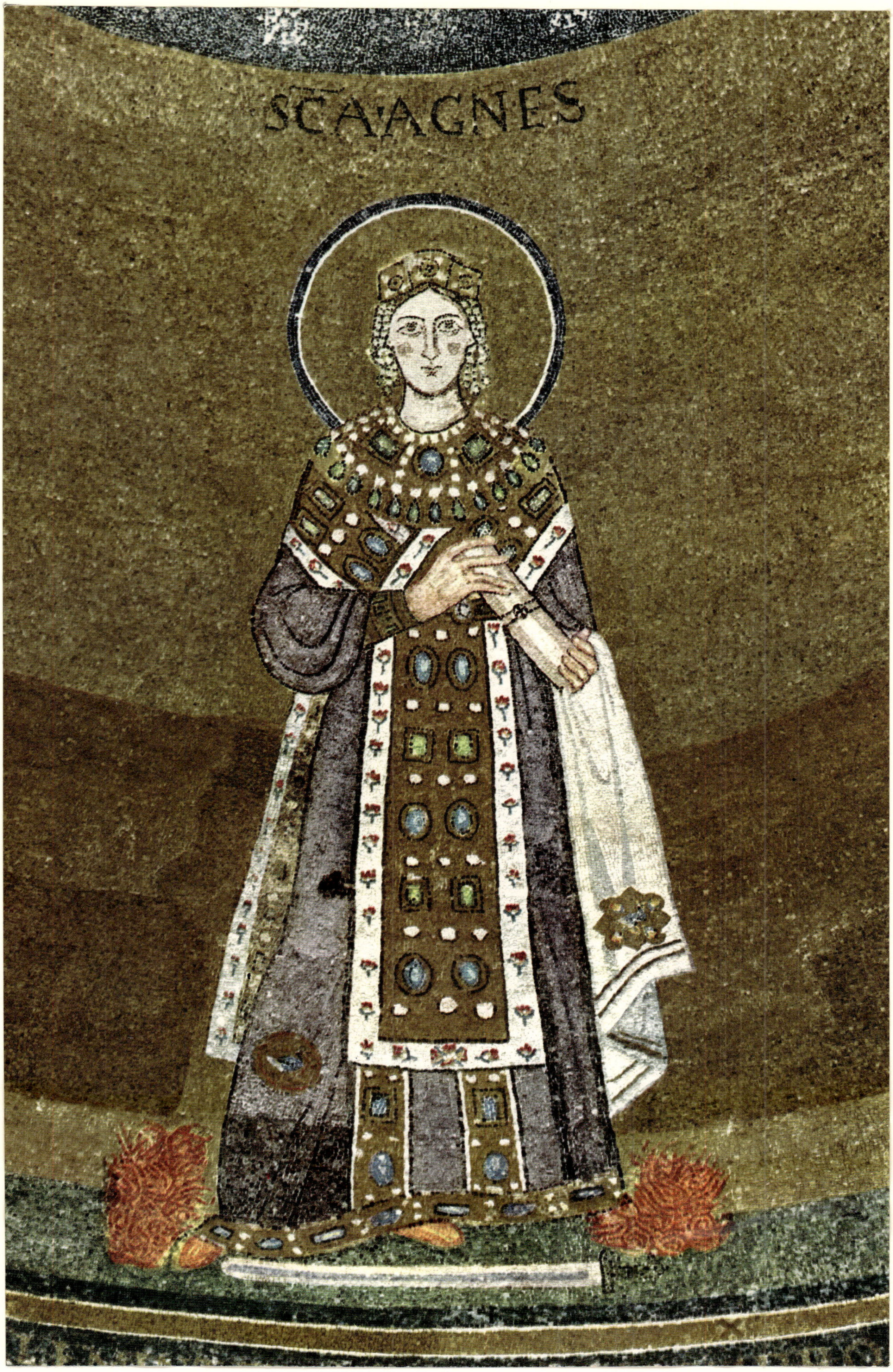

Byzantine art: S. Agnes, detail of the apse. S. Agnese, Rome

As well as the large number of Byzantine artists at work in Rome there must have been a great many local craftsmen, for Rome was an important city with an artistic tradition that was too old and too famous to be wholly submerged in the seventh century, even although it fell completely under Eastern influence and lost its individuality. From the seventh century onward there are to be found in Rome a great many works which, in their excessive rigidity of figure and composition, the accentuated breaking up of colours, and the emphasis on ascetic expression, seem likely to be copies and not original works by Byzantine artists. It seems highly probable that these were done by local craftsmen who, as usually happens with imitators, concentrated on superficial characteristics without penetrating the fundamentals. So there is no reason to suppose that genuine Byzantine art showed any signs of exhaustion in the seventh century.

The mosaics in the apse of the Oratory of S. Venanzio, near the Lateran Baptistery, which date from the time of John IV (640-642) are an example of work carried out by Romans imitating the Byzantine style. Christ is shown blessing the Madonna from above, between saints and two popes.

There is, too, the point that in Rome a great deal of the more popular type of Byzantine art has been preserved. The city was so large, and religious buildings so numerous, that the artists who had been summoned from Byzantium to carry out the great mass of work were hardly of the highest quality, or truly representative of court art. There were also a great many Greek monasteries in Rome, and many of the monks were painters. The tastes and outlook of this monastic school of painting were different from those of the court or Church at Byzantium. The journeymen carried out the tasks they were given, but in doing so inevitably introduced humbler or more popular trends; while they were likely in any case to have less technical skill. A proof of this is to be found in the frescoes in the Greek convent of S. Saba, at the beginning of the eighth century: despite a pleasing competency in the likenesses of some of the religious figures, the work is like that of amateurs, as in fact many of the Greek monks were. We can only form hypotheses, because of the scarcity of surviving examples in the chief centre of Byzantine painting, Constantinople. Yet it is significant that although there were close ties between Rome and the court at Constantinople, such works as have survived are not in the same class as those at Ravenna, which was a political capital of the Empire and the seat of the Exarchate. Compared with the works at Ravenna the very fine examples at Salonika strike a provincial note, and this is even truer of Rome, which from the seventh century onwards was artistically no more than a Byzantine province. The fragmentary mosaics from the Oratory of Pope John VII (705-707), now dispersed in several places (Lateran Museum, Opera of S. Peter, S. Maria in Cosmedin, S. Mark's at Florence and the Cathedral at Orte), are of course very well known. It seems probable (in view of the skilful colour effect which is contrived by contrasting blue, violet, white and gold), that these were carried out by an authentic Byzantine, or at least Eastern, artist, equally skilful in the technique of using very small *tesserae* to model the faces, achieving some liveliness of expression, and turning almost to caricature. Pope John VIII was a well-born Greek, and must have had close contacts with intellectual society at Constantinople. That he employed Eastern artists to decorate the buildings he founded is inherently possible. The frescoes in S. Maria Antiqua which date from his pontificate are undoubtedly the work of Byzantine artists: they are of much better quality than the mosaics in the Oratory, and it may be that they are truly representative of the great contemporary school at Constantinople.

The fresco decoration in the basilica of S. Maria Antiqua is the most important of all the works which have survived from the period covering the seventh to the tenth centuries. The walls are covered with paintings of various dates, sometimes placed on top of each other in layers, and strange contrasts of cultured and popular taste are to be seen there, mixing Greek and Roman traditions and inscriptions. Evidently S. Maria Antiqua, like S. Demetrius at Salonika, was decorated with a number of separate votive paintings, and provides evidence that icon painting was flourishing alongside the historical-monumental style.

Among the layers of paintings in the presbytery dating from the fifth to the ninth centuries, there must be some belonging to the time of John VII, for it is known that he ordered a complete redecoration of the presbytery. There are enormous painted figures of the apostles and scenes from the life of Christ, and above the apse is the Adoration of the Cross, with multitudes of beautiful angels, very delicate and feminine in flowing robes. Despite its fragmentary nature this work is of exceptional importance, because among the few examples which have come down to us it displays the persistence of the most cultured element in Byzantine painting, the memory of its classical origin, which is truly felt here despite all changes in feeling and mannered stylisation. It is curious that, so far as can be judged by the works which have survived, this remote Greek influence was stronger in fresco painting than in mosaics.

It is to a still earlier period in the seventh century, during the pontificate of Martin I, that it is usual to ascribe a fragmentary scene of the Annunciation where the body of the angel can still be seen: at this particular moment in Byzantine painting, the impressionistic style of brushwork, giving a rapid outline of the shape, and the dry, jerky drawing of the outlines, which give a suggestion of movement, are surprising elements, and it may be that the fresco was done by some Greek miniaturist. Illuminated books, often copies from other Greek manuscripts, were frequently used as models for decorations in buildings. Stylistically the angel in S. Maria Antiqua is

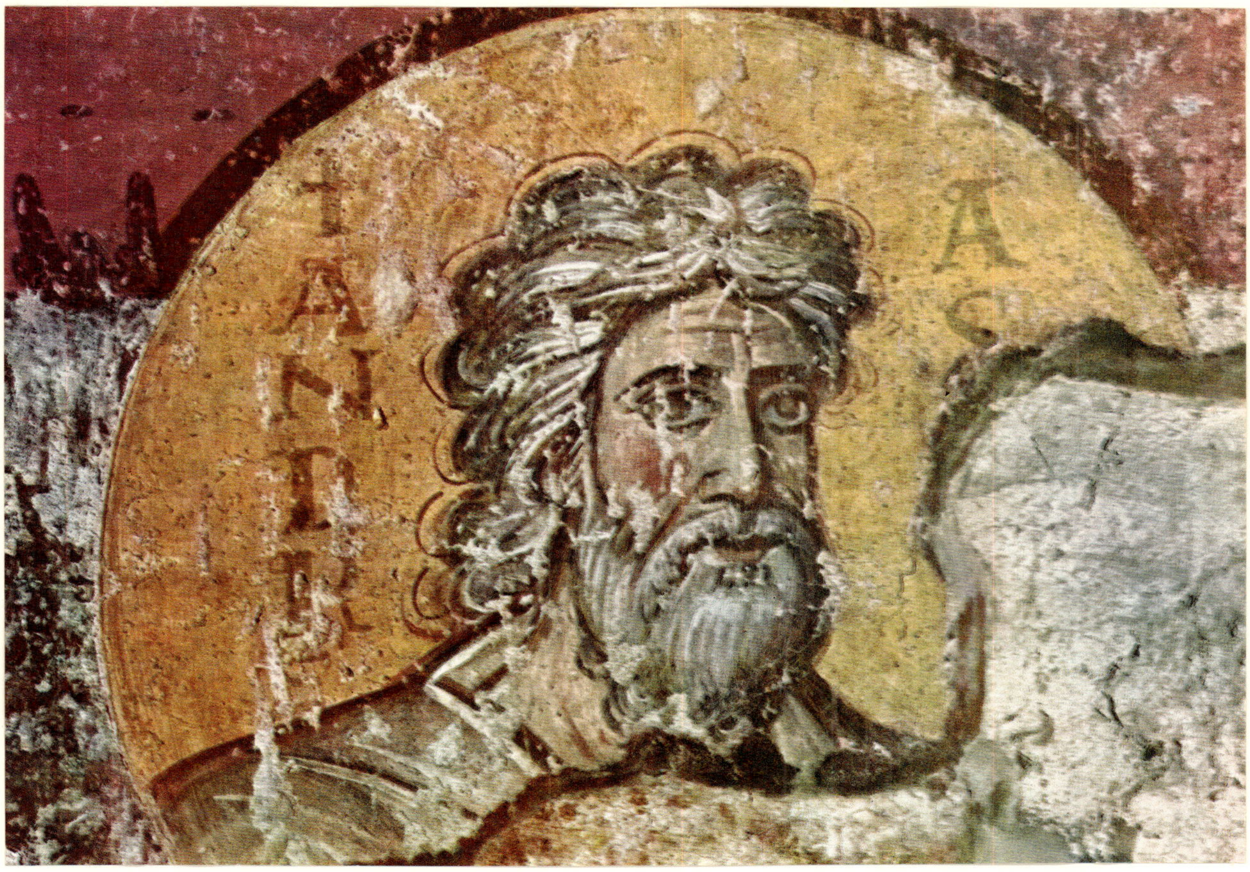

Byzantine art: The Apostle Andrew. S. Maria Antiqua, Rome

similar to the frescoes in the little church of Castelseprio (Milan), which present a very difficult problem in the history of medieval art. We shall return to these frescoes at Castelseprio — which are more Western than Byzantine in feeling — when we come to discuss Carolingian art.

The Iconoclastic movement began officially in 726 with the Edict of Leo III, the Isaurian. It was a sudden and violent explosion of the ancient antipathy, which Christianity had inherited from the Jews, to any representation of the human, or even more the divine, form. Latent and submerged beneath the opposing current which had prevailed under the influence of Hellenistic anthropomorphism, it had nevertheless continued to survive, especially in Asia Minor, and in fact was stronger in Syria than anywhere else. The strength and expansion of the movement, which was also found to a lesser degree in western countries, was due to a number of different causes. One was the excess to which the figurative movement had been pushed, until it was on the verge of becoming an idolatry. Another was the rise to power at the beginning of the eighth century of a Syrian dynasty of emperors who were opposed by virtue of their origins to sacred pictures. A third reason was political. The state believed that iconoclasm would weaken the material and moral power which the monks, the principal custodians of the best-known sacred pictures, were acquiring from iconolatry.

However that may be, the struggle against figural representational art, which was led by laymen and supported by a large number of churchmen, especially in the East, lasted for more than a century. It gave rise to a great deal of bloodshed, especially under Constantine V. Frescoes and mosaics and moveable pictures were all alike either destroyed or covered by whitewash. The iconoclastic movement is one reason why so few of the great works at Constantinople have come down to us. Not that iconoclasm led to a sterile period in Byzantine art; buildings were still being sumptuously decorated at Constantinople. But the subjects were no longer sacred, they were secular ; or more precisely they were no longer representational, but geometrical. This was due to the influence of Islam, then enjoying a period of conquest and expansion, for the Moslems were equally opposed to any representation of the human figure.

Nothing remains of this iconoclastic period. When the heretics were finally ousted, their opponents in turn destroyed the greater part of their work and substituted the traditional sacred subjects.

Except for a brief truce between 787 and 815, when the cult of figures was temporarily restored, the iconoclastic ban lasted until 842. In spite of the length of this struggle Byzantine religious painting was continued elsewhere by artists who had fled from persecution. These " Greeks " were made especially welcome in Italy, the nearest western country to remain outside the iconoclastic ban.

As a result Italy remained a Greek province in the field of painting, while other western regions assumed independent art forms, enriched by a new vitality typical of the barbarian state. The development of new forms and expressions in the western world was greatly helped by the iconoclastic movement, as well as by the freshness and vitality which characterise all " Barbarians " when they first enter into history and civilisation. As we have seen, Byzantine painting in the seventh century was beginning to show signs of weariness and exhaustion. By the time Byzantine art recovered its vigour and resumed its great programme of expansion and annexation after the iconoclastic movement, the western countries of Europe had already established artistic independence.

No examples of figurative art from western or central Europe have survived from the early centuries of Christianity. It may be assumed however, that they did not reach a high level. The lack of tradition; a probable and very natural hostility towards, or refusal to accept, the importation of Roman works of art whose purpose was to stifle the evolution of popular movements, whether Celtic or Germanic; and the migrations of people from one part of Europe to another, certainly did not provide favourable circumstances for the establishment of any individual school of figurative expression. Even when the Germanic tribes were converted to Christianity, and were brought into closer contact with Mediterranean civilisation, they were unable to absorb Byzantine art as the Latin peoples had done, because they had neither a Greek nor an Asiatic past. In spite of this, Byzantine art, usually conveyed by monks, did penetrate among the Saxons, Celts and Britons and other Germanic tribes who were permanently established in their respective regions and who, with the help of Christianity, had become part of contemporary civilisation. When these races did produce figurative work they borrowed and made use of Byzantine iconography, although with very un-Byzantine results.

Examples of their work, illustrating the transformation which took place in the North and West of Europe of models brought in from the East or from Rome, or directly from Byzantium, must once have existed in basilicas and other buildings. These have disappeared, but the changes can be followed very well by means of illumination.

The origins of pre-Carolingian illumination are still obscure, although some elements are common to the Irish, the Anglo-Saxons (the most important school), the Franks, Visigoths and Lombards. The paintings in most cases are entirely decorative; a geometric design, sometimes simple and sometimes complex, of straight lines, curves, diagonals, spirals, circles and zig-zags, combined with animals of fantastic shapes and sometimes even stylised, almost geometric, figures. Later, especially in England, a need was felt to illustrate specific subjects, but the geometric style did not change. Only a few colours are used, clear and flat between penned outlines: there is no gold at all. It is possible that this type of decoration may have been a simplification or a graphic interpretation of motifs which had come from the East, especially Syria, by means of textiles or the products of other minor arts such as gold work. The Irish were, after all, very skilful goldsmiths.

When we remember that Byzantium and Rome used to send superbly illustrated manuscripts, often copied from classical models, to the monasteries of the British Isles, it seems surprising that this new and equally beautiful decorative sense (perhaps even more beautiful from the purely ornamental point of view), seems to have been derived from the products of commercial art which were either Syrian or Egyptian. But apart from the fact that barbarian taste inclines towards the decorative, these examples of minor arts most nearly resembled the remote local traditions of the Eastern races and consequently were more congenial than the " decadent " Greek-Byzantine examples.

The monastery system is of fundamental significance in the history of the Middle Ages even for painting. Pre-Carolingian and Anglo-Irish illuminated manuscripts were very important, and since the work was done exclusively by monks they were widely diffused both in the barbarian world and in Italy. Furthermore, by the end of the sixth century the Irish monks had become great missionaries and travellers and they continued their journeyings all through the seventh century and even later, so that the decorative style of their manuscripts was to be found from France to Spain, from Germany to Italy (for example at Bobbio and Monte Cassino).

The most famous Irish manuscripts of the seventh century are the Book of Kells, and the Book of Armagh. The Gospel of S. Cuthbert (or Lindisfarne manuscript) and the Book of Durrow, which are examples of the Irish style done in England, possibly belong to the beginning of the eighth century, like the Bible of Ceolfrid (Codex Amiatinus, Florence, Laurentian Library). In these codices, where the feeling depends greatly on

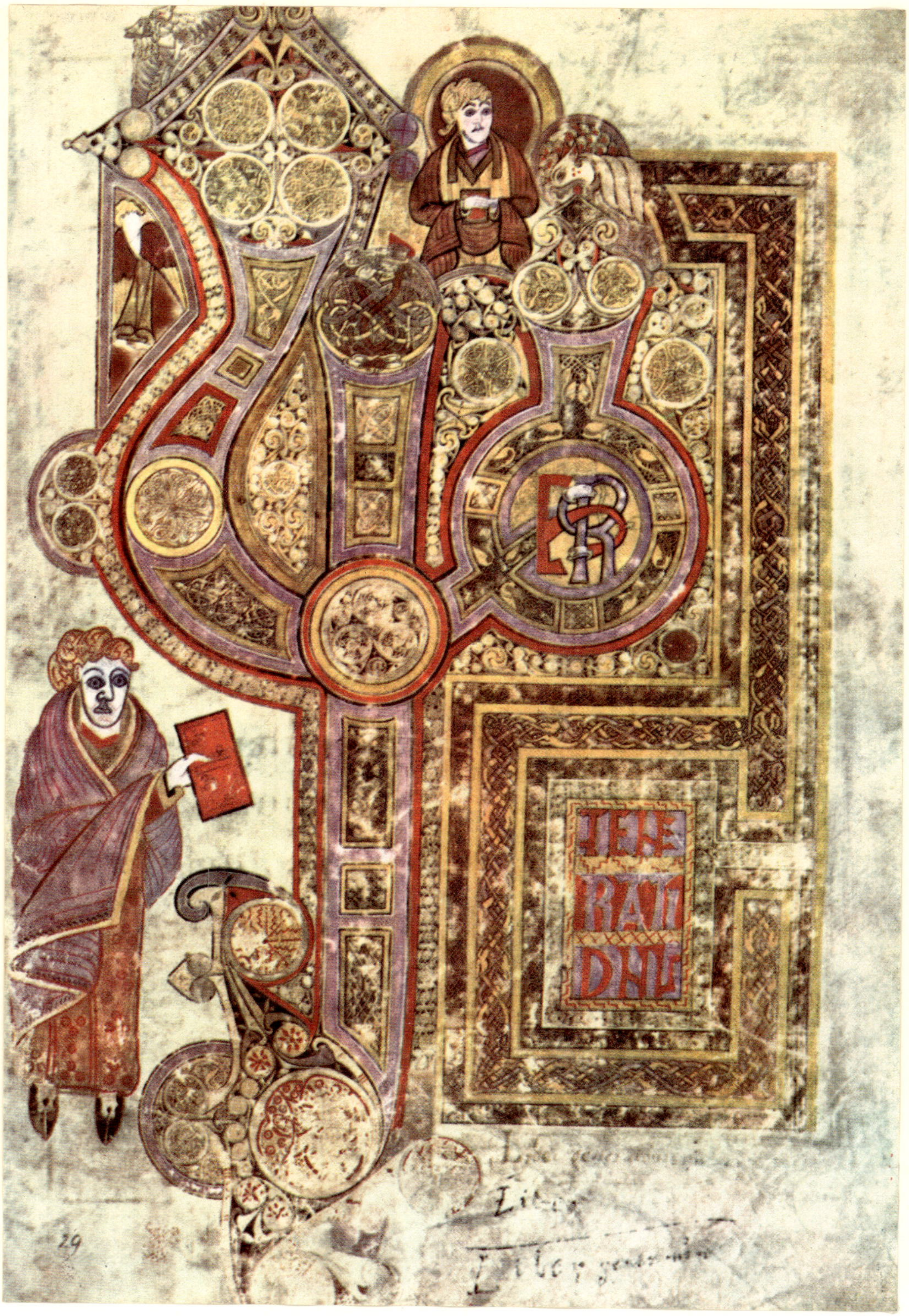

Irish art: Evangeliarium, known as the Book of Kells. Trinity College, Dublin

the linear quality, there is a wonderful harmony between the painting, the writing and the composition of the page. But what is surprising from the figurative point of view, and gives great originality to the work, is the expressive vitality of the outline in the case of both the human figures and animals which, although they are stylised, do not have the dry, emblematical eastern shapes. This is characteristic even of ribbons, strings and knots, although they conform to a strict geometric system.

The Irish invented the decoration of the medieval book. More than one motif from their elaborate geometric scheme was adopted by Frankish and Ottonian illuminators, and in spite of many changes lasted until the fourteenth century.

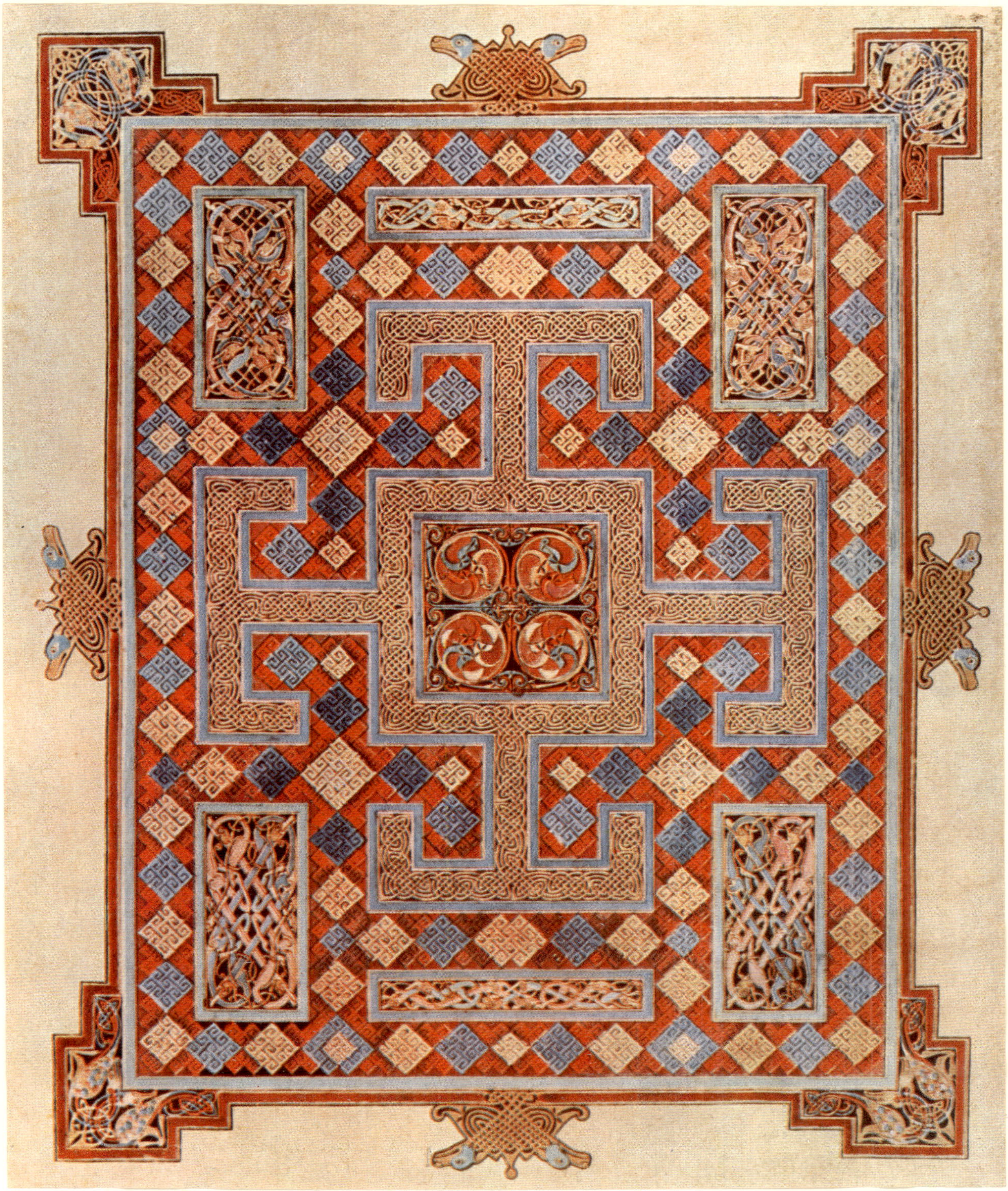

Anglo-Irish art: Evangeliarium known as the Lindisfarne manuscript, British Museum, London

Carolingian illumination, more complex pictorially and psychologically, was also more important in the artistic development of the new modern world of converted Christian-Barbarian people which was gradually emerging. Its birth is linked with Anglo-Irish illumination, but other elements are involved which combine to give it greater originality and to enrich it figuratively.

The great period of expansion in all fields of art which has been called the Carolingian renaissance was brought about by the exceptional personality of Charlemagne. Rough and uncultured as he was, he realised as well as the eastern Emperor — at that time deeply embroiled in the iconoclastic struggle — the political importance of art, and he became a great patron. He received strong support from the monastic orders, the section of the population best able to understand and further cultural interests at the time.

All the wall-paintings and mosaics of the finest period which decorated the basilicas and monasteries founded by Charlemagne and his successors in various parts of the Empire have perished. But it is important to note that there is textual evidence that this monumental painting did exist, and it is clear from the lists of German names that the majority of artists employed by Charlemagne were local. This demonstrates considerable independence of the all-powerful Byzantine, even if Carolingian artists relied on it for models and iconography.

Illuminated Carolingian manuscripts were numerous, and because of their wide circulation they were the most effective means of developing medieval painting, and we shall see that in Italy, for example, Carolingian manuscripts of the ninth and tenth centuries powerfully influenced some thirteenth-century painters. Carolingian illustration properly so-called began only towards the end of the eighth century. Its characteristics were however forecast towards the middle of the century in such works as the Gospels of Autun (754) and Flavigny, the Soissons Psalter and others, all of which show a strong British influence. Works carried out after this date show a sudden change and an internal homogeneousness, so that one cannot help thinking that a strong organising influence, that of the sovereign, lay behind the many schools and sub-divisions giving them a vigorous start and clarity of purpose. Thus Carolingian art too was created at court, or for a court, even when it was executed in the more distant monasteries. It too followed existing models from Rome, Byzantium and the East in general, which were invariably Byzantine in style. Like Byzantine art it tried to create afresh the beauty of ancient classical art. All these factors were common to both styles, but whereas Byzantine art incorporated ancient traditions, Carolingian art had the naivety and frankness of the barbarian sensibility. The artists were for the most part followers and pupils of Irish and Saxon monks from whom they had inherited a sharpness of outline, a carefully planned colour scheme, and a fundamental taste for orderly arrangement in their decorative schemes. They had too a great admiration for the ancient world, but no barbarian could, in the nature of things, create a soft and pleasing intellectual stylisation. Instead they produced a humble, ingenuous, admiring piece of work whose effect was the exact opposite of the model they copied. The classical models used by Carolingian miniaturists can rarely have been of high quality. Usually they would be mural paintings, mosaics, reliefs, or memorial stones, of which there were plenty of Romano-Gallic examples: productions of debased Roman or paleo-Christian style, which already showed many anti-classical trends. Naturally, however, the lavish effect of these manuscripts is a result of Eastern-Greek influence. The Carolingian miniaturist, unlike the Irish one, aimed at an effect of richness by using colours and gold. This was perhaps the only element in Byzantine art which could readily be assimilated by the Barbarians, who were spontaneously attracted by splendour and richness.

Eastern, particularly Syrian, influence is more clearly seen in the group of manuscripts which were commissioned personally by Charlemagne. This is the group known today as the Rhine school. The rich Gospel from the diocese of Magonza belongs to this group. It was composed for Charlemagne and his wife Hildegarde between 781 and 783, and is therefore the oldest known Carolingian manuscript; it has a purple background with gold lettering, and the geometric decoration reveals a knowledge of British illumination.

The other group of Carolingian illumination is very different from the Rhenish school. It includes the schools of Tours, Rheims, Metz, and the Franco-Saxon school,

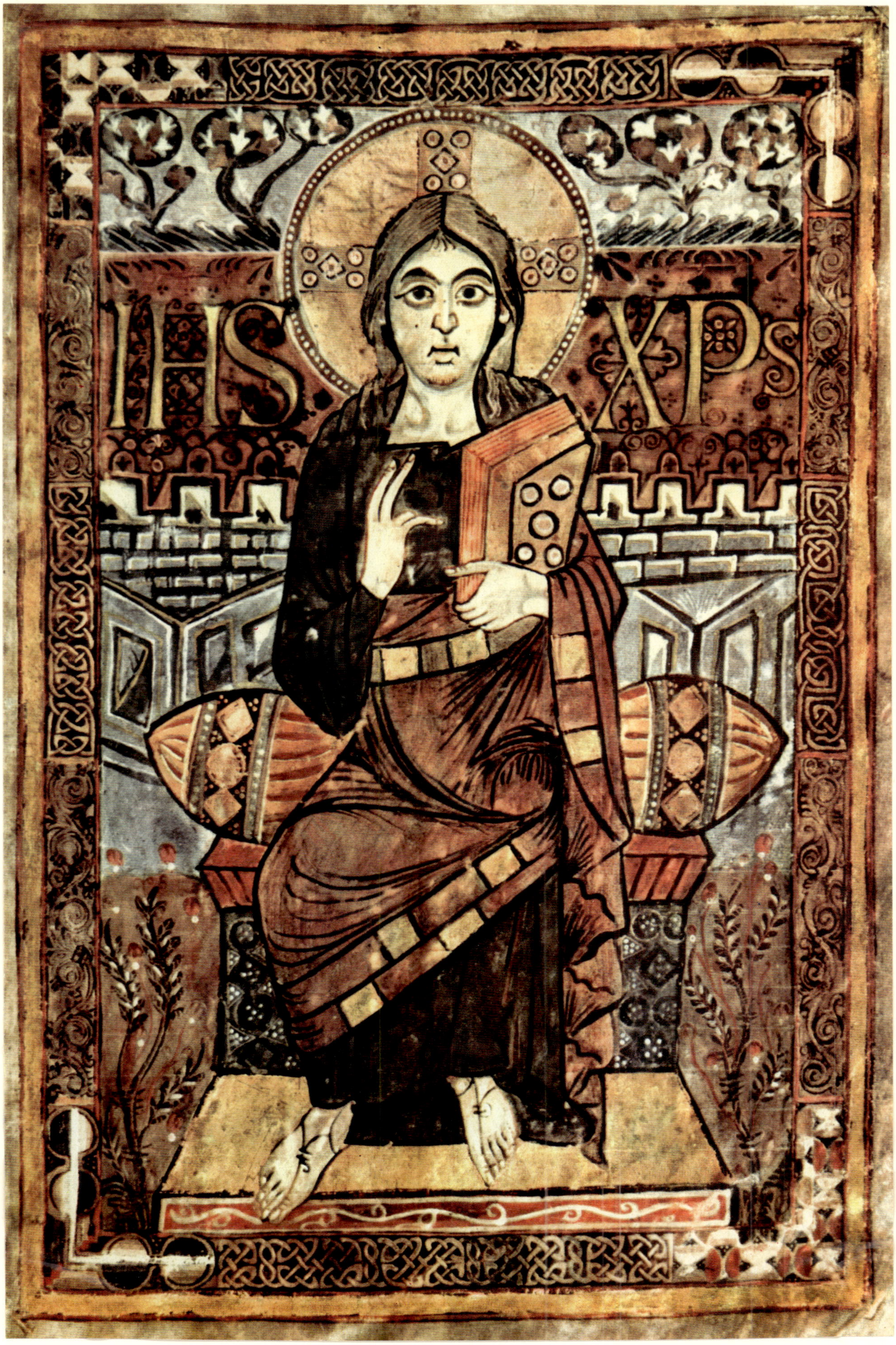

Carolingian art: Christ from the Evangeliarium of Charlemagne. (enlarged)

Bibliothèque Nationale, Paris

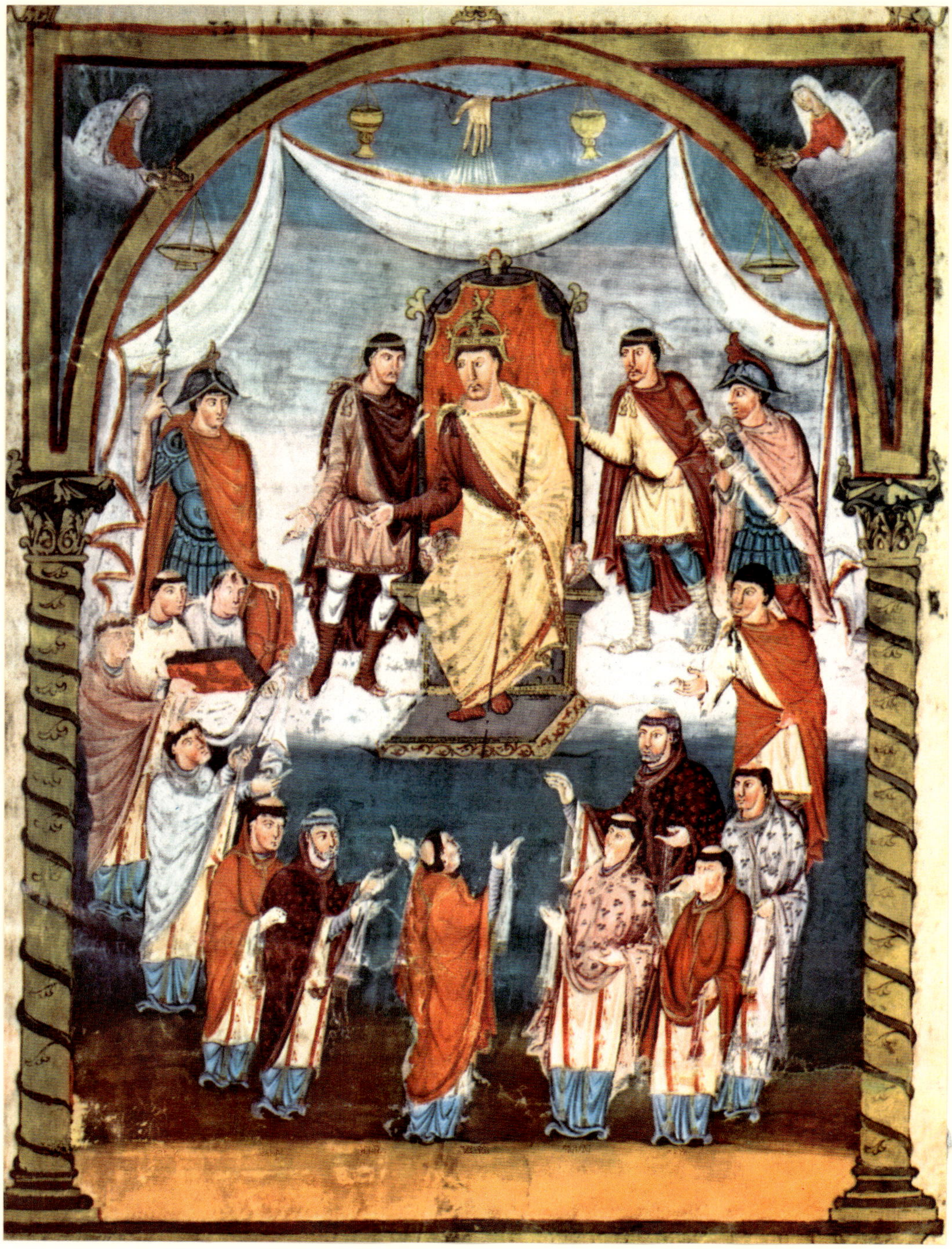

Carolingian art: First Bible of Charles the Bald. Bibliothèque Nationale, Paris

with further sub-divisions. They are all distinguished by their great enthusiasm for classical antiquity, not the equivocal reflection found in contemporary works of Greek-Eastern origin, but the purer style as seen in late Latin works of local origin. In manuscripts which date back to the end of the eighth century, for example, we can see the beginnings of architectural backgrounds, with arches, columns, and pillars, obviously copied from Roman buildings. This is a fact of some importance, because it indicates a more receptive artistic awareness which was a forerunner of the Romanesque movement. Romanesque art is indeed incomprehensible without some understanding of these Carolingian sources.

Credit for the first long and active campaign to distribute Carolingian manuscripts beyond local boundaries belongs to Tours, through the monastery of S. Martin and the dependent convent of Marmoutier. It is usual to attribute the origins of the school of Tours to the English monk Alcuin, a man of high culture, who was trained at York. But in reality the part which he could have played during the brief period when he was Abbot of S. Martin (796-804) is not clear. The manuscripts which date from this period have an appearance which is still almost pre-Carolingian, so much so that they cannot be very closely linked with later developments. Nor do we know of any which were actually commissioned by Alcuin, since all those which bear his name are of a somewhat later date, such as the London Vulgate. We know however that Alcuin brought a number of English manuscripts to Tours, and this may have inspired the foundation of the school on Anglo-Saxon models. At any rate masterpieces were inspired in the time of Alcuin's successors and pupils, reaching a peak in the time of the Count Abbot Vivien (845-851) in the reign of Charles the Bald. Vivien had the remarkable manuscript known as " The first Bible of Charles the Bald " written and illustrated for this king about the year 846. The ceremony of presenting the Bible is portrayed with life-like portraits of the people concerned, and is an unusual instance in western painting of the representation of a contemporary event. From now onwards, however, there is a tendency in Carolingian illumination to paint portraits and historical events. And history, whether sacred or secular (for example the stories of S. Jerome in the Bible of Charles the Bald), is narrated with all the liveliness and directness of a contemporary chronicle. Action is the keynote of the scenes, and a maximum of expression is conveyed by the gestures, by the use of a jerky design, with breaks and uneven lines. Rich and shining colour adds subtle metallic vibrations.

We are undoubtedly, in the tenth century, in the presence of an expressive ability of enormous potentiality which was the exact antithesis of the frozen Byzantine style. This trembling of life in the figures seems to reveal the astonishment of someone who has suddenly and miraculously, after centuries of painting composed according to an unchangeable canon, recaptured and eagerly mobilised all his expressive capabilities.

The peak of liveliness and complexity both in form and composition was reached by the school of Rheims, from which the masterly Utrecht Psalter has survived. Although it is only in pen work it is very important for the influence it wielded. The centre of the school was the Abbey of Hautvillers, and the leading spirit was the Archbishop Ebbon for whom the Abbot Pierre de Hautvillers commissioned, from the artist of the psalter, a gospel known as Gospel of Ebbon (Epernay, Manuscript 1).

It is noteworthy that this school, unlike the western school of illumination, had little or no love for decorative motifs, and often omitted them altogether. Their aims were more realistic and more pictorial and their affinity is perhaps with the more classical school of Byzantine miniaturists. The results, however, were very remote both spiritually and aesthetically from those of the Byzantine codices. Among Carolingian schools, the strongest interest in classical antiquity is shown at Rheims. The neighbourhood of Rheims happened to be very rich in classical remains, particularly bas-reliefs. And it is significant that the technique of the Rheims artists, which was very pictorial, at times almost " impressionist ", aspired towards plastic effects in the figures. To achieve this effect they used very small and frequent hatches which followed the waving outlines of the planes, so that the result bore a semblance to gold work. It is quite possible that objects in gold of classical or classical-Byzantine origin replaced sculpture as models whenever possible. Even from the archaeological point of view we can see how the miniaturists of Rheims loved antiquity. There is a profusion of classical buildings in their work; objects and costumes are faithfully reproduced, as well as landscapes in the neo-Alexandrian manner.

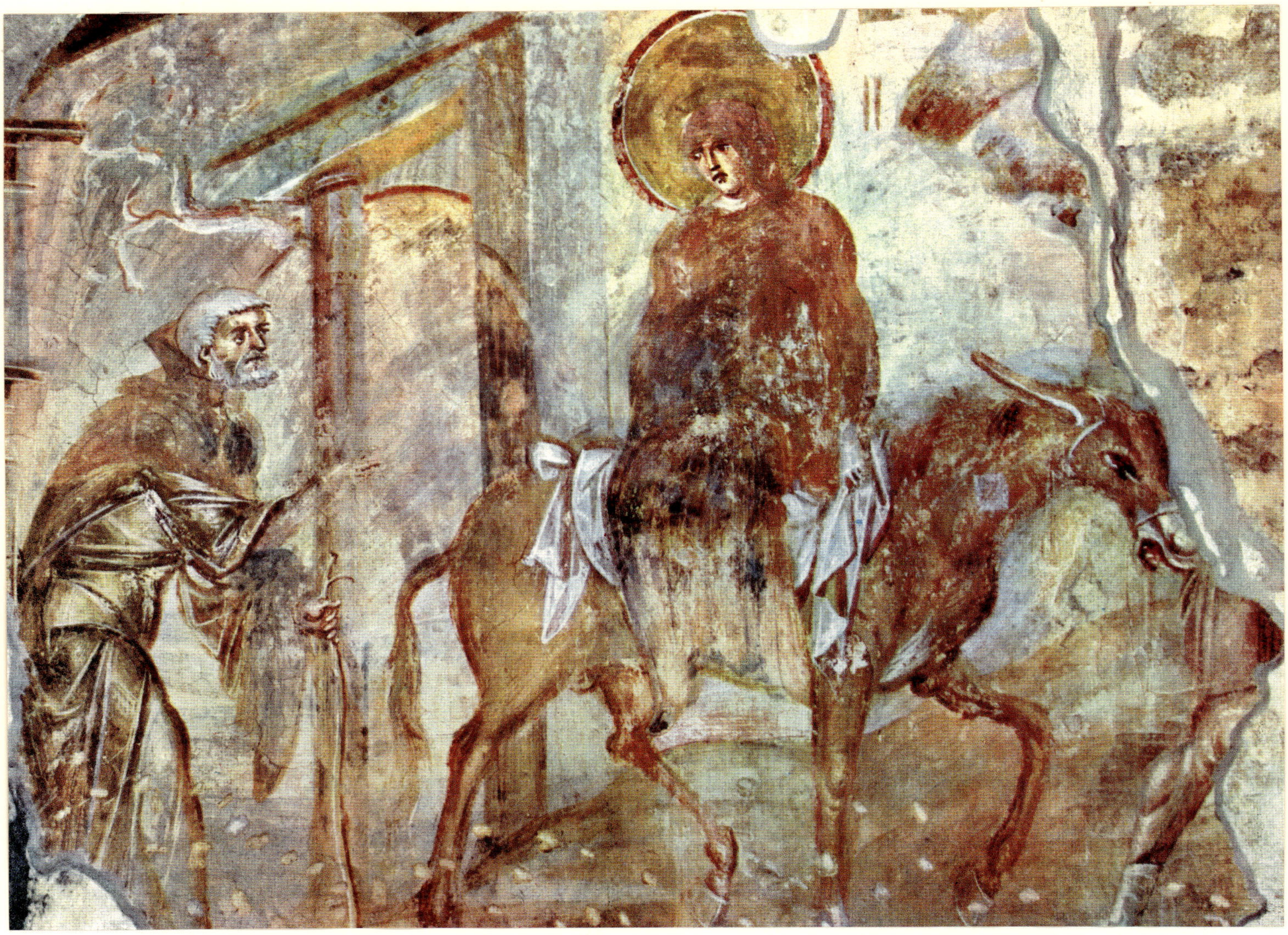

Master of Castelseprio: Journey to Bethlehem. Church of S. Maria, Castelseprio

spirit which eventually appeared in the heart of the Byzantine tradition, as a result of the adoption of a more deeply classical and western approach. But in Italy this renewal — authentic and not fleeting like the " Renaissance " of Constantinople after the Iconoclasts — only took place several centuries later, with the advent of Cimabue and Duccio. We do not know whether the painter of Castelseprio was Franco-Saxon or Italian, but judging by the Byzantine tone underlying the work the latter would seem to be the more likely. There is too little to compare his work with for us to form a judgment. But if Castelseprio does represent the first infiltration of western culture, it also demonstrates very clearly how slow Italy was to accept and assimilate this influence, and how she remained for a long time to come, we may say until Giotto, the last bulwark of Byzantine painting in the West.

With the exception of the frescoes at Castelseprio, there are no traces to be found in Italy of direct Carolingian influence. In other western countries however this influence was very strong, and owing to the circulation of manuscripts was very easily spread among courts and monasteries. It was particularly important because it resulted in the revival of the English school of illumination and provided a stimulus for the Germanic races during the tenth and eleventh centuries.

While the iconoclastic movement was occupying the Eastern Empire during the ninth century, painting was in a very flourishing state at Rome and elsewhere in Italy. But although there was a great deal of activity, there were unfortunately no new developments or awakenings, as there were in France and other Western countries. Throughout the ninth century Italy in general and Rome in particular must have been full of Greek workmen who sought refuge from the Iconoclasts. At Rome indeed there had always been a colony, but whereas formerly they had been temporary residents they were now permanent and organised into important workshops which were frequented by local artists.

The fact that the mosaics which have survived since the ninth century in many Roman churches show great similarity among themselves leaves no doubt that there was at the time a definite school, or a number of schools closely connected both economically and industrially. We can now see, and it may have occurred in Italy for the first time because historical and social circumstances were propitious, the phenomenon of the industrialisation of Byzantine painting, although there had been tendencies in this direction from the beginning, owing to the expansionist and imperialist systems which, one might say, gave birth to the style.

The flat, summary, schematic treatment of many eighth-century Roman mosaics seems to be accentuated in the ninth century, and to reveal a decorative conception based on colour and form. None of the mosaics dating from the time of Paschal I (817-824) in the basilicas of S. Cecilia, S. Maria in Domnica, S. Prassede, or in those of the time of Gregory IV (827-844) in the Basilica of S. Mark is of great interest either in design or content. The absence of any genuine creative feeling is so marked that it seems reasonable to suppose that these works were copied from long established models. Even the execution varies, possibly because commercial methods were so far advanced that specialist artists were employed for different parts of the composition; some for the faces, others for the drapery, others for the landscapes, and so on. As a rule the colouring is flat and uniform in the backgrounds and drapery, and uneven and patchy in the faces, so that the results recall the primitive " impressionist " painting. Generally speaking, contrasting colours are placed next to each other, but are blended to some extent by the typical technique of this period, of using glass *tesserae* with rough surfaces and of different sizes and shapes. This system caused the light to be broken up and reflected in various ways so that the colour effect was blended and multiplied.

The largest work of the Graeco-Roman mosaicists of the ninth century is to be found in S. Prassede, where the chapel of S. Zenone, built by Paschal I as a tomb for his mother Theodora, is of particular importance. The architecture, rich decoration and encrustations in marble and mosaic are all typically Byzantine, and the chapel has been called " a jewel of eastern art ". Although this was the greatest period of Carolingian art there is no trace of either Latin or western influence. Nor is there any sign of a new figurative, much less iconographical, treatment. The vault contains the well-known composition of the angels supporting a half-figure of Christ within a circle. The Descent into Hell between the Transfiguration and the Throne of God is of special interest because it is the oldest example of *Anastasis* which has survived. Artists employed fixed schemes which had become old, or rather old-fashioned, and which they followed mechanically. Their aim was to achieve an effect of dazzling colour by the most skilful use of their materials. These systems were particularly well suited to small buildings, such as the chapel of S. Zenone, which has indeed the enchantment of a fairy-tale jewel box.

It is unnecessary to add, after all that has been said, that paintings in the ninth century lost almost all contact with reality. Their character could have been more expressive if it had sprung from a stronger and deeper feeling for the Transcendent Deity. But instead the abstract quality seems like a mechanical simplification which is purely decorative.

Nor do the frescoes of the ninth and tenth centuries (now mostly in fragments) show any signs of invention or development, although there are numerous examples in and near Rome, for instance at Subiaco. They do however provide evidence of the enormous production of the period and, unlike the mosaics, show a variety of trends, many of which seem to be Eastern and provincial.

The quality is on the whole poor everywhere, and sometimes makes the attribution of dates difficult, so that the standard of wall-painting in Rome at that time is by no means clear. It would seem that either few of the best examples of Roman wall-paintings have survived or else the work was only done by inferior artists, possibly by monks from the eastern provinces. The most successful is possibly the famous Ascension in the primitive church of S. Clement, dating from the time of Leo IV (847-855). There is a great deal of movement in the scene, with the apostles at the bottom of the picture expressing their feelings by means of agitated gestures, and the angels above surrounding the aureole which encircles Christ. The Madonna is shown in an attitude of prayer. The two figures of S. Vitus and Pope Leo IV are so still that they appear lifeless, and are placed laterally like the wings of a stage. They strike the only " modern " note in the painting, the rest following the traditional theme of Byzantine Ascensions, used particularly in miniatures, and derived from the Ascension of the Syrian codex of Rabula in the sixth century (Florence, Laurentian Library) which in turn was copied from an even older model. In the wall-painting at S. Clement a certain delicacy of treatment accentuates the modelling and shows that it was copied from a miniature. But this vitality, which is more apparent than real, is obviously an imitation, and has nothing of the genuine, strong, constructive vigour of contemporary Carolingian illumination, although it has been suggested that the Ascension in S. Clement does have an affinity with this school.

When the iconoclastic period came to an end the ties between Rome and Byzantium were no longer so close as in former times. The Pope now obtained political support from the western Empire, although this did not result in a wide acceptance of Carolingian art. This is a proof of the extent to which Rome had combined with the eastern Empire from the outset in establishing and spreading Christian art, and how deeply rooted Graeco-Oriental traditions had been ever since the seventh century, possibly reinforced later by the influx of refugee Byzantine artists. Instead of receiving art from the West, Rome dispatched it there. Byzantine manuscripts were frequently sent to France and Germany, where they provided inspiration for the unformed imaginations of the miniaturists.

If we except Castelseprio — which remains an enigma — no important signs of the remarkable school of western painting can be found in Italy. Elsewhere painting was in a popular vein, and of a lower standard than in Rome. The supposed Carolingian influence, which is often referred to whenever a sign of life is visible in Italian painting of the ninth and tenth centuries, remained in fact so superficial that it had no effect on the fundamental Greek style. The only result which contacts with the little understood Carolingian art did have was the introduction of a popular, facile note into copies of the old eastern models, which continued to enjoy increasing favour and fame among local artists and craftsmen.

A case in point are the paintings discovered in Benedictine monasteries, which have given rise to talk — greatly exaggerated — of a Benedictine " Renaissance ", or rather a Benedictine school. In the ninth century frescoes in the chapel of S. Vincenzo at Volturno, the great Benedictine Abbey founded in the eighth century, there are signs of a new freedom in the treatment of old themes. For example the artist, probably a monk, divided the Annunciation into two parts, placing the angel and the Virgin on either side of a window. In the same way the Child and servants of the Nativity scene are placed on one wall while the Mother faces them. The Abbot Epifanio (826-843)

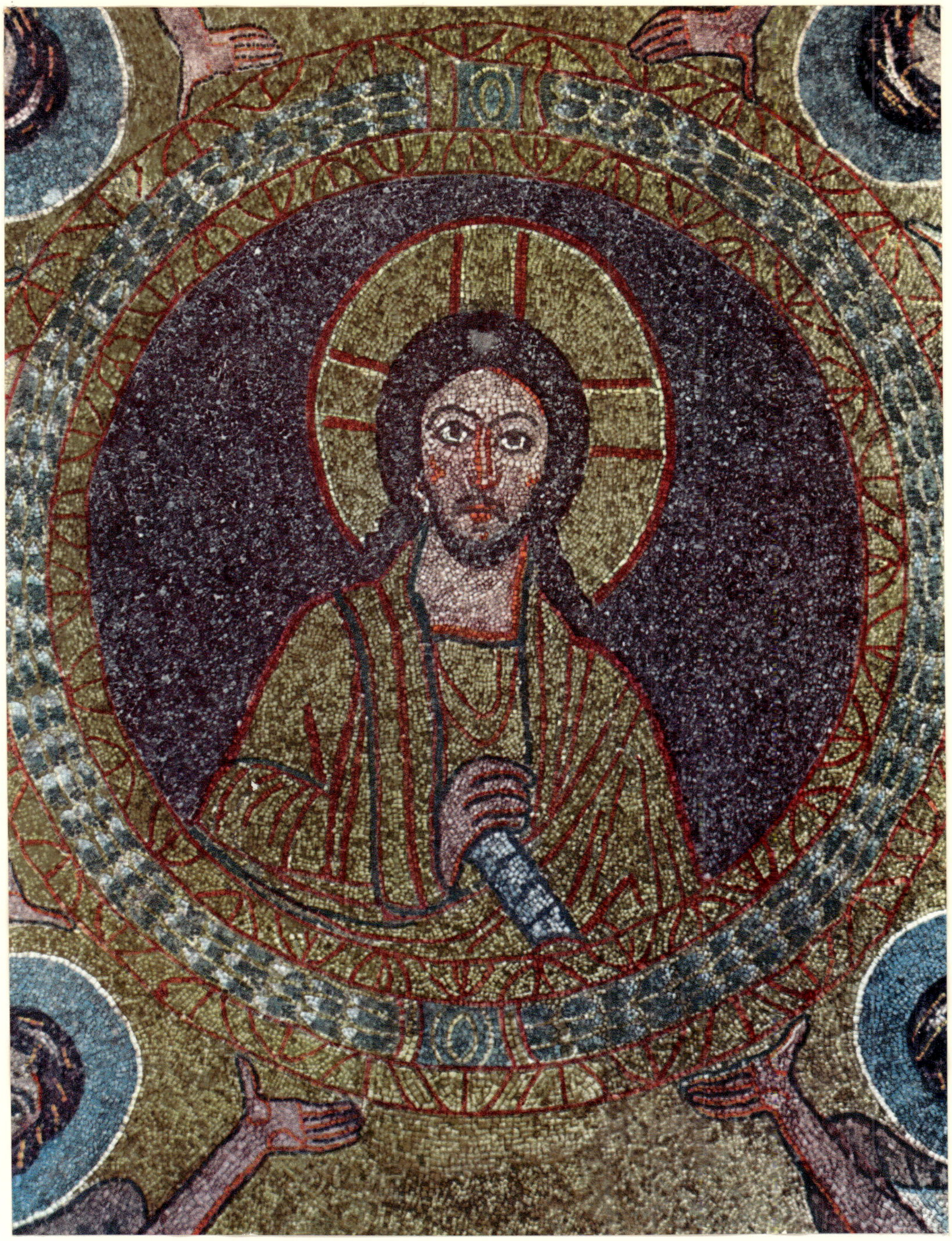

Romano-Byzantine art: Christ in Glory, detail from the vault of the chapel of S. Zenone.

S. Prassede, Rome

has been added to the Crucifixion and is shown kneeling outside the frame of the painting, giving an unusual impression of depth. There is an effort to create an effect of plastic form by gradations of light colours, and to convey expression by means of faces and gestures which, quite in the Carolingian style, are articulate or even violent. All these elements however seem to point not to a conscious attempt to create a style, but to a general acceptance of different pictorial trends, Roman, Carolingian, and Byzantine, which is understandable in view of the cultural activity of Benedictine centres, closely connected with both western and eastern monasteries. The latter always opposed the Iconoclasts, and it is worth noting that, especially in their illustrations to the Psalms, which were somewhat propagandist and polemical, their artists had shown signs of a lively popular style which seems to resemble the Benedictine rather than the Carolingian manner.

But the frescoes at S. Vincenzo in Volturno, like those in S. Crisogono in Rome, which are alleged to show the beginnings of the Benedictine school, remain essentially Romano-Byzantine, because this was the important element in their tradition; any impact which may have been felt from Franco-Saxon art was wholly superficial. Benedictine painting never became a school, because it had no genuine synthesis or originality, nor did it stimulate further developments; it remained a closed movement, limited to Benedictine centres of culture.

According to written sources, painting took an altogether new direction at Byzantium during the iconoclastic period. In order to avoid sacred images there had been a return to the Alexandrian school of primitive Christian art; and a naturalistic style of decoration was to be found in all buildings, even churches, showing birds, animals of various kinds, trees, and even landscapes, carefully arranged in decorative compositions. There was also a revival of classical themes. Portraits as well as historical paintings were of course continued, and recorded the exploits of the Emperors, or other contemporary events. This was a very different direction from that taken by " Byzantine " painting in Italy, especially in Rome, where, as we have seen, the old prototypes were wearily repeated, their decorative purpose being exaggerated in important works, elsewhere falling into a mechanical and popular dilettantism, very occasionally influenced by some western idea.

Except for fragments which are too small to permit even a hypothetical reconstruction, no paintings remain from the long iconoclastic period. After it was over the official guidance given to painting changed. In 842 the Church recognised the importance of images in a more precise way than before, and the use of sacred subjects for decorating interiors flourished once more.

The new flowering of painting, and of Byzantine art in general, was not entirely due to the end of the struggle against images; it was helped by the renewed political and commercial strength of the Eastern Empire. Once again, as in the early days of Christianity, and especially the sixth century, there was an expansionist programme for art. It was intensified under the Macedonian dynasty because, after the Moslem incursions had been halted, other regions were coming into the Constantinopolitan sphere, owing the fresh conversions to Christianity among such peoples as the Russians and Bulgarians. Economically, if not politically, Italy itself reverted to being a Byzantine province. Consequently Byzantine painting dominated Europe from Italy to the Balkans, from Russia to Armenia and Cappadocia, and also, of course, affected the more western countries, as far as Spain. Owing to Irish and Carolingian influence however the autochthonous characters of these countries were so deeply-rooted that although examples from the East were always treated with the greatest respect, imitations were automatically transformed into something wholly different.

The flowering of Byzantine art which took place towards the end of the ninth century under the Macedonian Emperors began again, after a brief interval, under the Comneni, and continued until the twelfth century, which is often called the " Second Golden Age." In painting it was characterised by a return to ancient classical sources. This return was a genuine attempt to make the classical element, in its purest form, dominate all the other influences which had contributed to the formation of Byzantine painting, and is a proof of the undoubted classical substratum which had always been present. But in spite of it, Byzantine painting remains substantially Eastern, because the principles on which it was based had been so firmly fixed and established from the fourth century in accordance with the political and religious system of the Empire that it was difficult to revolutionise or even modify it, so long as the all-powerful Byzantine theocracy continued. On the contrary these fixed imperial principles now acquired a greater value, when, after the defeat of the Iconoclasts, the Church officially declared that images possessed a particle of Divine energy and were consequently to be revered. It was probably mainly as a result of this declaration that the cult of icons spread enormously in the ninth century. Some of those judged to be particularly " divine " were repeated for centuries in Russia, where this was the only style permitted for religious paintings, right up to modern times. But before spreading to Russia icons became a kind of private or monastic cult. The same thing happened to some extent in icon-painting that frequently happened, for different reasons, in illumination, where the same pictures were repeated from the first century onwards, simply because the text had to be copied.

In monumental painting the fixed, unchanging principles applied above all to iconography, and developments which took place were entirely superficial. The new classical revival was neither spontaneous nor nostalgic; it was intellectual. It is curious, however, to note that Byzantine painting, with its intellectual formulae derived from innumerable artistic movements, prevented that total disintegration of the classical aesthetic which had been heralded since the decay of the Roman Empire, and at the same time also prevented a complete return to this aesthetic at least until the Italian Renaissance. It is something of a paradox that although the triumph of Byzantine art signified the death of classical art, it returned to this source every time a need was felt for new inspiration. This happened again, in the so-called revival in the time of the Paleologues, known as the " Third Golden Age ". It is evident that even if the classical element was not the most important, it was the co-ordinator and organiser of all the others.

This classical character is more obvious in illumination than in Byzantine painting. In the ninth century, and even more in the tenth, eleventh and twelfth, miniature painting often has an " antique " appearance. It has already been stressed that such miniatures were copies of genuine classical manuscripts, often from Alexandria. But expensive books of this sort, not only religious, were for the restricted circle of intellectual aristocrats, both lay and religious, who had conservative and literary tastes. Nor did they have so much influence as monumental or panel paintings. In the latter a classical spirit was shown by renewed effects of plasticity.

In a rather more popular — even crude — style, possibly of monastic origin, a plastic effect is attempted by means of sharper, more definite outlines which detach and almost cut out the background plane. In yet another, more cultured and polished style, which seems to have originated at court, and therefore was most likely influenced by the miniature painting of the court *atelier*, there is a gentle, mellow moulding of form by means of subtle colour passages. This second style seems to have developed a little later than the first, towards the eleventh century, and in the end it evidently prevailed, since its main characteristics can be found as late as the thirteenth and fourteenth centuries. Examples exist which contain both these styles, as well as others even more independent. Nevertheless, although this new flowering of Byzantine painting produced works of considerable excellence and importance, the intellectual approach ended by achieving consummate skill rather than genuine poetry. This style gradually became so loaded with learning, subtlety and flamboyance that the results were rather like commercial art, especially the enamel and gold work. It was not that a genuine feeling was lacking, but it was so studied that it was reduced to a mere theory or system of feeling. Art of this kind however has an undeniable fascination: otherwise it would not have lasted for so long, even with political and economic support. It has the fascination of dominating architecture, so that space becomes indefinite, or infinite; of creating pale ghosts, swathed in splendour, and fabulous visions of landscapes composed of blue and golden skies, enamelled fields, glass rocks and cities bathed in the evening

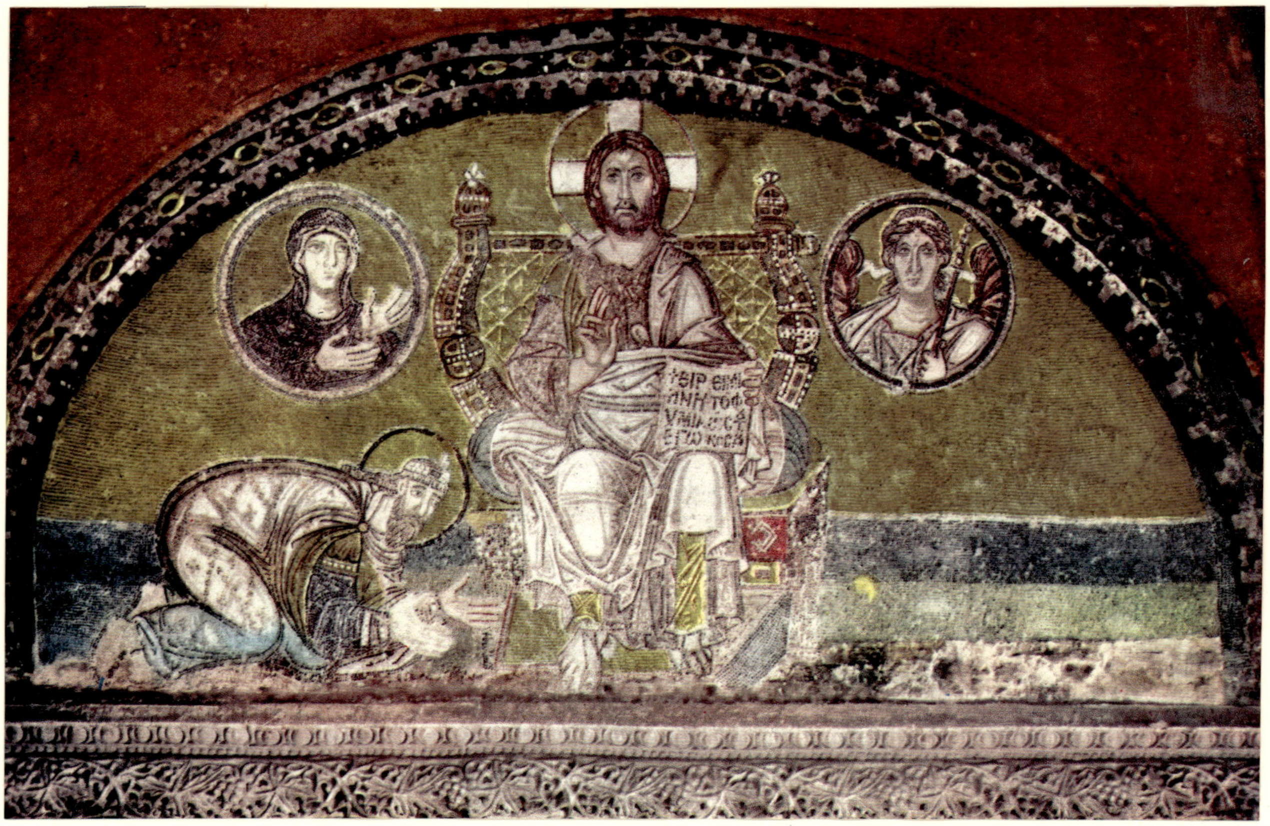

Byzantine art: Christ as Divine Wisdom with the Emperor Leo VI.

S. Sophia, Istanbul

sun. A luxurious art no doubt, even when it tried to be popular; but one which turned luxury into a worn-out, tragically inert form of poetry.

The final stage (we can call it this because it was to be the most lasting, the most famous and the most typically Byzantine) of painting can be studied in various parts of Europe, from Italy to Bulgaria and Greece, and even (which is unusual) in Istanbul. The interior of S. Sophia at Constantinople was completely covered in decorative-symbolic mosaic in the reign of Justinian and was given additional decorations at a later date which were more iconographically complex. Recent work has brought to light magnificent mosaics dating from the ninth century onwards.

From a fragmentary inscription it has been deduced that the mosaic in the apse was done immediately after the defeat of the Iconoclasts, in 843. The mosaics in the cupola and in the nave beneath it have not been dated, but it is possible that they are later than the tenth century, owing to delays in the work, and the enormous size of the church. Even so, the mosaics in the apse, the cupola and the nave, reveal a unity of conception. From that time onwards a coherent plan in series of works came to have great importance, either as liturgical sequences (representations alluding to the sacrifice of the Mass) or as narrative sequences (scenes from the lives of Christ, the Virgin and saints).

In the apse of S. Sophia the Virgin is shown enthroned with the Child, while angels portrayed on the arch seem to prepare the way. There are prophets and saints along the nave, and above in the cupola is the dominating figure of the Pantocrator. The symbolic unity of these pictures is clear, whereas the rest of the mosaics in S. Sophia are dedicatory and independent of one another. In the great days of the Empire they were gifts from the Emperors, but they have no inscriptions which would enlighten us

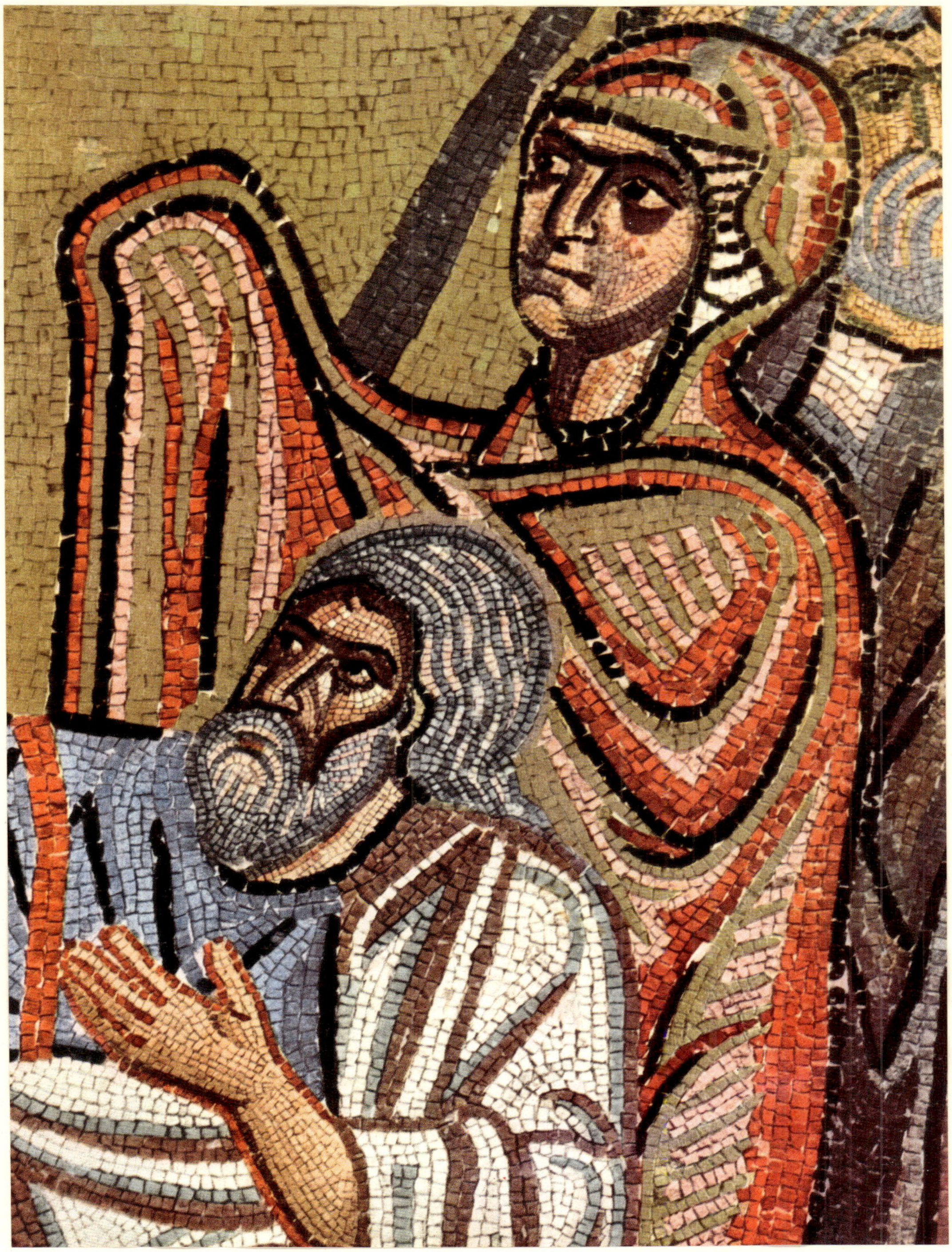

Byzantine art: Detail of the Descent into Hell. Nea Moni, Chios.

The series of mosaics, some of them merely fragments, in the church of Nea Moni (New Monastery) at Chios have a special importance in the eleventh century, at least within the confines of our actual knowledge of the history of Byzantine painting. The arrangement of this series corresponds to the principles of religious decoration of the post-iconoclast period, running from the choir to the single nave and narthex, with the Pantocrator (now destroyed), the Orans Virgin, saints and angels, and a series of fourteen scenes from the Gospels from the Annunciation to Pentecost. Their originality lies in the style: the figures are detached from a gold background by thick contours, and by so clear a contrast of light and shade that the forms are broken up into definite geometric planes. The black and blueish eyesockets, cutting into the white planes of the cheeks and forehead, are typical. The colouring presents clear contrasts which are harsh and discordant, sometimes bearing no relation to reality. For example, in the

Descent into Hades there is a king robed in dark blue, with a dark blue beard surrounded by a halo of green edged with red. Beside him is another king with a red halo edged with dark blue, and in the same scene Christ is robed in the same heavy dark blue, with deep folds of gold and with a slightly different shade of dark blue hair and beard. Generally speaking, the artist at Chios seems to like masses of colour which will stand out against the gold. The Marys of the Crucifixion are grouped together, a composition of blacks, greys and dark blues contrasting with the brightly coloured symmetrical group of S. John and the centurion. It is a style that reveals a passion for geometry even in the colour arrangements, which are dignified, carefully thought out, and clearly divided from the compactness of the golden background. The effect is one of heavy enclosed sadness, with little visual appeal.

The formal spirit of the painter of Chios, despite a certain aggressiveness, corresponds more to decorative than to psychological demands. This style of decoration, which reduces form and composition to a heavy geometric abstraction, would almost seem to suggest a figurative tradition of large, coloured, geometrical patterns in the style of Arabic ornaments. The comparison might seem too far-fetched — although the centurion of the Crucifixion is dressed as a Moslem soldier — were it not for the fact that many Moslem motifs came into the Eastern Empire during the iconoclastic period and that Moslem influence continued to be felt throughout the Mediterranean area. Nea Moni was a monastery which received monks of many different countries and cultures, and a possible contact with the elaborate Arab schemes of colour and decoration may explain this isolated example at Chios, because it is not merely an extreme case of the pictorial style of another monastery, namely S. Luke in Phocis. Again, we can see Moslem and Byzantine motifs co-existing, and sometimes merging together, in Sicily, for example in the Palatine Chapel at Palermo.

The mosaics in the church at Daphni in Attica are wholly different from the work at Chios, and are some fifty years later (c. 1100). As we have already said, Daphni represents the purest classical trend of all, developing almost academically in the time of the Comneni. The prevailing interest is in creating forms with a strong plastic suggestion between very thin outlines. The colouring becomes thinner and brighter by delicate contrasts on the gold, which is freely used to emphasise the outlines of drapery and mountains, as well as being used for backgrounds and decorative parts. The extent to which classical models were familiar to the painter, or painters, of Daphni is shown by the fullness of the regular, calm faces, and by the treatment of the nude (Baptism of Christ and Crucifixion) which strongly resembles miniatures copied from ancient texts in the ninth and tenth centuries. The religious theme of the decoration is a usual one, which is often found for example at S. Luke and at Chios: the Pantocrator in the cupola, the Virgin in the apse, angels, prophets and saints in the arches, vaults and niches, and finally a limited number of scenes from the Gospels — thirteen in the nave and six in the narthex.

The twelfth-century Sicilian mosaics in the cathedral at Cefalù and the Palatine chapel at Palermo offer a close parallel to the mosaics at Daphni. But the artistic merit of the Sicilian examples is greater. They date from the reign of Roger II and constitute the most important works in the pure Comnenian style.

The liberal fashion in which the Norman kings accepted the most diverse artistic and iconographical forms is remarkable. In fact for some centuries past, Sicily (and to some extent the extreme South of the Italian peninsula) had become accustomed to do so according to the invasions, conquests or various infiltrations to which it was subjected. But the island had above all a feeling for Byzantine art, having been a province of the Empire since the ninth century. There was also the spirit of emulation which all new monarchs of the West had felt (for example Charlemagne and the

Ottonians) for the Eastern Emperor, and it can easily be understood why Roger II wanted distinguished painters from Constantinople, versed in the style of the court, to work in the cathedral of Cefalù and the Palatine Chapel.

The mosaics which date from the reign of Roger II in the cathedral at Cefalù are those in the apse, dated 1148, and those in the presbytery, which are contemporary. The great figure of the Pantocrator dominating the space is a masterpiece of graphic delicacy and balance of colour, and seems immense in the apse, larger than all the other figures of the Virgin, the archangels and apostles. The regularity and symmetry of the decorative arrangement at Cefalù tend to isolate the figures in empty golden spaces; and their isolation is further emphasised by their geometric construction, well-matched by the sober colouring, which is none the less pure and radiant chiefly because of the way in which the blues and golds, the pale flesh tints and the blacks of the eyes and eye sockets stand out.

The art in the Palatine Chapel (1132-1140) is more heterogeneous and includes Arab motifs. Nevertheless, the mosaics are wholly Byzantine in spirit and workmanship, even if the iconography is not entirely eastern. The pure Comnenian style is to be seen in the series of icons of the saints which in their descriptive power and

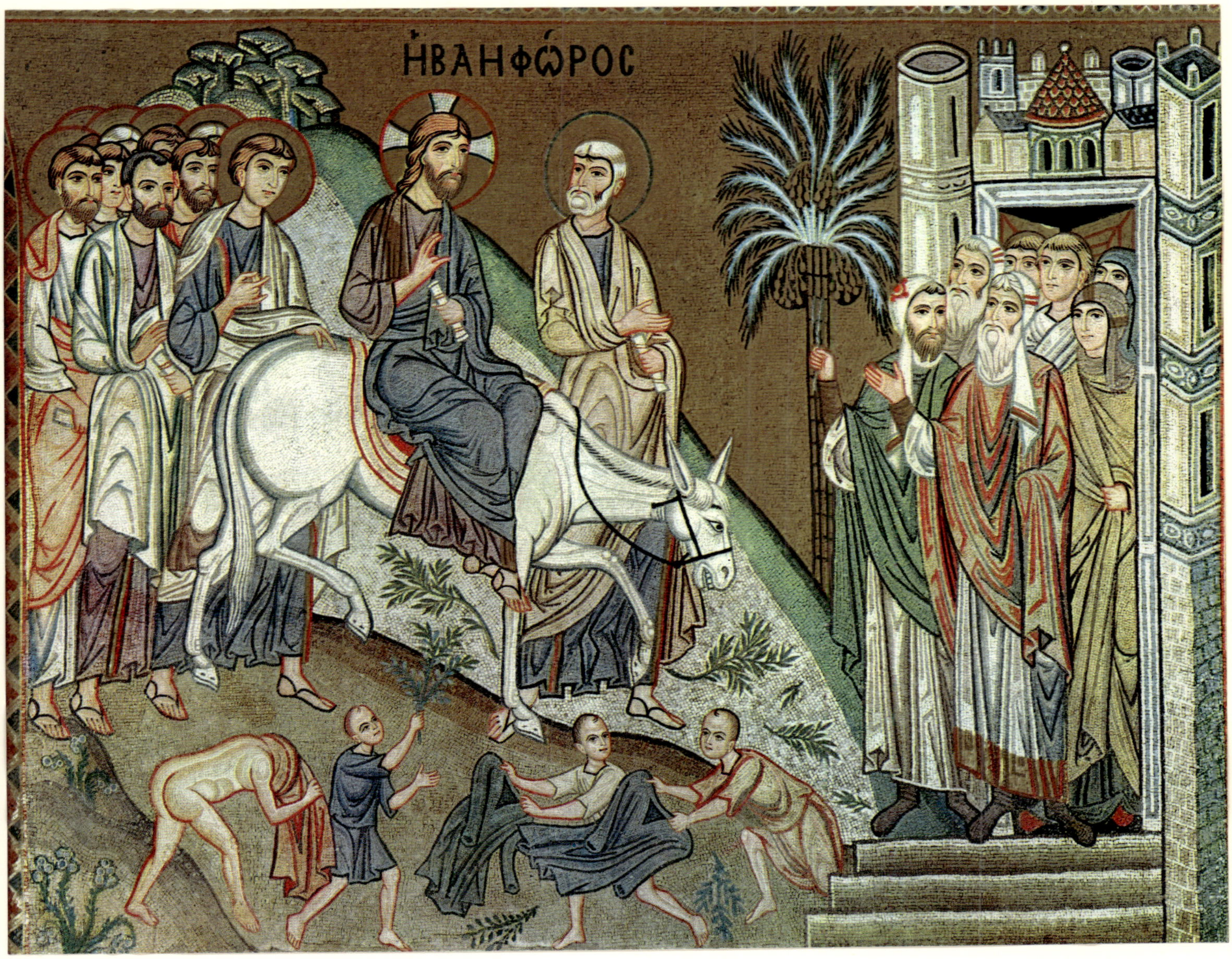

Byzantine art: Christ entering Jerusalem. Palatine Chapel, Palermo

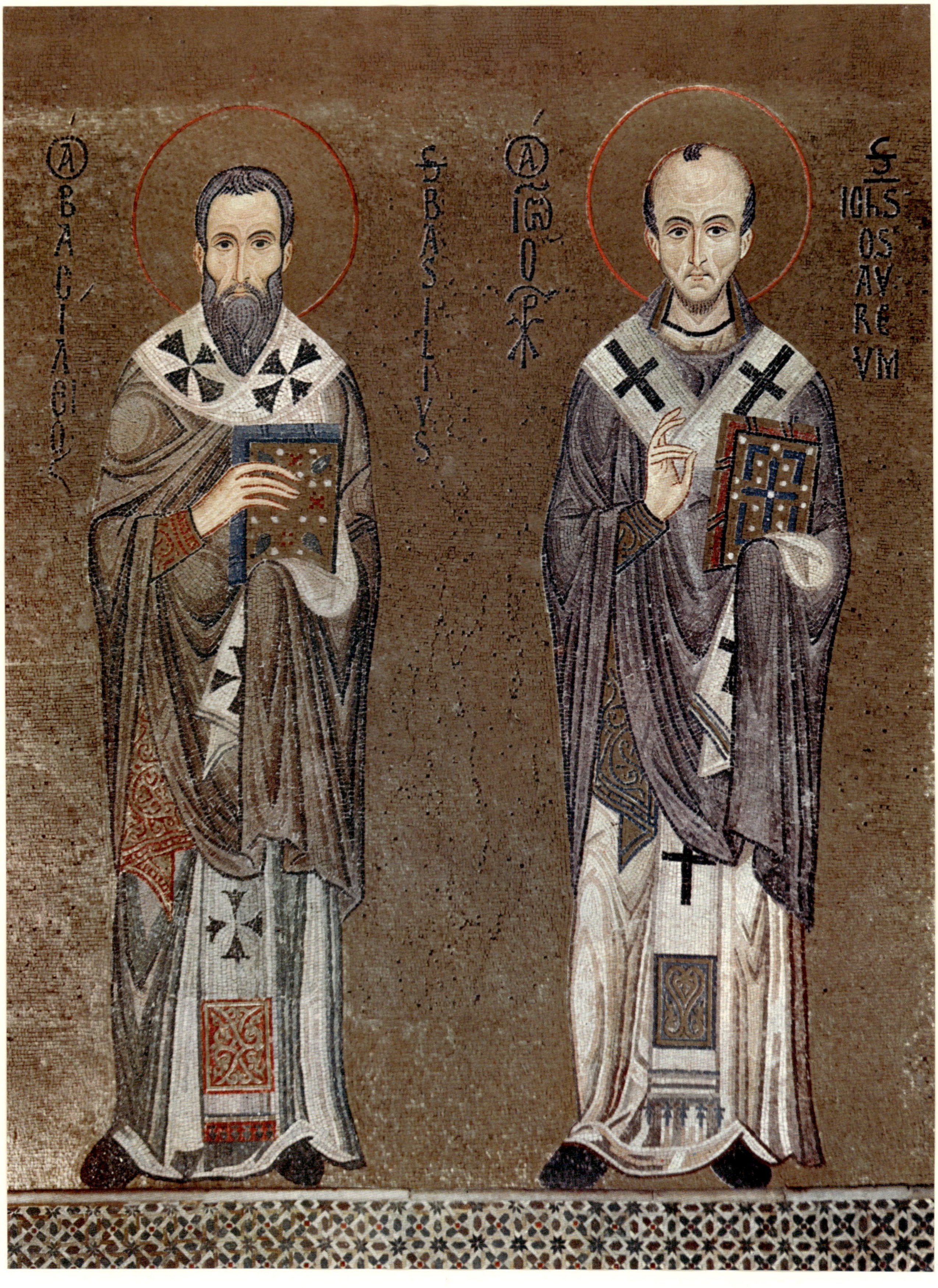

Byzantine art: SS. Gregory Theologue and Basil the Great.

Palatine Chapel, Palermo

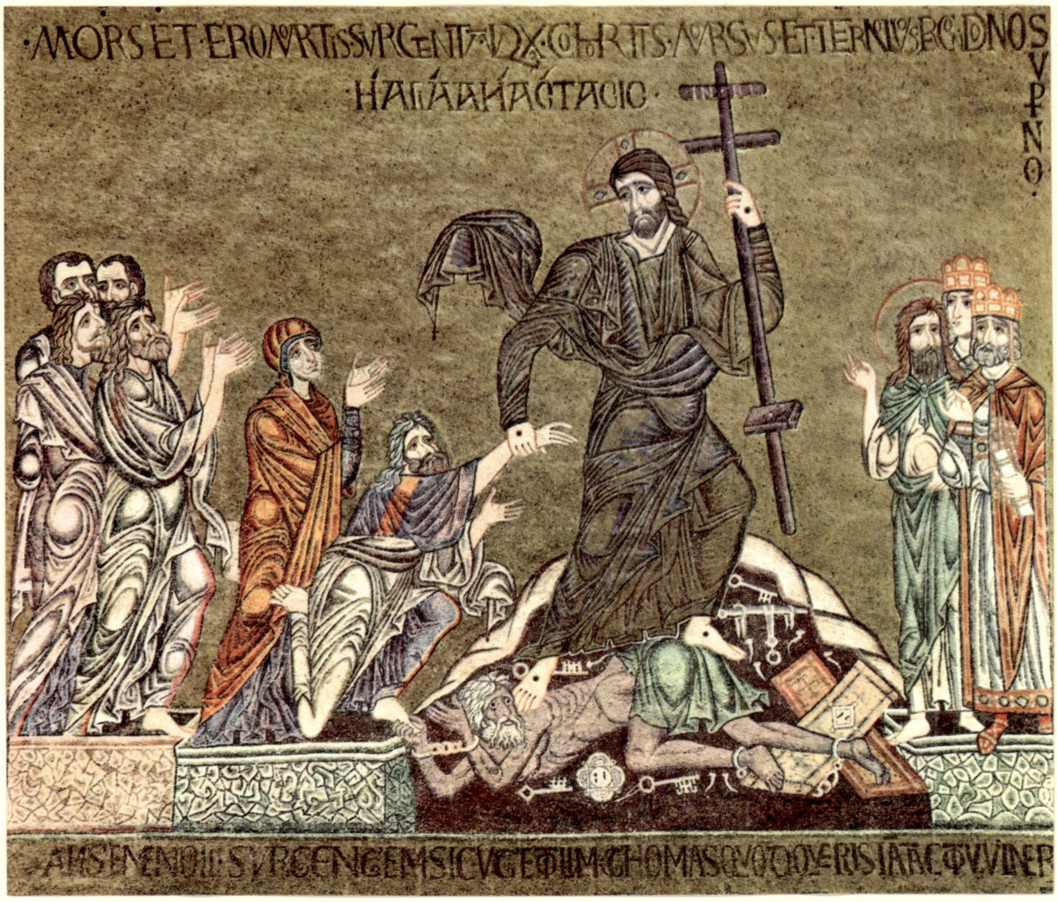

Byzantine art: The Descent into Hell. S. Mark's, Venice

superb design are among the finest examples known of the ascetic type of figure.

The scenes from the Gospels are among the greatest achievements of Byzantine mosaic art. The rich, often crowded compositions are elucidated by the delicate and carefully balanced arrangements of pale and spring-like colours, rose, white, greens, greys, ochre. A learned style, certainly, but one which was based on the supreme aesthetic of simplicity and order.

This calm, clear atmosphere is not to be found in the cathedral of Monreale where there are large numbers of mosaics, mostly later in date (c. 1182). Here we see a reflection of the style known as the " pathetic " which appears as far back as the ninth century and became more widespread from the eleventh century onwards. This " pathetic " style represents an attempt to break away from conventional stylisation into a more dramatic mood, but the consequent effect of " pathos " or suffering is false, because it is based on a mere change of rhythms mechanically employed, and is not the outcome of a genuinely fresh approach to reality. The result was that this development only accentuated the stylisation which had existed for centuries. And so a typical intellectual compromise resulted — if in fact the dramatic is the opposite of the conventional. But a change of this nature in Byzantine art, according to Toesca, " was not the work of a creative artist, whose individuality could never have been kept within the traditional limits but would have found methods of expression which were substantially new, and suited his own temperament; such a change was, on the contrary, produced by a continuous movement which became stronger with the years, but never altered the fundamental characteristics of Byzantine traditions... "

The decoration of S. Mark's in Venice, which was modelled on the Holy Apostles in Constantinople, was the work of centuries, possibly beginning in the late eleventh or early twelfth century, although the architecture was finished between 1077 and 1095. Here, in some parts of the interior, we have examples of the pathetic style, probably dating from the twelfth century. We see them in the cupola of the Ascension, which is iconographically similar to that in S. Sophia at Salonika, and in the cupola of the Pentecost. The prophets in the backgrounds show, somewhat comically, how this style manages to transform the Byzantine tradition of portrait painting which was based on the idealisation of a type, or of a class of persons.

It is possible that many of these Venetian mosaics were done by local craftsmen, supervised by artists from Constantinople. In view of the close contacts between Venice and Byzantium, especially from the eleventh century onwards, there must have been a large group of authentic Eastern mosaicists employed on S. Mark's. The scenes of Christ, most of which belong to the first half of the twelfth century, do in fact appear to be wholly Eastern in workmanship. They are typical of the dramatic trend, and are among the most frigid, mannered examples of this style. The mosaics inside S. Mark's have a decorative value, viewed as a whole, as a sumptuous and brilliant covering for the architecture, rather than any genuine aesthetic interest.

The frescoes in the crypt of the cathedral at Aquileia resemble the style of the scenes of Christ at S. Mark's. Even the vivid contrasts of colour between thick green and red outlines and strong white lights, recalls mosaic technique. Their close connection with Byzantium is clearly shown in the decorative sections, which are identical with those found in Byzantine miniature paintings. At Aquileia, however, the conventional Byzantine pathos in the Scenes of the Passion is of higher quality than in S. Mark's. One might almost say this is due to good theatrical direction, judging by certain arrangements in the composition — for example the way in which the grief-stricken group

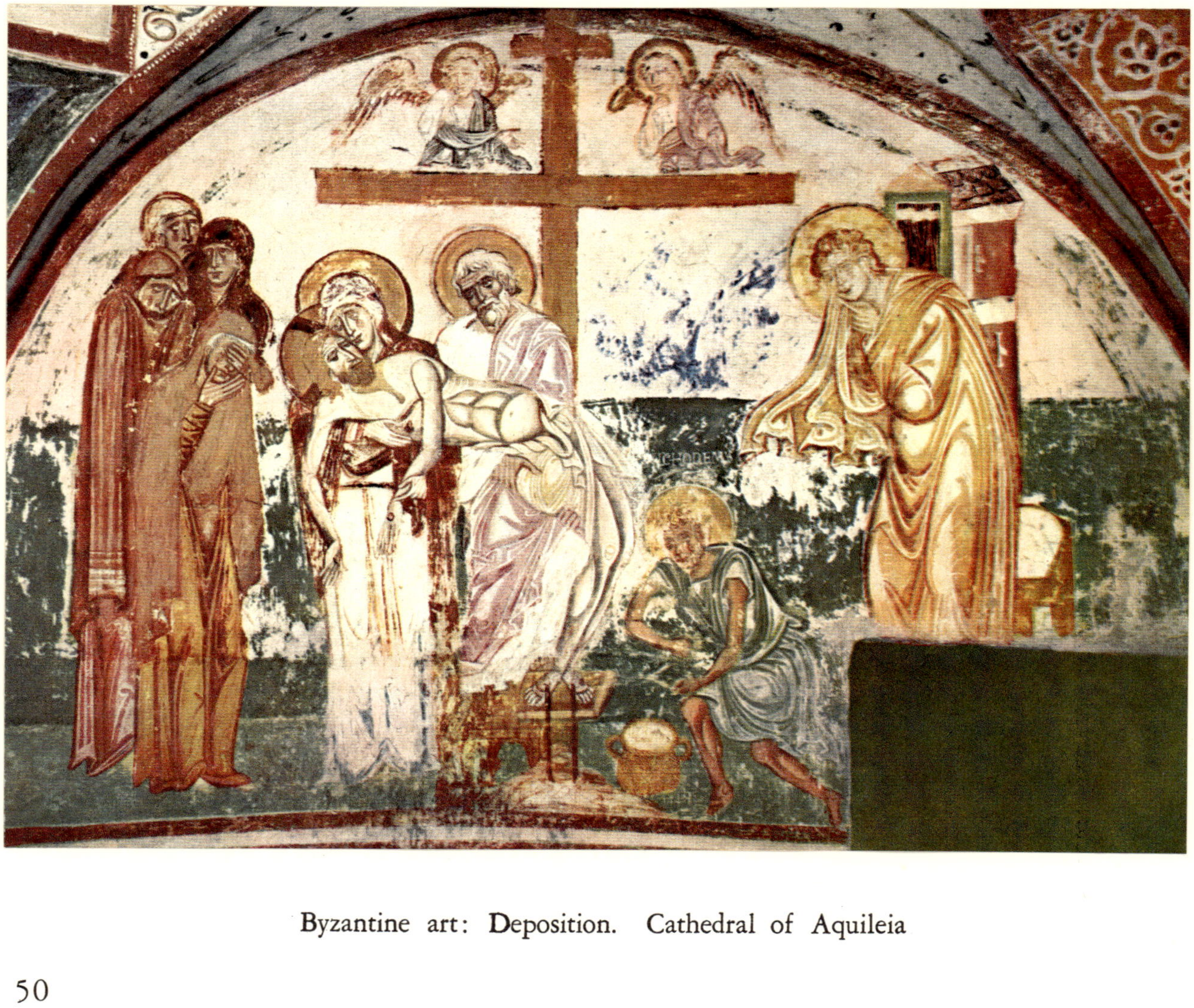

Byzantine art: Deposition. Cathedral of Aquileia

of the three Marys of the Deposition form a single unit. It may be that the higher quality of this pathos at Aquileia is due to new elements in Byzantine painting which are to be found in Serbia in the second half of the twelfth century. It is interesting to compare the wall-paintings in the crypt in the Church of Nerez (Macedonia) with the Scenes of the Passion, dated 1164. The wall-paintings at Nerez are an important point in the history of Byzantine art, since it would seem that both currents, the " academic " and the " pathetic ", meet here, to the advantage of both. The " pathetic " acquires dignity from the " academic " which in turn is revived by the " pathetic ". This balance in the pictures at Nerez (and other examples must have existed in Byzantine territory) shows the realistic detail, especially in small matters, such as costumes and objects, in a more striking manner than usual. The cultural style and feeling which are shown at Nerez must have been fairly easily copied in many Italian centres, because of this balance, for signs can still be discerned in a number of paintings of the first half of the thirteenth century: for example in the very " academic " style of Berlinghiero Berlinghieri, and the more " realistic " style of the Master of Vico l'Abate.

But in order to understand more fully the developments of Byzantine painting on Italian soil, developments which, with the advance of the thirteenth century, broke away from the original sources whether in Constantinople or less Eastern countries, such as Greece and Yugoslavia, we must consider once more the developments of western painting, which from the tenth century onwards was being diffused without the aid of the powerful organisation enjoyed by Byzantine art.

At the end of the ninth century Carolingian painting stimulated the development of other barbarian artistic movements. The most important was that of the Germanic tribes, and was closely related to the rise of a powerful monarchy, which took over the political role formerly held by the French monarchy. German art, whose best period coincided with the establishment of the Ottonian Emperors and is therefore called Ottonian, exercised an influence of the first importance until the end of the dynasty in the eleventh century. The formation of Romanesque art in western Europe was primarily due to the development of Ottonian art, soon to be mixed with French and English movements.

The very close contact between the German Empire and Italy resulted in a stronger and more direct classical influence than had ever been the case with Carolingian art. It was in fact the new interpretation of the classical element which was responsible for elucidating and organising both the raw barbarian influence and the various confused elements which had already been adopted from the Northern, the Latin, and Eastern races.

As in the case of Carolingian art, nothing or almost nothing remains of Ottonian monumental painting, so that once again we must look at miniature painting (probably very similar) to obtain an idea of the style. A great many descriptions of lost pictures and poems, called *tituli*, which were compiled as guides for artists in the decorations of churches, have also survived. Both point to a great development of wall-painting in churches in Germany between the tenth and the twelfth centuries. In view of the scarcity of examples those of S. George at Oberzell on the island of Reichenau are of the utmost importance, particularly since Reichenau itself was one of the outstanding centres of the Ottonian revival. The wall-paintings in the Convent of S. George probably date from the rule of the Abbot Witigov (985-997), except for the Last Judgment on the outside of an apse, which may belong to the eleventh century. In any case, the series of paintings in the central nave is of greater importance than the Judgment. Here we have scenes of the Miracles of Christ, figures of the apostles and half-length portraits of the prophets in medallions. All these pictures closely resemble the miniature painting of Reichenau, so we may conclude that, as in the case of Carolingian art, painting and miniatures were influenced by each other in the Ottonian age, and developed along parallel lines.

Ottonian manuscripts in general seek an effect of luxury by the use of colour (although gold and silver are used sparingly), and by designs which stand out with vigorous outlines and a strong feeling of movement, but are carefully balanced to present a symmetrical rhythm. The frequent incidence of portraits of the reigning emperors in the manuscripts, combined with their luxurious character, shows how closely this type of art was connected with the court: either the sovereign commissioned the books himself or he received them in homage. The portraits are intended to be not so much true likenesses as an apologia for the sovereign power which exists on earth through the will of God. Indeed the hand of God, crowning the head of the monarch, is often seen in this type of figurative work. The apotheosis often includes feminine figures surrounding the Emperor as Allegories, referring to lands which had been conquered in war or subjected politically. And it is significant that at times, even in the case of sacred subjects such as the figures of the Evangelists, the arrangement of the picture takes on a feeling of apotheosis. (Gospel of Bamberg, in the Bibliotek, Munich).

Like Carolingian miniature painting, the Ottonian school includes a variety of styles, suggesting the existence of local monastic schools even if most of their work was done for the court. There are two schools which have very distinct and definite characteristics: the school of Reichenau and the school of Trèves-Echternach.

The most important centre of activity was the Benedictine Abbey of Reichenau on Lake Constance. In its origins it was certainly influenced by the neighbouring abbey of S. Gall, a centre of Carolingian illumination since the ninth century. There are however no manuscripts of that date which can be attributed with certainty to the Benedictines of Reichenau, probably because they are indistinguishable from those of S. Gall. Examples from both S. Gall and Reichenau show an interest in pure decoration rather than in figural work, with special emphasis on the ornamental beauty of initials. The decorative work of the two schools began to be distinguishable in the course of the tenth century. During this period the initials of Reichenau became strikingly elegant in their spiral designs and exquisite colouring, and established a model which lasted throughout the whole of the Middle Ages.

Figural painting is found in the books of Reichenau only in the latter half of the tenth century, and shows a certain similarity to the Carolingian Rhine school. Among the most famous manuscripts of the Reichenau school are the Gospels (Darmstadt, Library, No. 1948), the Evangeliarium of the Abbey of Poussay (Paris Bibliothèque Nat. Cat. 10574) and the Egbert Psalter (Cividale, Museum). Egbert, the highly cultured archbishop of Trèves, was one of the principal founders of the Ottonian school, and his name is linked with the masterpiece of Reichenau, which even mentions the names of the artists. It is known as the Gospel book of Trèves (Municipal Library) or Codex Egberti, and is the work of Keraldus and Heribertus. This is the oldest known example of cyclical illustration, and includes many scenes from the lives of Christ and the Virgin, arranged in chronological order. Another innovation of the Ottonian book was the inclusion of a great many detailed illustrations of the Gospels.

The output of the Reichenau school was prodigious, and their productions were widely dispersed, some reaching Italy, where they contributed to a deeper understanding of the western spirit. The Carolingian school possibly made a greater impression in Italy because of its strength and clarity of design, and contributed to the organisation in the most constructive and monumental sense of medieval or Romanesque art up to the thirteenth century, as can be seen in Giunta Pisano and in Coppo di Marcovaldo.

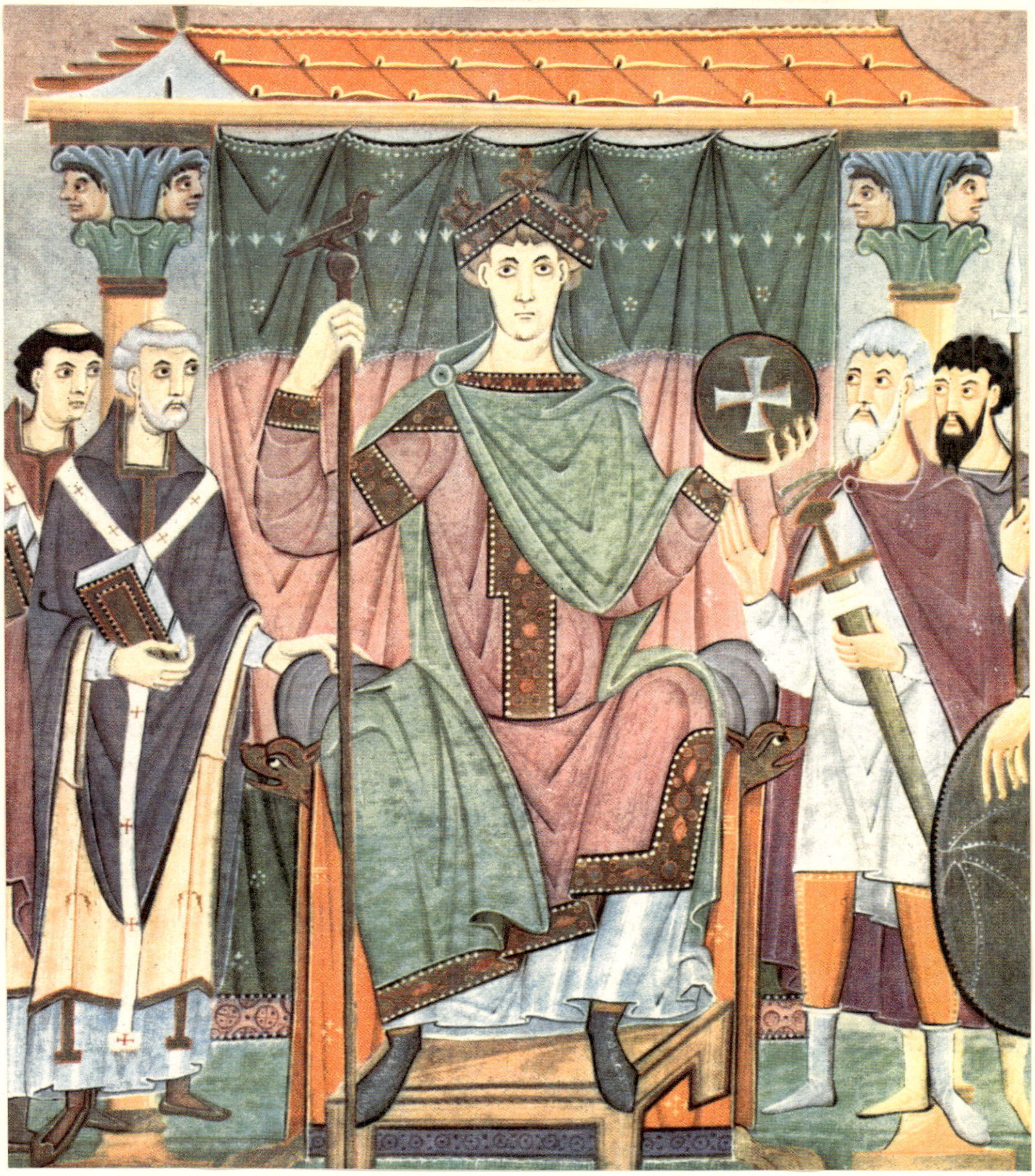

Ottonian art: Evangeliarium of Otto III. Staatbibliotek, Munich

Although less penetrating and skilful than the Carolingian school, Ottonian painting had more imagination and inventiveness in the treatment of subjects which made it important in the revival of the traditional palaeo-Christian-Byzantine iconography.

The other Ottonian school is Trèves-Echternach. The miniaturists can be subdivided into two groups, one with headquarters at the Benedictine Abbey of S. Maximian, at Trèves, and the other at the nearby Benedictine Abbey of Echternach. It is possible that Egbert, who was appointed archbishop of Trèves, inspired the first group. Judging by the few surviving manuscripts, the workmanship was both accurate and beautiful. The many examples which remain of the Echternach group are less polished in appearance and at times a little provincial, although equally sumptuous. Both schools started at more or less the same date, but the school of Trèves-Echternach supplanted Reichenau at the end of the eleventh century and received the important, especially the imperial, commissions.

The style of Reichenau is unusual because of the great importance attached to colour, rich in whites, greens, and violets, and always extremely luxurious. A preference for static figures and scenes helped to give an effect of great power, and also contributed a spiritual feeling in the work of Trèves-Echternach, whose artists lacked the imagination and inventiveness of the school of Reichenau, and preferred to repeat the same compositions and themes, once a plan had been established. The technical skill at Trèves may have been superior to that at Reichenau, possibly owing to a greater appreciation of Byzantine art. Illustrations of scenes from the Gospels are often separated by pages devoted entirely to decoration with motifs from Eastern textiles. The best examples of this school are two fragments, which come from a lost *Registrum Gregorii*, given by Egbert to the cathedral of Trèves. The one shows S. Gregory inspired by the dove, while the writer watches him (Trèves, Library); the other shows the Emperor Otto II receiving homage from allegories of the nations (Chantilly, Musée Condé). The most splendid and luxurious of all is the Gospel book given by Henry III and Queen Agnes to the cathedral of Spires, now in the Escorial.

There were many other active centres of illumination in Germany, notably in Saxony, in Bavaria (especially at Ratisbon), and at Cologne. Because they did not produce works for the court, however, they were less important. Only the school of Cologne is of some significance in the history of art, since characteristics of the Rheims school were developed there with some originality and very effective results and their influence was still visible in Rhenish painting in the thirteenth century.

During the tenth and eleventh centuries striking developments took place in English illumination. This had fallen off badly towards the ninth century, and been almost eclipsed by the splendour of Carolingian art, but now a highly individual and remarkable style appeared. Although it has points in common with famous examples of the Rheims school such as the Psalter of Utrecht and the Ebbon Gospel-book, its origins are somewhat mysterious. The extent to which the English style was based on the Rheims school is very obscure, the more so since the Carolingian schools had, as we know, been greatly influenced by the Anglo-Saxons. Relations between French and English monasteries were so close, and traffic between them so frequent, that it is difficult to establish priority of influence. The capacity for expression in design, already shown in the Psalter of Utrecht, is now carried to its limits, with special emphasis on movement and on the rapid, almost impressionist quality of the design. It is possible that the school of Hautvillers concentrated on the graphic qualities which had long been shown by the Irish and the English. Artists had now become so accomplished that they were able to create effects of illusion which as a rule are only achieved by the use of colour and chiaroscuro.

Colour itself is employed graphically. with short, swift strokes of the brush, so that the general effect frequently resembles a free sketch: so much so that the background is often the parchment page without any patches of colour, still less decoration. For the same reason gold and silver were sparingly used, and only in decorative details such as textiles, haloes, or some occasional object. Nevertheless the absence of rich colouring — a contrast to continental productions — does not imply a lack of feeling for colour. With their rapid picture sketches done with the point of the pen the English managed to convey a variety of shades in one colour. It was a way of simplifying painting, and resulted in a trend towards monochrome (in England and France) enriched by very subtle shading. For the English it was essentially the beginning of a new style of illustration, looser and freer, more descriptive and also impressionistic, which has continued up to the present day. During the fourteenth and fifteenth centuries, the great French illustrators found that pen illustrations were particularly well suited to narrative works such as the romances and poems of chivalry.

This English system of illustration is interesting because it shows a final break with the Byzantine miniature, traces of which continued to appear in French and German styles of miniature painting. Classical influences however do exist, although

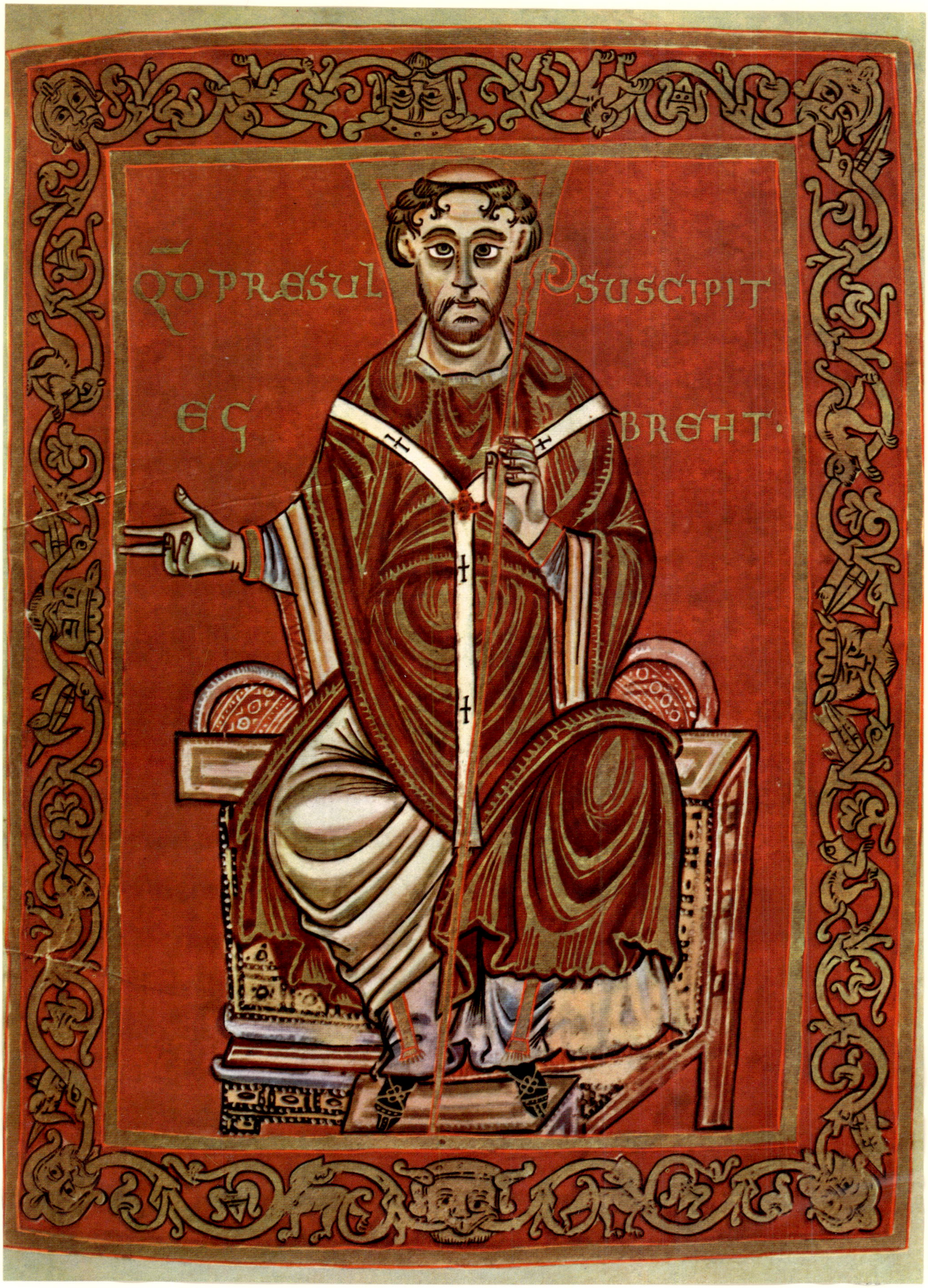

Ottonian art: Psalter of Archbishop Egbert. Museum, Cividale

English artists were more interested in an impressionistic treatment of form or a stylisation based on careful observation, than in producing a naturalistic rendering.

The most important school of illumination in this period was at Winchester; the masterpiece of this school is now at Chatsworth in the library of the Duke of Devonshire — the Benedictional commissioned by Archbishop Aethelwold (963-984) with scenes from the life of Christ and the saints connected with the various " Feast Days ". It is clear from the bold, sharp, free figurative interpretation of the Anglo-Saxon artists that Gothic painting is not far off, although it was actually to be developed in France.

While the English and German schools were producing brilliant work quite independently of each other, France seems to have passed through a period of creative inertia. The increasing weakness of the Carolingian monarchy was accompanied by a gradual disappearance of artistic traditions in the various centres throughout the century. During the tenth century political incompetence reduced France to a confusion and disorder increased by the invasions of the Normans in the North and the Arabs in the South. It was not until the beginning of the eleventh century that there were signs of an artistic upheaval, which produced extraordinary results in painting. But just as a break-up of political power resulted from the weakening of the French monarchy, so there was a lack of any co-ordinating power in art able to organise a national school, or even several closely allied schools as had happened in the Carolingian era. Instead there were many different styles, sometimes found in the same monastery, and each artistic centre worked quite independently. The level of French painting was very high, but no unity was possible since so many — usually foreign — styles were in operation, each one being transformed separately by a French imprint. The North, for instance, was greatly influenced by the English school, through the Abbey of Winchester, which was closely connected with a number of monasteries in this part of France. The Abbey of S. Amand near Valenciennes was particularly notable for illustrations of the life of S. Amand and other saints, and produced the best work among the monastic *ateliers* of the North. Ottonian as well as English influence is to be found at S. Amand, and in other Northern abbeys as well, such as S. Omer and S. Bertin where other styles, characteristic of the South of France, are also found. These various complications resulted from the frequent journeys which the artists made between one monastery and another.

The South had virtually no direct contact with the Anglo-Saxons, but was closely allied to Spain, the Ottonians and Italy. Italian influence was of course Byzantine, although modified by other trends, such as the Benedictine school.

At this period in the history of medieval art, France seems to assume the role of consolidating western styles of figurative expression, to which she had already made a notable contribution with the Carolingian renaissance. Her tradition enabled her to accept and transform a wide variety of styles and this distinctively French amalgam continued to be most influential and widely disseminated until the end of the Gothic period. In fact it was France that gave a particular style to western art, from the Romanesque period onwards, which was radically different from eastern art.

Painting in the South of France, which can be traced in important remains of frescoes, was more homogeneous than in the North, and is especially noteworthy for the trends which developed at Moissac and Limoges. But before studying this aspect of French painting we must consider some important developments in Spain.

Before the eleventh century very little is known about Spanish painting, and the origins of Spanish Romanesque art are by no means clear. It is known however that between 970 and 1050 a group of manuscripts were produced in Cantabria (those of Gerona, Burgo de Osma, Madrid and elsewhere) illustrating the commentary of the Apocalypse by the Abbot Beatus Llebana (the " Beatus " of Valladolid). These manuscripts are called Mosarabic after certain motifs, especially costumes and ornaments, which characterise them. In fact, however, the Arab element is on the whole superficial compared with others, and there is a note of fantasy which recalls the Irish school. Nothing, or practically nothing, has survived of any monumental painting which may have existed in this style. The earliest frescoes in S. Quirce at Pedret contain only a faint echo and are ingenuously popular in feeling.

The " Master of Bohi " who worked in the church of S. John of Bohi may be connected with this type of illumination, but his work seems to be quite separate from the characteristic style which was developed in the twelfth century, and was Romanesque. It contains a very strong, although indirect, Byzantine influence which may have come through Italian artists. However, this Byzantine quality is transformed by a wild, almost violent, power of design. Unlike the swirling linear movement of the Germans at Reichenau, the Spaniards evolved a scheme of carefully planned outlines which tended towards a structural solidity of geometric planes combined with severe, compact, contrasting colours which create an effect of polychrome wooden sculptures translated into paint. This is the style of the artist known as the " Master of Tahull ", who is possibly the greatest figure in Catalan painting. He is responsible for the striking apse of S. Clement in Tahull, with the full-length Pantocrator seated inside a mandorla between two archangels with half-figures of the Evangelists in medallions up above, while below are the Virgin and apostles. It is a typical Byzantine scheme, and the efforts made to introduce expression into the rigid forms are so insistent that an element of the grotesque appears, as it might in the work of any portrait painter with a malicious and too-penetrating eye. The work in S. Clement's is in fact tragically grotesque. But the striking contrasts of colour in the apse are remarkably decorative. The figures stand out harshly and severely against a background of large areas of ochre, dark blue and red.

Tahull is the principal centre of examples of Romanesque wall-paintings, and in the church of S. Maria there is important work by a painter known as the " Master of Manderuelo " where he also worked. He was probably a companion or follower of the first master, and although less sensitive to the power of colour, his designs reached a high level in both expression and composition.

The two Masters of Tahull are usually thought to have been foreigners, as their style has little connection with the few known examples of earlier Spanish painting, whereas it does have a strong Byzantine flavour. But if this is so it is strange that the Byzantine element in the two Masters was so transformed that it shows no clear connection with any other production of European art, not even with the Italian school with whom the Spaniards had often been in contact. It seems more likely that the two principal artists of Tahull reveal a personal interpretation of Anglo-Irish and Ottonian examples with their respective Byzantine backgrounds; apart from this common Byzantine cultural element I cannot see any connection with Italy.

The " Master of the Last Judgment " who is inferior to the other two, worked in both the churches of Tahull, decorating the lower parts. His name is taken from an Inferno painted at S. Maria, and he seems to have been unaffected by Byzantine forms in the sense that even when he followed them he re-invented them. He has moreover a certain primitive simplicity that contributes spontaneity to his compositions by means of an ingenuous distortion in the drawing, according to the necessities of expression. In this he resembles the Anglo-Saxons to some extent, but there is no trace of their careful geometric patterns; instead his work is free and almost child-like. The colouring is dignified and rather dull, as in the " Master of Bohi ". For this reason and because of his more obvious connection with earlier works the " Master of the Last Judgment " is thought to have been the only Catalan in this group. But it is more likely that they

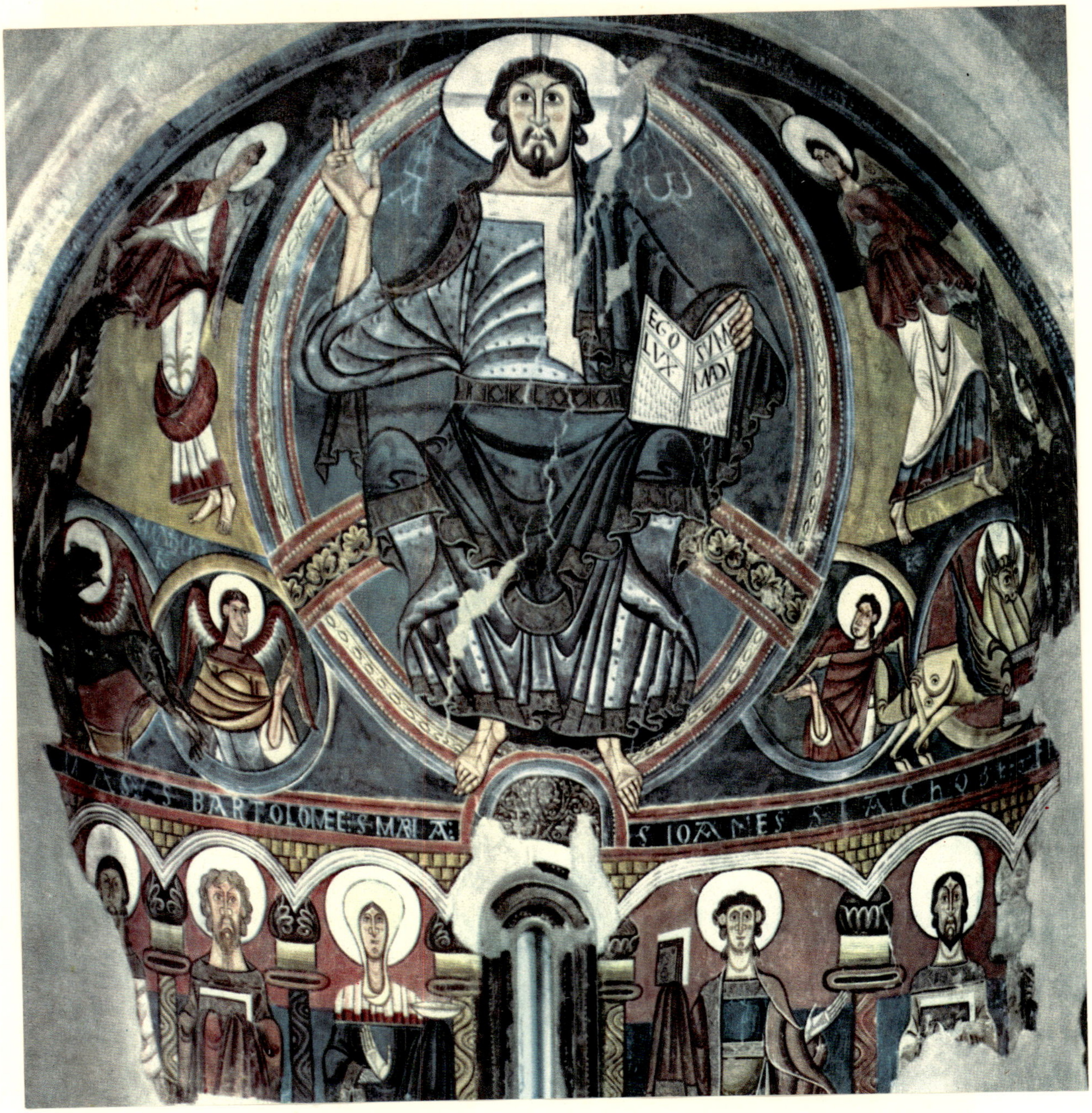

Master of Tahull: Apse of S. Clement of Tahull. Museum of Catalan Art, Barcelona

were all three Spanish with a more or less heterogeneous culture.

The work at Tahull is very important because of the influence it exercised elsewhere in Spain, especially of course in the North. It is interesting that throughout the Romanesque period there is ample proof that both artists and schools often moved about in France and Spain and what had already happened to codices and their authors now happened in wall-painting as well. The artists travelled from one monastery to another, so that the same trends are to be found far apart and the various styles influenced one another.

Another Catalan artist is the " Master of Pedret ", who was active about the middle of the twelfth century. A number of paintings which, if not actually his work, are similar in style and feeling, imply that he was the leader of a large school. This school developed in the valley of Noguera Palaresa, which runs from the province of Lerida to Barcelona, and represents the most interesting and successful attempt to achieve a personal style at a time when traditional and symbolic formulae were being abandoned.

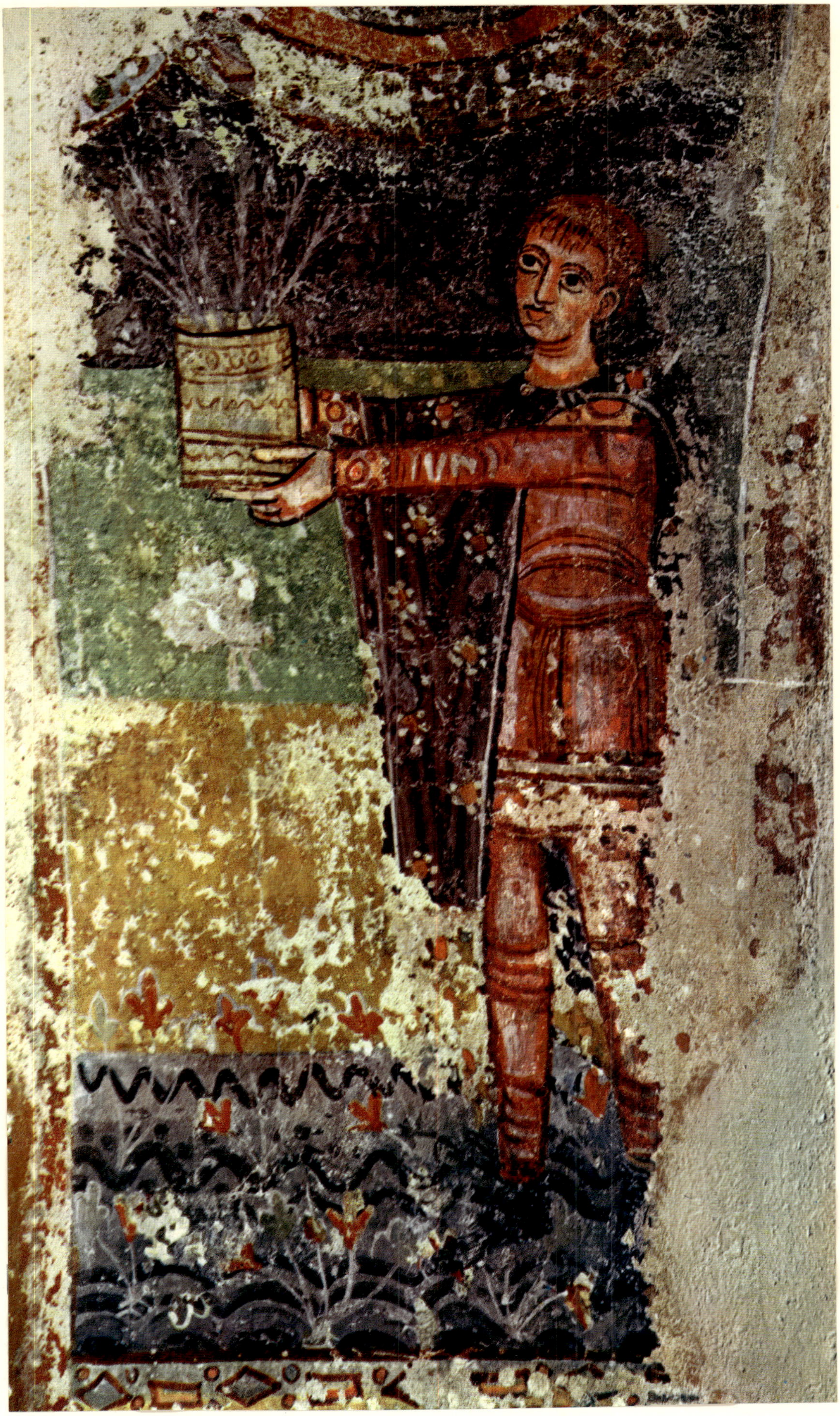

Master of Pedret: Abel offering flowers to God, from the central nave of S. Quirce, Pedret.

Diocesan Museum, Barcelona

With the Master of Pedret, whose chief work consists in the decoration of the church of S. Quirce at Pedret with scenes from the Bible and the Apocalypse, the tendency towards harsh, strong expression, which was evident in the earlier masters, is softened and deepened by a more subtle appreciation both of people and things, into a more natural human expression. His love of painting the most humble objects makes it possible to find in his work genuine " still life " for the first time in the history of painting. Ties with Byzantine culture were thus completely broken. Spiritually this simplicity and truth in representation, whether of human forms or objects in nature, animals and plants, is already a precursor of the Gothic conception of life, even if the artists' method of expression remains essentially Romanesque.

In sympathy with this tender and intimate feeling for life, the drawing is no longer sharp and hard, in the Master of Pedret and his school, and the outlines, although still very visible, tend to melt into coloured backgrounds representing natural surroundings, instead of being composed of abstract strips of colour. The whole appearance is more pictorial; colour is imposed with passages of continuous gentle modelling, without the sharp breaks and limited colouring of the painters of Tahull. The result is a closer union between colour and composition, whose development is based on calm, fluid, balanced colour arrangements.

An influence of wall-painting can be seen in panel painting, which probably started about the same time in Spain, and was certainly in some cases done by the same artists. A type of panel painting which is interesting because of a close connection with the wall-paintings at Tahull is to be found further north, at Urgel. Here the same artists worked in several media including wall-painting, panel painting, sculpture and gold work, relief decoration and plaster work. When compared with Tahull, even with the " Master of the Last Judgment ", the artistic tone is more prosaic and popular, and different techniques were often employed together. The inspiration was originally Byzantine, and gold and decorations were often combined with painting in the production of icons. But whereas Byzantine work kept a consistently high level of luxury, the work of Urgel is decidedly popular, in spite of an obvious and very Spanish attempt at expressionism.

At Urgel panel painting is employed for frontals (in front of the altar, near the ground) and canopies, which are typical of Spain, although in the fourteenth century they were to be replaced above the altars by the famous *retablos*. The oldest canopy to survive is that of Ribas (Museum of Vich) with the Pantocrator surrounded by angels. Technically it is akin to mural painting, and shows certain resemblances in style and feeling to the apse of S. Clement at Tahull; the obvious Byzantine quality may be due to a contact with the enormous workshop at Venice.

A departure from the more cultured style of the apse of S. Clement and the canopy at Ribas, towards a freer and more popular mood, still within the bounds of stylisation, is shown in the frontal of La Seo d'Urgel, with Christ between the twelve apostles. The frontal at Hix, with the Virgin Enthroned, is also attributed to the Master of Urgel, and there is in his work a decided resemblance to wall-painting in the monumental effect of the well-ordered, symmetrical and symbolic composition. At the same time he is interested in conveying a realistic note, especially in the case of the apostles. Compared with wall-painting his work is much richer in colouring, and is greatly enlivened by a new splendour and density, which stands out particularly well between the black contours.

To begin with, the subjects represented on these Spanish altarpieces must have been the Pantocrator and the Virgin enthroned, for they were the same as the pictures in the main parts of the churches, the cupolas, apses and triumphal arch, transferred on to panels. Slightly later, in the second half of the twelfth century, scenes of the saints began to appear, and panel painting acquired a greater freedom of composition, tending towards narrative painting.

Spanish taste — already evident in the Master of Pedret — inclines towards telling a story. The artist is apt to insist on some particular detail of feature or gesture, if necessary by distortion, in order to emphasise the salient point of the action. This is not done through movement as in the Carolingian and Ottonian schools, nor by impressionism as in the English style; it is done by emphatic underlining of the decisive point. There is something ingenuous and paradoxical about this method of expression, but it gives a singular fascination to Spanish painting, even if it rarely rises above the quality of popular art, especially in the school of Urgel. Popular feeling may have tended to keep Spanish painting far removed from academic Byzantine art, and maintained an independent originality throughout the centuries. Certain notes can be traced at the birth of Spanish art which are still visible in Goya.

The work of the artist who painted the altar frontal at Montgrony in the second half of the century, with the Saviour enthroned and surrounded by scenes from the life of S. Martin, demonstrates this intention clearly. His graphic powers are remarkable, and he uses the most arbitrary distortions in order to achieve the maximum of emphasis. The drawing is almost like a nineteenth-century French Impressionist in that line drawing is subordinated to an overriding will to give expression, so that even the smallest stroke has an indispensable part to play in building up the whole. The rolling eyes,

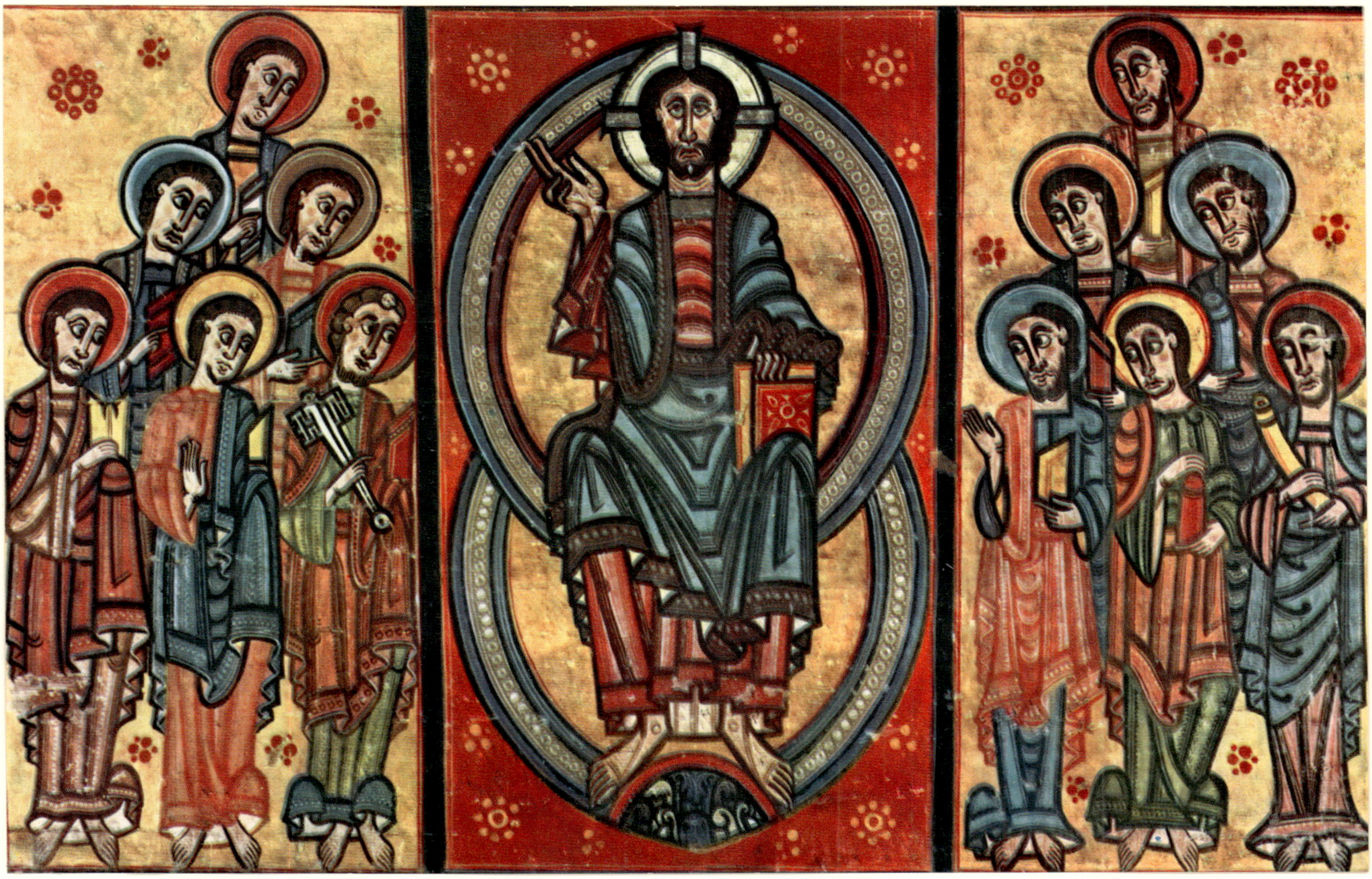

Master of Urgel: Christ and the twelve Apostles. Museum of Catalan Art, Barcelona

raising and lowering of eyebrows, the wrinkles, and dilation of the nostrils are particularly striking.

It is true that the placing of so much emphasis on details involves a danger of acute stylisation which could degenerate very easily into conventional popular mannerism, and all the more so because panel painting had always been inclined to cater for the masses. This in fact is what happened, and fairly quickly, since panels were a convenient medium for use in private worship, and were consequently distributed commercially. Soon Spanish works of this kind became very plentiful and were much in use among the pious country folk.

As the twelfth century advanced, memories of Byzantium, which had always been tenuous in Spain, began to disappear. More and more strongly men wanted a formal synthesis based on direct observation of truth, on the lines already indicated in the Master of Pedret, together with a greater freedom of design, and softening of colour. The same aims are to be found in the gentle, timid work of the " Master of Llussanès ", both in the wall-paintings in the tomb of S. Pablo de Casserres (Sonsona) and in the frontal with the Life of the Virgin. At the same time there is a search for greater unity and spiritual harmony, which results in a simple, dignified grace savouring of the archaic.

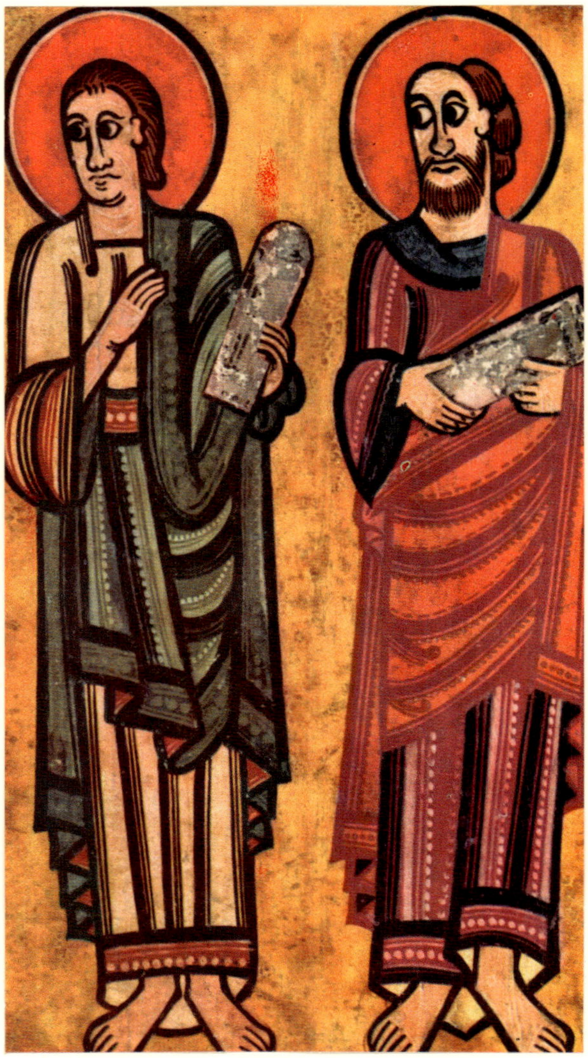

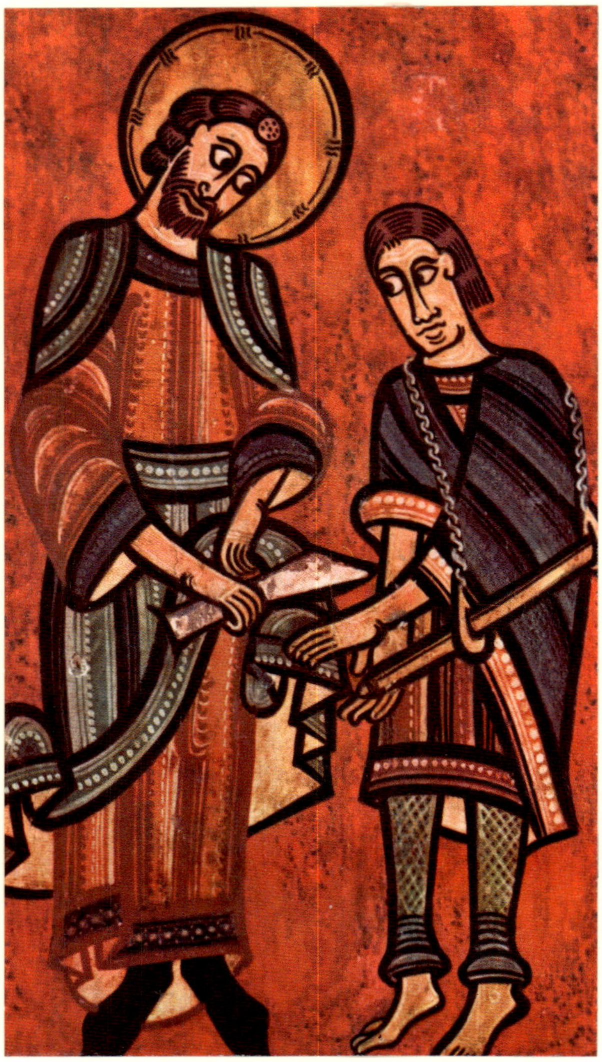

Master of Montgrony: The Legend of S. Martin, details. Archepiscopal Museum, Vich

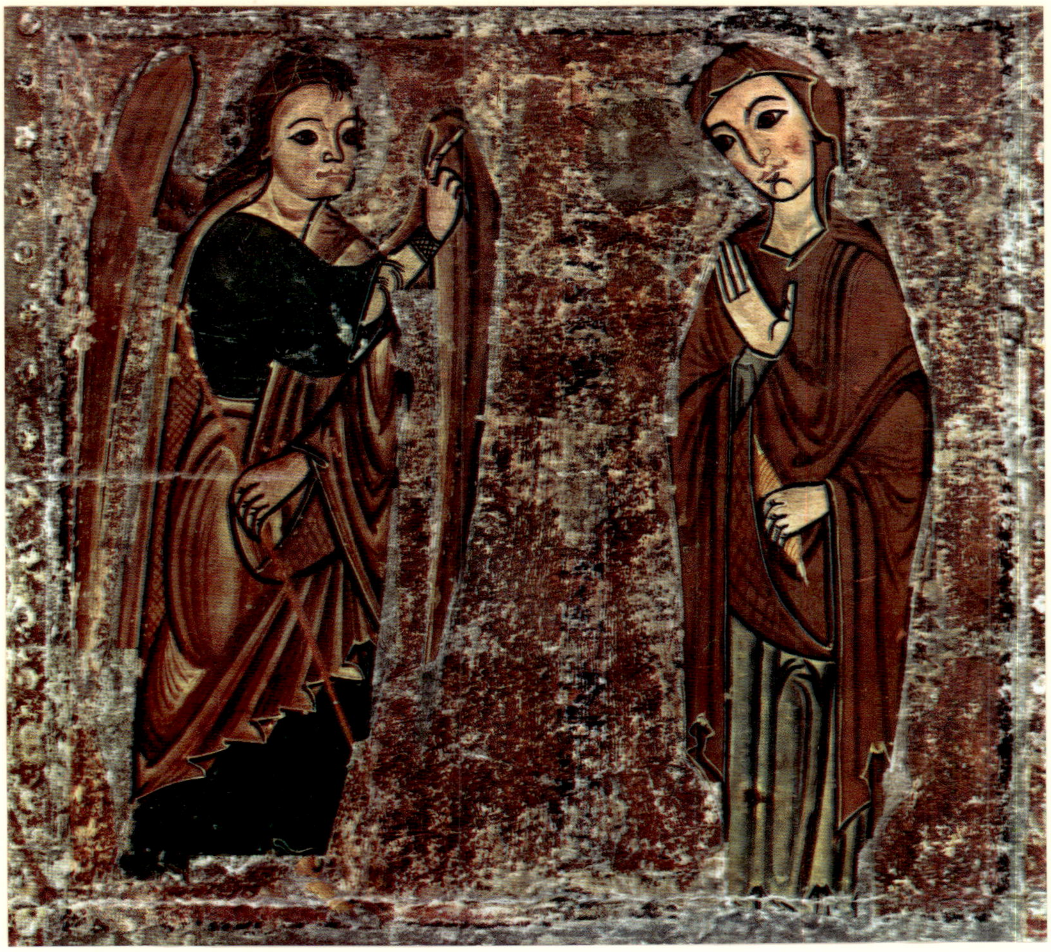

Master of Llussanès: Annunciation, detail from the Llussa frontal.

Archepiscopal Museum, Vich

And in a way it is akin, despite different origins, to the work of the "Master of S. Martino" who worked half a century later in Italy.

Meanwhile a strong French influence had made its way into Spain, coming over the Pyrenees by a route which led to S. James of Compostella. Both the Cistercian and the Cluniac orders sponsored this infiltration, and employed architects, sculptors and painters. These painters may have been responsible for the accomplished decoration of the Pantheon of the Catholic Kings in the kingdom of Leon at the end of the twelfth century, where the naturalistic expression is very different from the Spanish style.

Architecture too was affected by the French Gothic movement. Large windows appeared in church walls, and were filled with stained glass which must also be regarded as the work of French painters. Vast expanses of walls no longer required decorating, and pictures became increasingly limited to panel paintings or frescoes for tombs. Frontals themselves were modified, probably because they were principally used above altars rather than below. They were now sub-divided into a number of scenes, often in horizontal sequences, and were forerunners of the altarpiece, which was of course placed above the altar.

More important still is a change in feeling. A more worldly, secular note appears in paintings, even in those destined for religious purposes. This follows the change which was taking place in the social order — a transition from a monastic society, ruled by the religious orders, to a lay society in which authority was vested in the merchant guilds, kings, and other dignitaries. As society became more highly organised,

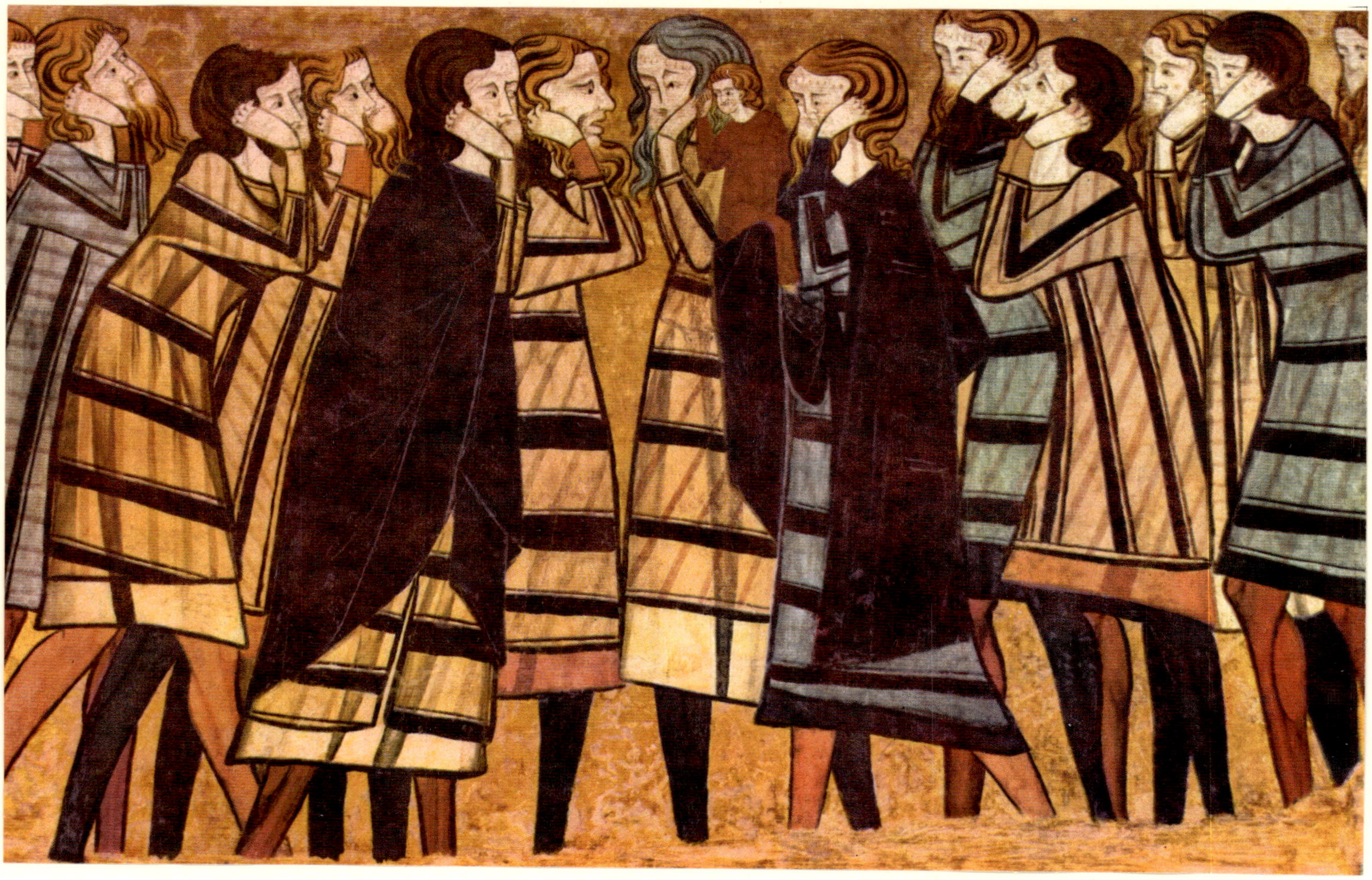

Catalan art: Funeral procession, detail from the tomb of Sancho Saiz de Carillo.

Barcelona, Museum of Catalan art.

brilliant and luxurious, pictures began to include keen observations of events, people and objects connected with daily life rather than with the feelings and passions of the soul. The panels from the tomb of Sancho Saiz de Carillo for example, at Mahamud, now in the Barcelona Museum, show a single scene with a funeral procession. Both men and women are portrayed with sharp accuracy in their grief-stricken attitudes, which are so extreme that they border on the ridiculous, and in their sad, severely coloured clothes. The figures are contained in an elegant and decorative stylisation, both in design and colour distribution (which however in its use of green and dark blue for hair bears little relation to reality), and resemble stained glass in appearance and technique. As we can see from the tomb of Carillo, or from the altar frontal of Suriguerola (Barcelona Museum) which also dates from the end of the thirteenth century, drawing had now become dry and jerky, with a lack of symmetry and a note of psychological inquiry which was morbid if not actually hysterical. Spanish artists were evidently deeply impressed by French drawing but transposed the sharpness of the current style into a typically Spanish mood of violence.

From now onwards Spain was susceptible to every kind of influence which came from the North (the Low Countries, France) or the East (Germany, Bohemia, Italy). But Spanish works always retain their typical individual note of heavy, passionate melancholy which is to be found at the beginning of her art history. This continuous note of detachment and originality may be due to the native autonomy which was established at the outset. As well as this note of passion an equally original feeling for colour persists. Indeed a Spanish painting can easily be recognised up to the end of the seventeenth century by the colouring alone. Although it is vivid, harsh and strong, it also contains a range of greys and ochre (one might almost say a shadow effect) and contrasts of browns, blacks and opaque whites which give a hint of tragedy.

Illumination in the south of France seems to derive a feeling for strong outline from the Spanish conception of art, so that it is linked to some extent with the old Irish and Franco-Saxon streams. Decorative motifs, whether of human or animal forms, were used mainly for initials, and show a strong Arab influence, caused either by direct contacts, or, more probably, through Spain. The most striking characteristic of illumination in the South, especially at the Abbey of S. Martial in Limoges, is a calligraphic, ornamental and emblematic style, sometimes subordinated to a lively inventiveness which seems more Ottonian than Spanish. It is not a very important episode in the history of art, and contributed nothing of significance to later developments in painting, which by the end of the twelfth century was already on the verge of the Gothic era and was to be bound up with events which had taken place in England and northern France between the tenth and twelfth centuries. Illumination in the south of France is memorable for some extremely skilful decorative illustrations to the Apocalypse. Artistic centres there seem to have concentrated on this theme, for there are many remarkable examples of a large size with plentiful miniatures. But even this type of illustration was Spanish in origin, and the French miniatures were done for a Commentary of the Apocalypse written by the Spanish monk, Beatus de Llebana. The masterpiece of this school came from the Abbey of S. Sever towards the middle of the eleventh century. The book was made for the Abbot Gregory Mutaner (1028-1072), and the artist was probably a certain Stephan Garsia whose name is inscribed on a column in one of the pictures. Spanish influence is very evident in the Apocalypse of S. Sever (Paris Bibliothèque Nat. Lat. 8878), in the frequent use of Arab motifs, the violence of the colouring, the animation of the figures and the grandeur of the compositions. But in spite of this influence the general tone remains typically French.

A number of influences met at the Abbey of S. Martial at Limoges, and inspired the creation of some truly remarkable works, especially Bibles in large format, which were used a great deal in the twelfth century in Italy, where they were known as " Atlantic Bibles ", probably because they first originated in Limoges. The best of them, known as the " Second Bible of S. Martial ", dates from the second half of the eleventh century. It is a masterpiece of the Limousin-Romanesque style, and was done by a painter of considerable talent, who reveals a personal taste and ability derived from the School of Tours in the time of Alcuin, as well as a number of southern influences, especially Albigensian and Hispano-Arabic.

The Gothic style first makes an appearance during the twelfth century, in the illustrations of a number of French Bibles from various centres. This type of Bible originated mainly in Cistercian and Cluniac monasteries, which were international centres. Their style reveals an English origin, as can be seen in those of Clermont-Ferrand (Bib. ms. 1), Souvigny (Moulins ms. 1) and the Grande-Chartreuse (Grenoble, ms. 17). The main stimulus to the development of French Gothic painting came from this English influence.

The French Bibles of the twelfth century were widely circulated in Italy, mainly by the Carthusians, and widely imitated; they may help to account for the revival of Italian painting in the following century.

In France there are considerable remains of Romanesque wall-paintings dating from the eleventh and twelfth centuries. But although they were discovered only in the course of the last century they are rapidly disappearing: many are scarcely visible.

For that matter monumental painting is in the same situation throughout western Europe. All over England, Spain and Germany an immense amount of wall-painting was done in religious buildings. And yet very few traces now remain of works which were completed before the thirteenth century, except in Spain and Italy, and even there a great deal has been lost. So we are fortunate in being able to gain some idea of French monumental painting from skilful copies made at the end of the nineteenth century, now preserved in the Trocadéro Palace in Paris. From these copies it is clear that the quality of French wall-painting was as high as that of the miniatures which it so closely resembled in style, while retaining a genuine feeling for harmony and for the relationship between architecture and decoration. As we know, this is equally true of stained glass decoration. But, unlike the Byzantines, the French subordinated painting to the requirements of architecture.

The Legend of Noah (c. 1100) which disappeared some time ago in the church of S. John the Baptist at Château-Goutier (Mayenne), showed a close affinity with the miniatures of a Life of S. Aubin (Paris Bibliothèque Nat., Nouv. Acq. Lat. 1390). Château-Goutier belongs to the Abbey of S. Aubin. The frescoes (Legend of S. Savin and S. Cyprian) in the crypt of S. Savin (Vienne) resembled the contemporary (end of the eleventh century) life of S. Radegonde (Poitiers, Ms. 250), while the scenes of the life of Christ in the chapel of S. Martin at Nohant-Vic (Indre) in the first half of the twelfth century were similar to the earlier *De Bello Judaico* of Giuseppe Flavio (Paris, Bibliothèque Nat. Lat. 5058) from Moissac, which was possibly the scriptorium with the most original and free style in the south of France. At Moissac, the painters must have studied local sculpture with interest, for even in the eleventh century this had achieved great force of expression. In the same way the frescoes at Vic have a rough chiselled appearance and an effect of violent dramatic movement, rather like reliefs. It was possibly this contact with Moissac which makes the paintings of Vic wholly different from those in the rest of central France. A great many other close connections between murals and miniatures could be quoted, and it is not impossible that the same artists worked on codices and walls, as they are known to have done in France during the fourteenth and fifteenth centuries.

Many other examples of French paintings could be mentioned, but it is difficult to discuss them in a brief survey, since all we know about them today is the bare fact of their existence, and they can be classified only according to somewhat individual trends and not ascribed to definite schools. The fact that different styles are found in the same limited area, while similar works may exist many miles apart, leads one to suppose that Romanesque artists travelled about, working first in one place and then another, and that they imposed their own personalities on their work according to their training and taste.

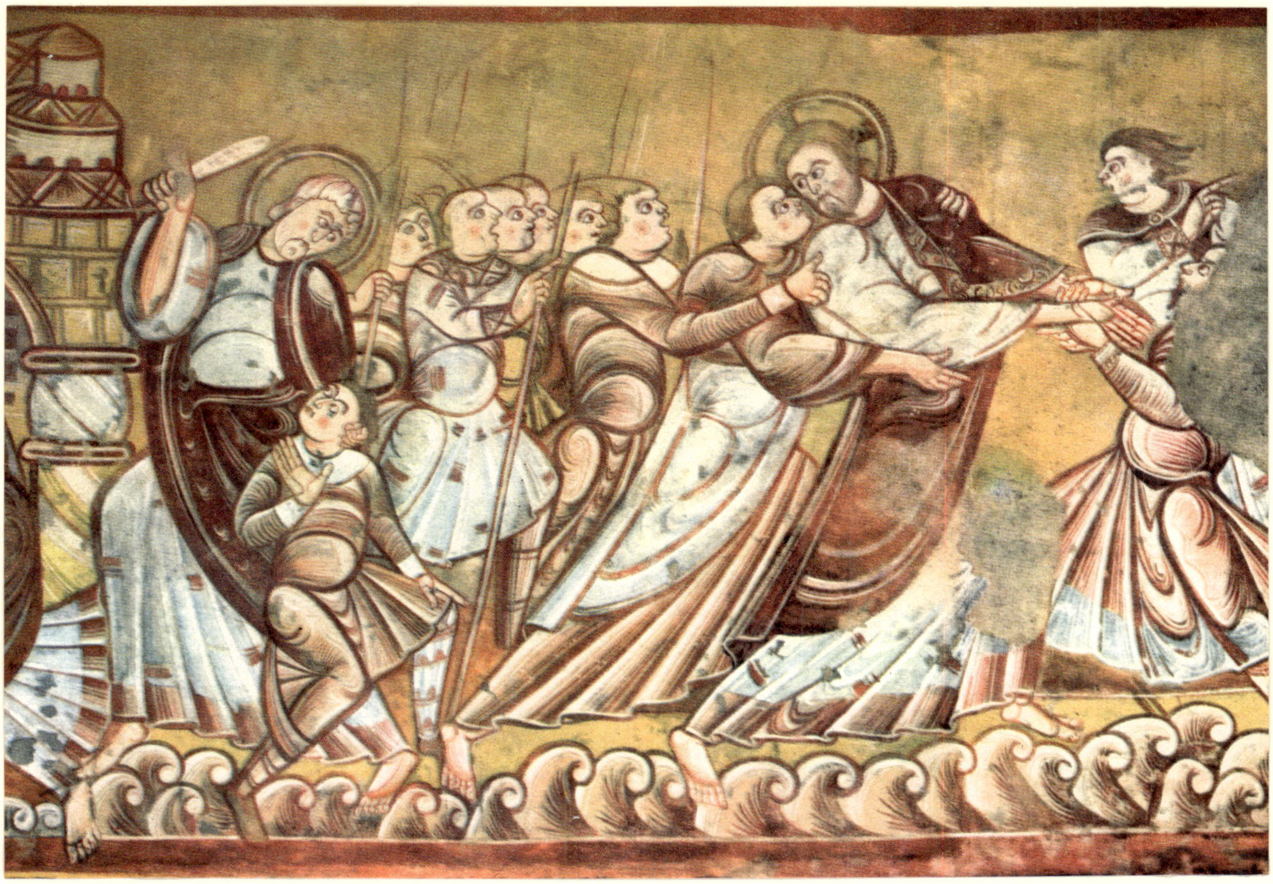

French-Romanesque art: The Kiss of Judas, from the church of Vic.

Musée des Monuments français, Paris

As we have already noticed, there are virtually no traces in Italy of genuine Romanesque painting, although Italian sculpture was far freer from Byzantine influence. The only region where infiltrations from north-western Europe might have met with success was in the north of Italy, and we have seen an example of this in the wall-paintings of Castelseprio, if they can, in fact, be dated to the ninth or tenth century. But the Byzantine stronghold of Venice was in the north and the reflection of Venetian art and taste spread across the lagoon and far beyond.

Apart from the enigmatic Castelseprio, Carolingian art, or Carolingian influence, produced a masterpiece of the goldsmith's art in Lombardy with the golden altar by Vuolvinius. Here a refreshing northern influence can be perceived through the preponderantly Byzantine style. The frescoes of S. Vincenzo di Galliano, painted about 1007, are also interesting. Contemporary Roman and Byzantine styles are mainly responsible for the iconography and style, and yet in the movement and emotional expressions, and in the strong plastic sense produced by means of violent lights on dark colours, there is a suggestion of earlier Ottonian painting, in the same way in which, for example, the painting at Vic was influenced. A great deal of the work at Galliano has been lost, but in the apse a large Theophany stands against a background of ultramarine, with archangels, saints, the prophets Jeremiah and Ezekiel, while beneath in the exedra are some scenes in the life of S. Vincent.

We can also see signs of northern infiltration in Lombardy (at Spigno for example, and at S. Ambrogio in Milan) from the ninth century onwards, and there are documents naming painters from Aquisgrana or from French monasteries as late as the eleventh and thirteenth centuries. But there was no real possibility of further development.

On the contrary, as time went on it seems as though Byzantine influence strengthened in Italy, at least in so far as commissions of important works were entrusted to Eastern workmen and their Italian disciples. In fact, in the twelfth century the immense influence of the Byzantine workshops in Venice resulted in highly stylised Eastern characteristics appearing in Lombardy, as in the wall-paintings of S. Pietro al Monte (Civate) with their scenes from the Apocalypse.

Yet about this time a symptom of Nordic influence is noticeable at S. Urbano alla Caffarella in Rome. The curious wall-paintings which are to be seen there (largely restored) date from the end of the eleventh or beginning of the twelfth century. Decidedly popular in feeling, they are both effective and amusing. The themes of the Annunciation and the Adoration of the Magi are told with great freedom in iconography and types of figure, and with an ingenuous primitive quality which imparts a feeling of folklore or legend if not of true art.

Mosaicists from the enormous centre in Venice spread all over Italy, and even at Rome there are traces of Venetian-Byzantine art as late as the mid-thirteenth century, when sculpture was already enjoying a very high level of free expression and individuality. But Venice in the twelfth century was still a great stronghold of Byzantine painting, although in the last mosaics in S. Mark's it is possible to discern a certain local autonomy. Beside a typical Byzantine group in the narthex of S. Mark's, for example, there are some which have typical iconography and colouring but show a Romanesque style of form and descriptive spirit, which tends towards narrative and was certainly influenced by sculpture. The subjects taken from Genesis are an example: sometimes attributed to the twelfth century and sometimes, probably more correctly, to the beginning of the thirteenth century, they are taken from miniatures in a sixth-century codex known as the " Cotton Bible ", but the artist has transformed his model into a more realistic version, with a narrative style which shows a different feeling from the Byzantine.

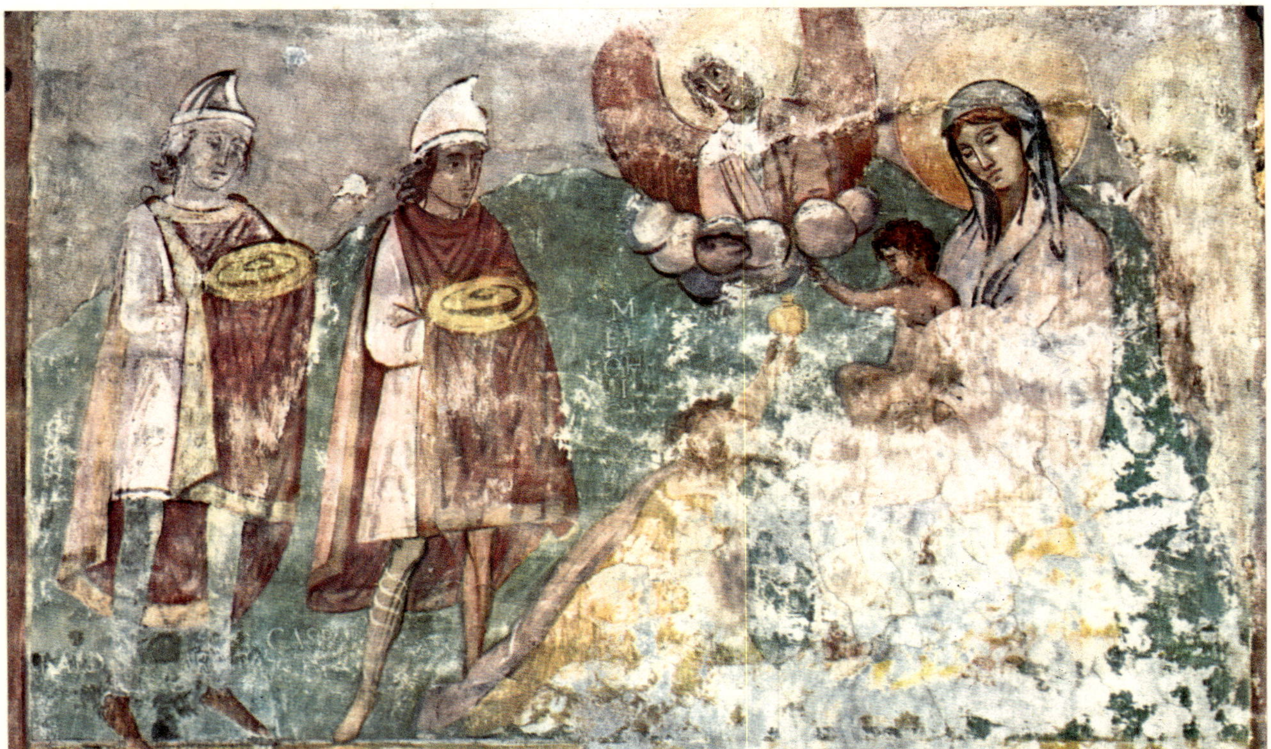

Roman art: Adoration of the Magi. S. Urbano alla Caffarella

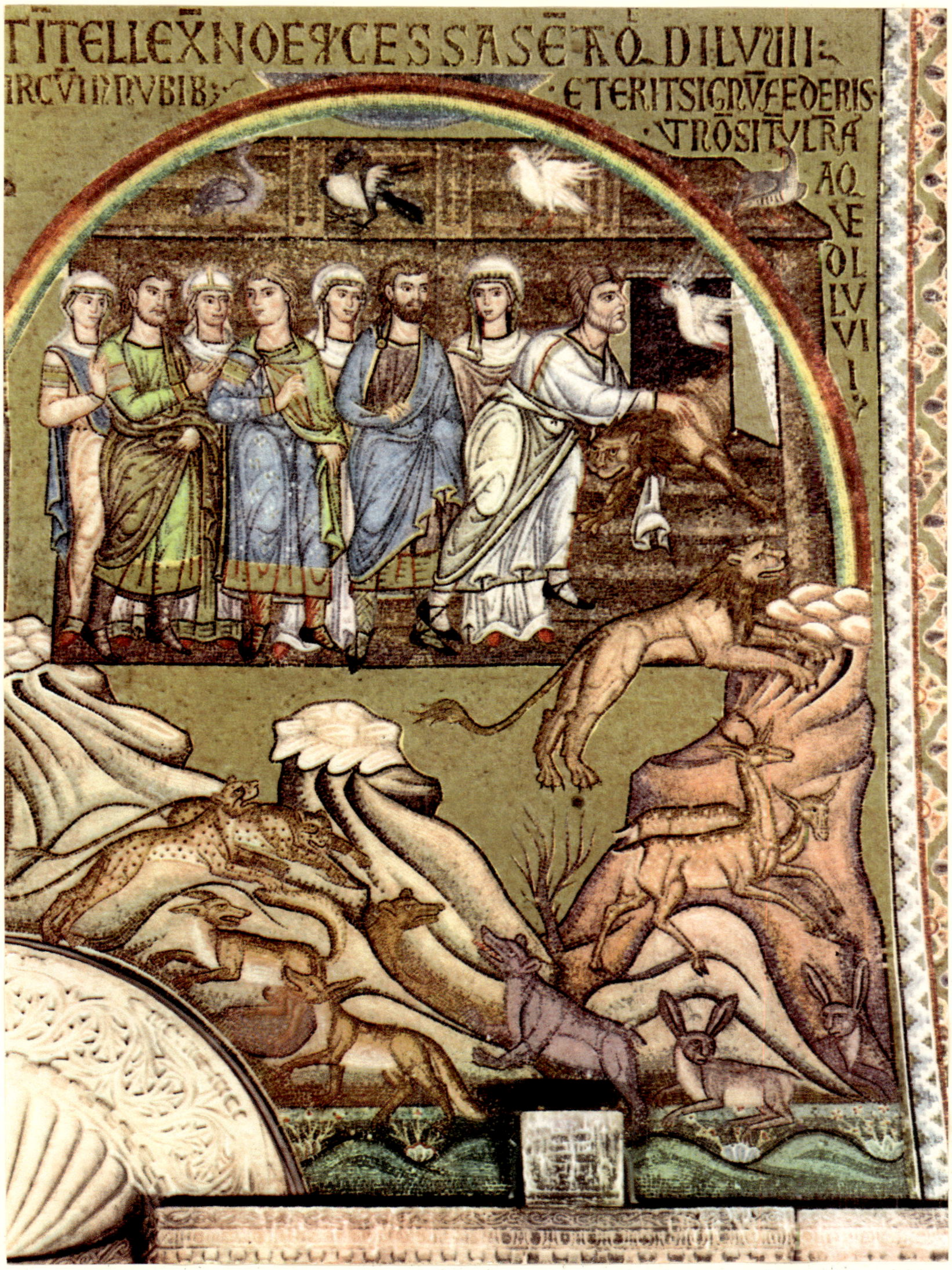

Byzantine-Venetian art: Noah freeing the animals from the Ark.

S. Mark's, Venice

The artist (or artists, for probably several were employed on the Genesis cycle) is no longer concerned with drawing up a composition according to fixed rules. There is a primitive feeling of spontaneity similar to that in contemporary Italian sculpture. But there are no traces of Byzantine grace and rhythm. It seems as though the artists had absorbed the technique without absorbing the culture; Byzantine symmetry, and nobility of gesture and expression are equally lacking. The artist prefers to group his characters effectively according to the requirements of the scene, and sometimes, as in the scenes from Noah, there is a trace of humour in the expressions. In spite of this however, the scenes from the Genesis at Venice never reach a high artistic level, nor even a

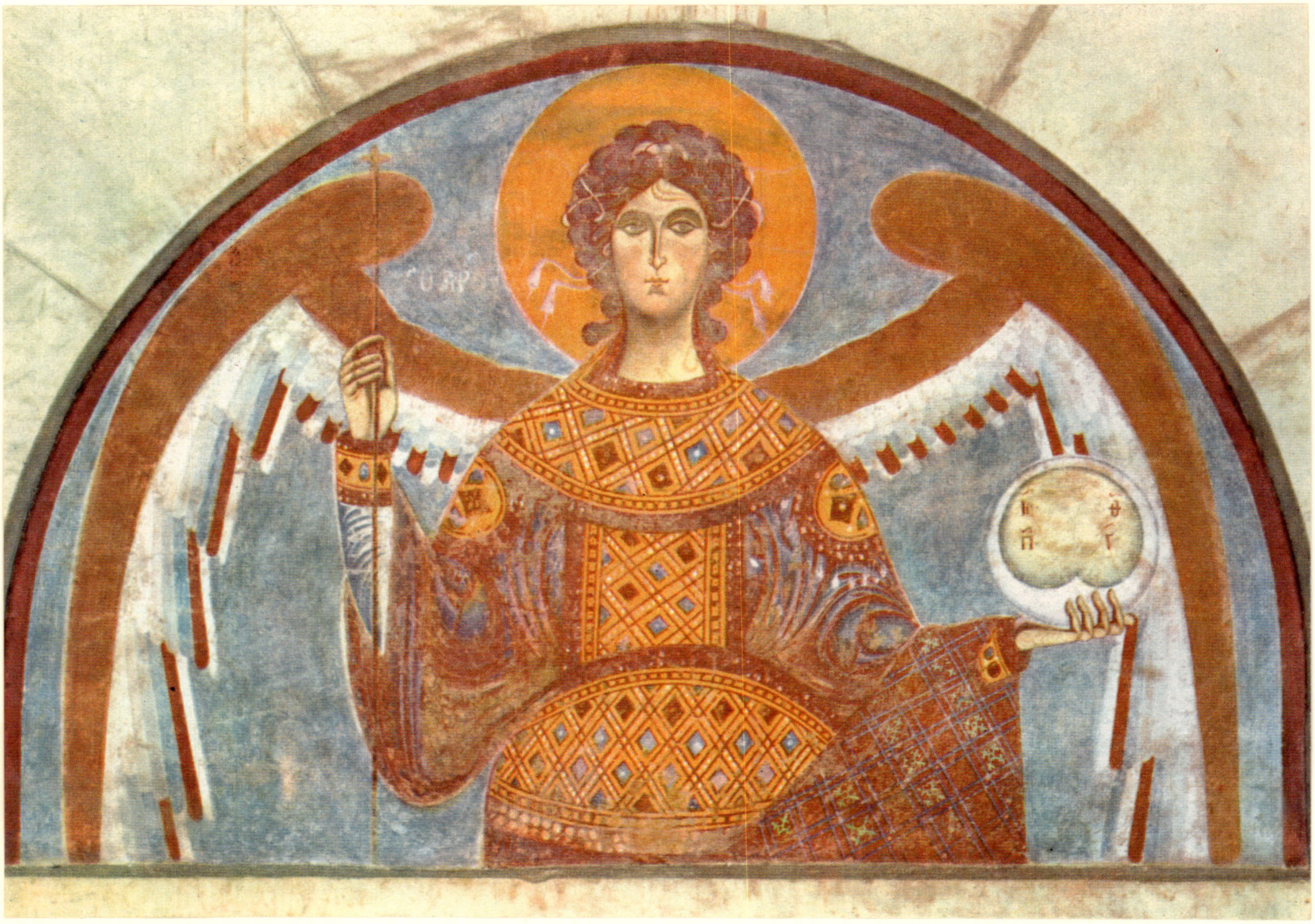

Byzantine art: S. Michael Archangel. Sant'Angelo in Formis

very important one; their interest lies in the new spirit which they represent.

Meanwhile, between the eleventh and twelfth centuries, Benedictine painting had attempted some complex and complicated cycles of which there are important examples in Castel S. Elia near Nepi, at S. Peter in Tuscania, at S. Angelo in Formis (Capua), and in Rome in the Legend of S. Clement and S. Alessio in S. Clement's, and some fragments in S. John Lateran and S. Cecilia in Trastevere. The Benedictine school continued to have the same characteristics which have already been noticed in the previous century — a prevailing Byzantine iconography and style modified by northern influence. Possibly this barbarian note appealed to the neo-Latin spirit of the Benedictines, but it was still Byzantine culture which they held in the highest esteem. The contrasting mixture of Byzantine imitations and original touches gave Benedictine painting a distinctive appearance during the eleventh century. Yet it was not destined to be very important for the future development of Italian painting, for there are in fact no traces of the Benedictine style to be found in the great masters of the thirteenth century. Apart altogether from style, the close connection between Benedictine painting and the Byzantine world is illustrated by the fact that the Abbot Desiderius (1058-1087) summoned Greek masters to Monte Cassino to decorate the Abbey and teach the monks. The decoration of S. Angelo in Formis was ordered by Desiderius and was chiefly carried out by Benedictine " pupils ", although there are touches of the style of the " masters ". A S. Michael Archangel and an Orans Virgin above the door of the church cannot be attributed to Benedictine craftsmen, for in their polish and obvious contact with the classical element in court painting at Constantinople, these paintings contrast strongly with the remaining frescoes. The same style can be perceived in some of the mosaics of S. Sophia; in the Virgin in the apse at Murano; and in some parts of the Venice mosaics: a refined, decadent, mysterious and petrified art which the Benedictine monks tried and failed to imitate, reproducing only the external characteristics and not the inner feeling and ancient tradition. In spite of their Byzantine masters and their wish to imitate, the Benedictines created a popular art, eastern in appearance although with some western touches. They had a good deal of facility in interpretation and rapidity of execution, which might easily be mistaken for immediacy. There is an unmistakeable character in their work, partly due to their great — sometimes too great — facility of execution, and partly to the simplicity and ingenuousness of their representations, which was the only lively element in their painting, and which sometimes made their crude, disjointed colours

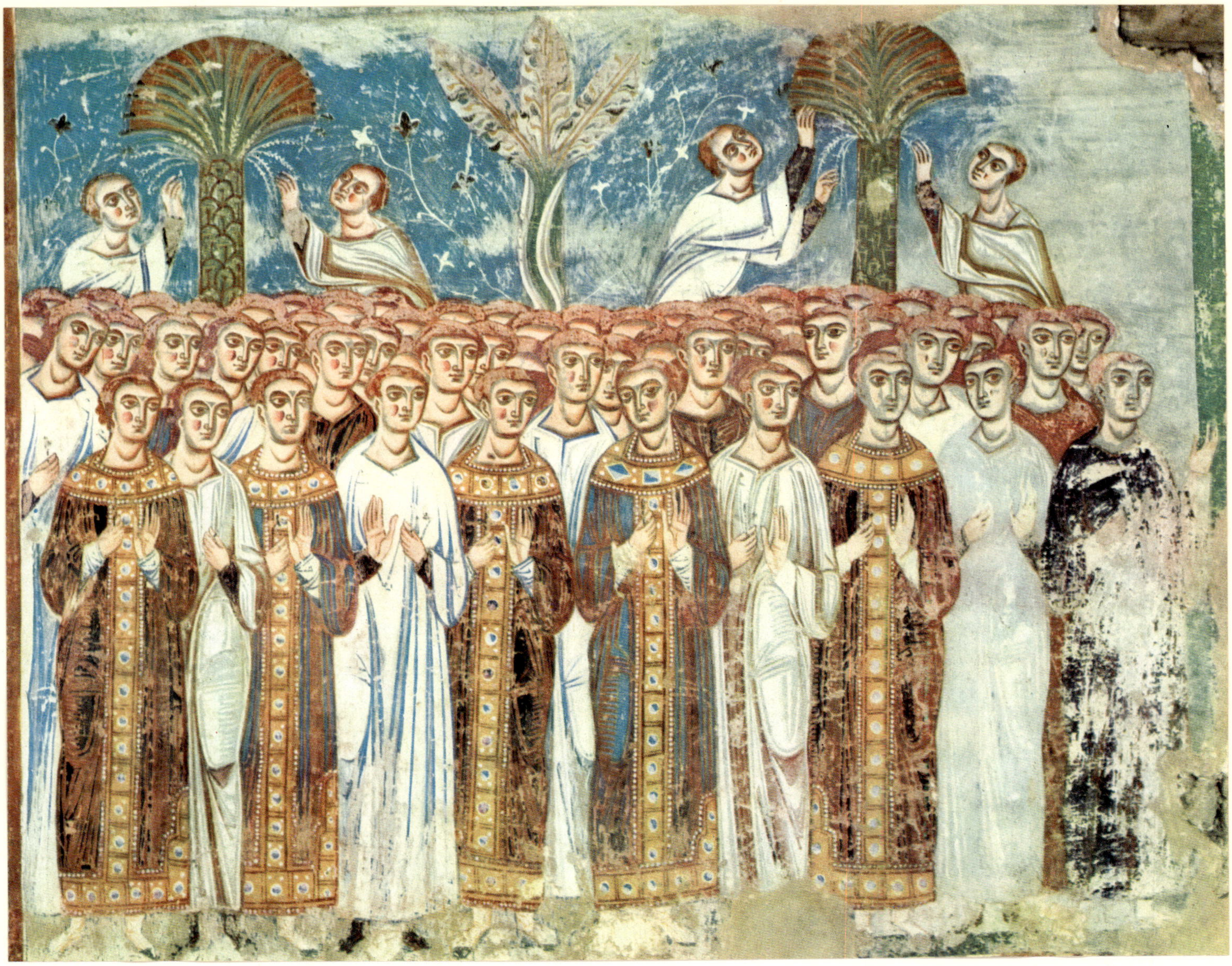

Benedictine art: The Elect, detail of The Last Judgment, Sant'Angelo in Formis

pleasing or at least entertaining. Almost all the frescoes in the interior of S. Angelo date from the time of Desiderius, of whom there is a living portrait (with a square halo) in the apse, in the act of offering the church to God. Although this is not all the work of one hand, it shows a remarkable uniformity, indicating the unity of Benedictine painting, and equally the lack of any outstanding individual personality. If such a person had ever existed, Benedictine painting might have occupied an important position in the evolution of Italian art. However, the wall-paintings of S. Angelo have an iconographical importance, forming a vast cycle of liturgical representations of events of the Old and New Testaments, even including the parables. In the apse is Christ between archangels and symbols of the evangelists; on the walls of the principal nave are scenes of Christ and the parables; in the side naves are scenes from the Old Testament and on the inside of the façade is the Last Judgment. There are also pictures of Benedictine origin on the outside, with legends of the Hermits, dating possibly from the thirteenth century, although they differ in style from the work inside. It is unfortunate from the point of view of the history of Italian art that even this outburst of Benedictine painting cannot be called " Romanesque ", since it remained too closely bound up with the Byzantine system.

Nor can the famous scenes painted in the lower church of S. Clement in Rome at the end of the eleventh century be truly classified as Romanesque. The Romanesque style was western, and implies a victory over the domination of eastern painting, whereas the painter (or painters, because there were at least two, belonging to the same school) of S. Clement shows a basic knowledge of the court style of Byzantine composition and decoration. Behind this cultural framework there is an evident narrative interest at S. Clement's or rather an interest in unfolding a series of events without analysing the factors necessary to give importance and effectiveness to the story. So that in spite of the restless attitudes of the characters, no authentic impression of drama is achieved.

The three scenes from the life of S. Clement, one from the life of S. Alessio, another from the life of S. Biagio and a scene of Daniel among the Lions are divided into squares decorated with yellow palms on a black background, which recall classical motifs. Other classical touches derived more from Roman surroundings than from Byzantine tradition, are to be found in the same paintings. For example the background architecture is neo-Hellenistic-Byzantine in origin, but has a certain decorative grace, which together with the wide, calm expanses of colour, clear and flat, and bright with pink, yellow and green shades, gives it a harmony which conceals its sketchiness.

The pictures in S. Clement's are superior to those in S. Angelo in Formis, but they are none the less Benedictine, for they have the same figurative system and ease of execution, while also exhibiting a richer, more deeply assimilated culture — probably because the artist was trained in Rome, and was acquainted with good examples of classical Byzantine or even paleo-Christian work.

The same Benedictine figurative facility can be found in the Church of S. Elio near Nepi, where the Roman monks John and Stephen, and their nephew Niccolò, covered the transept and apse with frescoes showing Christ among the saints and various visions from the Apocalypse divided into squares. This work dates from the beginning of the twelfth century.

In these Benedictine paintings at Rome dating from the end of the eleventh and beginning of the twelfth centuries it is possible to see an influence which is not directly due to the Byzantines, although it may have been inspired by them. It belongs to a local tradition of skilful figure drawing, combined with a conception of solemn, human dignity, both in the classical style. It is a sign, still very weak it is true, of the growing awareness that an autonomous revival might be possible in art, taking up where the

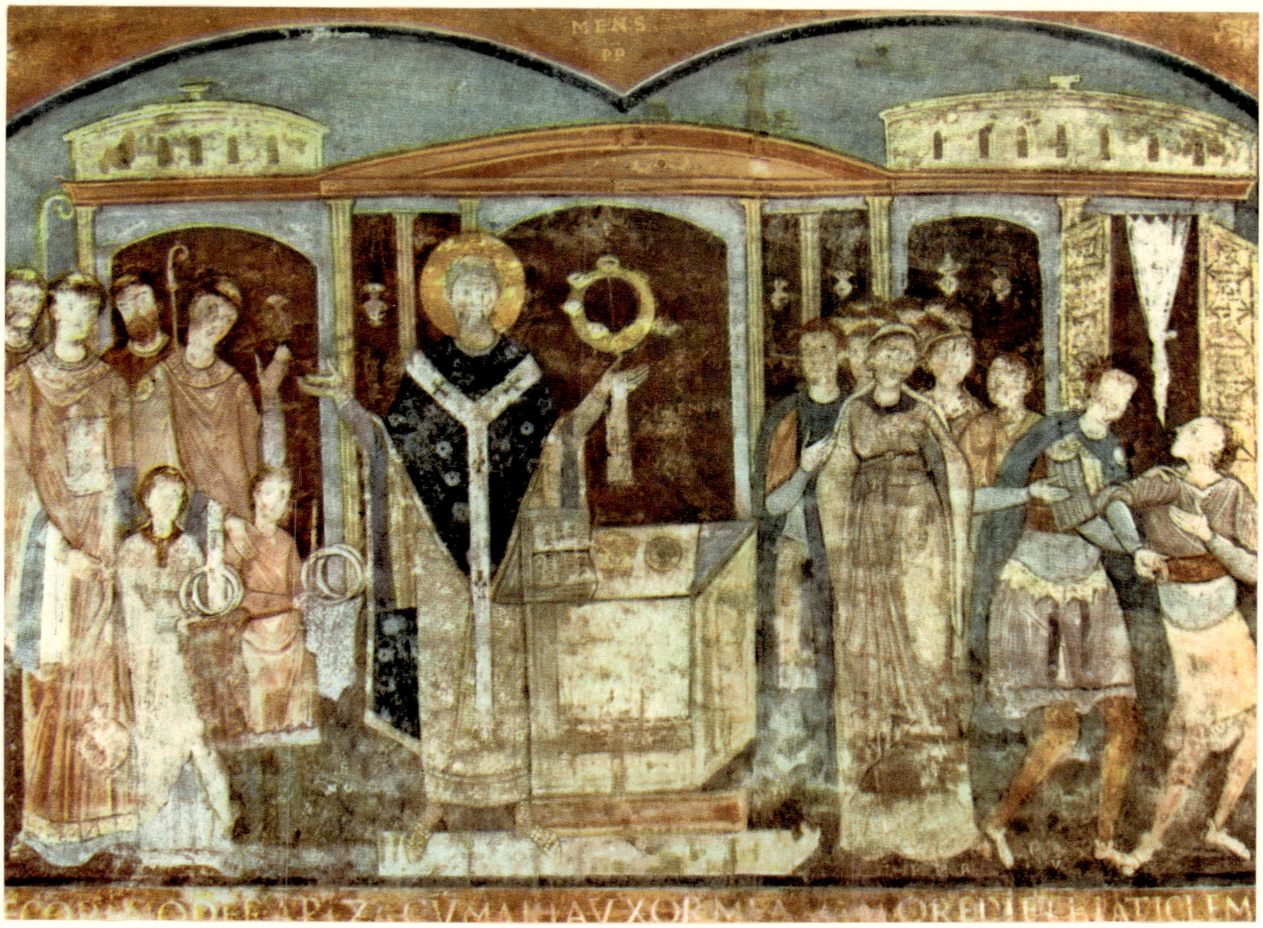

Romano-Benedictine art: Mass of S. Clement. S. Clement's, Rome

ancient Latin races left off, before the rise of the age-old, and now worn-out, academic Byzantine style.

It was a feeble symptom, because in fact Rome was not free from Constantinopolitan influence until the end of the thirteenth century. Nevertheless, even this very small indication gives a hint of the stronger, more perceptive spirits of the thirteenth century, such as Cimabue, for whom contemporary sculpture was the chief stimulus which led him to follow a new path.

In Roman mosaics too we can see the same searching for a more genuinely " antique " spiritual feeling, although the technique remains closely bound up with Byzantine prototypes. The same kind of effect is produced by the calm solemnity of the mosaic of Christ with the Virgin enthroned, in the apse of S. Maria in Trastevere, dating from the time of Innocent II (1130-1143).

This faint local movement is also found in panel painting, of which various examples can be found from the twelfth century onwards. A badly damaged icon preserved in S. Maria in Trastevere of the Madonna della Clemenza is usually attributed to the eleventh century. In the parts which can still be clearly seen there is a classical feeling of the neo-Hellenistic type which seems to forecast the Palaeologue period. The angels, especially the one which is best preserved, have a compact and well-blended colour impasto which suggests a full, soft modelling, and leads one to suspect the hand of a true Byzantine artist, and not a Roman, working at the end of the twelfth century, or more likely in the early years of the thirteenth century. The triptych in the cathedral of Tivoli, on the other hand, belongs to the Roman school and is more or less contemporary with the mosaics in S. Maria in Trastevere, showing very much the same taste and style. It represents the Saviour between Mary and S. John Evangelist, and scenes of the Death of the Virgin and Pentecost. The work is of very high technical quality and skill in execution, and is wholly Byzantine in feeling, with the well-known characteristics of sumptuousness and decadence (Christ has a robe which is entirely golden, the drapery being indicated by small red lines so as not to diminish the brightness); but the detailed drawing of shapes diminishes in the faces and hands, thus giving a slight feeling of the modelling of planes bounded by strong black contours, and the same effect of gentle seriousness which has already been noted in the mosaics in S. Maria. This Roman version of academic Byzantine painting must have reached other parts of Italy, such as Umbria and Tuscany. The same gentle, grave figure of Christ which we see in Tivoli is also to be found in the earliest known painted Crosses, such as the Crucifix in the cathedral of Spoleto, painted in 1187 by a certain Alberto Sotio, who was also the painter of some frescoes in the church of S. John and S. Paul; or the Crucifix in the cathedral of Sarzana, painted in 1138 by one Guglielmo, painter of the Holy Sepulchre now in the Pisa museum. Another is that of S. Maria of the Servites at Lucca, possibly belonging to the thirteenth century. These great Crosses were usually placed on the iconostasis of the churches and may have been used more frequently in Tuscany than elsewhere, for there are a large number at Pisa, Lucca, Florence, Siena and Arezzo, belonging to the fourteenth century and beginning of the fifteenth.

The prevailing style towards the middle of the thirteenth century is that of a living Christ with open eyes, head erect and a calm expression, symbolising the triumph over death (*Christus triumphans*). This is regarded as a Romanesque feature, or at any rate as being of western origin (possibly from France), as opposed to the other iconography, typically Byzantine, of a dead Christ with bent head and closed eyes (*Christus patiens*) which was later adopted in Italy. The first style may have been spread by the Benedictines, but even if it is genuinely western in origin, the examples which are to be found in Italy, up to the Crucifix of Berlinghiero at Lucca, are nevertheless very Byzantine in technique and feeling.

In the thirteenth century Italy was still producing Byzantine paintings. We have seen how long the importance of the Venetian workshop continued — the Byzantine feeling lasted along shores of the Lagoon until modern times in the so-called "madonneri". The "Greek" or Venetian-Greek masters travelled all over the peninsula, taking pupils. The maritime republics, with their commerce, helped the importation of "models" from Constantinople and other eastern cities. As the thirteenth century progressed, relations with the East became even closer so far as painting was concerned, although at the same time a great school of independent painters was growing up in Italy, owing to the work of a few outstanding artists.

Even in the mid-thirteenth century important works were entrusted to "Greek" masters and their local workmen who carried on and spread the style, while lowering the quality. The Baptistery of Parma (c. 1260-1270) was entirely decorated by talented Byzantine artists, possibly under the direction of a leader of exceptional personality, since the whole cycle, which is about S. John and the Old Testament, shows great homogeneity of style. The Parma frescoes are particularly interesting because they are among the best and most complete examples of the neo-Hellenistic style, and give a foretaste of the Palaeologue renaissance.

Many traces of this are also to be found in the Serbian churches, especially at Milesova (c. 1235) and Sopocani (1265). Between the eleventh and fourteenth centuries, Serbia, like Venice, became a notable centre of Byzantine painting. Chronologically the paintings of the Parma Baptistery can be placed between those of Sopocani and the later ones of Gracanica (1320 c.). They are probably nearer to the latter, although the Paleologue style is very evident at Gracanica. Owing to the lack of works from this period in the capital and the immediate surroundings, it is not known whether the artist of Parma was Serbian or from Constantinople, or whether the workmen were local or from Byzantium. In the case of Gracanica the work can be compared with the mosaics of Kahrieh-Djami, which are more or less of the same date. Although they are not so good, their style seems to be a provincial variation of the attenuated elegance of Kahrieh-Djami. In the first decade of the thirteenth century the neo-Hellenistic Byzantine style took on a rather vague note of what might be described as chivalry and courtly life, a little idyllic at times, with easy, calm rhythms. The iconography too changed slightly, but the pictorial systems remained the same as they had been for centuries.

Pisa was another very active workshop of Byzantine art in Italy between the twelfth and thirteenth centuries, especially for panel painting. A great many icons must have been imported — crosses, altarpieces, and moveable pictures — most probably directly from Byzantium. These served as models for local painters, and were possibly used in other parts of Tuscany as well, at Lucca, Florence and Siena. Even today there are still panel paintings in Pisa which are obviously pure Byzantine, whereas local products were often rather mechanical and crude imitations, such as the famous frontal of S. Catherine, now in the Museum of S. Matteo.

In the early years of the thirteenth century a complete new mosaic covering for the Baptistery was begun at Florence, and craftsmen were brought in from Venice. The work went on for a hundred years, and even in the early years of the fourteenth century the names of Venetian (that is Byzantine) masters are to be found in documents, although Giotto was then at the height of his powers. The mosaics in the cupola of the " bel S. John " date from this time, and side by side with a number which are still Byzantine in form, there are others which reveal clearly the style of the great Italian master, Giotto.

The decoration of the Baptistery was an immense undertaking, and at least until the middle of the thirteenth century was a very important factor in the development of Florentine painting. Cimabue certainly began his career in the Baptistery alongside the " Greek " artists who were working there. With so monumental an enterprise in progress, and with so vast a workshop, artistic life at Florence could hardly stagnate; the old Eastern ideas gave way before Florentine vigour and the new artists had a personal and well-defined individuality, despite their submission to Byzantine, Venetian, or Roman rules. For not all the artists were Venetian: through the years different generations succeeded one another in the Baptistery, and it is probable that some of them came, if not from Byzantium itself, then from elsewhere, especially Rome. There is no doubt that the oldest mosaics in the church — those in the gallery with the Virgin enthroned in the centre, signed by a Franciscan Friar called Jacopo, and dated 1225 — show a close relationship to Byzantine design, an elegant solemnity, slightly doctrinal, such as one might find round the Venetian Lagoon, especially at Torcello and Murano. Fra Jacopo must also have begun to decorate the cupola. Parts of the upper sections, with God as the Creator of angels and the hierarchic angels, are equally distinguished by their Venetian style: Vasari says that these mosaics were by a Byzantine named Apollonio from Venice, and one of his pupils Andrea Tafì, a Florentine. Mythical names for us today, but nevertheless Vasari's record throws some light — if the style of the works were not sufficient in itself — on the Byzantine atmosphere of the Florentine school in the thirteenth century.

The fact is that during the thirteenth century the commerce in works and artists in Italy was more lively than ever, and consequently Byzantine schools were flourishing.

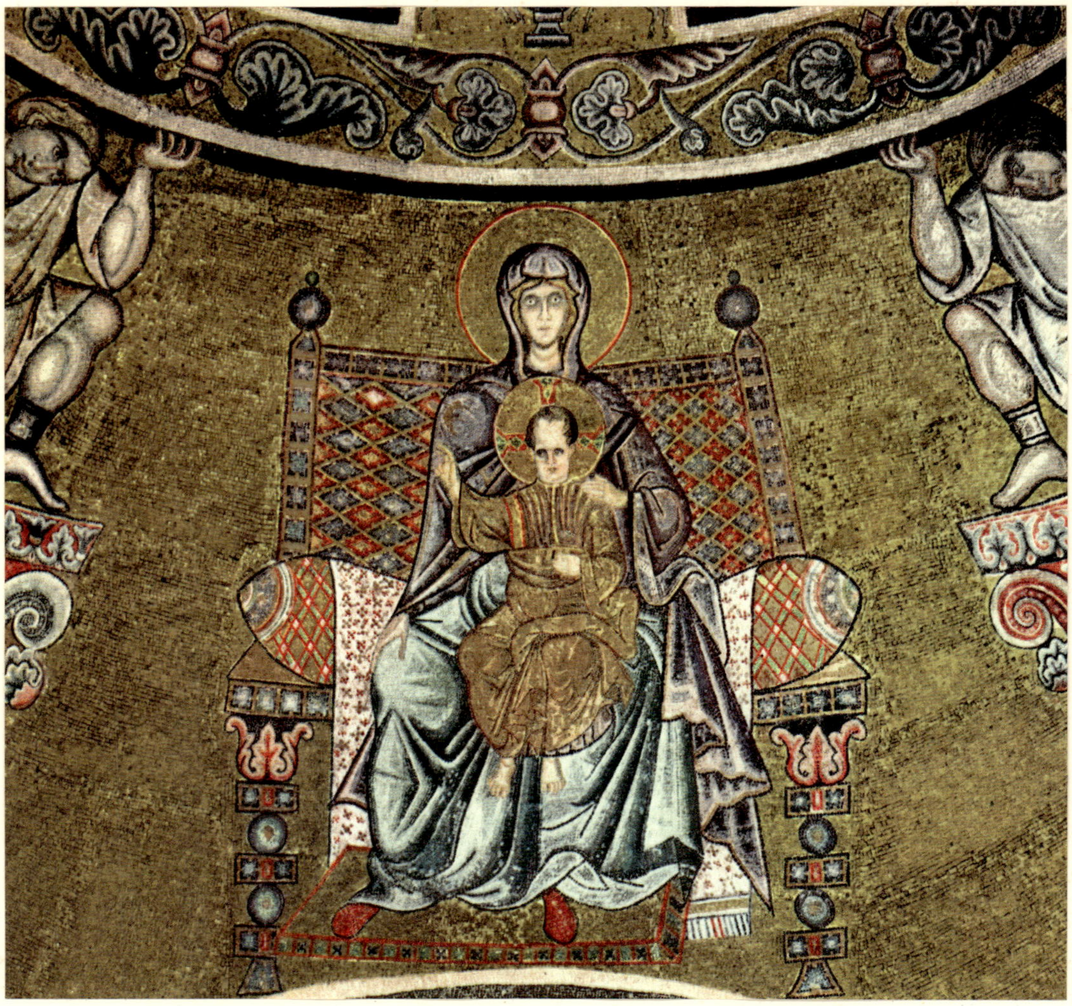

Fra Jacopo: The Virgin Enthroned, Baptistery, Florence

In Rome itself, and in the surrounding country, which had always possessed local schools occasionally displaying feeble signs of independence, there were still in the thirteenth century traces of a pure Byzantine style in the neo-Hellenistic manner. And curiously enough it is due to this strong neo-Hellenistic feeling in thirteenth-century Byzantine painting, both at Rome and at Florence, that a more deeply conscious local school grew up. It is almost as though a more truly indigenous classical feeling had awakened among the Latin peoples, more authentic than the other, which had absorbed so many deep-rooted Eastern elements.

Venetian mosaicists came to Rome for the apse of the old S. Peter's (c. 1198-1216) and for that of S. Paul Outside-the-Walls (c. 1218), of which some fragments remain in the famous " pathetic " style, found in many parts of the great Basilica.

And it would certainly seem that artists from Byzantium or nearby were responsible for the wall-paintings which remain in the church of the Greek abbey of Grottaferrata. These are painted in an accomplished Hellenistic style, a little dreamy, achieving a gentle effect of modelling by means of colour impasto and by softening the outlines, and giving a foretaste of the style of Pietro Cavallini.

But of all the many complex cycles which can still be seen in and near Rome, and which are either Byzantine or under Byzantine influence, or even in an archaic style based on paleo-Christian examples, perhaps the most important is that in the crypt of the cathedral at Anagni, since among the many painters who worked there

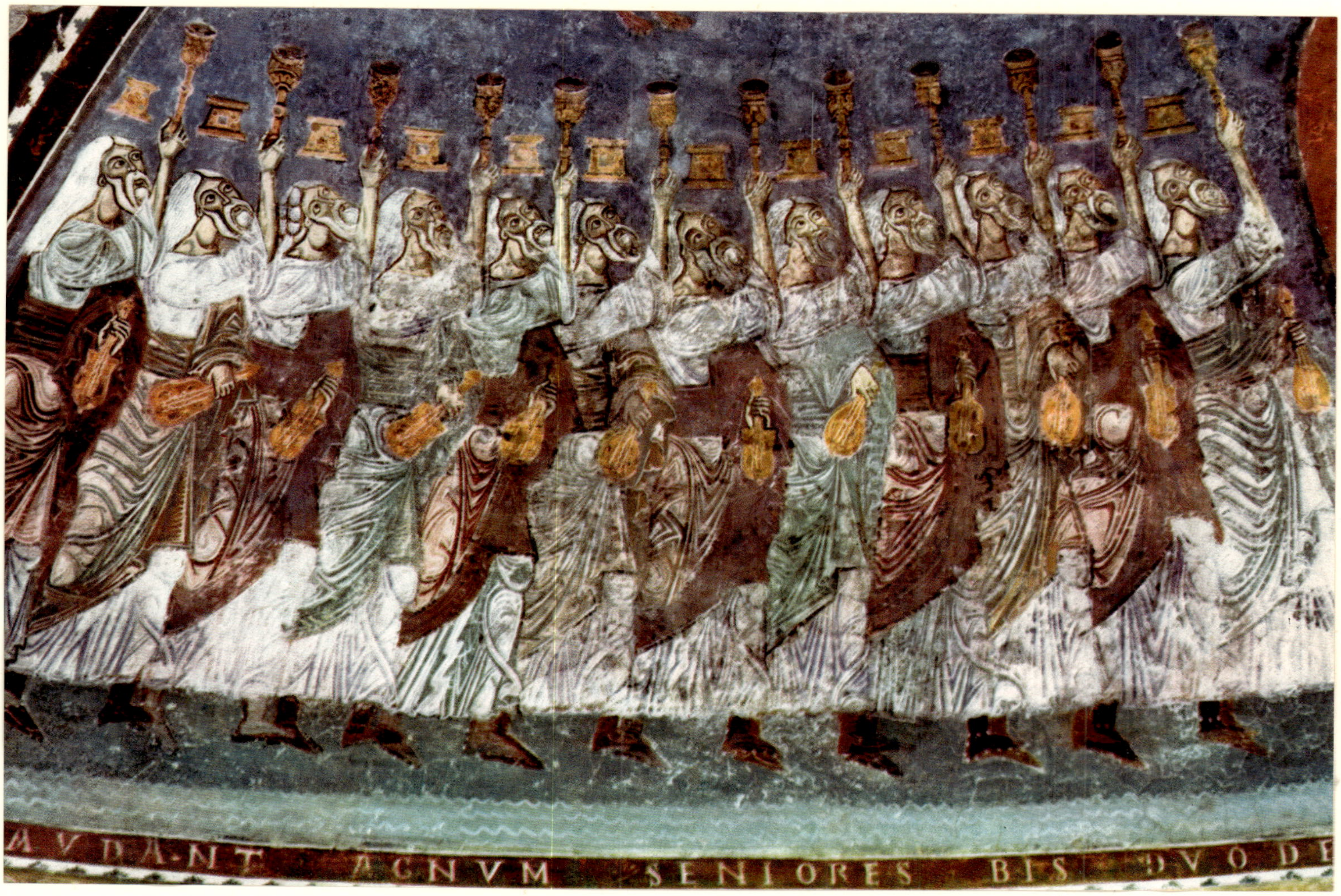

Master of Anagni: The Old Men of the Apocalypse. Cathedral, Anagni

between 1230 and 1255 we can begin to see a movement towards independence which followed a direction opposite to that in which the Byzantine school was moving.

The Anagni cycle is vast and complex. It begins with the creation of the world and humanity by a meeting of the four elements, according to the doctrines of Hippocrates and Galeno (portrayed in the church) and goes on from legends of the ark to lives of the patron saints of Anagni, down to the most recent canonisations.

The various styles of the painters who worked there show not only the diversity of trends then to be found in Rome and nearby, but also a new ferment, a vague restlessness and intolerance, a sign of some revolutionary, or at least schismatic event, in the heart of a tradition which had endured for centuries.

At Anagni, alongside the tired and trite examples derived from the mechanical Byzantine style of S. Paul Outside-the-Walls, there are others which show a deeper classical feeling. The Master, with the help of various collaborators, painted the vaults: and his Pantocrator, for example, interprets the neo-Hellenistic Byzantine movement with a breadth and solidity of form based on a secure, firm foundation and of vigorous, dense colouring, accentuating the planes with strong lighting. In this way he achieves a heavy, solemn style, with its own serene grace: it is a style and feeling which, like Grottaferrata, gives an idea of the complex world of eastern, paleo-Christian and classical influences in which Cavallini developed.

Outstanding among the artists of Anagni is the painter of the scene with Hippocrates teaching Galeno, the scenes of Samuel and the Old Men of the Apocalypse, as well as some other parts in which he was helped by pupils. It is in his work that a real attempt can be seen to break away from the mechanical Byzantine style, and from the Greek influence contained in it: an attempt to return to the classical forms in use up to the sixth century, with a personal interpretation, as the Carolingians and Ottonians had done in their turn. And we can discern a wish to find, for painting, a neo-Latin language as opposed to a neo-Hellenistic one polluted with Eastern ideas. The traditional schemes now seem to be refreshed and revived, transplanted into the congenial atmosphere of the ancient world. And so the feeling of the ancient legends dawned afresh in art, going back beyond history into the world of myth. This feeling, at once new and " antique ", was conveyed by clear, crystal colouring, rich in ultramarine and emerald, whites and pinks; and although the effect was rich, it was not due to the supremely skilful alchemy of the Byzantines. On the contrary, it was due to a poetical abstraction of personal impressions drawn from the natural world. Design gives way to an expressive rhythm similar to the Carolingian. This feeling for line, very different from the irregular and broken line of the Byzantines, leads one to think that the " Master of Anagni " represents the first symptom in Italy of a genuine " Western " stirring, whose interest lay in the native Latin civilisation and not in the foreign, Greek civilisation of Constantinople. It has been said (by Longhi) that the " Master of Anagni " opened the way for the " Master of S. Martino " and Cimabue.

Meanwhile, a sure sign of a new and growing movement is that in the middle of the thirteenth century in Italy a number of schools can be distinguished, each with special characteristics according to its situation. The names of the leaders moreover were beginning to be known.

From the middle of the thirteenth century onwards, Italy became the great source of painting and the fount of promise. She acquired her new position partly because of the strong personalities of the Italian artists who mark the beginning of individuality in art, a modern conception quite contrary to the collective anonymity of the Middle Ages; and partly because of the vast cycles of frescoes and great altarpieces and icons which were produced. Italian painting became increasingly monumental, with a preference for cycles and narrative legends, as in Spain.

Throughout the rest of the western world, with the exception of France, where the Gothic style developed brilliantly during the thirteenth century, a period of stagnation set in. But in France (although sculpture and painting reflected the perfection of its style), architecture was the dominant art.

No wall-paintings have survived in France. No doubt they existed in private residences and castles, but the new style of architecture no longer permitted the pictorial decoration of churches. The great expanses of wall had disappeared, giving place to great expanses of window. Representations of divine figures and holy scenes were transposed to glass.

The art of stained glass began about the tenth century. It is known that Adalberon, Bishop of Rheims (969-988), ordered stained glass with figures and scenes for the cathedral. But nothing is known about the origin of the technique, not even if it is French, although this seems likely in view of the close connections with Gothic architecture, which was born mainly in France. References in the " Treatise " of Theophilus, at the end of the eleventh century, say that as the Byzantines reached perfection in the art of fresco, so France reached it in stained glass. But very little stained glass now in existence can be assigned even doubtfully to the eleventh century.

Possibly only the fragment with a head of Christ from Wissenbourg, now in the Museum of Notre Dame at Strasbourg, judging by a strong Ottonian tone, dates back to the middle of the century.

From the twelfth century, however, works of high quality can be discerned: the fragments of the Basilica of S. Denis, with scenes of S. Vincent, symbolical figures and decorative motifs (c. 1145); the Virgin and Child from the church of the Trinity at Vendôme (c. 1150); the fine panels with the Crucifixion, scenes from the Old Testament and S. Stephen (c. 1135) from the cathedral of Chalôns-sur-Marne; and others as well. It is significant that these fragments of stained glass show a stylistic likeness to sculpture and not to illumination. This is because of the way in which stained glass and sculpture were bound up with, and subordinated to, architecture. Stained glass, especially that from Chalôns-sur-Marne, also shows a close connection with gold and enamel work of the kind produced in the region of the Meuse and the Rhine, which is explained by the basically decorative function of stained glass and by the superb quality of the gold work of this area. In the twelfth century the most important stained glass was at S. Denis: during the reconstruction of the Abbey by Abbot Suger an important *atelier* was established, and craftsmen were summoned from all over France, and even from England — for the same style is to be found in the famous glass at Chartres, Le Mans, and York Minster, where there is a Tree of Jesse similar to those at Chartres and S. Denis.

From about the middle of the twelfth century stained glass windows tended to increase in size, partly for the practical purpose of letting in more light, and partly because of the superb skill of the artists. It is not unlikely that one of the reasons for the development of Gothic architecture was the increasing attention paid to stained glass, so that walls had to be reduced in size, and therefore supports had to be strengthened. However that may be, there is no doubt that stained glass and Gothic architecture flourished together, closely linked with each other and with sculpture, which was used mainly for external decoration. These three manifestations of art were so closely welded together during the Gothic period in France that together they form a single imaginative creation, almost the poetic dream of a single mind. Soon a Gothic building seemed like a magical choral glorification under the guidance of a chorus-master.

The master craftsmen of S. Denis moved to other places and were responsible for the formation of other schools: thus the glass of the cathedrals of Poitiers and Angers, which dates mainly from the end of the twelfth century, has its own characteristics, while showing a clear connection with that of Chartres and Le Mans.

Stained glass probably reached a peak of perfection in the twelfth century: we can distinguish at this time a supremely accomplished skill in execution combined with great powers of decoration and expression. Later on the technique became even more perfect, but the quality and adaptability of the style could not be improved upon or extended. During the thirteenth century stained glass developed enormously, but structurally it was less bound up with architecture. While tending to make the window-spaces brighter than ever with a vast number of coloured lights, the compositions became more elaborate and restless, as though they were emulating contemporary miniatures. At the beginning of the century the style of S. Denis was developed and can be seen in the later windows of Chartres and the church of the Trinity at Vendôme.

But at the end of the century the great importance of the workshop at Notre Dame at Paris, which had been formed in order to complete the church begun in 1165, also gave importance to the *atelier* for stained glass which was attached to it. As a result other centres — especially the neighbouring Chartres — were strongly influenced, and an important centre developed there at the beginning of the thirteenth century. Today we are accustomed to speak of a kind of stained glass dating from the first half of the thirteenth century as belonging to the " Chartres school ". We cannot speak of the school of Paris or Notre Dame, since although there is a great deal of thirteenth-century glass all over France, none survives from the great cathedral itself. It is probable that the Paris *atelier* was transferred to Chartres and continued the same kind of work there. The greater part of stained glass in France in the first half of the thirteenth century is undoubtedly closely connected with the school of Chartres. And not only in France: the same style is to be found in England, for example at Canterbury. Evidently at this period Chartres exercised the influence formerly held by S. Denis.

In the second half of the century the dominating influence was once more to be found in Paris — if indeed it had really been there when the original stained glass was made for Notre Dame — owing to the building of the Sainte-Chapelle (consecrated in 1248) and the new transepts in Notre Dame. Now however there is a slight feeling of decadence especially in the harmony of the colours: violet is the prevailing background colour in Paris, and it does not blend well with the kaleidoscope of brighter colours, nor does it make them stand out so vividly, as did the typical brilliant blue of the older glass. The decorative parts moreover lost their quality of elegant display and were impoverished. But in spite of this the decorative value of French stained glass remained very high, owing to the skill with which it was adapted to architecture.

The masterpieces of the Sainte-Chapelle school are the windows with the Life of S. Martial in the cathedral of Tours. Their general effect is very similar to that of the great windows of the Sainte-Chapelle, although the style is more accomplished, and there is a sensitive, sinuous feeling of movement in the design that recalls the illumination of the time of S. Louis.

The close relationship which formerly existed between illumination and wall-painting is now to be found in the relationship of form and feeling between illumination and stained glass. This does not mean that as a general rule the same artists worked on the codices and on the preliminary cartoons for the stained glass: the two arts were too different in purpose and function, and there was too much specialised activity in both fields. It is truer to say that illumination and stained glass had a reciprocal influence on each other.

The earliest artists in stained glass seem to have been unacquainted with illumination. Theirs was a medium which called for complete submission to the requirements of architecture. This tendency to attach special importance to the architectural whole has already been shown in the fresco decoration of Romanesque building and now, at the beginning of the Gothic period, architectural features are introduced into painting, even when architecture is not directly concerned, and this was no doubt due to the influence of stained glass.

Later in the thirteenth century illumination itself began to resemble stained glass. To begin with, it was a matter of modifying the miniature pictures by introducing architectural settings in reds and blues (the favourite colours in French stained glass), with foliage borders like those of the windows. But later on, windows were divided into an arrangement of circles and squares like the pages of a manuscript. But the fact that illumination was influenced by the decorative and architectural quality of stained glass shows how important the latter had become in French artistic life at the beginning of the thirteenth century and how greatly it was admired and imitated. Nevertheless the French school of illumination expanded and flourished on its own account, and exercised immense influence in the thirteenth century. A wholly new and original poetical interpretation grew up as well as an independent capacity for invention, and an unsurpassed technical skill. Moreover a revolution had taken place in the system of production: there were now lay schools directed by artists who imposed their own personalities rather than those of the monasteries. They produced great quantities of books on all subjects, from the profane (stories, learned theses and scientific works) to the religious. Gradually the names of the heads of schools and the great miniaturists began to be mentioned. The first to be known is that of Honoré, who was active at the end of the century and was responsible for the development of illumination in the fourteenth century. Even in the monasteries lay artists from Paris worked among the monks, who continued their traditional occupation. For Paris had become the unquestioned centre of illumination. Probably the fact that book illustration had become localised is connected with the importance of the University, and the constant demand for books on various subjects. But the high quality, the exquisite tone of elegance and richness of many thirteenth-century manuscripts are certainly not due to the Sorbonne, whose main interests were practical and didactic. Once again, in fact, as in the days of Charlemagne and his immediate successors, it was the Court which took the initiative in book decoration, especially for the Bibles, psalters, and evangeliaries, which were constantly used by devout laymen. The books which were produced for the French royal family reach the highest peak of perfection ever achieved in this type of work in the Gothic period: from the thirteenth-century Psalter of Queen Ingeborg (Chantilly, Musée Condé) wife of Philip Augustus (which still shows traces of the English school as well as the S. Denis school of stained glass), to that of Blanche of Castile (Paris, Arsenal 1186) mother of S. Louis, where for the first time scenes are placed in medallions like stained glass. The masterpiece of the Paris school, the Psalter of S. Louis, reveals the great change in taste and style which took place in the second half of the century.

S. Louis took a lively interest in the decoration of codices, and the manuscripts which he commissioned constitute the masterpieces of the Paris school, in particular the Psalter mentioned above and the Bible *moralisée* which is now divided between the Bibliothèque Nationale and the British Museum.

The famous S. Louis Psalter, which was done between 1253 and 1270, contains 78 full-page pictures, showing scenes from the Old Testament in rich harmonious colouring enhanced by the use of gold in the backgrounds and decoration. It is supremely elegant, but owing to the delicate balance of the soft and springlike colours, it cannot be called sumptuous. This new and vernal vision of the world is also seen in the rhythm, which is almost like a dance, controlling the gestures and creating a composition from a free, easy design always disciplined by the style. The sharp graphic feeling of the Carolingians seems to flower in a tender, yielding, and graceful manner both in space and movement. The outline turns, bends, slides, on a compact golden plane or on other areas of flat colour, so that a feeling of depth and modelling is rapidly created. It is a kind of illusionism which was the outcome of a rather down-to-earth view of life. A treatment of space, inspired by Gothic architecture, emphasises the vertical lines of both figures and composition. The influence of Gothic architecture is very plainly shown in the Codex of S. Louis by the presence of ogives with pinnacles, columns and perforations, which are used to crown the pictures. These motifs are derived directly from the Sainte-Chapelle, and it is very possible that the architect, Jean de Montreuil, was asked by the King to collaborate in the designing of these remarkable pictures.

Gothic painting had now reached a stage of development which remained unchanged until after the middle of the fourteenth century. It spread over most of Europe by means of books, especially scientific manuscripts from the University, and

Bibles. It was particularly important in England and Germany, where it underwent changes. But it also reached the Byzantine countries, although more slowly and with less understanding. A certain sinuous and elongated development of the neo-Hellenistic form in the time of the Palaeologues probably owes something to the gracefulness of thirteenth-century Gothic; a blending of the imaginative, the realistic and the capricious. This development is evident in the mosaics of Kahrieh-Djami and in some frescoes at Mistra. And certainly the poetic truth, mysterious grace, epic and " courtly " feeling of Duccio owe a great deal to the Paris school of illumination in the reign of S. Louis.

Nevertheless, in spite of the evolution and expansion of the French Gothic style, the strengthening of Byzantine influence in a commercial rather than an artistic sense can be seen in other European countries besides Italy. It is true that this did not hinder the other, more vital and modern influence of Gothic art, but it persisted, and although it was modified by the new style it never disappeared altogether except in those parts of France which were furthest from the Italian and German borders.

In countries such as England and Germany which adopted Romanesque and Gothic art at an early stage, the last breath of the Byzantine influence in the West produced a curious hybrid style, generally considered to be " baroque " in flavour, and attributed to a period of transition. The term transitional is usually applied with special reference to painting in England and Germany. It was in fact a style of brief duration, or crisis, which ended by ensuring the triumph of Gothic. In a sense this crisis also reached Italy, as we can see in the work of Giunta Pisano, the Master of S. Francis and Coppo di Marcovaldo: indeed, it seemed more natural in Italy, where painting had always been Byzantine, and where a new upheaval resulted from contacts with forms which had already been developed for centuries in more western countries. This crisis was very beneficial to Italy, and gave rise to conceptions which were truly revolutionary and modern. North of the Alps, on the other hand, it was a crisis in the other direction and resembled the behaviour of children who, having strayed too far from home, suddenly want to get back — in this case to the great matriarch who was primarly responsible for Christian art, Byzantium. The Crusades, the mercantile power of Byzantium and the Italian maritime republics who acted as intermediaries, all contributed to this phenomenon. The Crusades brought a touch of western patina to the age-old Byzantine forms, and at the same time they created a renewal of interest in the East. The transition period may have represented something of a spiritual crisis as well, because painting both in England and in Germany — and even in Italy (*vide* Giunta) — gives an impression of restlessness and of genuine stress.

In England the transitional style had a negative result, and simply arrested the Gothic movement which had begun so splendidly. But the new style was introduced by a great artist, a men of limitless talent, Matthew Paris: historian, painter, sculptor, and goldsmith. His miniatures, preserved in the British Museum and at Corpus Christi College, Cambridge, still have the sense of grandeur, and the designs in a few colours, which belong to the Romanesque epoch. But they also have a restless grace within the rigorous framework of Byzantine iconography, as can be seen in the great Madonna at the beginning of his History of the Conquest of England (British Museum). This style reached a peak about 1250, with brilliant results in the illustrations of the Apocalypse, of which a notable example is at Trinity College, Cambridge (R. 16.2). The subjects in the Apocalypse are of course usually well-suited to the anguished note of the style.

In Germany, on the other hand, where the transition style is limited to the period between the death of Frederick Barbarossa (1190) and the end of the Hohenstaufen dynasty, it brought great originality into German art, though more to sculpture than to painting. The latter was of secondary importance even compared with architecture, which had completely adopted the French Gothic style.

The great welcome given to Byzantine models was due to a desire for something new, possibly as a result of contacts with Italian culture at the end of the twelfth century, when the German Emperors, the heirs of the Normans, transferred their capital to the south of Italy. And, of course, to the Crusades.

The most remarkable " crisis " in Byzantine art took place in Limburg, where between the end of the twelfth century and 1235-40, painting is characterised by an effort to achieve a monumental solemnity. Elsewhere, especially in Westphalia, Byzantine iconography and monumental feeling prevailed, producing a certain fixity of expression; but these motifs are embodied in a design which, curiously enough, gives a very strong impression of the Gothic feeling for movement in the drapery alone. And so we find hieratic, stylised Byzantine figures clothed in pointed swirling robes that flow and quiver. All the vitality of the style seems to be concentrated in the draperies, which are sometimes so exaggerated that they suggest the baroque. The oldest examples of this style are perhaps the wall-paintings in the Baptistery of S. Gereon at Cologne, and some miniatures of the Saxon-Thuringian school, such as the Psalter of S. Elisabeth, now in the Library at Cividale. The most important example of this strange mixture of the Byzantine and the Gothic in Westphalia is a Madonna, very largely restored in the sixteenth century and now in the Bargello Museum at Florence. The picture is by the artist who, between 1250 and 1272, painted the altar frontal with the Trinity which comes from the Wiesenkirche in Soest, and is now in the Kaiser Friedrich Museum in Berlin. This Madonna reveals even more clearly

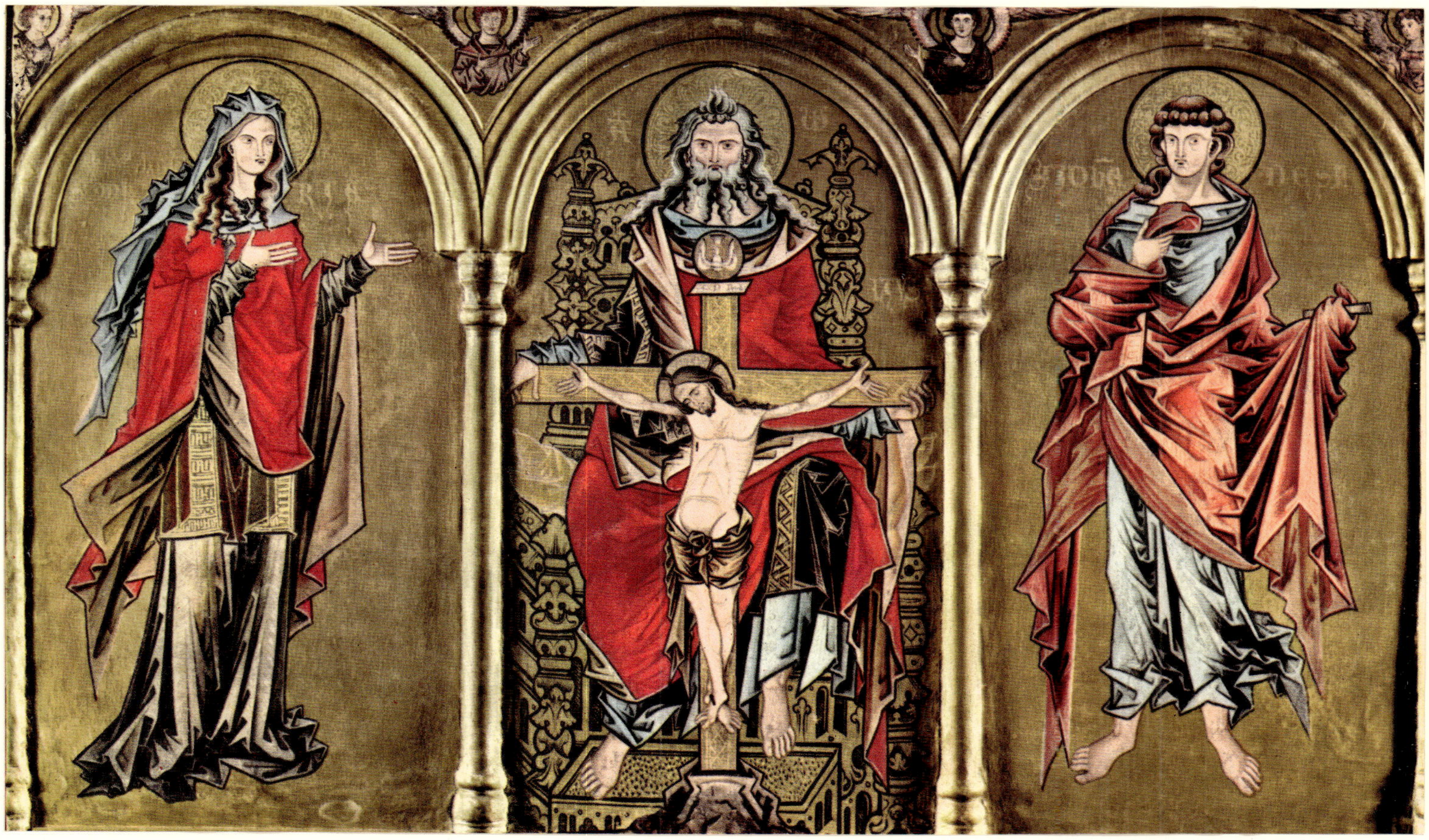

German art: The Trinity from Soest. Kaiser Friedrich Museum, Berlin

the transposition of a theme of Byzantine iconography (the Eleusa) into a taut and nervous form that is wholly German.

The German version was certainly copied from a Byzantine painting, but the artist's approach was over-intellectual and the result is essentially mannered. In fact in the last decade of the thirteenth century only the Gothic element of the transition period, that is to say the flowing, pointed drapery, remained alive. In all other respects German painting fell into line with the more genuine Gothic movements which came from France in the West and Bohemia in the East, where through the influence of illuminated manuscripts French culture had long been widespread.

Between the twelfth and thirteenth centuries in France the foundations were laid for a new conception of life, and a modern spirit appears in every field of culture. In Italy, towards the middle of the thirteenth century, there were signs of the upheaval which resulted a few decades later in a revolution in painting and in the emergence of individual personalities. But even in the first half of the thirteenth century schools began to emerge bearing the imprint of their leading artists. This did not always imply great originality, or artistic independence, but it was a symptom of developments along personal lines.

The first important name to appear in the early decades of the thirteenth century is that of an artist from Lucca, Berlinghiero Berlinghieri. In 1228 he is referred to as being already dead, and in another document of 1242 he is mentioned as having been the head of the Lucca school of painting and also the founder of a family of painters. One of his sons, Barone, was a painter, and another named Marco was an illuminator, but nothing has survived which can be definitely attributed to either of them. Another son, Bonaventura, signed and dated an altarpiece with S. Francis and scenes from his life in 1235 for the church of S. Francis at Pescia.

The only signed work of Berlinghiero is the Crucifix from the Monastery of S. Maria degli Angioli in Lucca, and, on analogy, some other paintings are attributed to him. His work is closely bound up with the neo-Hellenistic Byzantine style, but he introduced a personal note of calm solemnity, recalling the Roman-Byzantine style, into the fixed schemes of iconography. His rather academic manner was copied for many years, almost until the end of the century in Lucca and the neighbourhood. About the middle of the thirteenth century his influence reached Florence, and is seen to some extent in the work of artists like the " Master of the Bigallo ", so called after a Crucifix now in the Oratory of the Bigallo in Florence.

His son Bonaventura, so far as can be judged from his one signed work at Pescia, kept to the same technique and style, but was rather more provincial, and also adopted a more gloomy Byzantine note. Nevertheless in Florence his influence was greater than his father's, and affected painters of greater talent than himself, such as the " Master of S. Francis Bardi ", named after a picture of the saint in the chapel of that name in S. Croce. Both this painter and another, whose work is so similar that they cannot always be distinguished from one another, the " Master of Vico l'Abate ", broke away from Bonaventura's style. The " Master of Vico l'Abate " and the " Master of S. Francis Bardi " are either the same person or two artists whose work was remarkably alike, both inspired by a Balkan, that is to say a provincial version of Byzantine culture and yet showing a certain Romanesque feeling, especially in the relationship between the background and the figures, so that surroundings are always subordinated to the action. In the pictures attributed to the " Master of S. Francis Bardi ", and the " Master of Vico l'Abate ", there is a plastic feeling which is regarded as being the immediate forerunner of Coppo di Marcovaldo's style.

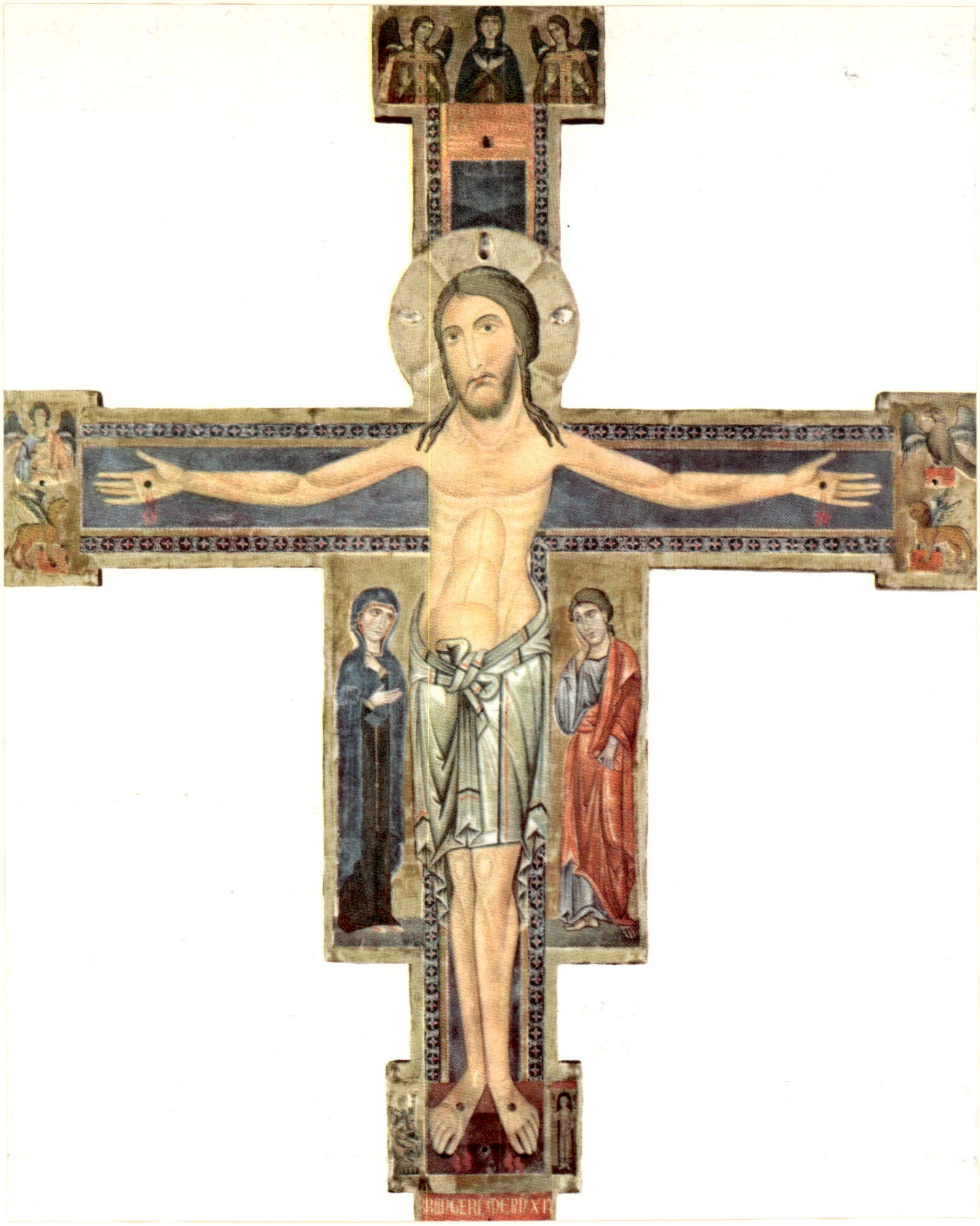

Berlinghiero: Crucifix. Pinacoteca, Lucca

Coppo di Marcovaldo and Giunta Pisano are jointly associated with the first crisis in the history of Italian painting of the kind that had occurred in other European centres, but for different reasons and with different aims. Deeply troubled by their knowledge of the mechanical nature of the Byzantine systems in force all over Italy, they made confused efforts to change the situation, but finding no solution to their problem they merely aggravated it.

Giunta Pisano was trained in his own town, doubtless by studying icons which merchants brought back from eastern countries. But his work was done mostly in Umbria. Documents of 1229 and 1259 record him as still living at Pisa. Nothing remains of his work except Crucifixes, of which three are signed, so that possibly he did not paint anything else. That in S. Maria degli Angeli at Assisi is the oldest; another is in S. Ranierino in Pisa and the third in S. Domenico at Bologna. In all his Crucifixes he faithfully follows the Byzantine models of Christ in agony.

Yet his work has a very personal dramatic feeling, conveyed by a jerky linear style that suggests an interest in the expressionism of western art, of which he may well have seen Carolingian and Ottonian examples. As time went on his work moved steadily in this direction, concentrating on a feeling of suffering. Possibly his years in Umbria contributed to this change, for the presence of monasteries there meant that contacts with the West were more frequent than at Pisa. His great dramatic qualities are especially evident in the fine Crucifix of Bologna, which is monumental and so charged with passion that the effect of despair verges on the grotesque. Giunta's influence was widely felt in central Italy as far as Emilia, and was of great importance in the formation of the Umbrian school in the thirteenth century.

The Umbrian " Master of S. Francis ", so-called from the picture with the figure of the Saint in S. Maria degli Angeli in Assisi, based his style on Giunta's latest work. Three other paintings and a great Crucifix at Perugia, dated 1272, can be attributed to this artist, which enables us to establish the dates of his work as being roughly between 1250 and 1280. The " Master of S. Francis " is one of the most remarkable and most original Umbrian painters of the thirteenth century and, like Giunta, showed that it was possible to overcome the rigid Eastern schemes by expressing a deep personal feeling. His line drawing is more subtle and his colouring softer than that of Giunta, who expresses his violence and pathos, whereas the Master of S. Francis imparts a feeling of pity and grief.

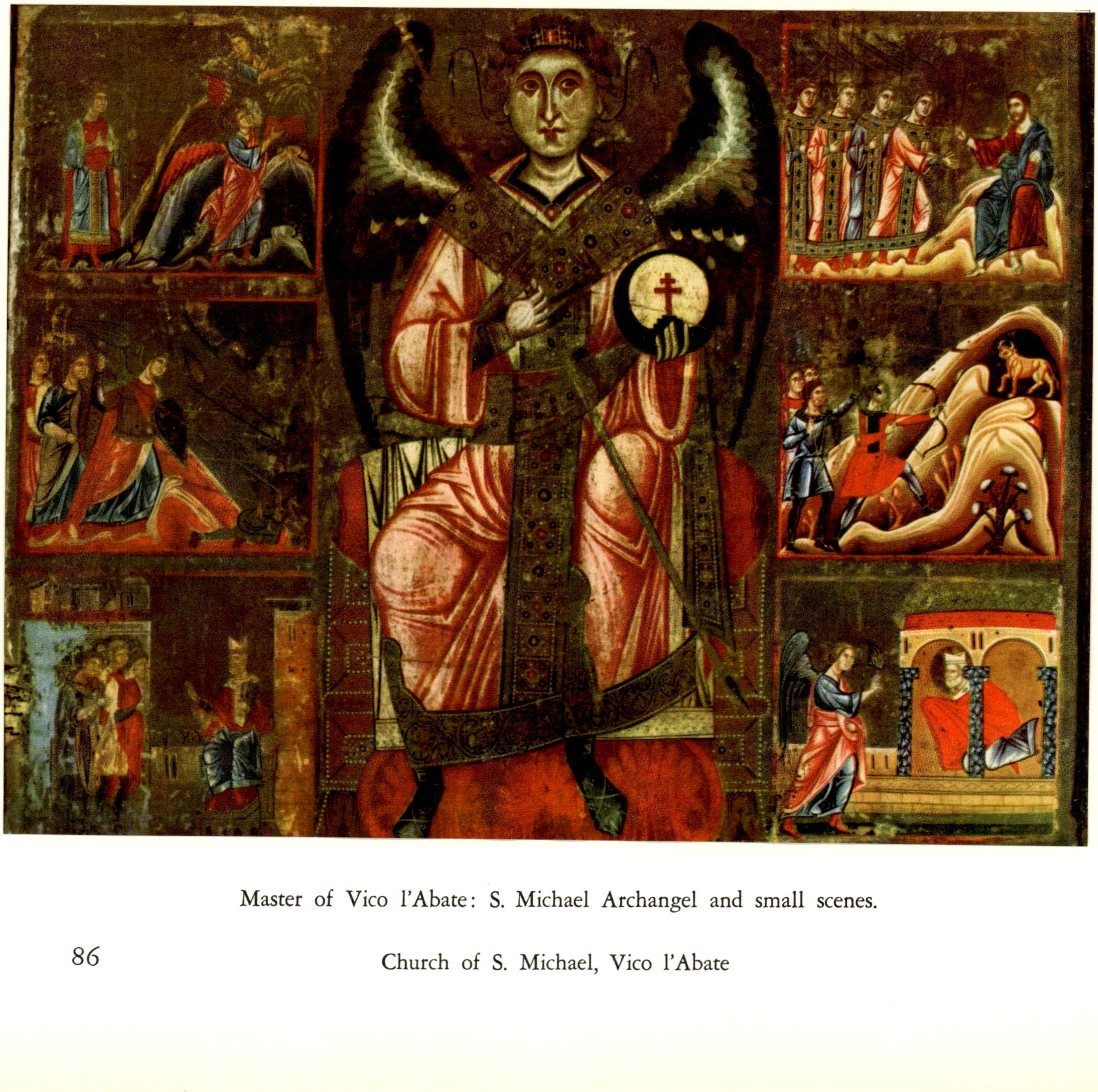

Master of Vico l'Abate: S. Michael Archangel and small scenes.

Church of S. Michael, Vico l'Abate

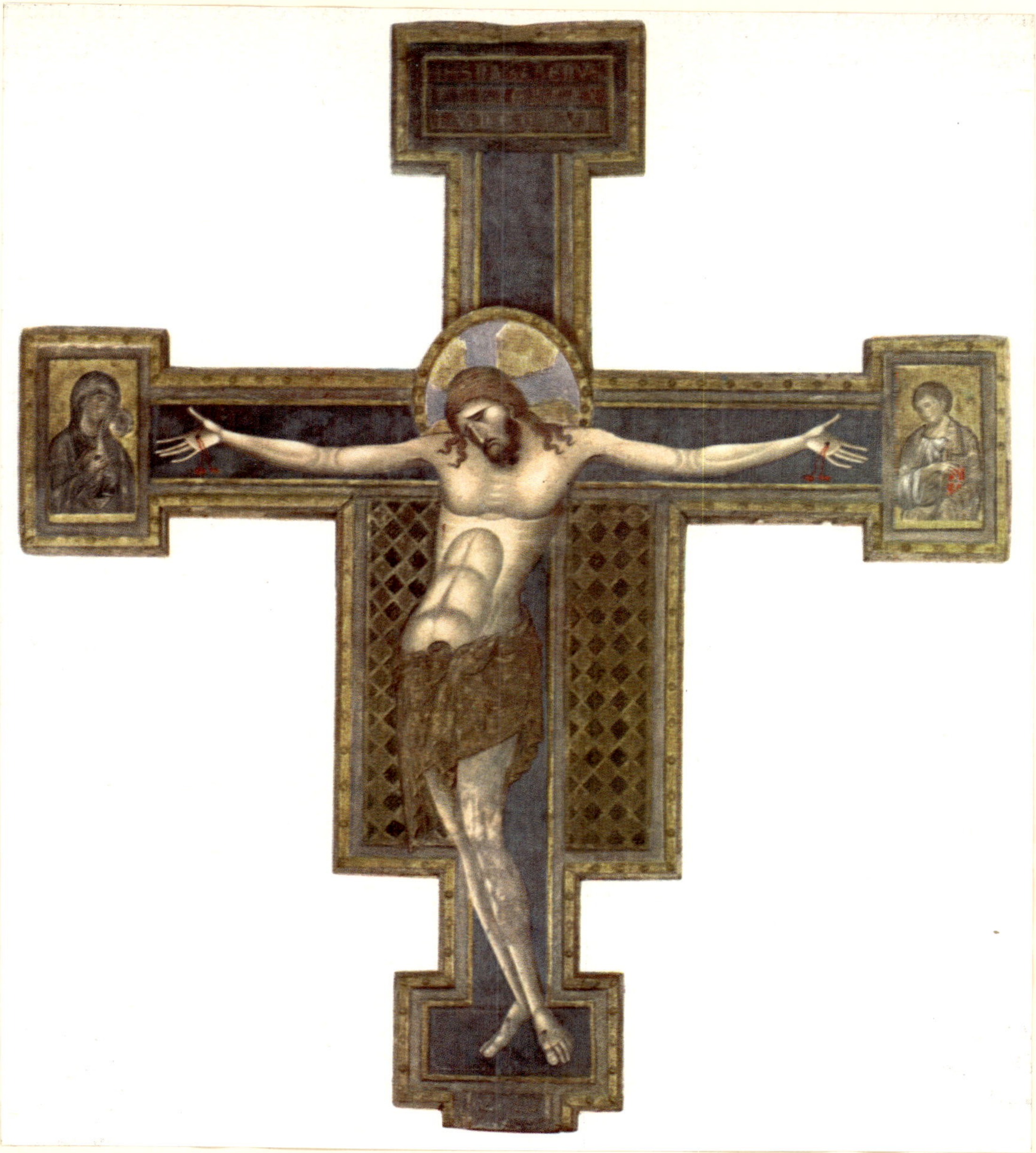

Giunta Pisano: S. Domenico, Bologna

The art of the Florentine painter, Coppo di Marcovaldo, belongs to this atmosphere of crisis. Trained by Byzantines and Venetians, he worked on the mosaics in the Baptistery. He is known to have been in Florence in 1260, and is listed among the combatants of the Battle of Montaperti (1260), when he was probably taken prisoner by the Sienese, since in 1261 he signed the Madonna del Bordone in the Church of the Servites at Siena. From 1265 to 1274 he is known to have worked at Pistoia. The oldest picture known to be by Coppo is the Crucifix, dated between 1255 and 1260, now in the Museum of San Gimignano. It appears to be a direct copy of a Byzantine model, although there is a lively dramatic feeling which leaves no doubt that he too was acquainted with examples of western art, possibly Carolingian miniatures and Rhenish enamels. Stylistically it resembles the terrifying, violent Inferno of the Last Judgment in the Baptistery mosaics at Florence, which is accepted as being his work or that of one of his pupils (according to Longhi) towards 1260. It was certainly the influence of western culture, combined with a strong personal feeling, that caused Coppo to introduce a new emotional and expressionist tendency into the weary Byzantine formulae. His style is distinguished by large, vigorous forms, strong con-

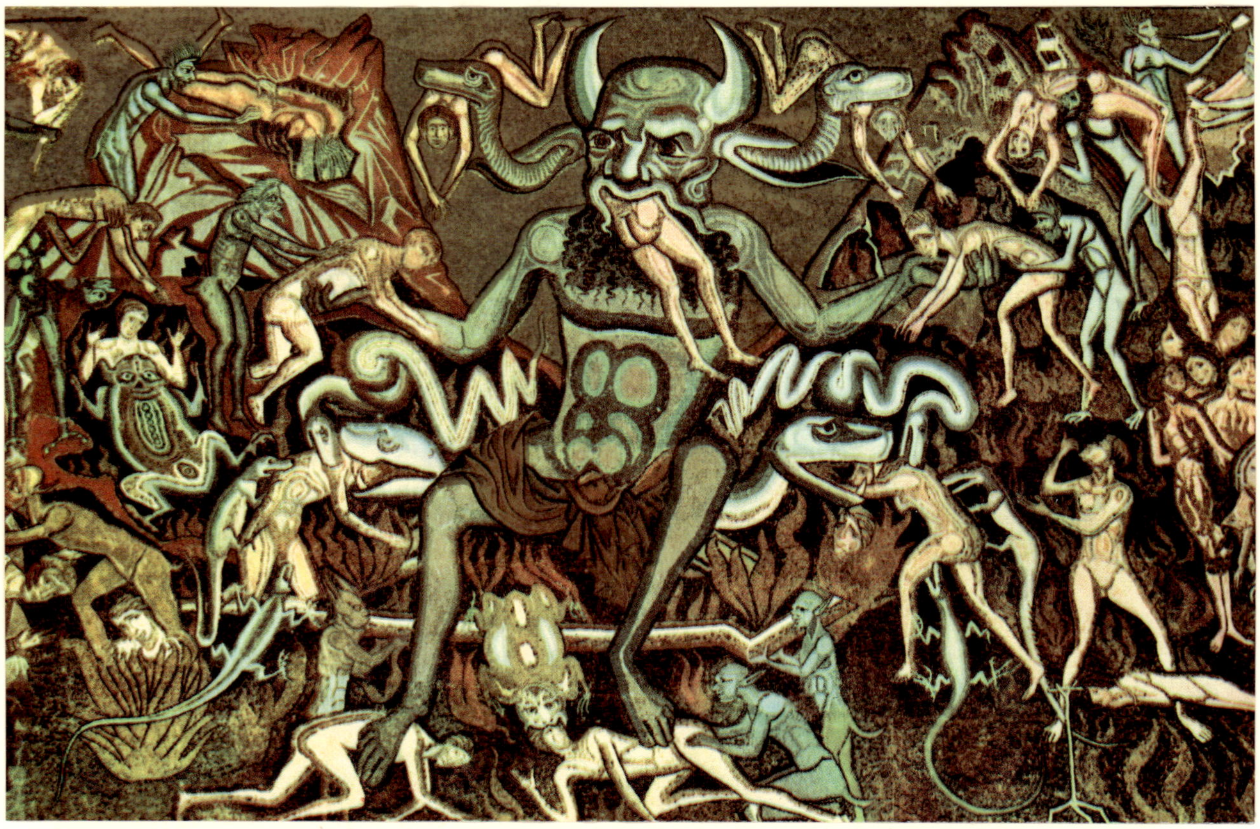

Coppo di Marcovaldo: The Inferno. Baptistery, Florence

trast of light and shade, and heavy contours, with sharp breaks in the drapery. In the Madonna, painted possibly before 1265 for the Church of the Servites at Orvieto, his style is seen to be developing: he shows a feeling of humanity which is more tranquil and regular, and sadness rather than drama now pervades his work. He combines strong chiaroscuro with strong colouring; even the gold becomes magnificent. It is probable that the change in his work was occasioned by his visit to Siena, where he had the opportunity of seeing examples of Byzantine art from Constantinople itself instead of from the provinces. After the victory of Montaperti Siena became a very prosperous commercial city, and many artistic products of high quality must have come there both from the East and from the West.

Coppo's work is important because his influence contributed to the formation of the Florentine school, where the power of his monumental vision was transmitted to Cimabue, and also because it inspired Sienese painting. Guido, the first painter to show the characteristics peculiar to Siena, took over from him; and possibly the earliest, somewhat obscure influences in Duccio are derived from Coppo. In Siena there was no tradition of monumental painting (there had been nothing like the building of the Baptistery at Florence at the beginning of the thirteenth century), and artists drew inspiration from the work of the Florentine school, which had already become firmly established between 1240 and 1260.

In the second half of the thirteenth century a conscious effort to organise and weld together the two distinct trends of Eastern-Hellenistic and Roman-Archaic influence can be discerned in Rome, and Jacopo Torriti is a typical representative of the new spirit. A similarity in style, especially in the plastic treatment of the colouring and in the composition, is to be seen between Torriti and his younger contemporary, Pietro Cavallini, and suggests that they belonged originally to the same artistic group. If so, however, no examples of his work at this period have survived.

There is only one signed work by Jacopo Torriti: the mosaic in the apse of

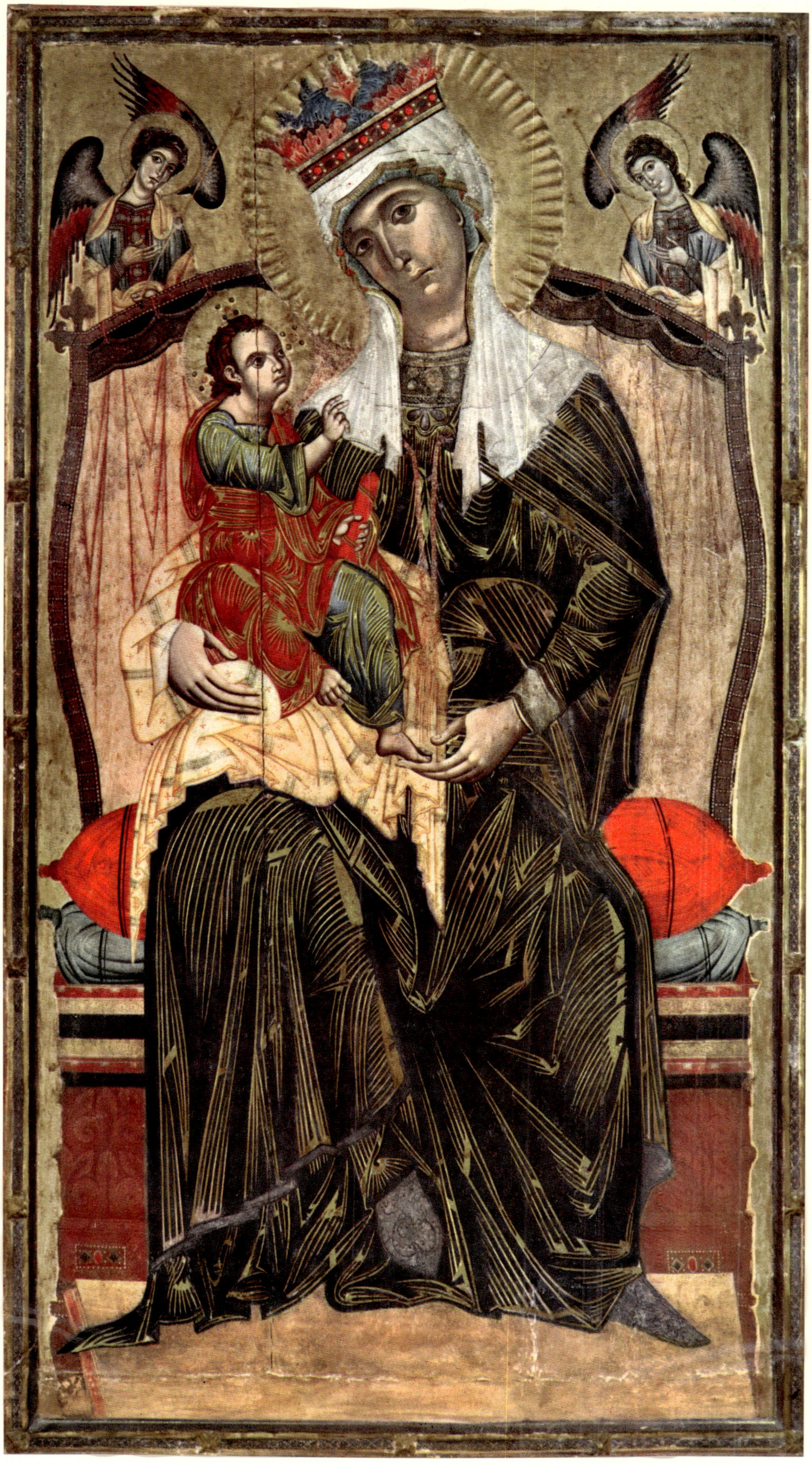

Coppo di Marcovaldo: Madonna. S. Martin of the Servites, Orvieto

S. Maria Maggiore, with the Coronation of the Virgin in the centre, and other scenes from her life in the fascia below, dating from 1295. Cavallini was by then at the height of his career, and his work had developed in another direction. The other mosaic by Torriti, in the apse of S. John Lateran, done in 1291 in collaboration with a certain Jacopo da Camerino, has undergone too much restoration for any opinions to be formed about it. But early examples of his work and that of his pupils are to be found in the upper church at Assisi, a fact which demonstrated the importance of this Roman school in the latter half of the century. For judging by the choice of Cimabue, Giotto, Stefano, Simone Martini and Pietro Lorenzetti, it would seem that only artists of the highest quality were permitted to work in the Basilica of S. Francis.

And so there belongs to Rome the honour of producing the first independent school of painting, or at least to Rome goes the honour of deciding to follow a path which was to lead to new developments. But the honour does not belong so much to Torriti personally, for he remained essentially a learned academician working within the bounds of the Eastern system, as to the more independent and original " Master of Anagni ". The unknown painter of the Madonna, and the Legends of Joachim and Anna from the church of S. Martin at Pisa, also followed the same plan, seeking inspiration from antiquity, and giving a personal version. Judging by the qualities of the painting from which his name is taken, very few other works can be attributed to him with any certainty.

In the new dignity of the " Master of S. Martino " there is no trace of the sterile Pisan atmosphere, still imbued with neo-Classical Byzantine characteristics in the thirteenth century. The old repertory and established formulae seem new, since they are enveloped in an atmosphere which is at once Arcadian and elegiac, and are transported into the timeless world of pure poetry. The severe, traditional Odigitria of the icons has become softer, with a calm and — at long last — a *natural* expression, although the large Byzantine eye sockets are still there. The Child, a serious young prince, is weighed down by golden Byzantine ornaments, but His expression reveals the charm and tenderness of childish affection. Within the curved outlines, which form a gentle Gothic rhythm, is the broad, full modelling — not merely suggested but actually present — contributing to an effect of perfect control and deep serenity. In the same way the portraits of the saints, arranged in familiar schemes, appear as real people with thoughts and anxieties, something unprecedented in Italian painting. The innovations of the " Master of S. Martino " are seen to even greater advantage in the " legends " where he feels more at liberty than in the icon paintings, and where he seems to rely principally on his happy vision of a humanity with a truer, more intimate feeling, which he seems to have encountered almost by accident in " antiquity " and recognised as being the real origin of his own race. In the same way the Carolingians had benefited by their " barbarian " origins, and the Romanesque painters of Catalonia by their primitive feeling for passion. In Italy only the remarkable " Master of Castelseprio " had expressed a similar poetic truth outside the old established culture before the " Master of S. Martino " and the " Master of Anagni ". And now at last, many centuries later, there was no further question of using the Byzantine tradition of antiquity, which had been borrowed and cultivated like a hothouse flower by people who began as " mannerists " and ended by being " neo-classicists ". For the " Master of S. Martino ", like the " Master of Anagni " before him, and Cimabue immediately afterwards, it was a case of learning afresh an ancient language in order to take up the civilisation of their own race from the beginning, and to enter on a struggle — sometimes regretful and sometimes almost desperate — to break the chains of the age-old Eastern influence. The most important and significant example of this period of transformation in Italian art was in Pisan

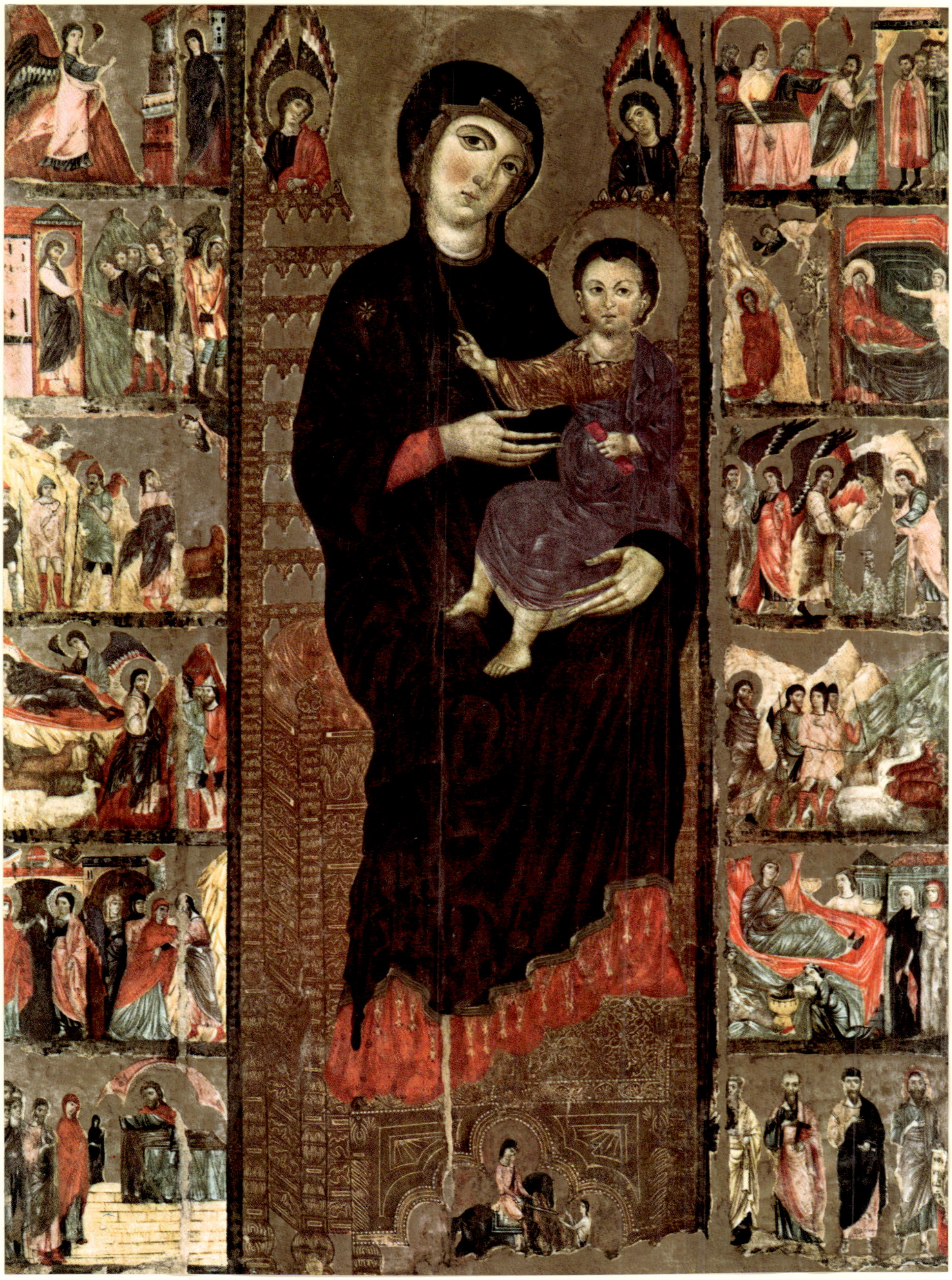

Master of S. Martin: Madonna and small scenes. S. Matteo Museum, Pisa

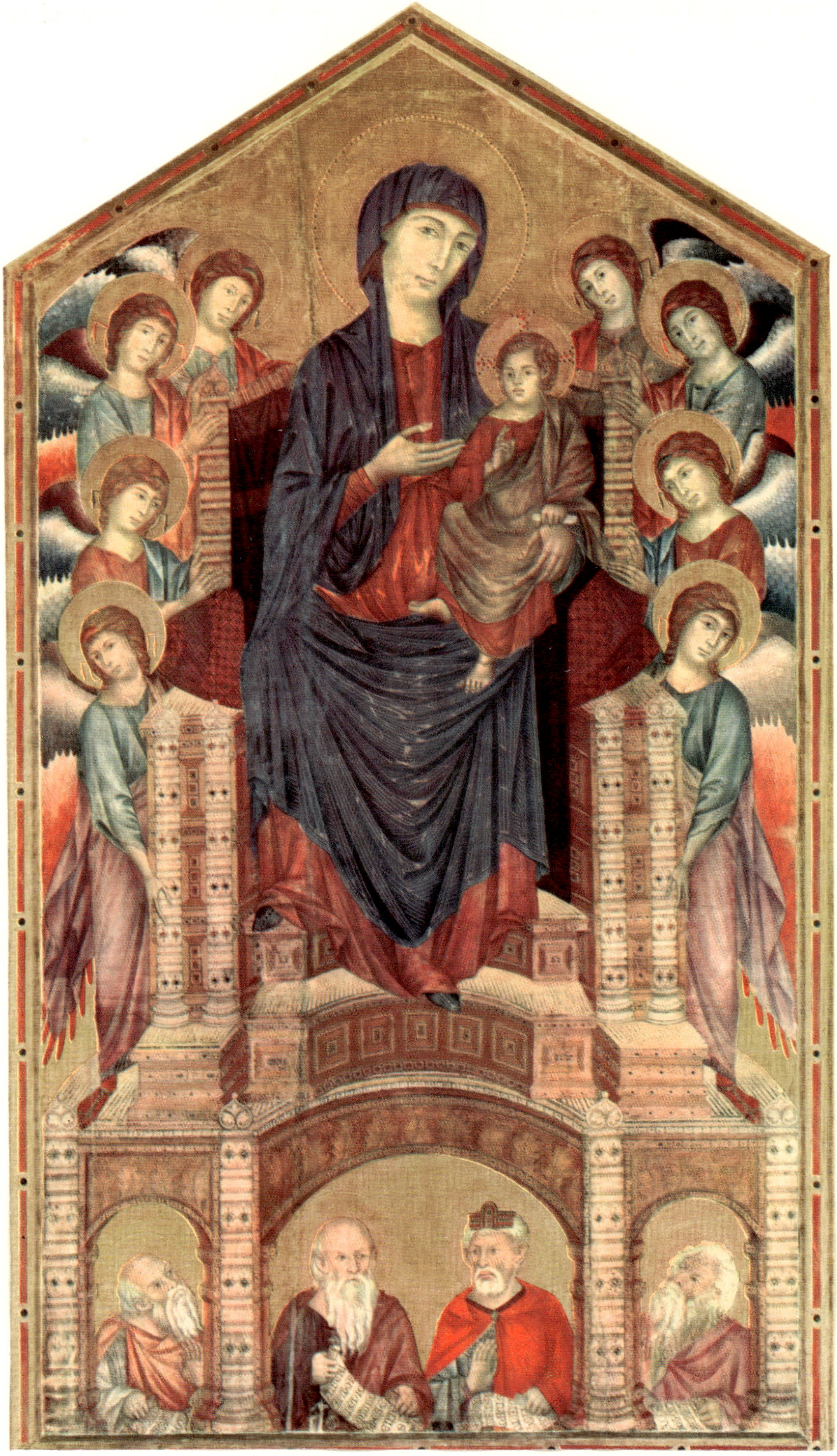

Cimabue: S. Trinità Madonna. Uffizi, Florence

sculpture. While the " Master of S. Martino " was in Pisa in 1260, the great Nicola Pisano was engaged on the pulpit, and his work shows that he too was simultaneously archaic, Byzantine and Gothic.

About Cenni di Pepo, or Cimabue as he is usually called, very little is known. According to Vasari he was born in Florence in 1240; he is recorded as being at Rome in 1272, and at Pisa between 1301 and 1302. At Pisa he continued some mosaics in the apse of the cathedral which had been left unfinished by a certain Master Francesco, and carried out the figure of S. John. It is probable that he died shortly afterwards in 1302-1303. As the S. John at Pisa, which is not a very important work, offers the only documentary evidence there is about Cimabue, the chronology of his work is one of the most difficult problems in the history of art. Efforts to establish one are all based merely on hypotheses and degrees of probability, although its artistic character seems fairly certain, chiefly owing to information handed down by Vasari. In this way the historical position of Cimabue the painter is very clearly defined. When he says that Cimabue was a pupil of " Greek masters " settled in Florence, we can accept Vasari's statement in the sense that Cimabue's art is rooted in Byzantine culture, although his version is entirely Western and Italian.

The most youthful work which can be attributed to him with any certainty is the Crucifix in S. Domenico at Arezzo, dated between 1260 and 1265. It is very evident that he began in the well-worn Byzantine tradition, dramatised with western feeling by Giunta Pisano. Another very important influence in his work is Coppo di Marcovaldo, from whom he derived his broad, firm design whose aim was to be monumental and plastic. These qualities, which were to become an essential part of Cimabue's art, are seen to better advantage in the later Crucifix in S. Croce at Florence — possibly the masterpiece of the painter's youth, if, as seems likely, it can really be dated at 1275, that is to say ten years later than the work at Arezzo. In this Cimabue showed that from the tragic sadness of Giunta and the solemn grief of Coppo he could envisage a means of transforming the old Byzantine scheme into a simpler and more constructive design, and of introducing a deeper note of truth and humanity into the formal balance.

He had a wonderful intuition, at once classical and modern, in realising that the simplicity of a figure can contribute to its expressiveness. This perception, still confined within a conventional Byzantine outline of faces and drapery in the Arezzo Crucifix, achieves its fullest expression in that of S. Croce. The scheme remains in the Byzantine tradition which only Giotto succeeded in destroying, but compared with an authentic Byzantine work it seems to be plastic and to be capable of absorbing the iron framework of Byzantine drawing in the vigorous, deep chiaroscuro of the modelling. A trace of the traditional tautness in the design remains in the attitudes, and in certain details of the faces; but the creation of figures with an essential plastic quality, a skill which seems to have been recaptured only with great, almost despairing efforts by painting, is entirely new and personal.

These new constructive qualities are seen even more clearly in the Madonna in the Uffizi, from S. Trinità, which was painted some time before the Crucifix of S. Croce.

Before considering the Madonna of S. Trinità however, we must consider Cimabue's work in the mosaics in the cupola of the Baptistery at Florence: his style is seen very clearly in the figure of a young man in the Baptism of S. John. Other parts of the scenes of S. John the Baptist and those of Joseph may also have been done by Cimabue; in any case, these two series of mosaics — whether or not by Cimabue himself — show that the artist had a knowledge of his work. In the meantime, according to the records Cimabue spent some time in Rome in 1272, and it was very probably during this time that he perfected his mosaic technique.

An earlier visit to Pisa must have been equally important. Although there is no contemporary record of this visit, it is mentioned by Vasari, and it is very probable that it did take place. If, as seems likely, his Roman experiences led Cimabue to soften the sharp, jerky modelling (which he used in the Crucifix at Arezzo under the influence of Giunta and Coppo) and adopt a fuller, more detailed style giving an effect of volume, it was his studies at Pisa which showed him how to overcome the worn-out Byzantine formula by returning, like Nicola Pisano and the Master of S. Martino, to a distant and authentic classical source of inspiration.

Cimabue must have been deeply moved by these experiences, and the date at which he introduced a more profound and personal feeling into his style seems to be indicated by the beautiful Madonna of S. Trinità, probably done between 1272 and 1275, that is to say slightly before the frescoes at Assisi, which are in his mature style. The spirit in which the Madonna is conceived still shows, more clearly than the work at Assisi, a decided Byzantine influence as well as that of Coppo and Giunta.

The frontal position and effect of a transcendental vision give the figure the solemnity of an imposing monumental icon. The richness of the gold and colours and the arrangement of the composition, based on a sweeping, curved rhythm, whose purpose was to suggest the luminous quality of a mosaic wall, reveal the artist's knowledge and experience of this medium. But the most striking element is the Hellenistic feeling with which the whole painting is imbued, and which, far from giving an academic or learned appearance as it would have done in a work of pure Byzantine origin, actually constitutes the most original and most surprising feature of the whole work. Byzantine abstraction is in fact supplanted by this classical feeling, which is no longer a studied imitation of an element in composition. It has become a form in itself, or rather the inspiration behind the form, a genuine inner feeling. So the classical feeling of *Beauty* returns in a new manifestation as *Humanity.* It is this new interest in humanity which creates so successfully and so simply the youthful grace of the angels, the austere femininity of the Virgin, and the sacred dignity of the prophets. We have come a long way from the insistence of the old Byzantine painters on a definite physical type, according to a conventional classification of people, feelings, and actions. To see this new, almost pre-humanist classical feeling we must look at the pulpit in the Baptistery at Pisa which was finished in 1260 by Nicola Pisano, who was profoundly affected by classical antiquity. If Nicola's figures have an archaic rather than an antique appearance it is because he went directly to the classical sources which had already given rise to both Romanesque and Byzantine art.

The new feeling which emanates from the paintings of Cimabue is similar, so it seems likely that, stimulated possibly by the work of the Master of S. Martino, he had studied Pisan sculpture carefully. It was natural that painters — those of genius like Cimabue — should study contemporary sculpture carefully, as this had radically changed in Italy, whereas generally speaking in the field of painting "the Greeks" were still increasing the number of their *ateliers* and their sterile productions. It may be that his interest in the work of Nicola brought Cimabue into contact with the work of Arnolfo di Cambio, whose style was fully formed by 1270. In some of the concise plastic and spatial effects, parts of the wall-paintings in the upper church of S. Francis in Assisi recall Arnolfo as well as Nicola.

The great cycle of wall-paintings at Assisi constitutes Cimabue's chief work. Although they can be dated with a good deal of certainty in the years between 1280 and 1290, they have been so badly damaged by time that their style provides little help in establishing the chronology of Cimabue's work. The colours have altered so much that they no longer convey a correct idea of the greatness of the artist. Their vast size and evidence of a change in style make it seem likely that Cimabue completed them during at least two different periods. It would seem likely that he first painted the Evangelists in the vault of the presbytery, then the scenes from the Life of the Virgin in the apse, and finally the Crucifixion and the scenes from the Apocalypse in the left transept. In spite of their bad state of preservation, all the pictures, superbly conceived and executed, possess a tragic expressiveness, a vehement prophetic pathos, a feeling, at once heroic and grief-stricken, of human destiny. So much strength of feeling and vision found an appropriate means of expression in the harsh plasticity, and the emotional effects always appear natural, although possibly excessive. It is therefore far removed from the conventional cold, broken line of the Byzantines; and although it may be closer to the sharp restlessness of the Carolingians, it has been transformed by an infinitely more exalted and noble conception both of humanity and of God.

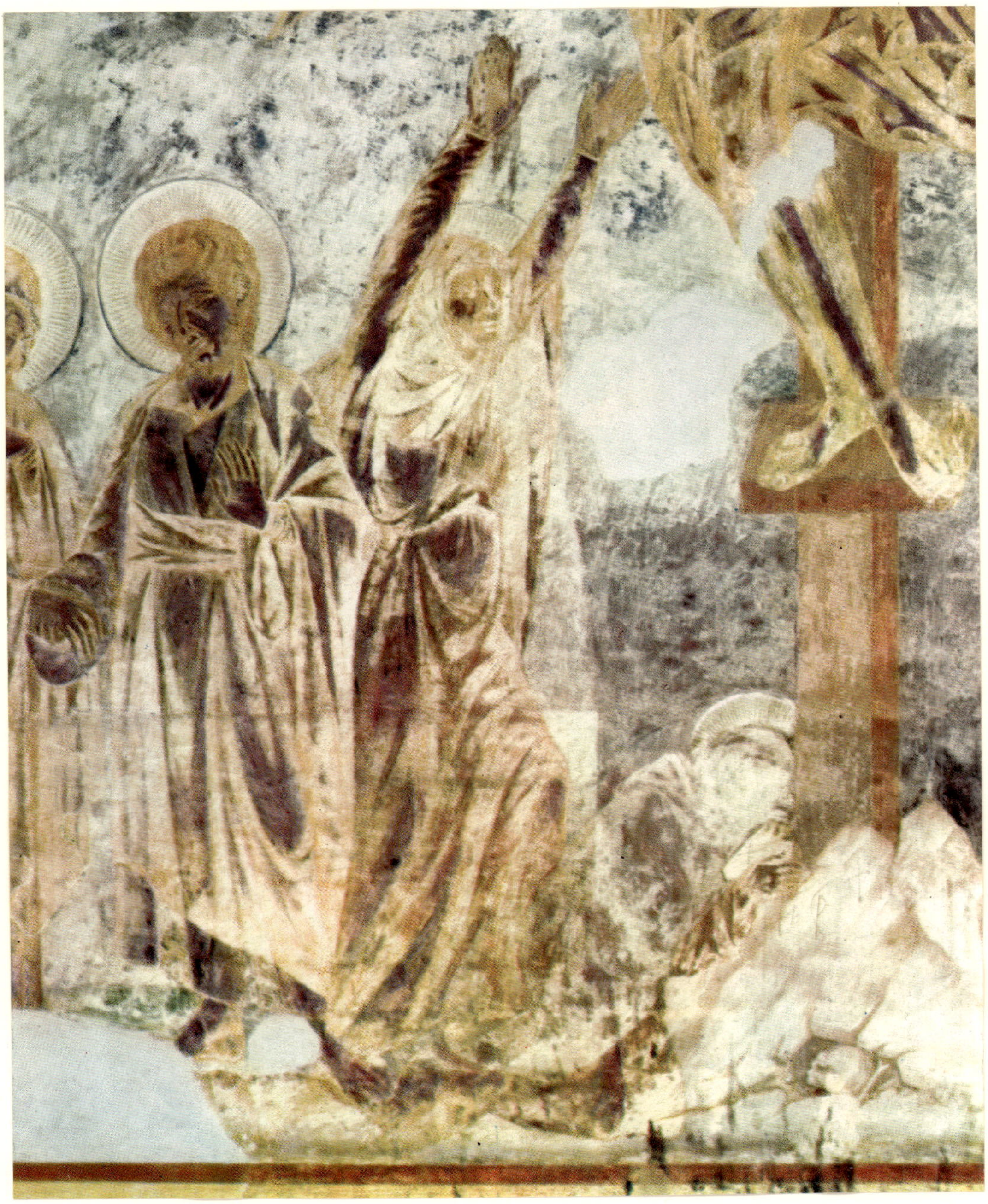

Cimabue: Detail from the Crucifixion. S. Francis, Assisi

In the later frescoes, including Christ and Mary enthroned, the Crucifixion in the right transept, and the scenes of the Apostles which were completed with the help of assistants, Cimabue's harsh plastic quality seems to soften, the action becomes less strained, and the whole composition of the picture more fluid, as though the artist were making a slight concession to the Gothic style which by that time, 1280-85, must have been fairly widely known in Italy. The Madonna enthroned with Angels and S. Francis in the lower church seems to belong to this more mature period, so far as can be judged after the restorations done in the eighteenth century. The beautiful Madonna enthroned among Angels, now in the Louvre, may possibly belong to the same period as the earliest wall-paintings at Assisi or even before, for it contains a suggestion of the work of Arnolfo. But it cannot have been painted much after 1280, because it was probably the model for the Rucellai Madonna of Duccio di Boninsegna, painted in 1285. The painting in the Louvre has usually been regarded as a late work because it came from the church of S. Francis at Pisa and has therefore been connected with the only known visit of Cimabue to that city in 1301. The Madonna of the Servites in Bologna is certainly a late work, and shows a far more decided Gothic sense than the last wall-paintings at Assisi. But it is rather an inferior painting, possibly done between 1290-95, and shows an outward compliance with the Gothic style in a greater freedom of composition, and gentleness in the actions, which were wholly outside Cimabue's personal conception of figure painting.

Cimabue is the central and dominating figure of Italian painting in the second half of the thirteenth century: his influence, particularly through the wall-paintings at Assisi, where his assistants came from Florence, Umbria, Rome, Siena, and Emilia, was immensely strong even in the early years of the fourteenth century, although Giotto was already working by then. His importance was eclipsed only by the advent of a wholly new conception of art and of humanity.

Cimabue was the Italian artist who brought to an end the mechanical repetition of works imported from the East. Although he never renounced the Byzantine tradition personally, he was aware of the new trends and he developed the influences to be found in sculpture and western styles of painting from Carolingian to Romanesque. But his art was not a true innovation and was certainly surpassed by the modern conceptions of Giotto.

His important followers, such as Vigoroso da Siena, Corso di Buono, and the Master of Città di Castello, also show great quality, but they lacked originality. Duccio di Boninsegna, the Sienese who made an equal contribution to the greatness of thirteenth-century painting, must also to some extent be regarded as his follower. But many other elements and conditions contributed to the formation of Duccio's artistic character, and it was wholly different from that of the Florentine master.

The battle of Montaperti (1260) ended in a victory of the Florentines over the Sienese, and resulted in Florentine painting reaching Siena, where it was eagerly welcomed. The city had no important tradition of monumental painting such as had been established at Florence with the mosaic decoration of the Baptistery. Duccio was born probably about 1255, and grew up while Florentine painters were working at Siena; they included Coppo di Marcovaldo and Meliore, the author of a signed painting dated 1271 now in the Uffizi, and Vigoroso, whose work is in a Byzantine-Cimabue style, and who is the author of a polyptych dated 1276, now in the Pinacoteca in Perugia. Following in the tradition of Coppo and Meliore was an artist named Guido da Siena, who was active probably between 1260 and 1280, in spite of the date 1221 on his Maestà in the Palazzo Publico. This date has given rise to endless controversies on the subject of who was born first, the Florentine or the Sienese. The year 1221 has certainly some religious significance and it probably refers to a venerated portrait of the Virgin belonging to an older period which was supplanted by that of Guido. At any rate, although Guido must have had a vast workshop, his art does not seem to have interested the young Duccio, perhaps because it was somewhat provincial, nor to have contributed to his development, unless it helped to give him some idea of Florentine painting.

It was the presence of Florentine paintings in Siena (possibly, as at Arezzo, there may have been some early work by Cimabue) and the sculpture of Nicola Pisano which together made Duccio aware of the need for a more monumental and constructive style. At that period — probably between 1275 and 1280 — such a feeling would inevitably send a talented artist in search of Cimabue. And so it was with Duccio, who probably met the great Florentine master for the first time at Assisi (as Longhi has recently stated); alternatively as a young man Duccio may possibly have worked with Cimabue at Florence. These close contacts with Cimabue would explain the presence of the Rucellai Madonna in Florence in 1285; otherwise, as Cimabue was alive and at the height of his fame, it would seem extraordinary that so important a commission should be awarded to a strange and still youthful painter.

The Rucellai altarpiece painted for S. Maria Novella is the earliest surviving work which can be attributed to Duccio with any certainty. (There is documentary evidence for this attribution, although even in modern times tradition continues to ascribe it to Cimabue, and a number of distinguished art historians are still doubtful). The influence of Cimabue is evident: there is a clear reflection of his style in the Assisi period and the Louvre Madonna. But although the Rucellai Madonna has the majestic vision of Cimabue it achieves a very different effect. It is contemplative rather than dramatic in spirit, and the monumental scheme is carried out in an airy texture which swells and trembles with waving lines and pauses that lighten the ample proportions by accentuating exquisite details and imparting a feeling of graceful melancholy.

The soft, graduated colouring contributes to these intimate, sensitive qualities and has the delicacy of a miniature. So clear a break from Cimabue, even in the interpretation of his own style, cannot be accounted for simply by a difference in temperament. Before meeting the Florentine painter, Duccio, although still a young man, had already been exposed to many other influences. There is little documentary evidence, but from 1278 onwards he is often mentioned as painting wooden coffers and book bindings, so he must have practised the art of miniature painting. And indeed, judging by the feeling of his work, it seems very possible that Duccio began as a miniaturist, copying either Eastern or French manuscripts of high quality, and thus absorbing both Byzantine and Gothic culture simultaneously. As a result he developed great skill as a colourist and decorator, qualities which remained fundamental to his art. In the Rucellai Madonna, now in the Uffizi, it is obvious that Cimabue's " reforms " have been taken over by an artist of genius, whose style is based partly on ancient Byzantine Greek models, and partly on others which were Western in feeling. Duccio derived his graceful magnificence and fairy-tale quality from the richness of Byzantine colouring, which he rendered more human by Gothic line drawing, so that the architectural schemes which he took from Cimabue are articulated in a lighter, freer, manner.

There was a great trade in Byzantine and French miniatures and ivories at Siena, especially after the battle of Montaperti, since Siena had no artistic tradition of her own. By 1270 or 1280 these had even influenced the provincial school which followed Guido. It may be that after he returned to Siena, Duccio adapted the teaching he had learned from Cimabue to a more Gothic style, although he had not entirely cast off Byzantine influence. The little Madonna of the Franciscans (1290-95) in the Pinacoteca in Siena is thought to be later than the Rucellai Madonna, and is clearly influenced by French illumination, with echoes of the Carolingian style in the quivering figures of the three Friars at prayer. The small dimensions of this work also recall miniature painting, in the very fine, rich workmanship, in the chequered background which is typical of so many French Gothic miniatures, in the Gothic drapery of the Virgin's swirling robe, and in the sinuous outline of the whole figure. But despite this Gothic effect Duccio did not relinquish his more monumental conception. The composition of the little painting is so arranged that both breadth and extent are suggested in the very limited dimensions which it occupies. If Duccio was able to create a work with strong Gothic tendencies based on a careful study of the expressive use of line, without renouncing his previous teaching in the formal style, this was because he was working in Siena at the same time as the greatest sculptor in the Gothic style, Giovanni Pisano. Between 1290 and 1300 Duccio moved away from Cimabue and evolved a style in which both Western and Byzantine influences were mixed, and showed that he was aware of the sculptural developments in the work of Giovanni Pisano, as well as those of the new young Florentine painter, Giotto. He remained essentially faithful to the Byzantine style both in iconography and technique, but his spirit was so Western that he introduced an unusual narrative quality into the old themes, and gave them an epic and " courtly " flavour, while his colouring developed a very personal style of shading.

This can be seen in the Maestà, in the Museum dell'Opera del Duomo at Siena, particularly in the numerous scenes of the life of Christ and the Virgin, painted on the predella and on the back of the picture. This is the second authentically documented work that has survived, and it is actually known that Duccio signed a contract for it on 9th October, 1308. It was finished in 1311, and on 9th June in the same year it was solemnly transferred from the master's studio to the cathedral and placed above the high altar.

This magnificent and complex work is Duccio's masterpiece, and shows his complete mastery of Byzantine, Gothic, and Florentine influences. It is evident that the strongest element among the many which contributed to his development is that highly accomplished neo-Hellenistic strain in Byzantine art and yet this seems to be wholly renewed or rather abandoned, not because it is crowded out by other influences, but because the personality of the artist himself towers above and overshadows the whole. From now on the authoritarian system of the Pope and monasteries was overcome. The ancient conventional forms, even when they were used, were linked with human and realistic values which finally absorbed them completely.

The style which Duccio revealed in the great altarpiece of the Maestà laid the foundations for fourteenth-century Sienese painting, of which he is justly regarded as the founder and leader. His style did in fact have a longer and more lasting effect than that of Cimabue, largely owing to the Gothic element which was so important in his work. The feeling which he expressed in his Maestà is to be seen in Siena throughout the whole of the fourteenth century, although very soon, in 1315 (while Duccio was still alive, for he died in 1319), the modern, cultured and fascinating personality of Simone Martini makes its appearance.

The third innovator in thirteenth-century Italian painting, still working within the Byzantine framework, is the Roman painter Pietro Cavallini. He was probably born about 1250 and lived to a great age, at least until 1340. Very little is known about him, and there are very few references to his work, the greater part of which has been destroyed, especially that belonging to his early period. His output was however, enormous, both at Rome and elsewhere. Ghiberti, who ranked him above

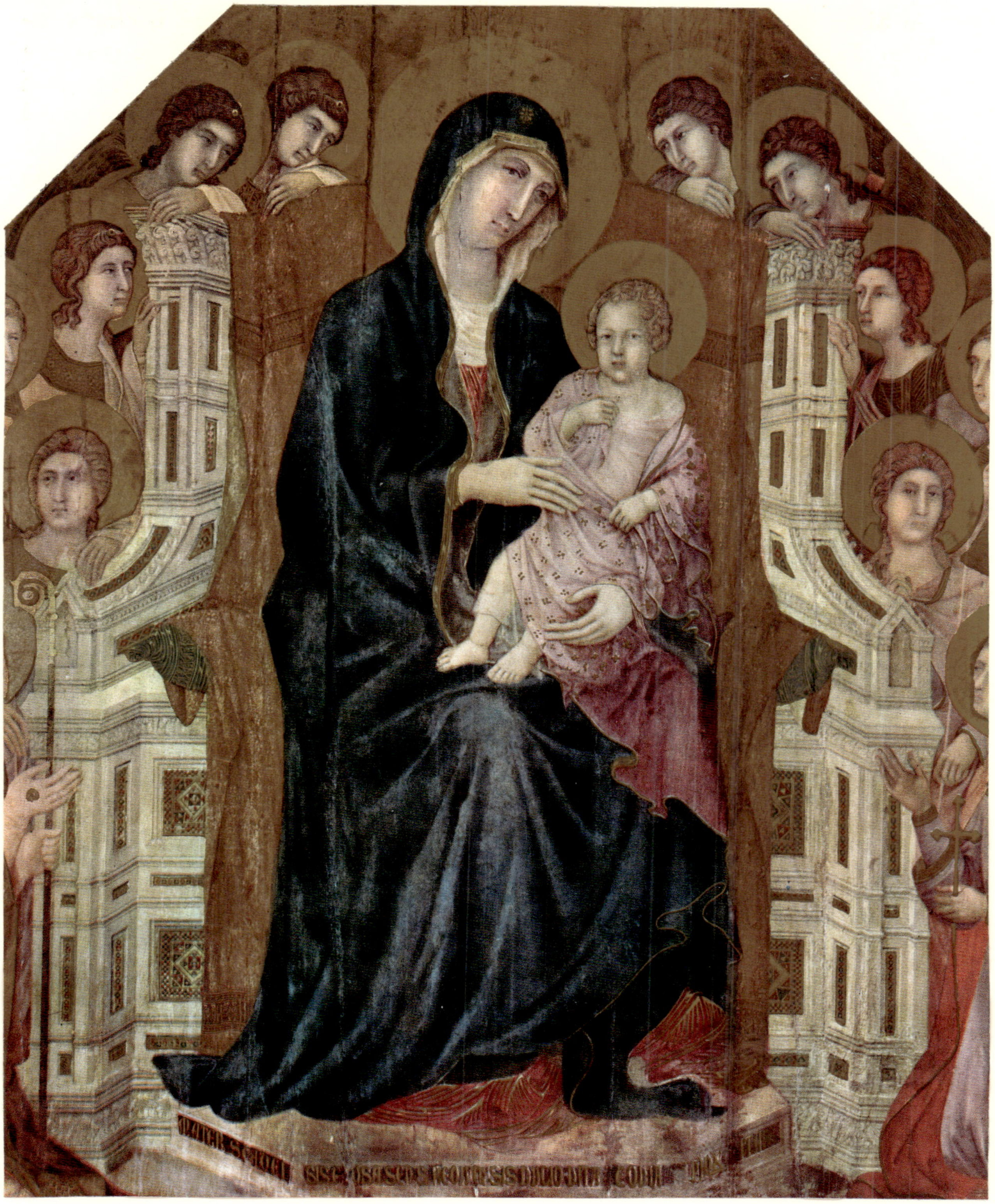

Duccio di Boninsegna: Central part of the Maestà. Opera del Duomo Museum, Siena

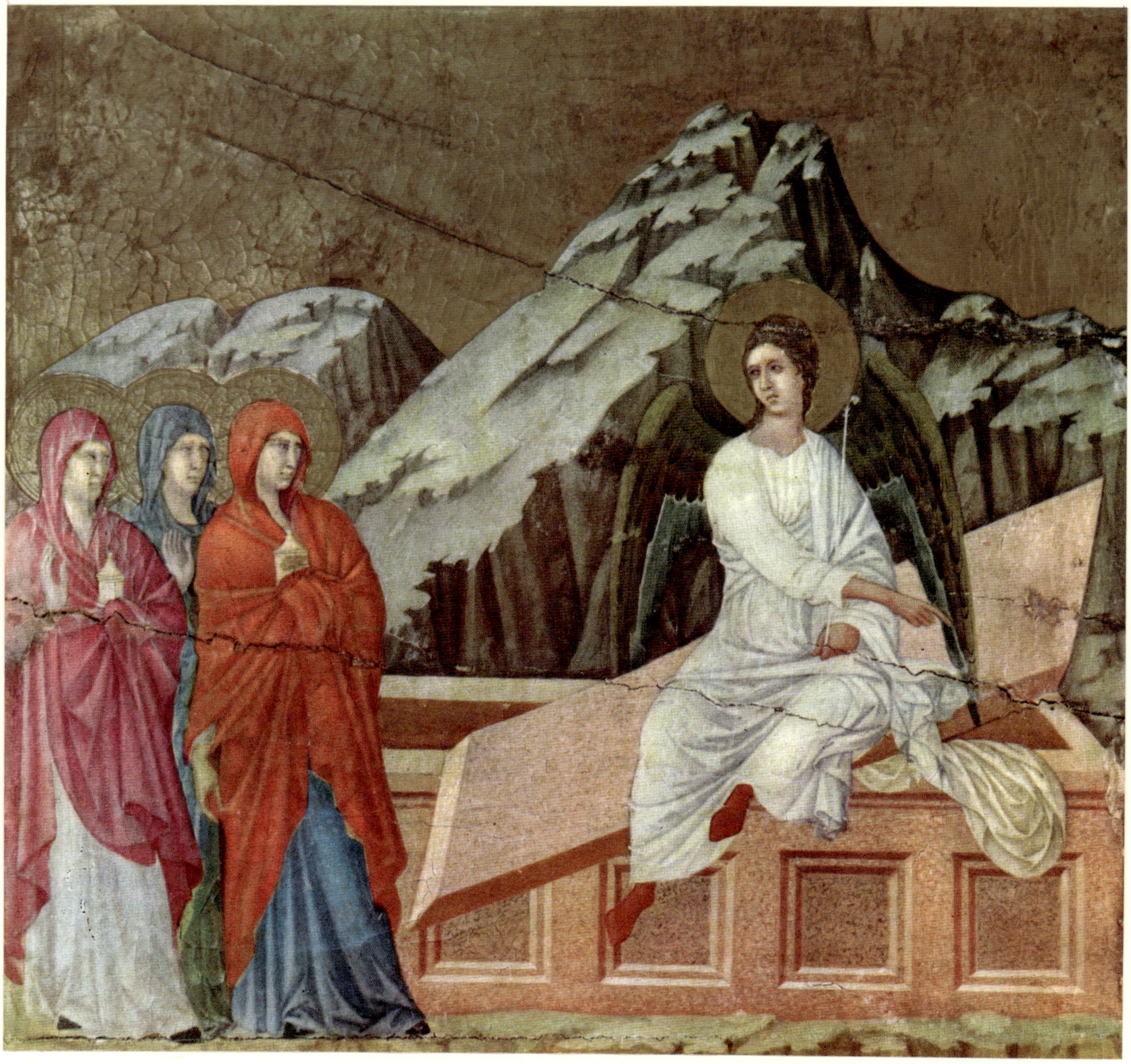

Duccio di Boninsegna: The Maries at the Sepulchre, detail of the Maestà.

Opera del Duomo Museum, Siena

all other Roman painters of the time, and praised his skill in mosaic and wall-painting, mentioned that he worked in a great many Roman churches: S. Peter's, S. Crisogono, S. Maria in Aracoeli, S. Paul Outside-the-Walls, and many others. Out of so much there remain only the mosaics in the lower part of the apse in S. Maria in Trastevere, part of the great cycle of frescoes in S. Cecilia in Trastevere, the fresco with the Madonna and Child between two saints above the tomb of Cardinal Matteo d'Acquasparta in Aracoeli (c. 1302), and the much damaged fresco with Christ between the Virgin and S. Peter and S. George, in the apse of S. Peter in Velabro. Many other minor works have been attributed to Cavallini, but in Rome, which is the centre for studying his work, there remain only the mosaics in S. Maria in Trastevere and the frescoes in S. Cecilia.

The mosaics with the Life of the Virgin were commissioned by Bertoldo Stefaneschi, and completed in 1291; although they belong to Cavallini's mature period, they reveal his Byzantine training. It is the purely classical aspect of Byzantine art which is to be found in his work, following the tradition of other earlier works which exist in or near Rome, such as wall-paintings at Grottaferrata and Anagni. Cavallini must of course have seen manuscripts from Constantinople in the superb style of the twelfth century, but his own style was formed in the same Roman circles as Jacopo Torriti. Cavallini, like Cimabue, was interested in re-discovering a classical feeling outside academic Byzantine-Hellenism, and closer to the original. Judging by his style, however, it would seem that he had studied paleo-Christian works, or works of the fourth or fifth centuries, and not genuine classical antiques which at that time were not clearly distinguished. This is suggested by the particular colouring of his work, especially in the mosaics of S. Maria in Trastevere. Cavallini uses colours which are not very rich, but which contrive to convey an impression of volume and space independently of the design. They seem to be a personal development resulting from study of late Roman and paleo-Christian wall-paintings, such as the oldest mosaics in S. Maria Maggiore. In the mosaics of S. Maria in Trastevere, the iconography is pure Byzantine, especially in the Nativities of Mary and of Jesus, and in the Death of the Virgin, yet the artist introduces his own plastic effects and feeling of depth into the recognised scheme. The most original aspect of Cavallini's work is his extraordinary perception of the constructive and illusive capabilities of colour, which can be used to convey volume and perspective. If Byzantine art suggested the use of colour for modelling, Cavallini certainly carried the suggestion to its conclusion. His colour seems to vibrate continuously, partly because of the richness of the tone, partly because of the skilful gradation of light and shade, which he constantly uses to model his forms. The modelling emerges soft and gentle under the bright colours and strong shading. In keeping with these gentle, luminous shapes, the action of the scenes is peaceful — suffused with grace and Byzantine elegance, it is true, but relaxed in a more human and natural Italian version. More human and natural than the severe style of Cimabue and the mysterious, fragile, sad style of Duccio, Cavallini's work does not present a personal interpretation of a tradition so much as a reflection of a way of feeling and seeing in painting that was already widely spread. And in fact for some years past Italian painting had possessed a new vitality and a new set of concrete and realistic values, while maintaining a very high spiritual level which it derived from the work of the young Giotto, who had been active since at least 1285.

In 1293, barely two years after the scenes from the Life of Mary, Cavallini with various assistants undertook the whole fresco decoration of S. Cecilia. Today only a few fragments remain: part of the Last Judgment (Christ between the Virgin and S. John with the Apostles seated); Angels assembling the Saved and the Damned; and parts of the scenes from the Old and New Testaments. The Last Judgment cannot be attributed with certainty. Cavallini's personality seems to be greatly heightened both in style and feeling, not entirely due to the freer technique of the fresco. The forms are more plastic and built-up, although they have the typical mobility and shading of colour, and the composition has a new grandeur and solemnity. Even more surprising is the expressive power of the characters, who seem to have grown in stature compared with those in S. Maria in Trastevere, and to have a more profound conception of life.

And here, for art critics, is the problem of Cavallini. Although his style is very clear, the scarcity of his surviving works means that any reconstruction of his personality must remain hypothetical. He is regarded by some authorities as the immediate predecessor and chief influence on Giotto; by others Giotto is thought to have had a decisive influence on Cavallini. This second view is based not on ancient written sources (Vasari and others), who say that Cavallini had been a pupil of Giotto, but on the transformation of his style in S. Cecilia, which is thought to resemble the youthful style of Giotto. But whatever may be decided in the specific case of

Giotto and Cavallini, one fact is certain: that Giotto very soon began to exercise an influence on his contemporaries, even those older than himself, whether they were Florentine, Sienese, Umbrian or Roman; followers of Cimabue or Duccio; Latin or Byzantine. Even so it is possible that as a very young man Giotto, while studying classical art at Rome, had also at one time studied the art of Roman painters in the Classical-Byzantine tradition, such as Torriti and Cavallini. In any case, the technique and means of expression of the two masters remained wholly different and opposed.

In 1308 Cavallini is known to have been at Naples, where he remained probably until 1316, working first for Charles II and then for Robert of Anjou. He had a large following of pupils and imitators in Naples, but there are very few traces of his own work. In the frescoes which remain in the cathedral, his hand can be distinguished from the work of his collaborators only in the Tree of Jesse, while in S. Maria Donna Regina, only the apostles and prophets in the Last Judgment recall the grandeur of the same subject painted in S. Cecilia in Rome. Having returned to Rome (according to Ghiberti) in the time of John XXII (1316-1334), he worked at the mosaics on the façade of S. Paul Outside-the-Walls, which have been so restored and altered that they cannot be judged today. Nothing has survived of his panel painting, nor is anything known about it.

Cavallini's school developed in Rome and Naples, but now that painting had taken a wholly new direction in Italy, the results were dull and old-fashioned. Among his Roman pupils the name of Filippo Rosuti is known, since he signed the mosaics of the upper part of the façade of S. Maria Maggiore (Christ among Angels in the mandorla): this however shows no development of the master's style, and in fact is more like the work of Torriti.

An echo of Cavallini's work can be found in Umbria and in the Romagna, probably because work was done on the upper church at Assisi by men who were colleagues and pupils of Cavallini. Nor is it improbable that Cavallini himself went to Assisi, although there is no direct of convincing proof of his work there. In any case his influence was soon to be overshadowed by the more powerful influence of Giotto, which inspired such remarkable and important developments in fourteenth-century Italian painting.

A knowledge of the work of these three great figures of the thirteenth century demonstrates very clearly that Byzantine painting was redeemed in Italy not through the work of eastern artists, but by men who were profoundly Italian, or Latin, in spirit. They were men who had laboriously come to realise that a western civilisation now existed, or rather had already existed before the Byzantine one, and that they belonged to it. The reign of Byzantine art was over in Italy, and the lost classical source had been found once more. At least in essence it was over, although Byzantine art continued to exist for a long time to come in other countries; but deprived of any means of renewal, it was slowly and inevitably destroyed by a long process of involution.

Cimabue, Duccio and Cavallini bring to a glorious end a long period in the history of painting, but they do not begin a fresh one. Their originality consisted in some exceptional quality of temperament which each possessed, and in their consequent efforts to bring individuality to their work.

L. M.

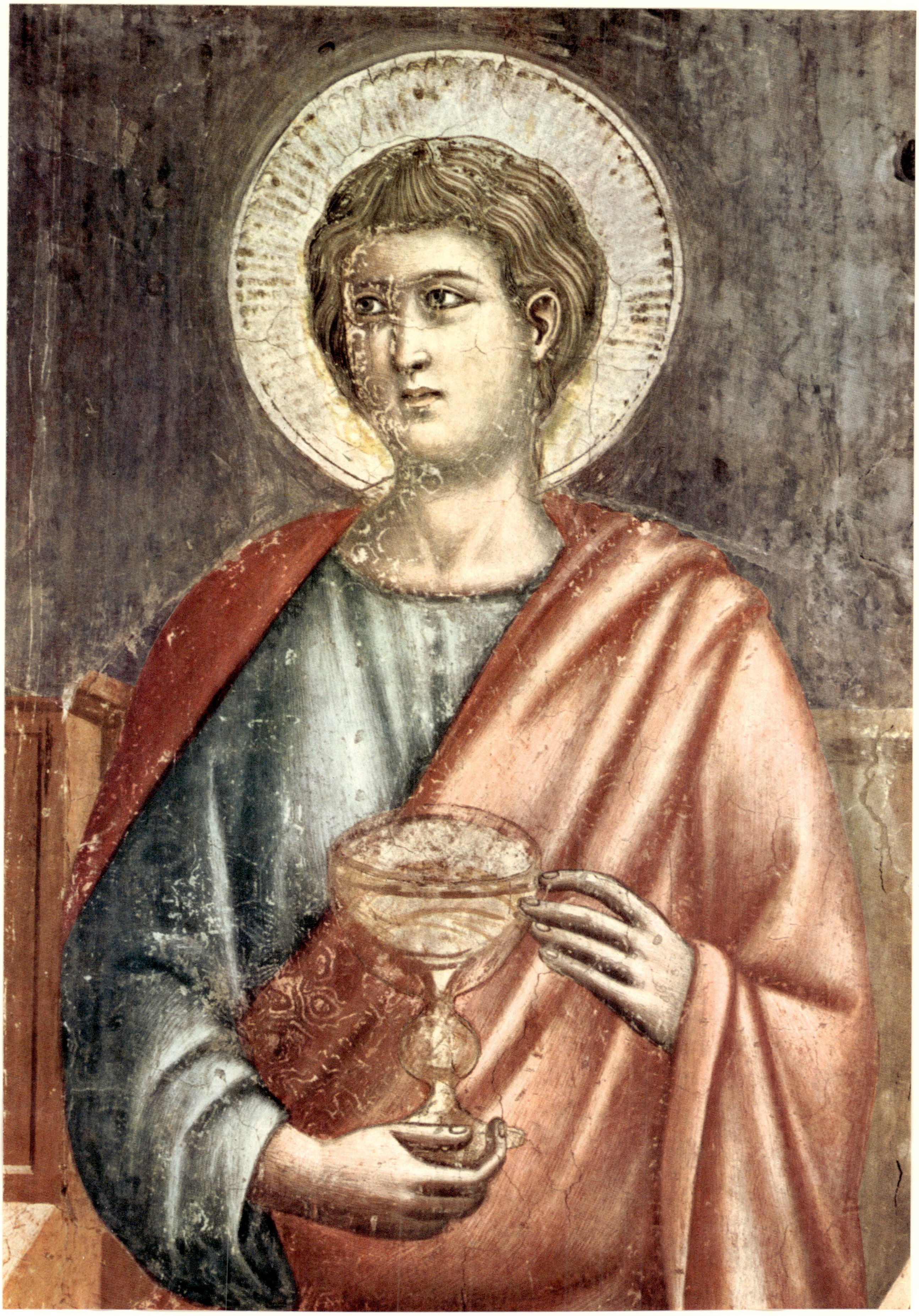

Pietro Cavallini: An Apostle from the Last Judgment. S. Cecilia in Trastevere, Rome

THE FOURTEENTH CENTURY

No discussion of Giotto is possible without some knowledge of his immediate predecessors, particularly Cimabue and Pietro Cavallini. In order to appreciate his importance as an innovator it is necessary to have some understanding of Florentine painting at the period when Giotto, then scarcely more than a child, followed Cimabue to Florence. This has already been fully dealt with: we have reached a point at which the dominating influences were Cimabue's harsh style and powerful design, the soft colouring of Pietro Cavallini, and the somewhat popular style of those Florentine painters who were still working in the Byzantine tradition, such as the Master of the Magdalene, or Coppo di Marcovaldo. Florence had already some knowledge of the graceful quality of Gothic line, modified by the pure Byzantine rhythm of Duccio, who had painted his great Madonna for the company of the Laudesi in S. Maria Novella a few years earlier.

A new way of life was beginning to stir in Italy, especially in Florence, and Giotto's work was to be one of the most important consequences of the cultural and spiritual revival which had begun at the end of the thirteenth century. Above the fanatical crowds inspired by moralists scourging the frivolities of the day, there had now arisen the powerful figure of Frederick II of Swabia. Frederick's court was a highly cultured one, well versed in the classics, and this was also the age in which the charming vernacular style of the *Dolce Stil Novo* was spreading through Italy side by side with the new spirit of the two great religious orders founded by S. Dominic and S. Francis.

The great civilisation of the fourteenth century, which sprang from this combination of the old and the new, was essentially an Italian phenomenon, and has left its mark in the vast Gothic cathedrals, in Dante's *Divine Comedy*, and in Giotto's masterpieces. Politics too were changing and maturing in this period. After the failure of Henry VII's enterprise, so cherished by Dante, and the voluntary exile of Pope Clement V, the great city states of Italy began to emerge — Florence, Siena, Bologna, and Milan. The exception was Naples, where the Angevins were still in power.

These events signify a change in men's ways of thinking, a reaction from the contemplative abstraction of the preceding era. The cult of the individual, and an interest in his nature and behaviour, were now established. The discovery of man, the understanding of his soul, became important, and instead of seeking complete effacement in God men tried to approach Him through works. The anonymous singers of religious hymns, love songs, and epics had disappeared, and in their place were individual poets with names, styles and thoughts of their own. Gone too were the nameless workmen who had built walls, carved capitals and columns, or composed superb mosaics; they had been replaced by artists with clearly realised personalities. These new artists, moreover, were mainly of the first rank, as though the human race had suddenly burst into flower after being imprisoned for centuries in darkness and uncertainty, nullified, as it were, by the grandeur of the Universe and its Creator.

It was this maturing of the spirit which prepared the way for the new thought, the transforming of the religious spirit of Christianity from a remote theological assertion into a wonderful supernatural reality. Christ, through His grandeur and the immense tragedy of His Passion, had entered into the heart and soul of man, and the Gospel became an easily understood story of the God who became man, endowed with all the gifts and all the sorrows of humanity.

The creations of Dante and Giotto, the two greatest figures in fourteenth-century culture, were the immediate results of this new spiritual feeling that was epitomised by S. Dominic and S. Francis. S. Dominic, searching for a rational explanation of the miracle of the Incarnation and the human manifestation of Christ, laid the foundation for the vast edifice of scholastic theology later built up by S. Thomas Aquinas, in whose orbit Dante wrote his poem. S. Francis, whose faith enabled him to accept divine miracles, wore himself out in a fervour of adoration, and in complete simplicity of spirit re-lived the truths of the Gospels. Giotto was inspired by this simplicity, and in his superb and deeply human art — which contains no trace of self-flagellatory exaltation — he is concerned exclusively and constantly with the celebration of the human spirit.

There is no doubt that Giotto knew Dante personally. This is evident from the way in which certain dates in their lives coincide; in any case they were both Florentines and may even have spent some time together in Padua, Ravenna and Verona, when Giotto was carrying out commissions in these cities and Dante was in exile. Dante's famous reference to Giotto reveals both admiration and friendly feelings: " Cimabue thought that he held the field in painting and now Giotto is supreme... ". Finally there is the portrait of Dante by Giotto or one of this assistants in the Podestà chapel of the Bargello Palace at Florence. This knowledge and friendship is evident in the similarity of their profound and vivid images; in their ability to seize on the essentials both in life and mankind; in the depth of their human feeling, the way in which they both threw off the stylistic and moral fetters which bound them to their predecessors.

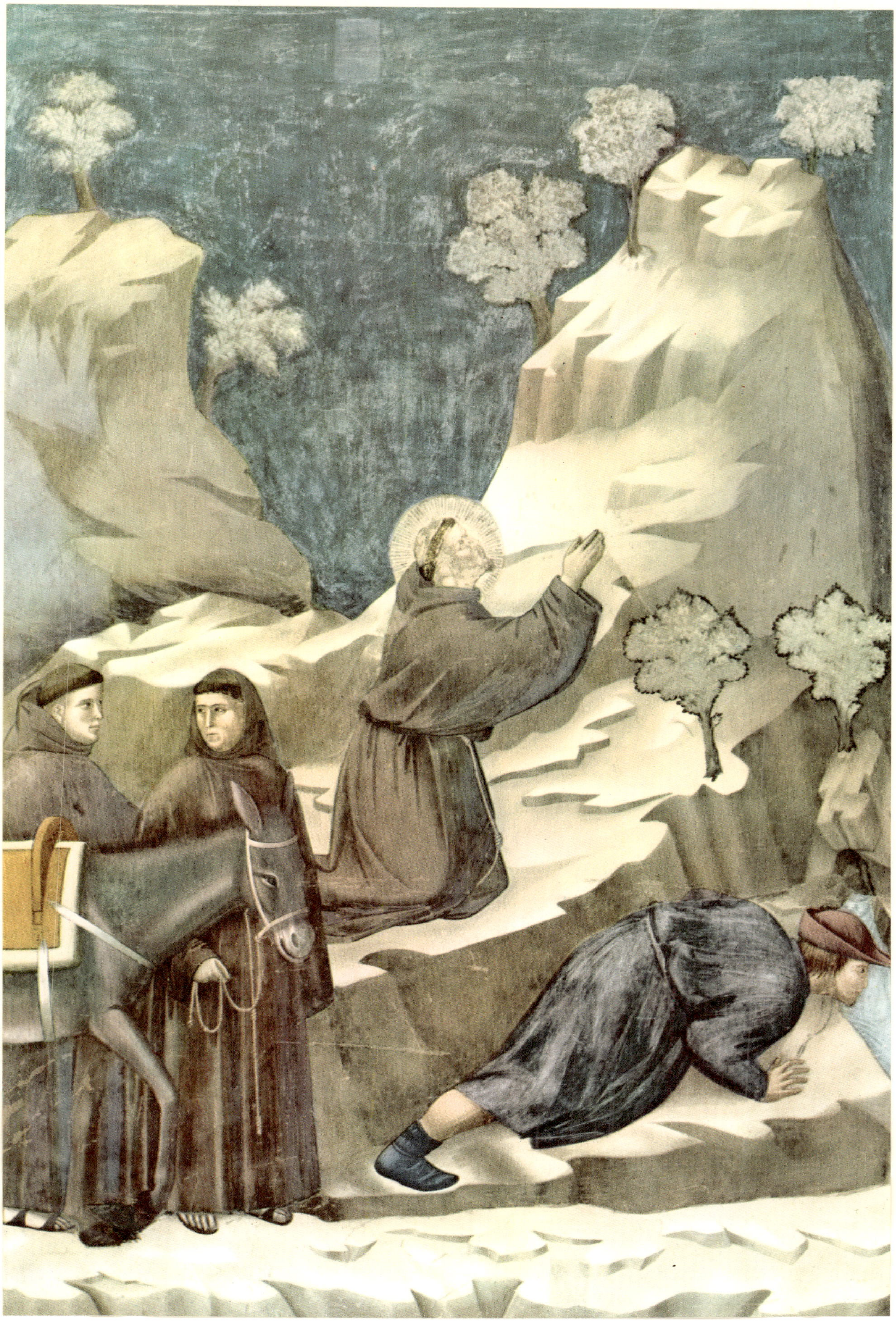

Giotto: The Miracle of the Spring. S. Francis, Assisi

Giotto was influenced by Cimabue and Cavallini, while his overwhelming interest in plasticity also laid him open to the influence of contemporary sculpture, particularly that of Arnolfo and later of Giovanni Pisano. At Padua, for example, in the Massacre of the Innocents, Giotto spoke the same tragic and forceful language as the great Pisan sculptor. Florence at this period was becoming one of the most modern and lively intellectual centres of the West, and Giotto absorbed this atmosphere. But when taste began to turn away from the classical world towards the easier linear and decorative manner of the French Gothic style, Giotto rebelled against its indefinite qualities. All abstraction, whether Byzantine or Gothic, repelled him; his method was to endow ideal concepts with concrete forms, and although his art tended towards the universal, he never created spiritual abstractions. The expression of the human spirit is the very essence of Giotto's art, and it is for this reason that he may be described as classical. He has the serene contemplation of life, the self-control, the balance and perfect sense of adjustment between the physical and the moral worlds. And so he brought back to the West a long-forgotten world, and, more than any humanistic learning, it was his work that prepared the way for the Renaissance.

This is the spiritual essence of Giotto and the world in which he grew up. Without some knowledge of these circumstances he would appear like a gigantic and inexplicable accident. As it was, his greatness was immediately felt, and even his earliest biographers have remarkable things to say about him. There is the verse by Dante; the praise of Boccaccio; the assertion of Cennini that " Giotto turned painting from Greek to Latin "; and the poetical image of Ghiberti, who referred in his Commentaries to Giotto's birth as though it were a miracle: " A child was born of a wonderful genius, who drew from nature ", implying that even as a child Giotto's talent was outstanding.

This remarkable child was born at Vespignano di Mugello, near Nicchio, in 1267. About his youth little is known, and legend is apt to be substituted for history. The story has the artist as a poor shepherd boy, drawing a sheep on a stone, and Cimabue discovering him and taking him to Florence. Whatever this story may be worth, it does suggest precocity, and provides a poetical account of the young Giotto's arrival in the city, and his entry into the celebrated studio of the great Florentine.

It was Giotto who created a new spirit in painting. This has never been disputed, and has been repeated through the centuries by Dante, Giovanni Villani, Lorenzo Ghiberti, Leonardo, Vasari, down to Lanzi and Goethe; in our own time the assertion is truer and stronger than ever before. Yet it would be absurd to see the new painter emerge immediately. To begin with, he worked and painted according to the circumstances and tastes of his time, and there are aspects of his mature style which still reveal his debt to Cimabue. In particular the striking quality of Cimabue's design became in Giotto an expressive force whereby he controlled his tremendous volumes by his outline and gave that immediacy to his gestures which was one of his strongest characteristics. There is no doubt that he also adopted some of the more human aspects of Byzantine art, which he transformed and strengthened, while keeping in mind the nobility and bearing of classical art and the heavy, barely articulate masses of Romanesque sculpture. His balance and imperturbable clarity result from all these elements, and — once the golden barriers of Byzantine art were broken down — he saved painting from the violence and exaggerated expressionism of fourteenth-century Gothic sculpture, from the Master of Naumburg to Giovanni Pisano.

The history and personality of Giotto are still subjects for study and discussion, since nothing is known for certain about his earliest works. What is certain is that he emerged at once as a tireless renovator, even in his own work, for he was continually trying to find new and better ways of understanding and expression. In working out Giotto's personal history, scholars have envisaged him following his master to Assisi, where he probably worked before 1290, perhaps between 1270 and 1280, on some of the legends of Isaac and on the Deposition of Christ. During recent years critics have been deeply interested in the attribution of these frescoes and have ended, with some dissenting opinions, by falling back on an anonymous "Master of Isaac", of Roman origin, closely linked with Cavallini but better acquainted with Cimabue's scenes from the Old Testament. With a good deal of reserve, critics are inclined to ascribe the scenes of the Passion to a youthful Giotto. Some of these are however in fragments, particularly the Deposition, where an artist of a later period than the "Master of Isaac", but less mature in style, composed the closely knit group of mourners, and the vertical masses of those who take part in the drama, in a real and admirably composed landscape. The dignity of the gestures, the intensity of the expressions, the calm dramatic power of this vision, which is no longer choral, but human and individual, does in fact suggest that this work may contain the first known example of the great art of Giotto. He had already cast off the weight of the Byzantine tradition and come into contact with the Roman style of Pietro Cavallini (a contact which was to be renewed in Rome shortly afterwards), and he now began to establish his own personality and style, drawing away from the harshness and violent drama of Cimabue. He had become the most important link between the old and the new; the greatest manifestation in art of the new movement which was taking place in the history of civilisation. In his earliest works his efforts to build afresh were harsher and more intense, but already he had made it clear that his interest lay in creating space, volume and mass, and that for him colour was inseparable from chiaroscuro and was a descriptive element which accentuated symmetry, masses, connecting passages and breaks. His primitive backgrounds, consisting in his first Deposition merely of bare rocks, established him as a creator of landscape, which seems to grow and live with his characters; but his main preoccupation was always with the human soul and its expressions. The strength of these qualities in his early works is almost violent, but later this violence, as is normal after a victory, was gradually modified.

In the frescoes in the upper church at Assisi, Giotto appears as a controversial innovator. Painted probably in 1290, these frescoes are now almost universally ascribed to him, just as they were by Ghiberti (1450) and Vasari (in the second edition of his "Lives", 1568). Recently there has been some some attempt to deny that they are by Giotto, or even that they belong to the Florentine school, but in fact they are the first authentic examples of his art, and the best foundation for a study of his later work.

Although he had considerable help from pupils and assistants, whose work, especially that of the "Master of S. Cecilia" is more obvious in the final scenes, the imprint of Giotto's mind is clearly evident in all of them. When he studied the life of S. Francis he was fascinated by its poetry and by the gentle nature of the miracles, which he paints with the same simplicity as the earliest disciples used to describe them in the "Little Flowers".

For the first time Francis of Assisi, the saint who appeals universally to the heart and mind, is portrayed not as a remote ascetic, as he had been in the thirteenth century, but as a living man filled with love and charity. Giotto, who had a genuine understanding of all that was simplest and most human in S. Francis, exalted his silent heroism, and above all, humbly praised the saint's humility. These supremely beautiful, simple legends were a spontaneous creation; the most delicate feeling is contained in flowing, simple images and backgrounds, according to "a synthesis of plastic character which reduces every visible appearance to an architecture of volume". Even when a note of drama is called for, every irrelevancy is whittled away, and this emphasises the wide gap between Giotto's style and the exaggerated liveliness of Giovanni Pisano. In his early work Giotto was in fact spiritually far removed from Giovanni Pisano, although later, possibly as a result of common interests and work, he did adopt something of the sculptor's violent dramatic feeling. He was, as we have seen, much closer to Arnolfo, possibly because in their decidedly archaic yet lively taste, and in their simple, sometimes even harsh forms, they both had the same classical antecedents.

The figure of the thirsty drinker in the " Miracle of the Source " strongly resembles the work of the great sculptor. The greedy, almost bestial gesture of throwing himself on the spring which has hardly begun to flow through the rocks recalls one of the thirsty figures in Perugia, drinking water at the edge of the basin. In all these scenes there is a perfect relationship of mass between people and landscapes, and the powerful figures stand out in the light against the huge, desolate and jagged rocks. The strength of the composition is however slightly softened in the gentle figure of the saint, absorbed in prayer; in the questioning and incredulous glances of his two companions; and in the patience of the ass, also looking eagerly at the water. In this painting Giotto touched the highest peak of Florentine art, whose essence was defined one hundred years later by Leonardo: " Place your figures in such an attitude that this is in itself sufficient to express what the figure has in his mind: otherwise your art will not be worthy of praise ". Where could one find a more perfect exemplar of Leonardo's dictum than this picture in which the painter has portrayed the actions and the souls of his characters so vividly, so forcefully, and so unmistakeably that they can almost be identified with the general concepts of thirst, faith, curiosity and patience? The light strikes the rocks and the figures, accentuating the sharpness of the one and the physical nature of the other, and the colouring stands out here and there in an unexpected way, giving touches of red and green shadows to the faces, and vivid, unexpected highlights. This is one of Giotto's simplest compositions, most consonant with his spirit, like the Sermon to the Birds and the Gift of the Cloak, where however there is a lively directness in the relationship between the characters and nature. Equally vivid is the depth of feeling in the loving gesture of S. Francis, bending over to talk to the birds, in his identification with nature. This gentle movement contrasts with the motionless figure of his companion standing against a tree. The same depth of feeling may be seen in the generous impulse of the young man giving his cloak to the impoverished old knight, in a gesture which expresses humility and vanquished pride both in the exchange of glances and in the action. From here it is a short step to the Miracle of Greccio: in this work the action is more complicated and operates on several planes. The backround is no longer the mountainous harshness of La Verna, or the gentle countryside of Umbria, but the interior of a church, where " Blessed Francis, in memory of the Birth of Christ, orders the cradle to be prepared... and preaches on the nature of the poor King... ". Giotto sets the scene in a choir, that is to say, against a monumental background which anticipates the Renaissance. Among a crowd of onlookers and friars, he portrays the miracle of the Child in the arms of Francis, who places Him gently in the cradle, the focal point of the composition. There is a great deal of movement and excitement both in expression and in the figures. Some of the friars, so deeply absorbed in chanting, are realistic to such a degree that one can almost hear the sound. The women behind the iconostasis press forward, curious to see what is happening, but only one astonished man who was " pure in heart " was aware of the miracle. There is perfect harmony in the representation of the characters, their feelings, their physical features, their clothes and all the other objects which are placed against the simple background of a marble wall, a pulpit in perspective, and a cross suspended in the void.

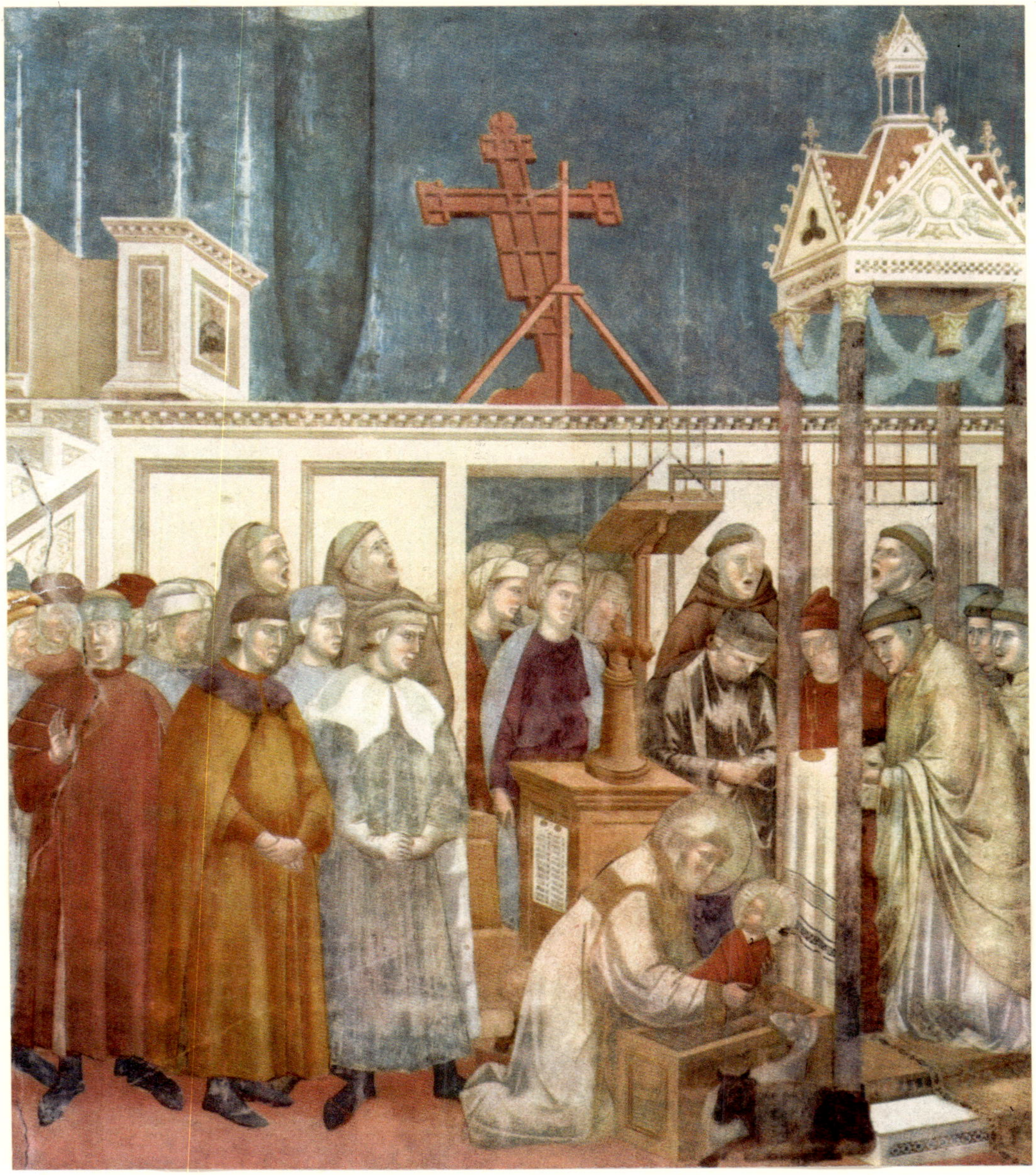

Giotto: The Cradle of Greccio. S. Francis, Assisi

In all the paintings of S. Francis for which Giotto was himself responsible the predominant note is one of depth and relief. He made use of his artistic inheritance to further his own aims, employing the Byzantine manner of shading to demarcate planes, and the simple landscapes with ultramarine skies, which belonged to the medieval tradition, to strengthen his feeling of spatial depth. His style of colouring underwent a complete transformation. Beginning with green and greyish shading he gradually adopted lighter tones, and produced delicate transparent effects which established a new criterion for the treatment of light.

In 1300 Giotto went from Assisi to Rome for the Holy Year, and worked in S. John Lateran on the wall-paintings of the Proclamation of the Holy Year, which have been restored, and on the mosaic of the apostles' boat in the atrium of S. Peter's, which has also been restored. Two angels remain, one in the Palazzo Venezia and the other in the Petriano Museum. The latter, in its pale colouring, imbued with light, reveals a new and important contact with Pietro Cavallini. Giotto was also at this time moving once again closer to Arnolfo, who was in Rome, and seeking to develop a truer quality of plasticity. Evidence of this new contact is seen in the lovely crucifix of S. Maria Novella, which Giotto painted after returning to Florence from Rome,

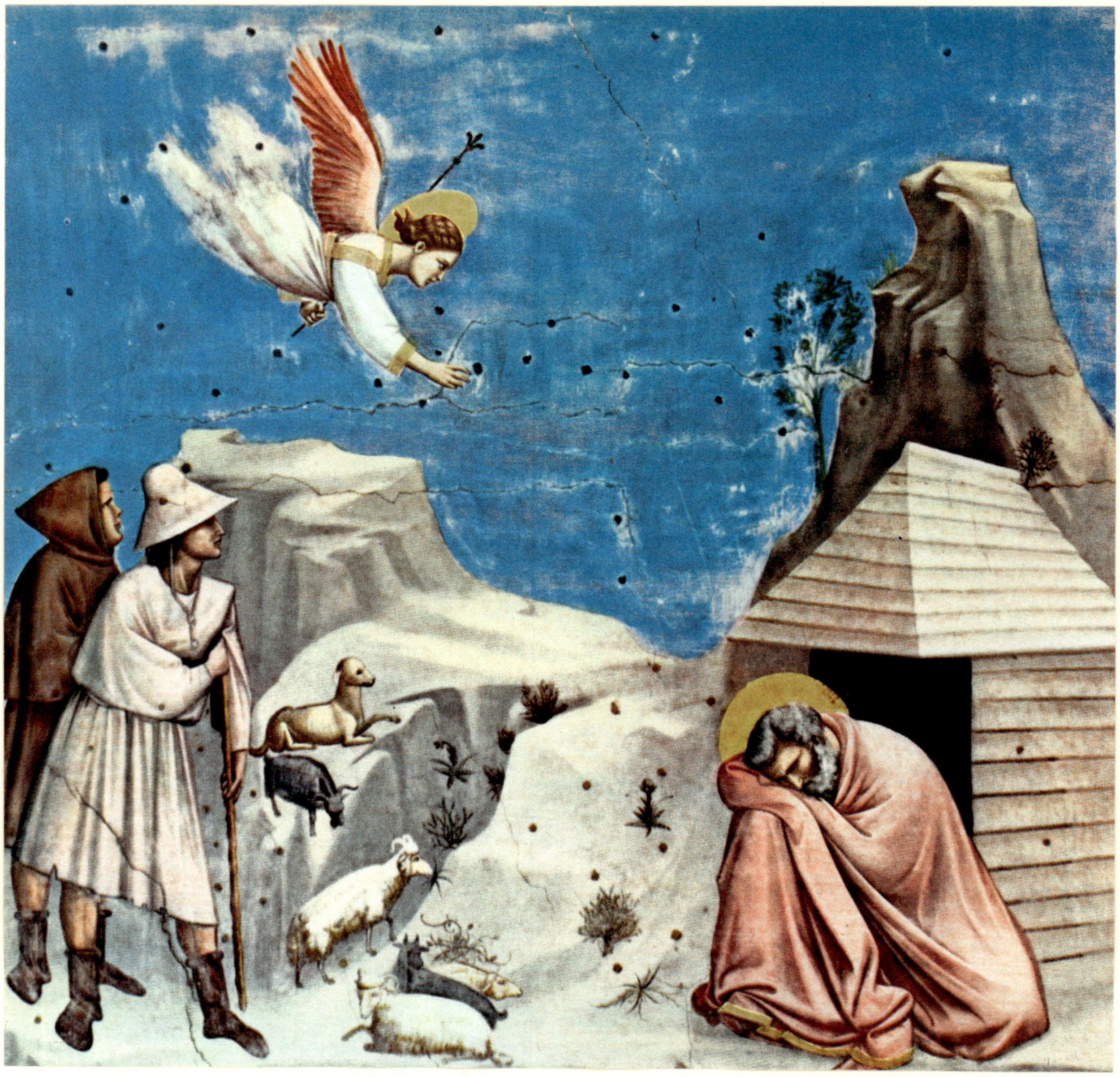

Giotto: The Dream of Joachim. Scrovegni Chapel, Padua

and from which it is clear that he was well acquainted with contemporary sculpture " in the plastic though peaceful representation of the body ", and that " combination of grandeur and humanity which create an absolute masterpiece ".

By 1305, when he carried out the wall-paintings in the Arena chapel in Padua for Enrico Scrovegni, Giotto was already famous. The chapel is a small building with a single nave on whose walls Giotto painted the Life of Christ in 37 scenes (beginning with stories of Joachim, Anna and the Virgin) up to Pentecost, and ending with the Last Judgment, showing Heaven and Hell. The barrel vault is covered with a star-sprinkled blue sky, and on the fascia there are monochrome allegories of the Vices and Virtues. This work was largely done by assistants. Even today the world which Giotto created " remains in the memory as something immense ". His style was now fully developed, and the note now struck is gentler, yet even more impressive. Colour, light, and chiaroscuro blend and clothe the figures, so that they seem almost to rise up. The masses are more powerful than those at Assisi, and, with the artist's new treatment of light, are more polished in appearance and have entirely discarded the harshness of his early work. There are still closely-knit groups planted in empty space, as for instance the sleeping figure of S. Joachim, wrapped in the warmth of his rose-coloured cloak with its softly shaded folds. The lighting is so arranged as to make the straw in the little country hut shine golden in the background. Opposite Joachim, in the deep silence of the rocky landscape, are the stocky figures of the shepherds, square and rough like the rocks, nature within nature, apparently indifferent and cut off from the humiliation of the forsaken saint. This dramatic quality gradually diminishes in the Padua wall-paintings, and Giotto reveals his profound understanding of the human spirit. From painting to painting, from scene to scene, his deep psychological intuition is as evident as his high moral sense and his ability to express it. The stories of the Virgin are more solemn and hieratical, whereas in the Life of Christ we see a straightforward narrative quality. Giotto has not only learned humility and grace from S. Francis, but penetrated the deep humanity and the transcendency of the divine goodness of Christ. The scenes from the Life of Christ change gradually; the childhood scenes showing a return to the bas-relief style with rocky landscapes harmonising with

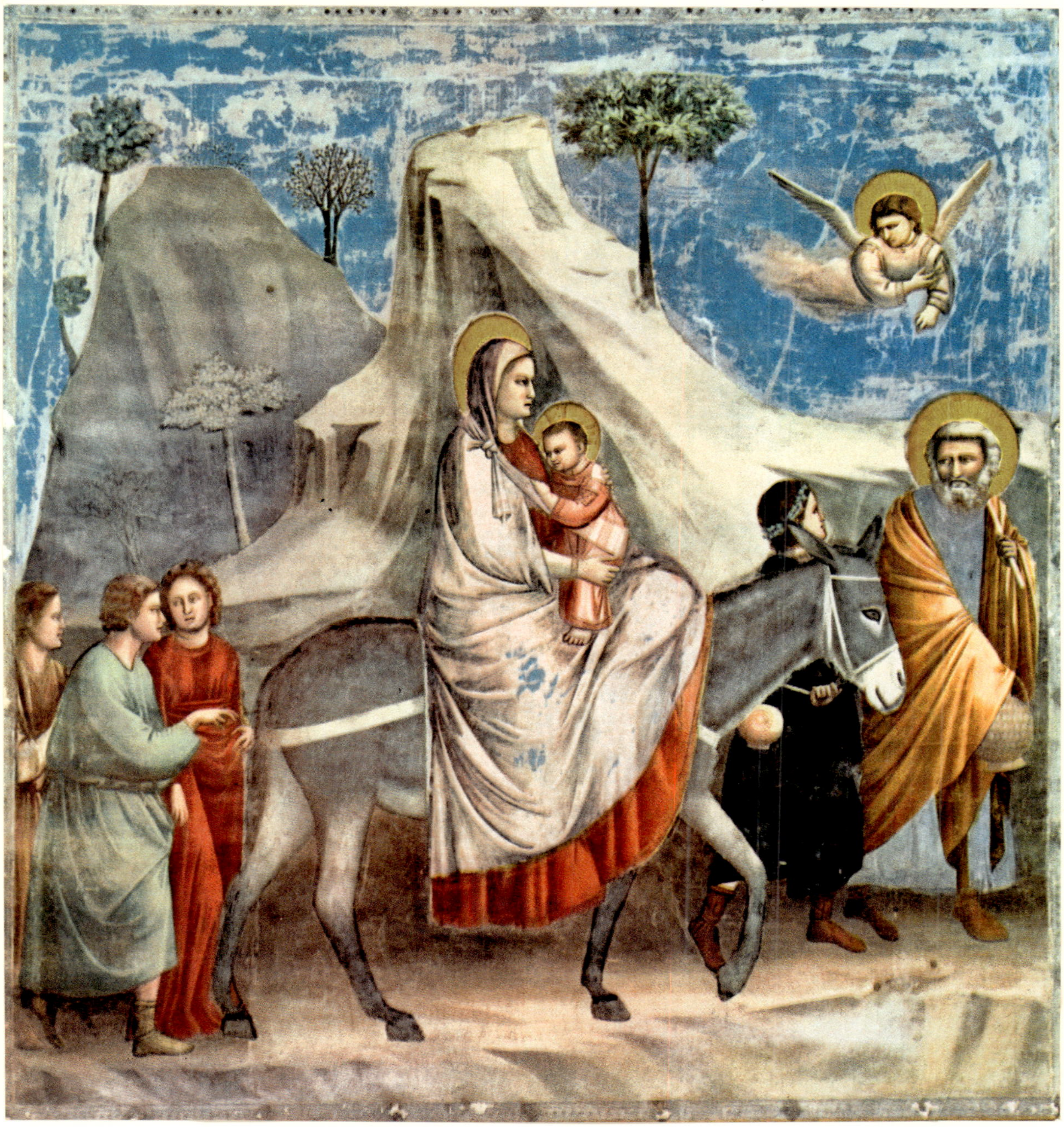

Giotto: The Flight into Egypt. Scrovegni Chapel, Padua

the squat figures. In the Flight into Egypt, for example, the relationship between characters and landscapes is perfect; the central rock balances the dignified figure of the Virgin, lost in contemplation of the cruel fate of her Son, whom for the present she holds gently in her arms. The ass moves slowly under his burden, while a young man, tired of walking, turns towards Joseph, who is thinking only of his family. It is the simplest, most direct kind of poetry, deeply moving in the feeling of tender love which is conveyed in the expressions and the actions. At the same time it possesses an impressive, religious solemnity.

Giotto's dramatic power, which appears in this case only in the Virgin's miraculous vision of the future, reaches its height in the Deposition. While life is suspended all around, the two rocks lead the eye swiftly towards the head of Christ. Grief cries aloud in the landscape, in the bare tree and the despairing angels who hover in the livid sky. This feeling is stronger and more controlled in the motionless figures behind the Mother, who has ceased weeping. Immediately behind her is the striking

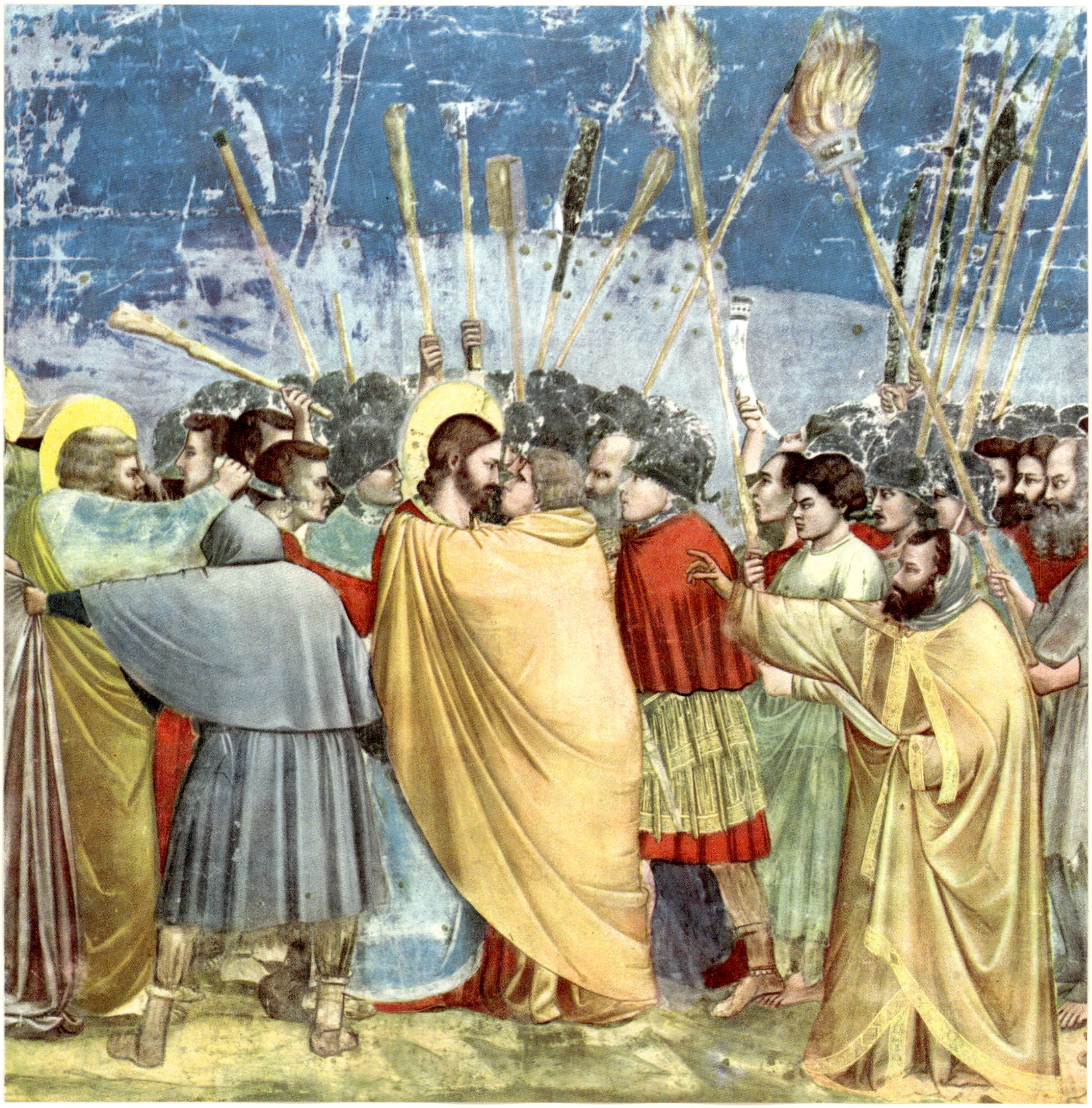

Giotto: The Kiss of Judas. Scrovegni Chapel, Padua

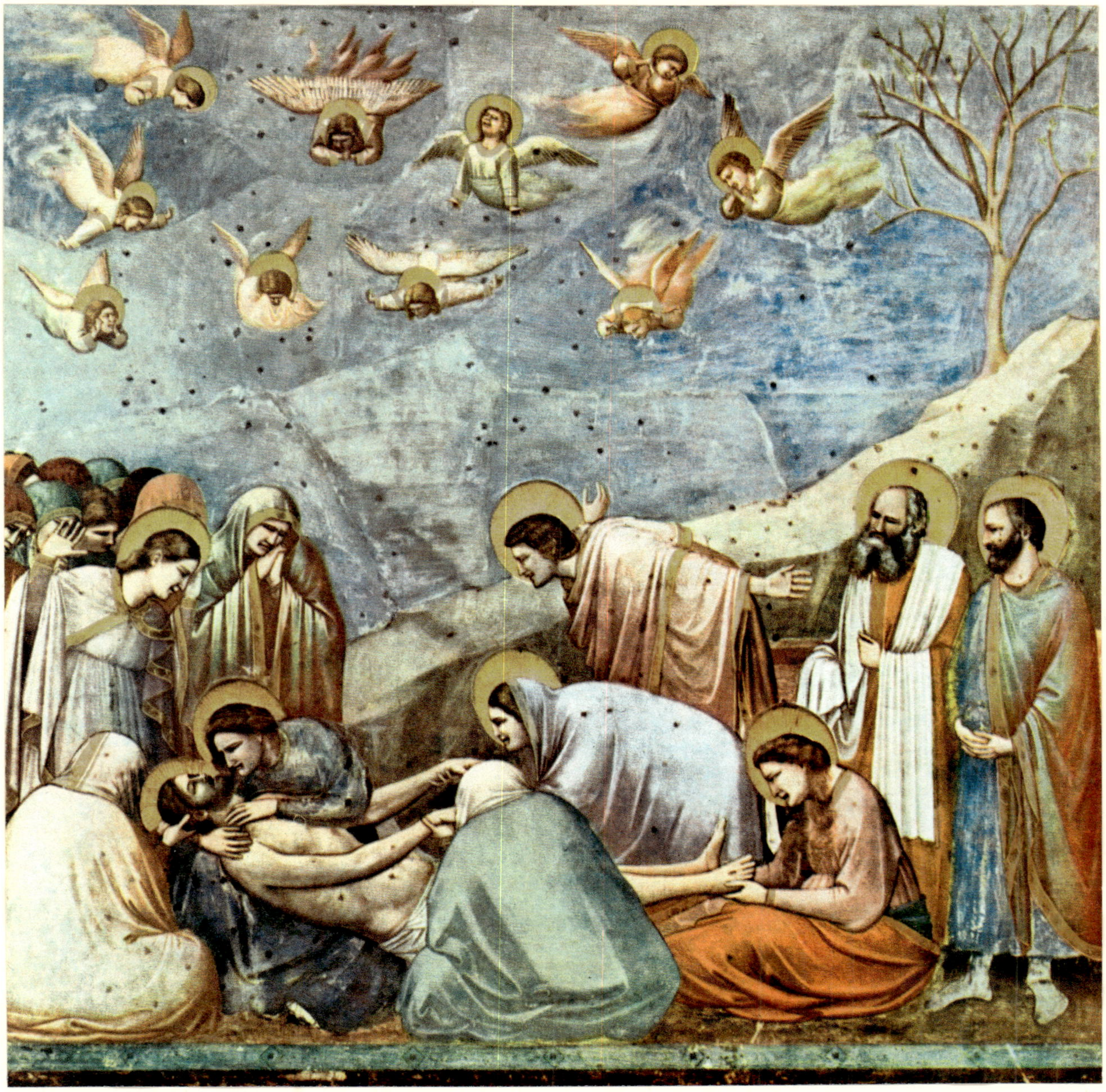

Giotto: Deposition. Scrovegni Chapel, Padua

figure of S. John who, in the beatiful, wide-spreading gesture of his arms, seems to sketch a despairing embrace and to recall the symbol of the suffering on the cross.

The drama is expressed in the arrangement of masses and in the gestures which create a chorus of grief, becoming more restrained as it approaches the focal point and culminating in the superhuman calm of Christ. This is His final expression after a long series ranging from mystical rapture to command, sorrow, disdain, and human suffering.

The colouring emphasises the feeling of despair: in the strong red tone of the mantle of the mourner at Christ's feet; in the reddish shades of the grey cloak of the woman who weeps over His hand; and in the wide scale ranging from strong green to yellow, and the alabaster-like pallor of Christ, which fades away into the dull grey of the rocks in the background, and finally in the dark blue of the sky.

As at Assisi Giotto used colour to emphasise his most vigorous plastic effects. It is now blended in a variety of tones which may harmonise or contrast. In almost every picture there is a dominant colour surrounded by a harmony of different tones, sometimes strong and sometimes gentle, so that each picture is like an island of blue, pink, grey, or golden light. The treatment of light is not violent as at Assisi; it is subdued and peaceful.

In every scene throughout the whole composition, Giotto's most mature style is evident. Superfluous detail, which was almost eliminated at Assisi, has now entirely disappeared, and every feeling is conveyed as simply as possible. A smile, a glance, a hand, each in turn may express sorrow, grace, betrayal, or goodness. And if at times Giotto concedes something to the dramatic violence of feeling, as he did in the Deposition and again in the Seizing of Christ and the Crucifixion, he nevertheless imparts a calm and solemn tone to the story. Every scene is dominated by an expression which has an absolute value: the scrutiny of Christ portrayed in the diabolically rapacious face of Judas, the betrayer; His ecstasy at hearing the voice of the Father speaking to Him from the splendour of the heavens above the Jordan at His baptism; the violent emotion of Mary Magdalene in the *Noli me Tangere*.

While Giotto's influence was spreading over northern Italy, he returned to Florence and painted his Ognissanti Madonna, now in the Uffizi. This is no longer a solemn iconic representation in Glory, as it was for Cimabue, but a firm plastic figure, which the delicate Gothic throne is barely deep enough to contain, moving round the central axis of the composition in an attitude that is calm yet human. The chaste femininity of the Virgin is nevertheless not without some feeling in the half-shut lips, and in the soft tenderness of the transparent robe, which gently emphasises the full firmness of her young breasts. Here we see the triumph of the colouring which Giotto began at Padua: in this song of blue, pink, greens and whites, the splendid golden background is no longer a symbol of the infinite, but a tangible, magnificent golden space.

Giotto could not have painted the Bardi and Peruzzi chapels, as well as two others in S. Croce (these have now entirely faded) before 1317. It is possible to date this work because of a portrait of S. Louis, who was canonised only in that year. In the Bardi chapel Giotto portrayed the legend of S. Francis, thus returning to a theme of his youth; in the other he painted scenes of the two saints named John. In these paintings the composition is freer and the rhythm and feeling are calmer, as though after his tremendous efforts and experiments to create a fresh style Giotto felt satisfied. The colouring of the faces and materials has become so delicate that they are almost diaphanous or transparent, but although solidity gives way to light, fleeting impressions of movement are still present.

With their ample, classical spirit and their singing colours, the compositions are pervaded by a gentle harmony, the result perhaps of a study of Sienese idiom, especially that of Ambrogio Lorenzetti. It has become easier to enjoy these paintings, which represent the ultimate stage in Giotto's work, since the recent restoration which got rid of all the eighteenth-century additions in the legend of S. Francis. On the walls of the Bardi chapel there are fragments which illustrate the extremely delicate colouring of his later years, combined with the surprising ease in the treatment of the faces and gestures, in a wonderfully spatial atmosphere.

Between 1329 and 1332 Giotto was in Naples, and in 1335 he went to Milan to carry out, first for Robert of Anjou and then for Azzone Visconti, works which have now disappeared. Evidently he was very famous by this time, and he is known to have worked in Rimini, Verona, and Ferrara. But nothing remains of his work in any of these cities, nor is anything known of his last years. Some pictures in the Louvre, and in Florence, Rome and Berlin bear the name of Giotto, but their style indicates that they were either wholly or partly the work of assistants.

Meanwhile, between journeys, he returned from time to time to Florence, where in 1334, with great solemnity, he was appointed head of the construction of the

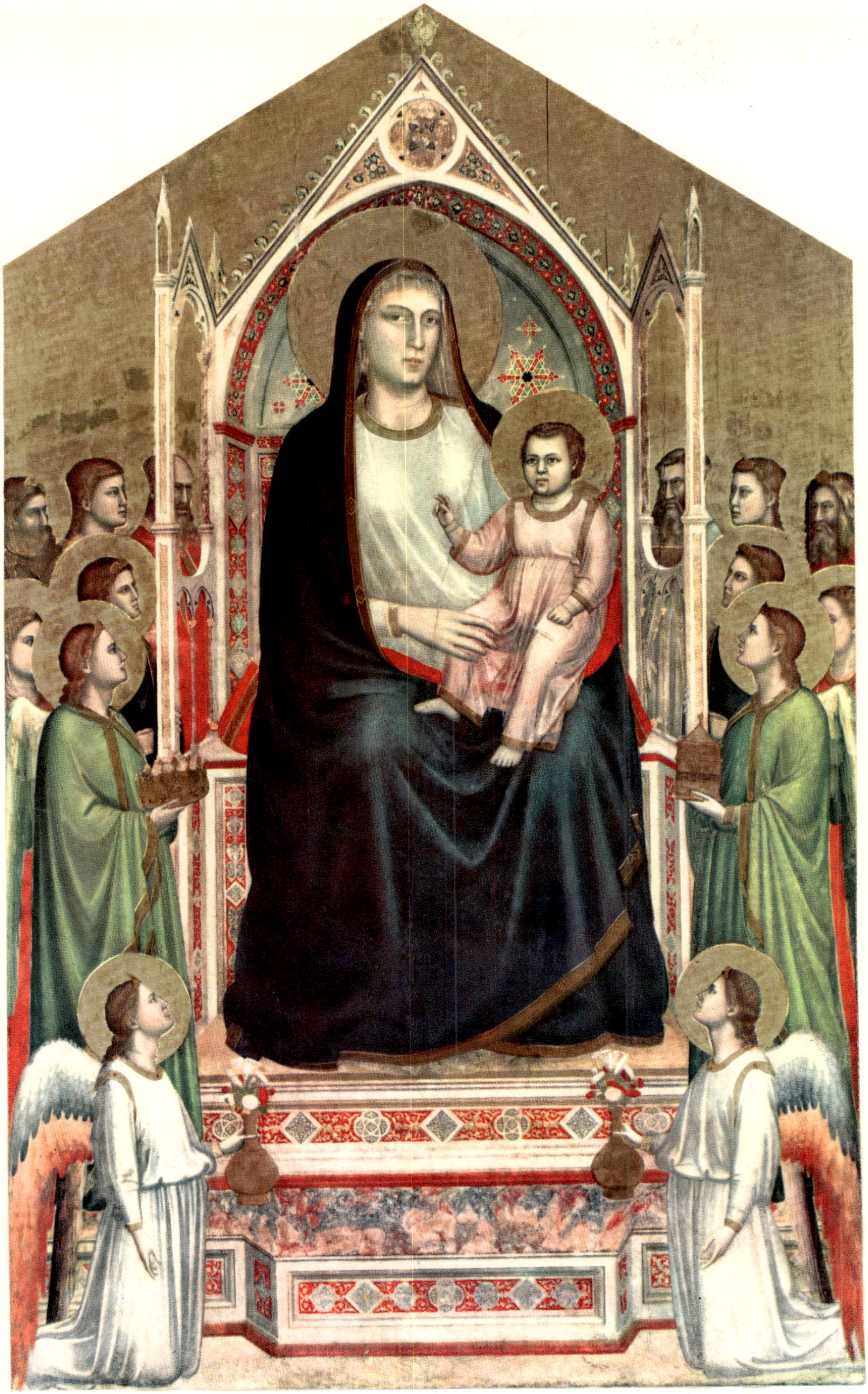

Giotto: Ognissanti Madonna. Uffizi, Florence

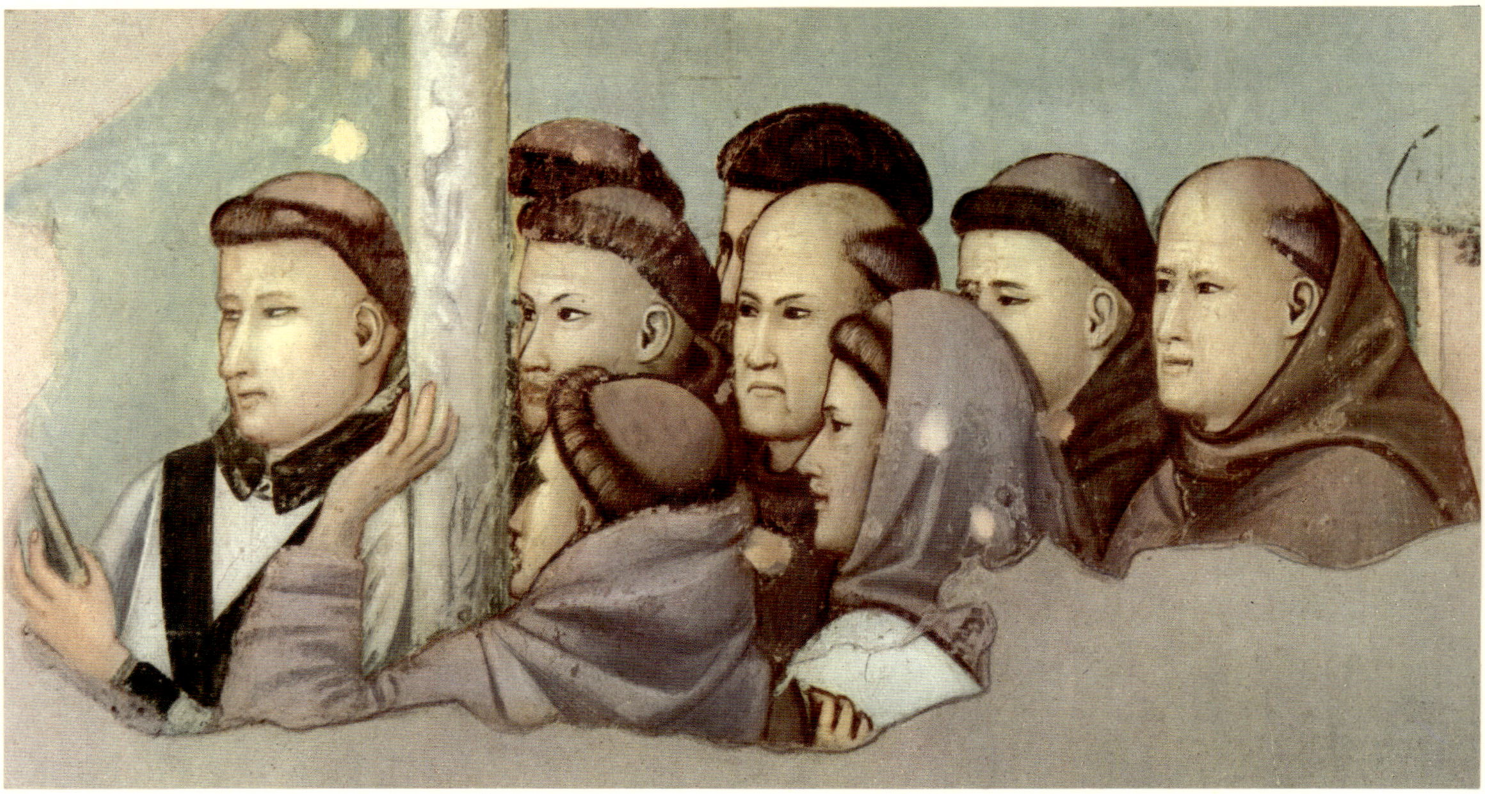

Giotto: The Vision of the Bishop and Brother Agostino. S. Croce, Florence

Cathedral. From this time until his death in January 1337 he devoted himself to the campanile which was to bear his name and which, in the plasticity of the architectural whole, corresponds to his pictorial style. He was also responsible for the decorative idea of the small reliefs which represent the story of man and his progress.

Throughout his long and varied career, Giotto, who belonged to the Middle Ages, brought art into line with our modern taste, providing a balance in the relationship between man and the world, and introducing into painting, as Dante did into poetry, the popular language which we still speak and understand today. In his later years he extended his activities into the fields of architecture and sculpture, and he remains today the first example of the many-sidedness of the Italian genius, which heralded the universal man of the Renaissance.

While Giotto was creating a new style of painting at Florence, undistinguished followers of Duccio were working at Siena and producing numerous Madonnas copied partly from his models, and partly from Cimabue. Among these artists are the anonymous masters of Badia a Isola and of Crevole; and especially Segna di Bonaventura, who was active about 1331, and Ugolino da Siena, who worked in Florence at the same time as Giotto and produced many examples of Sienese art. But the inspiration derived from Duccio was fading, and finally Ugolino came under Giotto's influence. The three most important painters in fourteenth-century Sienese painting are Simone Martini and the two Lorenzetti.

It is difficult to establish whether Simone or Pietro Lorenzetti was the elder. Ambrogio was certainly younger, but since tradition places Simone Martini immediately after Duccio di Boninsegna as head of the Sienese school, we too will begin the fourteenth century with his name.

As Duccio had worked at the same time as Cimabue, so Simone was contemporary with Giotto, although he was hardly aware of Giotto's ideas. Sienese painting was, from the outset, very different from Florentine, and the manifesto of 1355 enunciated very clearly the Sienese conception of painting: " We are, by the grace of God, witnesses for ignorant men who cannot read, of the miracles worked by virtue and in virtue of the holy faith ". The images of the saints, the Virgin and Christ which were created by these Sienese artists seem almost like the illustrations of a vision of a far-off world; and sacred history becomes a graceful legend which flowers spontaneously in their contemplative imagination. From the very beginning this fabulous and imaginative character of Sienese art was radically different from the reasoned and precise art of Florence, and justifies the eighteenth-century aphorism of Padre della Valle: " that Florence belongs to the thinkers and Siena to the poets ". It seemed almost as though the Sienese painters found the origins of their inspiration in some world remote from our own.

It was to this Sienese world of graceful accomplishment, which was at once the ultimate repository of the Greek style and (as the art of Duccio reveals), the fount of northern Gothic, that Simone Martini belonged. It was a society of crusaders and knights who kept alive the Eastern tradition, a small circle of merchants, aesthetes, pleasure seekers, and scholars, closely allied to French civilisation. With his gem-like colouring, subtle and transparent, and his sensitive and delicate outline, Simone Martini is the most typical painter of the Italian Gothic school. It has been suggested that his style was influenced by contacts with the Far East, and this may well be so, since contacts between Western civilisation and the Orient became frequent after Marco Polo had aroused the taste of Europeans for the exotic. Merchants, following in his footsteps, brought textiles, jewels, and Eastern *objets d'art* to the West, and Siena, which had long been a commercial centre, particularly for handwork and rich materials, was particularly affected by the tastes thus created.

Simone's star was at its zenith when he painted the fresco of the Maestà in the Mappamondo room of the Palazzo Pubblico at Siena in 1315. This is not a prelude; it is a masterpiece. In it the artist uses an idiom more cultured and polished than that of Gothic art, and clothes his figures with a warm humanity. It was an advent as unexpected as it was masterly, since in Siena the streets were still ringing with applause for Duccio's Maestà, the masterpiece of an artist who was still alive and greatly honoured.

A few years later Simone's Maestà appeared with the same grandeur as Duccio's, which indeed it resembles in many ways. But it is imbued with a Gothic linear rhythm which modifies the poses, drapery and expressions. The saints are no longer closely grouped around the Virgin, beneath the graceful, elegant canopy; they move and breathe with new life. The two kneeling angels are offering the perennial homage of " flowers of the angels — roses and lilies — with which the celestial meadows are adorned ", to the Queen of Heaven, who is seated on the delicate golden throne like the sovereign of a visionary court.

This is Simone's technique, with light-toned modelling, a warm, shadowless chiaroscuro, and colouring which, according to Ghiberti, who saw it at a time before it had faded into diaphanous transparencies, was vibrant. At times, in the plastic solidity of some of the figures, there is a memory of classical sculpture, and elsewhere one can see a suggestion of the graceful fluency of Gothic statues in wood, marble or ivory. More striking still is the likeness to illumination and the art of the goldsmith in the chiselled work, precious filigrees, enamels and jewels which cover and adorn Simone's figures, from the splendid court surrounding the Virgin in the Maestà to the sinuous arabesque of the Angel of the Annunciation and the curved outline of the Virgin in the same picture, now in the Uffizi. A Gothic note is also seen in the materials, the carpets and golden splendour of his backgrouds. Although Giotto's influence tended to curb the new excitement, Simone's general outline became freer, enabling the figures

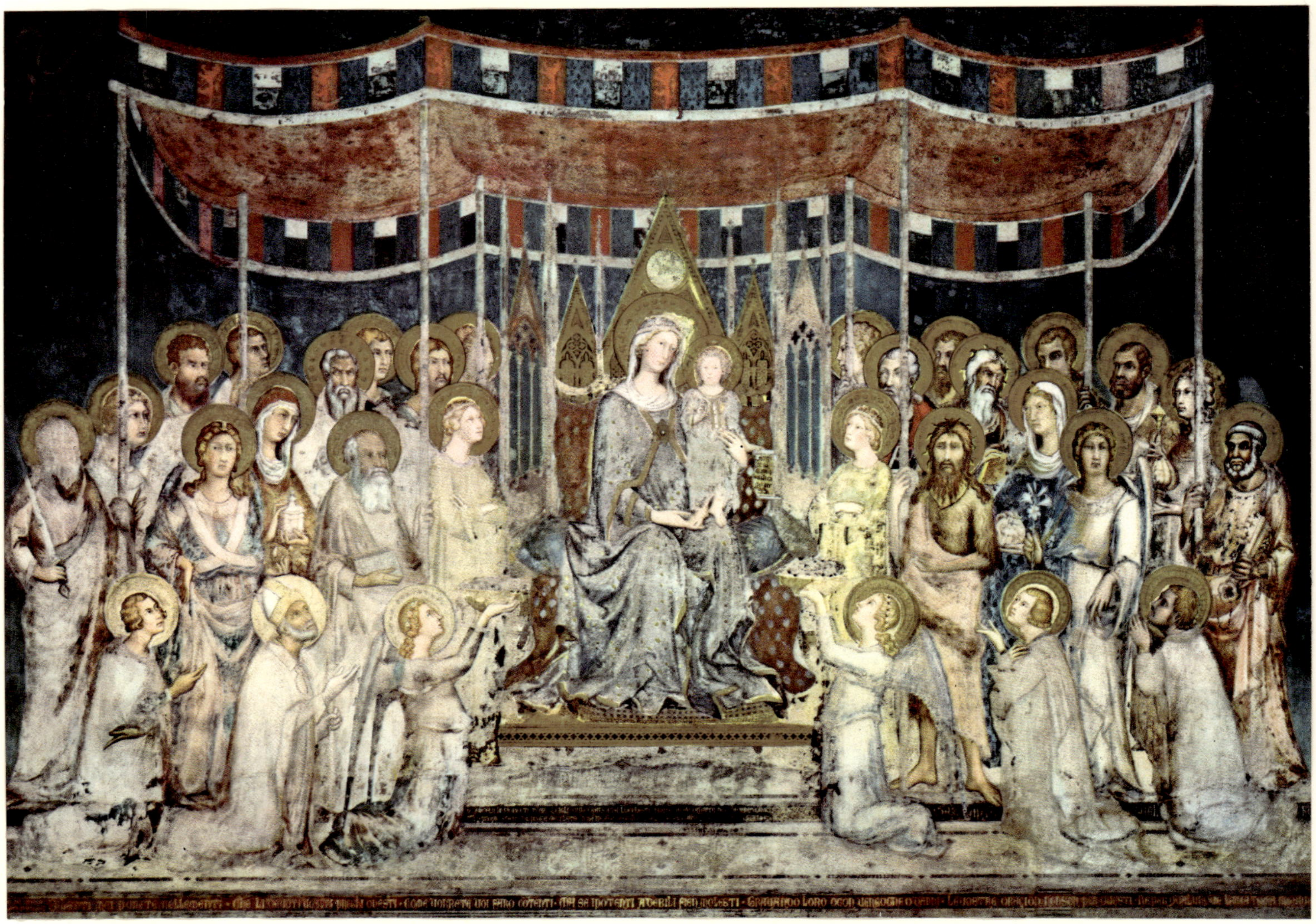

Simone Martini: Maestà. Town Hall, Siena

to breathe freely like celestial creatures in a world of infinite space nourished by a fresh narrative stream. This harmonious outline contains hidden volumes, like transparent, iridescent forms of the most delicate blown glass, while a soft, luminous colouring which ends by becoming pure light, surrounds and illuminates them. But the lyrical art of Simone Martini is not always the same. His mood changes, and while he never withdraws from the external world, he alters his tone from time to time according to his surroundings. Thus at Siena, as can be seen in the heavy forehead of the Virgin with the large crown, he was influenced by Giovanni Pisano, and he also translated the quivering vitality of Giovanni's figures into the swirling drapery and intense absorption of the angels who offer flowers and adoration to their Queen. At Assisi he studied the work Giotto had done there twenty years before. But throughout his work there is a constant reflection of his love of beauty and preoccupation with a sublime world above all the ugliness and reality of the human world.

After the Maestà there are very few works of Simone Martini which are known, or dates that are certain, as though time had spared only the most beautiful. In 1317 he is known to have gone to Naples where he was knighted by Robert of Anjou. This visit is recorded by a splendid picture, S. Louis being crowned by his brother Robert. It is a work whose external appearance is immensely rich, with the brilliant gold of the brocades standing out in the mitre and the crown, and the almost chiselled effect of the motifs in the background providing a frame for the two motionless

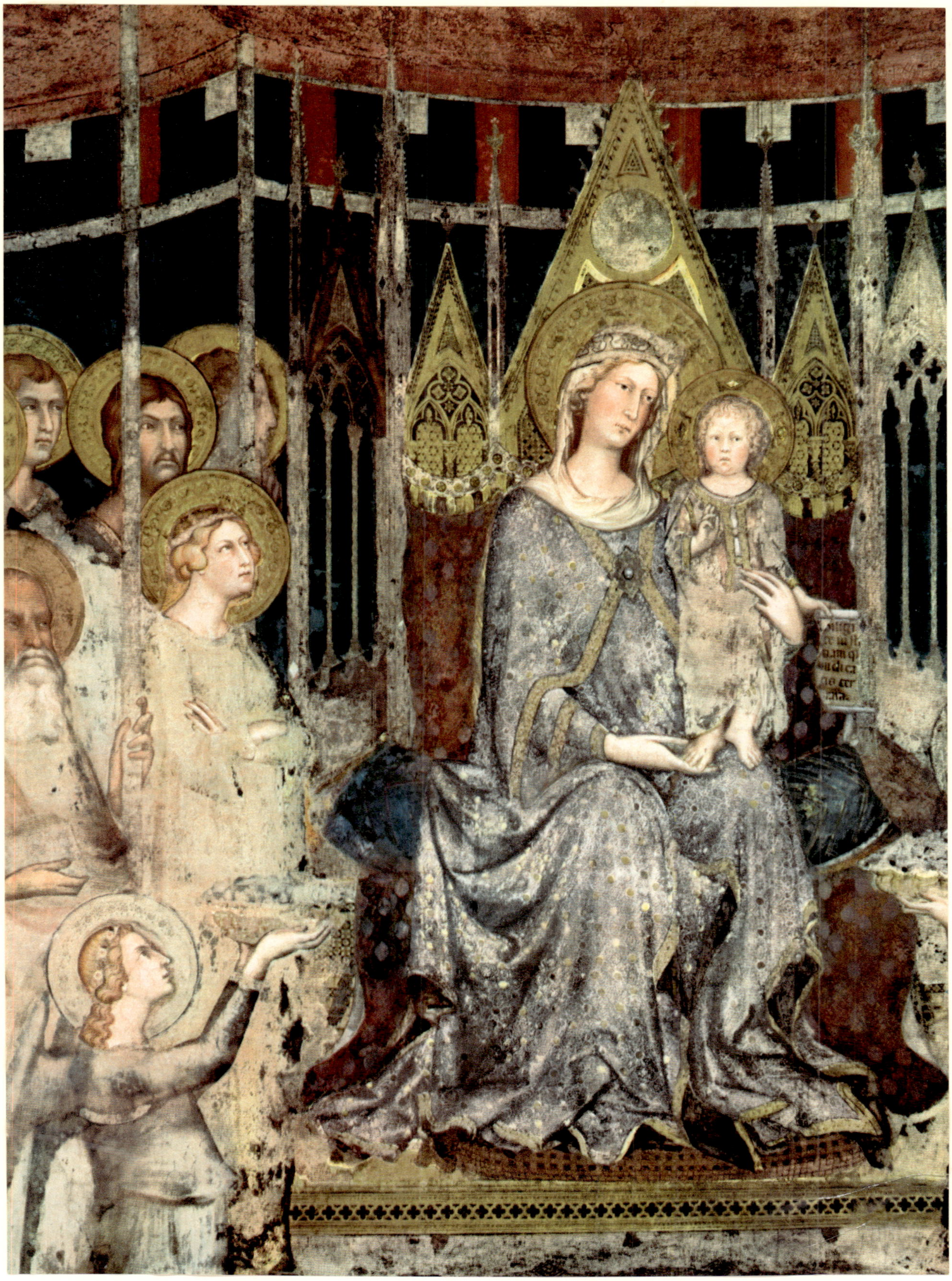

Simone Martini: Maestà, detail. Town Hall, Siena

visionary figures. Simone's poetical quality is diffused in a tone of pleasing and languid melancholy, balanced by the direct narrative liveliness in the little scenes on the predella.

About 1319 the artist was in Pisa, where he painted a great polyptych, with the Virgin and various saints, for the church of S. Catherine. Here he seems to return

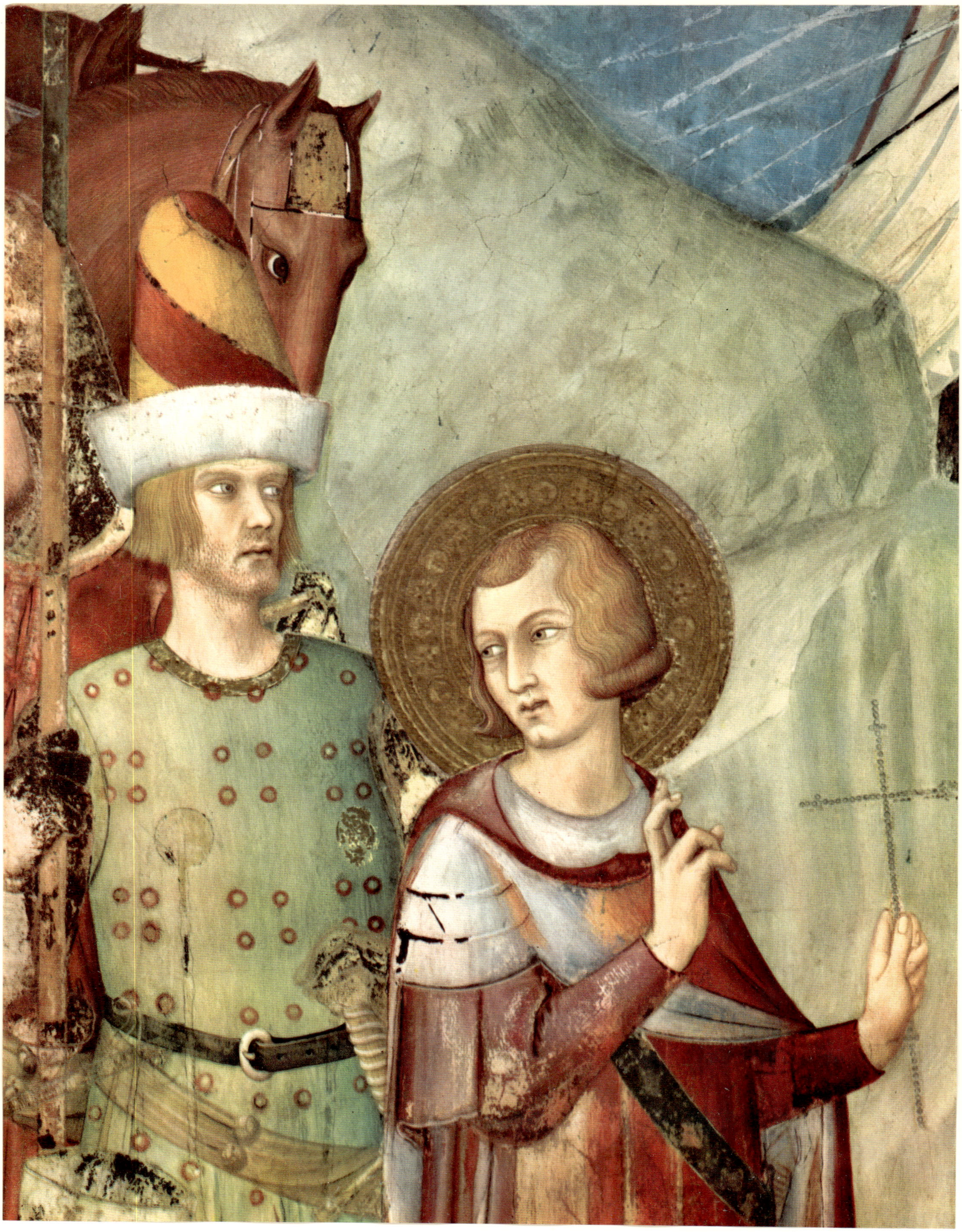

Simone Martini: S. Martin relinquishing his career as a soldier, detail.

S. Francis, Assisi.

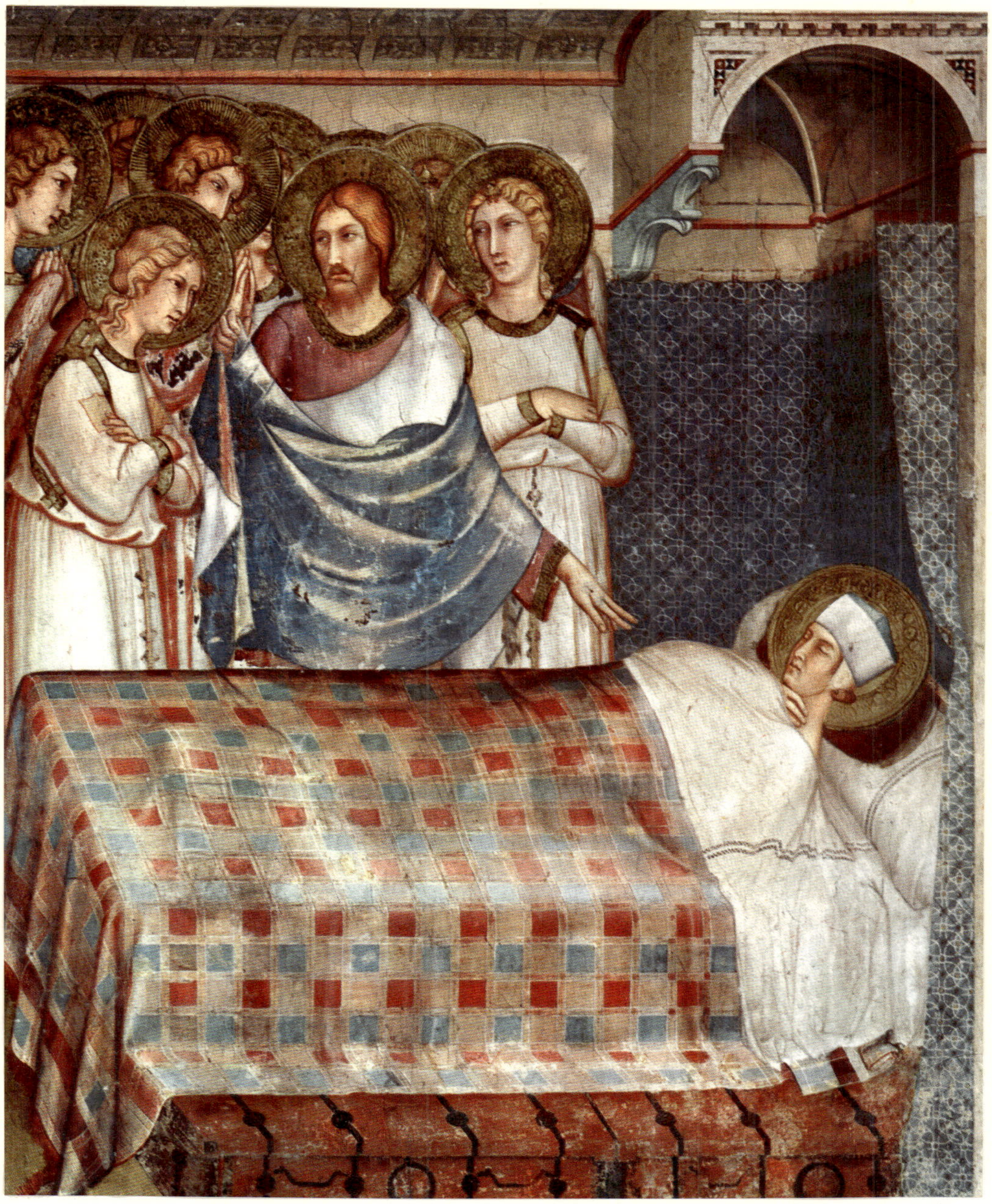

Simone Martini: The Dream of S. Martin. S. Francis, Assisi

to the style of thirteenth-century Sienese art, although he surpasses it with his warmth of expression and warm enamel-like colouring, composed of extremely pure tones and subtle passages.

In 1320 he began a work for the church of S. Domenico at Orvieto. Only five panels of this work remain in the Museo dell'Opera, although there are others in various places all over the world. The spatial arrangement of the figures is more balanced and the line more decided and sure, so that he may possibly have been swayed by the influence of Giotto's final period. Before he began his work at Assisi there is evidence of his current style, and of his daily contact with Giotto, in the polyptych of the Blessed Agostino Novello, in the church of S. Augustine at Siena. This large picture, composed of the hieratic figure of the Saint surrounded by small scenes with gay streets, courtyards, and the noisy squares of Siena, shows Simone to be a delightful narrative painter. But the musical development of line and colour, the idealised faces and graceful backgrounds transform this chronicle of city life into a lyric.

Simone's poetical style is now fully developed, and the legend of S. Martin, which he painted (probably between 1322-26) in the chapel founded by Cardinal

Gentile Partino di Montefiore in the lower church at Assisi, is quite spontaneous. Here, as in all his work, there is a strong yet sweet poetical treatment of nature, and an ingenuous, sympathetic observation of all aspects of creation. Detailed attention is paid both to the style and to the rich material of clothes and headdresses. Simone applied the same care to his rooms, architecture and furnishings, from the checked bedcover of the young, sleeping Martin to the strange musical instruments of the Imperial courtiers in their outlandish Eastern clothes. In every scene the colour is blended harmoniously, and follows the pure Gothic outlines and visionary appearance of the whole, from the silence above the angels surrounding Christ, the vision of the sleeping Saint, the thrust of the armed knight, the religious absorption of the bishop celebrating Mass, to the calm funeral service of the saint. It is not a genuinely narrative account, because the scenes are not connected with each other; it is rather a repetitive pattern of lines, planes and colours. The compositions are formed by lyrical cadences and harmonious rhymes; the figure of S. Martin, either as a blond young man or as a dignified bishop, moves from one scene to another, rapt in mystical ecstasies which transport him beyond the action. His investiture as a knight, and his relinquishing of his career, are chronologically the final scenes of this *chanson de geste*, and are among the happiest examples of Simone's art. His imagination has free play, and nostalgically relives the life of enchanted adventure in a world of chivalry which was now drawing to a close. Martin himself leaves this world when, armed only with a fragile, shining cross, he abandons the Imperial camp in favour of the hard reality of the rocks in the background. As he goes he casts a gentle look of farewell at the astonished Emperor, and the powerful contrast between the young exile and the splendour of the warriors who surround him is conveyed in the perfect balance of delicate greens, blues and pinks, which are now however fading into the background of the walls.

In this work we can see a foretaste of the impressive abstraction of Guidoriccio da Fogliano, which Simone painted in 1328 in the Mappamondo room at Siena, opposite his Maestà. This was commissioned by the Governor of Siena in honour of the leader who had won the battle of Montemassi and Sassoforte in that year and so preserved Sienese independence. Simone Martini has shown the tireless and determined progress of his knight, so rigidly posed as to seem almost lifeless, on a horse covered with the funereal black and golden cloth. He moves forward, hardly touching the clay-coloured earth, in a desert landscape, where there is no other figure to distract the eye from the obsessive movement of the horseman in the narrow space between the conquered castle and the deserted, terror-stricken little city, as he looms huge above the rigid stockade of the camp and above the repeated black and white emblems of the Republic.

The abstract decorative quality of Simone Martini's final period, which is forecast in the heraldic figure of Guidoriccio da Fogliano is seen at its best in the Annunciation painted in 1333 for the cathedral of Siena, and now in the Uffizi. Space exists only as a magnificent golden background, on which the outline, more harmonious than ever before, creates a magnificent arabesque which winds round the waving cloak of the angel, the flowing ribbons, the sinuous curves of the delicate Virgin, and the sharp thorn-like leaves of the lilies. Light takes control of Simone's line and transfers his images into a sublime empyrean where everything is shining: the rich materials, the dark blue of the timid Virgin, the bright flashes of strong red, the mother-of-pearl faces, the robe of the angel splashed with gold, the transparent, iridescent wings, the soft glow of the lilies and the way in which the olive branch melts into the gold. Everything flows into the lightest of rhythms which are complete in themselves. Life and reality become a mere breath, and everything grows light and intangible, seeming as though it might disappear at a glance like a miraculous vision. It is the final strophe of Simone's lyricism, towards which his art had been moving since the distant days of the Maestà.

No doubt the lost work at Avignon continued in this vein. Simone worked at Avignon between 1339 and 1344, having been summoned by Benedict XII to decorate the Papal Palace and the Cathedral. Nothing remains of this visit except a few badly damaged wall-paintings in the church of Notre Dame at Avignon, and the record of his friendship with Petrarch, for whom he painted the wonderful page of Virgil now in the Ambrosian Library at Milan. Ample in design, whith light colouring, the figures, the actions and surroundings are Gothic, and even the most delicate objects are carried out with a depth and penetration similar to that achieved much later by the Flemish painters.

Simone may have painted a polyptych at Avignon with scenes of the Passion, now divided into a few surviving fragments among the Museums of Berlin, Paris and Antwerp. In these the very brilliant Gothic colouring is skilfully used in the modelling, and the dramatic feeling is kept within bounds by the small size of the work as a whole.

As we have said, Simone and Petrarch met at Avignon, and each found in the

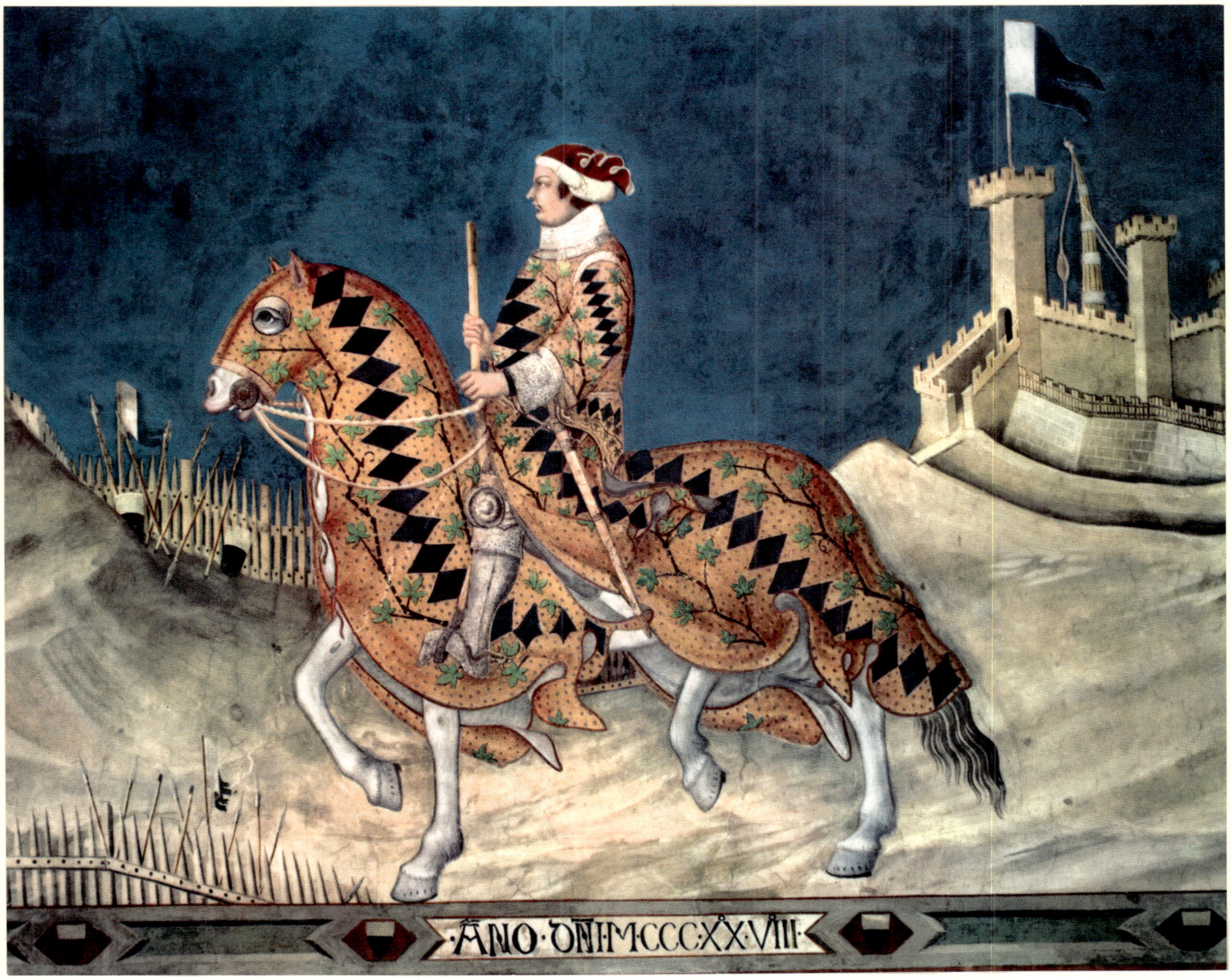

Simone Martini: Guidoriccio da Fogliano. Town Hall, Siena

other a congenial spirit, as Dante and Giotto had done. Better than anyone else Petrarch understood that the pure, direct beauty which filtered through Simone's glittering, sparkling art was the most intimate and also the most powerful element of his work. Simone brought to France an enriched version of the elegant linear Gothic style which he had acquired in his youth, and he thus initiated in western painting a movement towards graceful elegance which, combined with a sympathetic observation of reality, became pure poetry.

Artists in France, Catalonia, Bohemia and Flanders all owe a debt to Simone, for he was the real inventor of Flamboyant Gothic, the style which carried his rich, decorative and chivalrous spirit all over Western Europe at the end of the fourteenth and beginning of the fifteenth centuries.

The period that saw Simone Martini's influence spreading in Italy, and the countries north of the Alps, also saw the development of the style of Pietro and Ambrogio Lorenzetti. It is probable that, like Simone, they both began as followers of Duccio. But soon they broke away, especially Ambrogio, and developed styles that were wholly different both from Duccio and from each other. Later, as they both sought that ideal beauty which fulfilled the religious concepts of their age and their society, the distance between them diminished. Of the chronology of their lives very little is known, and very few dated works exist on which an accurate appraisal of their development can be made. Both may have died during the plague

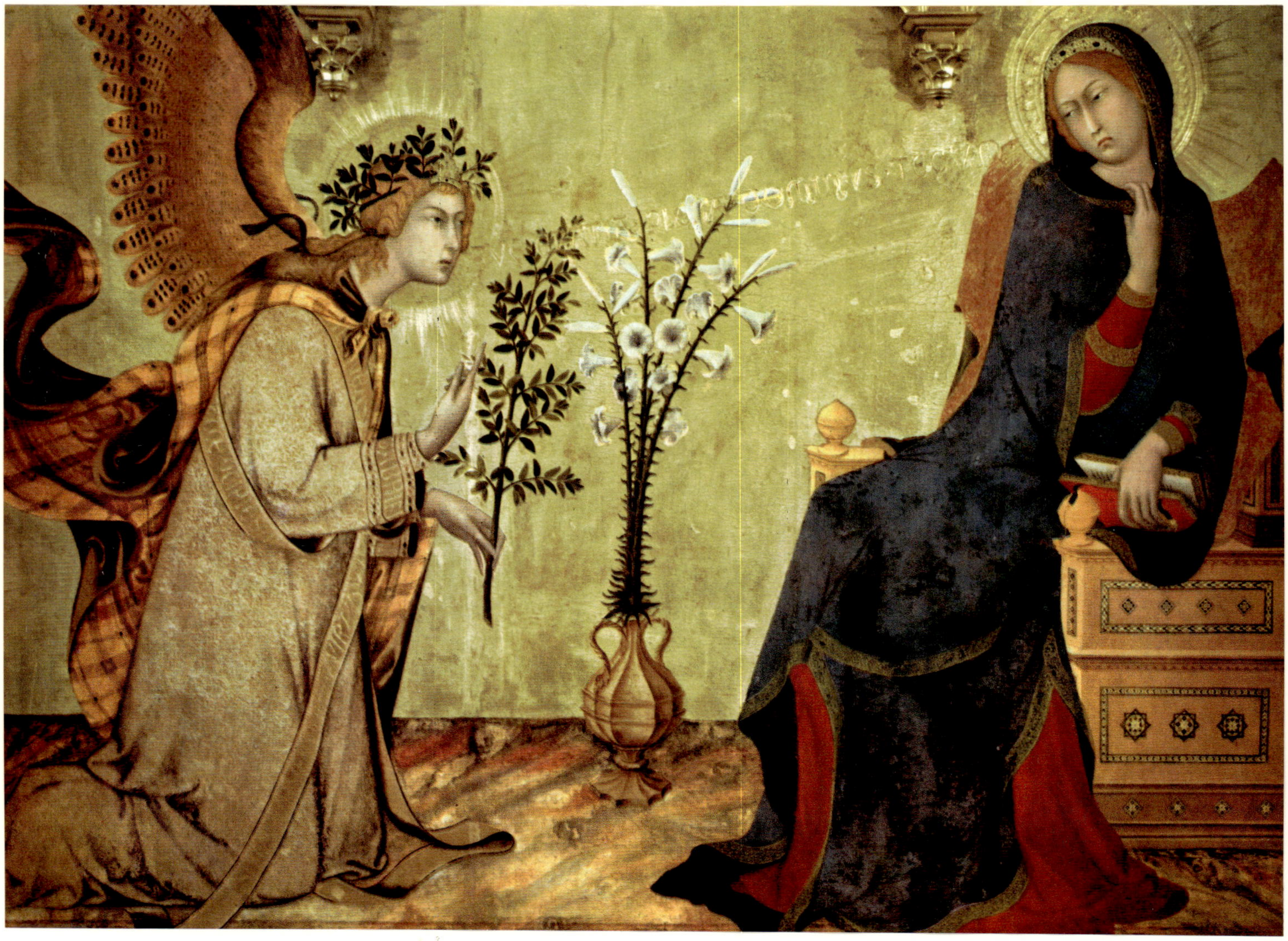

Simone Martini: The Annunciation. Uffizi, Florence

of 1348, because nothing is known of them after it.

Pietro, the elder, was probably born about 1280. In his youth he was influenced by Giotto, and his early polyptych of Blessed Humility, now in the Uffizi, shows this influence strongly. Composed of a few primary colours such as are to be found in Giotto's severest manner, it has a sculptural quality. Even in Siena Pietro neglected the brilliant world of Simone Martini and preferred to follow the old pupils of Duccio, in mourning for the recent death of their leader. At the same time he felt an increasing interest in Florentine art, particularly the simplicity and complete lack of all those decorative trifles which had now become part of Sienese art. He developed a simultaneous appreciation of Giotto's work and of the sculpture of Giovanni Pisano, then working on the cathedral of Siena. Pietro's study of this remarkable sculptor (second only to Donatello) who had the same passionate emotional intensity and the same love of restless humanity as he had himself, is perhaps the most powerful element in his art up to the time of his first dated work, the polyptych in the parish church of Arezzo, painted in 1320 for the Bishop, Guido Tarlati. Pietro's debt to Giotto is evident in the general framework, the strong chiaroscuro, and the quality of immediacy which this picture possesses. But the vibrant spirit of Giovanni Pisano lives again in the passionate, silent exchange of looks between the Mother and Son. The intensity of this exchange is so powerful that for a moment one forgets the great decorative richness of the Virgin's robes. This is Pietro's most memorable work and certainly the art of the great sculptor was present in his bold and concentrated modelling. The brilliant, luxurious colouring is denser, and the matter becomes almost plastic, with the result that the form is taut and strong. The outline is not composed of musical cadences as in Simone, but develops in broad sweeps, sharp breaks and incisive contours. From now on there develops in his art " a spiritual tension, a feeling of aloof severity, a foreboding of drama, all contained in an astonishing atmosphere of rich colouring ". Drama has been suspended in the enthroned Madonna in the Cortona Museum, where the intensity of feeling gives way to the gentle exchange of looks and the maternal gesture, which becomes a caress of the chubby Baby. The other Virgin with S. Francis and S. John on the wall of the lower church at Assisi is equally plastic, with a strong form, firm outlines, and intense colours harmoniously blended. His style is finally and clearly seen in the frescoes of the Passion: the Crucifixion, the Deposition, the Burial, Christ in Hell, and the Resurrection, painted probably between 1326 and 1329, in the lower church at Assisi. The culmination is perhaps to be found in the Deposition, where the strong, almost dark, colouring, composed of a few shades, emphasises the whole composition, unforgettable for the feeling of abandonment in the body of Christ, which is being carried by the mourners who are grouped round it in unrestrained grief. The diagonal line of the emaciated body, which seems to have almost no weight, is the centre of all the figures who form a rhythmical pattern of emotion, rather like an airy pyramid. The hands are very light, and very slightly opened. The only strident note of sorrow is in the powerful taut figure of the Magdalene at the foot of the Cross, and in the silent kiss of the Virgin on the motionless face of her Son. Space lives and breathes only in the diagonal line of the figure of Christ, and the stiff Cross broken by the archway. The remaining frescoes, which complete the Life of Christ, were painted by his pupils after the master had left Assisi. The pupils were wholly absorbed in a fantastic world of ornament and colour, emphasising details of actions and expressions and unconsciously anticipating the detailed style of the future miniaturists of the Books of Hours belonging to the French nobility.

It seems likely that at a later date Pietro changed back to the calm style of Giotto, and also renewed his contacts with Ambrogio, two factors which help to account for the broad, monumental style of his last works. One of these is the great Nativity of

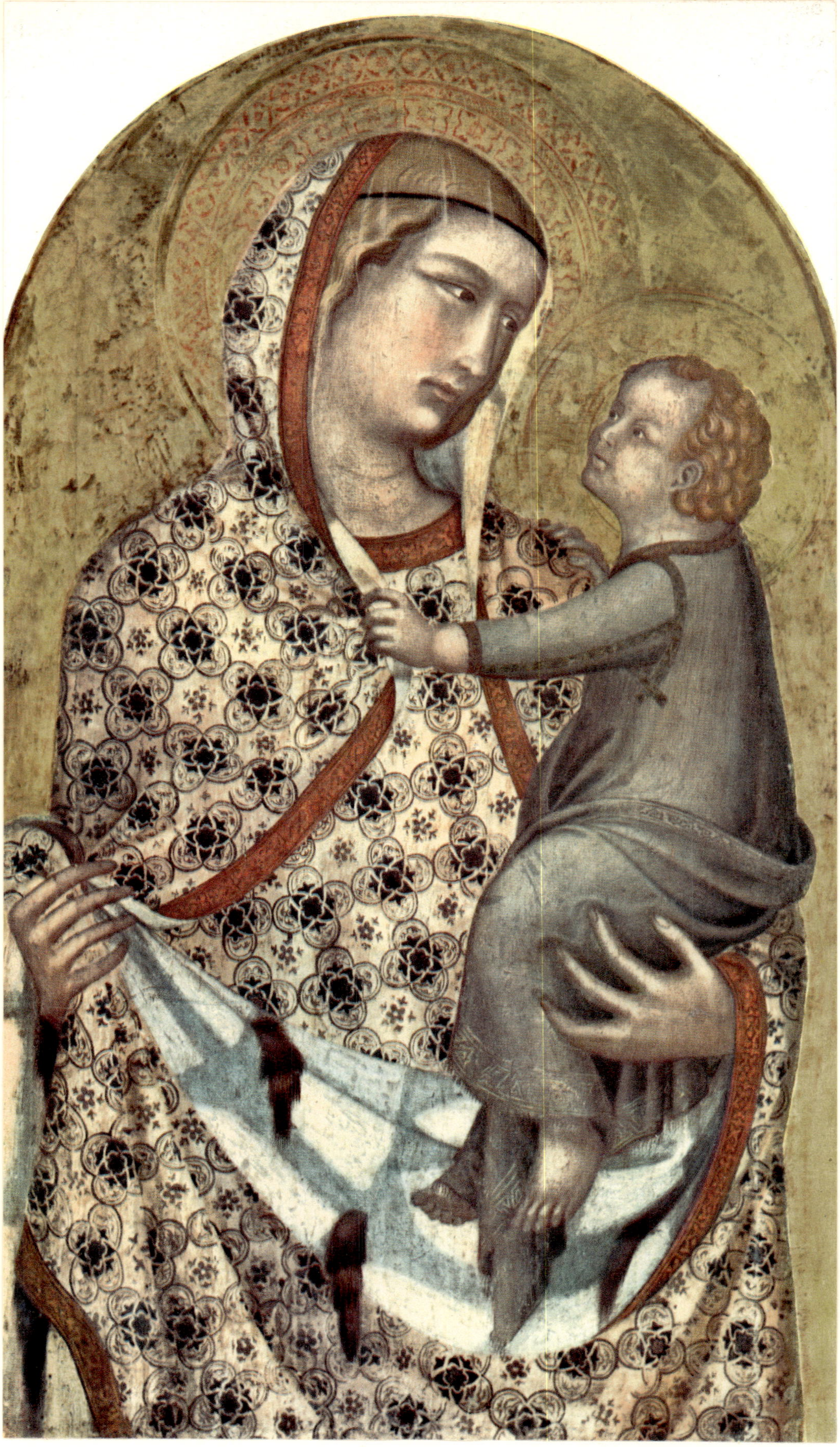

Pietro Lorenzetti: Polyptych, detail. S. Maria della Pieve, Arezzo

the Virgin, dated 1342, in the Opera del Duomo Museum at Siena, which resembles the contemporary Presentation at the Temple by Ambrogio, now in the Uffizi. The figures, placed against a landscape, have calm proportions and monumental poses which recall the severe style of Arnolfo although " they are really between Giotto and Piero della Francesca ".

As well as the passionate dramatic element in his art, and his forthright manner, Ambrogio Lorenzetti has a subtle lyricism which reveals a learned and sophisticated personality. The course of his development is an enigma. Possibly, instead of following Duccio and Giovanni Pisano, he clung to the older, more intricate Florentine traditions, both Byzantine and Romanesque, of the Master of the Magdalene, Arnolfo and the mosaicists of the Baptistery. He certainly had a very clear appreciation of Giotto's style, particularly in his detailed plastic modelling, which resembled Giotto's powerful style to begin with but was later transformed into something softer and more naturalistic, which gave a strong luminous quality to his figures, and made them very beautiful in the wholly Giottesque synthesis of gestures, expression and surroundings.

His first dated work, the Madonna of Vico l'Abate of 1319, is so hieratically solemn and remote from reality that it recalls the most exalted and difficult styles of an earlier age. There is no trace of Duccio or Simone Martini in Ambrogio's work, but the still, frontal position recalls very vividly a distant memory of the stiffness of Romanesque. The light modelling and rich colouring suggest an eastern ancestry, and give some feeling

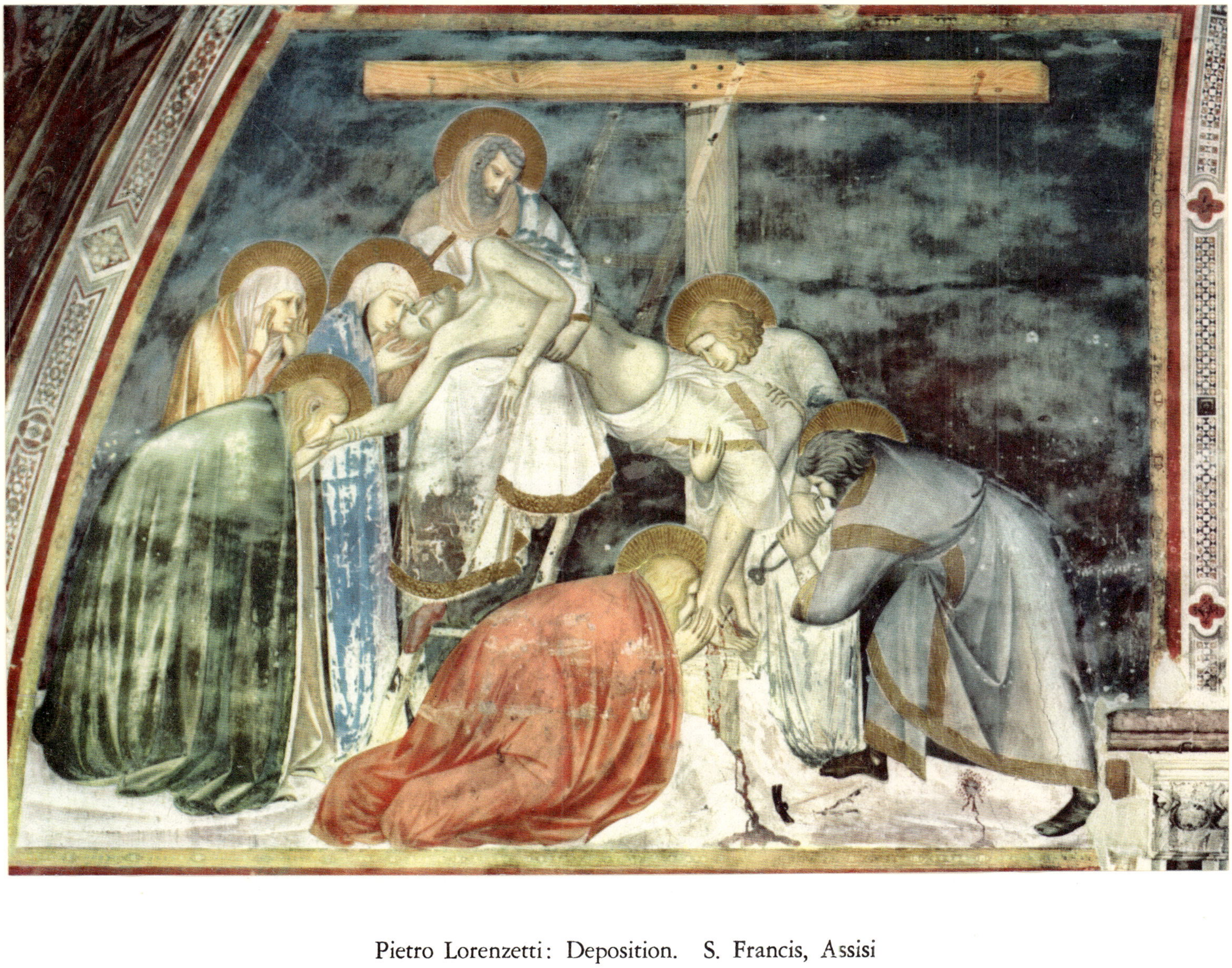

Pietro Lorenzetti: Deposition. S. Francis, Assisi

of life to the still statuesque figure. The artist was probably still at Florence in 1321, and returned home shortly afterwards to plunge into a study of Sienese art, no doubt paying particular attention to the immediate predecessors of Duccio and Simone. He carried out a series of wall-paintings in the church of S. Francis, but these have nearly all disappeared. In the surviving fragments his art is seen to have greater breadth, with a note of calm contemplation, a lyrical vision of the world, a slow, endless rhythm and warm, very natural colouring. This free play of the imagination was to remain characteristic of his poetical world, and the predominant motif in his art, although he paid another visit to Florence from 1332 to 1334 and renewed his contacts with Giotto, Maso, Stefano and other members of Giotto's school. Indeed the result of this meeting may have had reciprocal effects, as distant perspective and strong colouring, which are still visible in the legend of S. Nicholas which was painted during these years, was to find a sympathetic echo in the works of those early followers of Giotto, while the taste for moderation in the gestures and the plasticity of the Lorenzetti is Florentine. Meanwhile Ambrogio had become famous through commissions given to him by the Republic of Siena, and in 1337 and 1339 he painted the frescoes of Good and Bad Government in the Sala dei Nove in the Palazzo Pubblico. The representations of Bad Government and its consequences have almost disappeared, but the two great murals of Good Government have survived. Their didactic purpose placed them in great danger of dullness and dogmatism, but Ambrogio's talent overcame any such dangers, and even in the allegorical sections he avoided an abstract, pedagogic tone. He was particularly successful in the lively, direct, poetical portrayal of town and country life in a small, peaceful state, shown as a fanciful map of the surroundings of Siena, with its rolling countryside and its hills, or the closely packed towers, houses and doorways of the cities. In this work Ambrogio salutes his own world, his city and the Sienese landscape. He accepts his native land as it is, with both beauty and ugliness: and the whole scene is imbued with the poetry of his own soul. The barren countryside of Siena turns into a well-cared-for garden, dotted with houses and trees. The dark, turretted city is transformed into a collection of dream palaces with battlements and mullioned windows, bright colours and light refracted from many-sided buildings. With the same intimate feeling of familiarity and affection, he describes the townsfolk of Siena, or the peasants, busy with their endless work and simple amusements, with a charming taste for rich colouring and gay images. The landscape also plays an important part, and with it the spirited variety of its inhabitants, lovely children dancing, builders at work, a lady on horseback, gamblers at the inn, the schoolmaster in the balcony, and above all the fascinating spirit of the artist himself. But the most powerful and intimate expression of Ambrogio's feelings is revealed in his panel paintings, for example in the polyptych of S. Dorothy in the Pinacoteca at Siena, especially in the gentle blond figure of the Saint who is holding a bunch of delicate, many-coloured flowers on her lap which is a pale, and yet warm violet shade. Absorbed in ecstasy, she is offering the flowers to the Divine Child. Another example is in the wonderful series of his Madonnas, where, in the painting belonging to the Seminary at Siena, the motif of a silent exchange of glances, so dear to Pietro, becomes a tender embrace which unites the Virgin and Child so closely that they seem as one. There is a visionary sweetness in the small Maestà in the Pinacoteca at Siena, and a gentle kiss in the Maestà of Massa Marittima. In this work, possibly in 1330, Ambrogio renewed the theme of the choir of Saints surrounding the Virgin, and with a wonderful manifestation of spiritual and physical beauty he created an impression of depth at the sides of the throne. He gave life to the composition of angels and the three theological Virtues in a harmony of exquisite and sometimes evanescent colours; the white robe of Charity, for example, at times seems to melt into the whiteness of the marble steps.

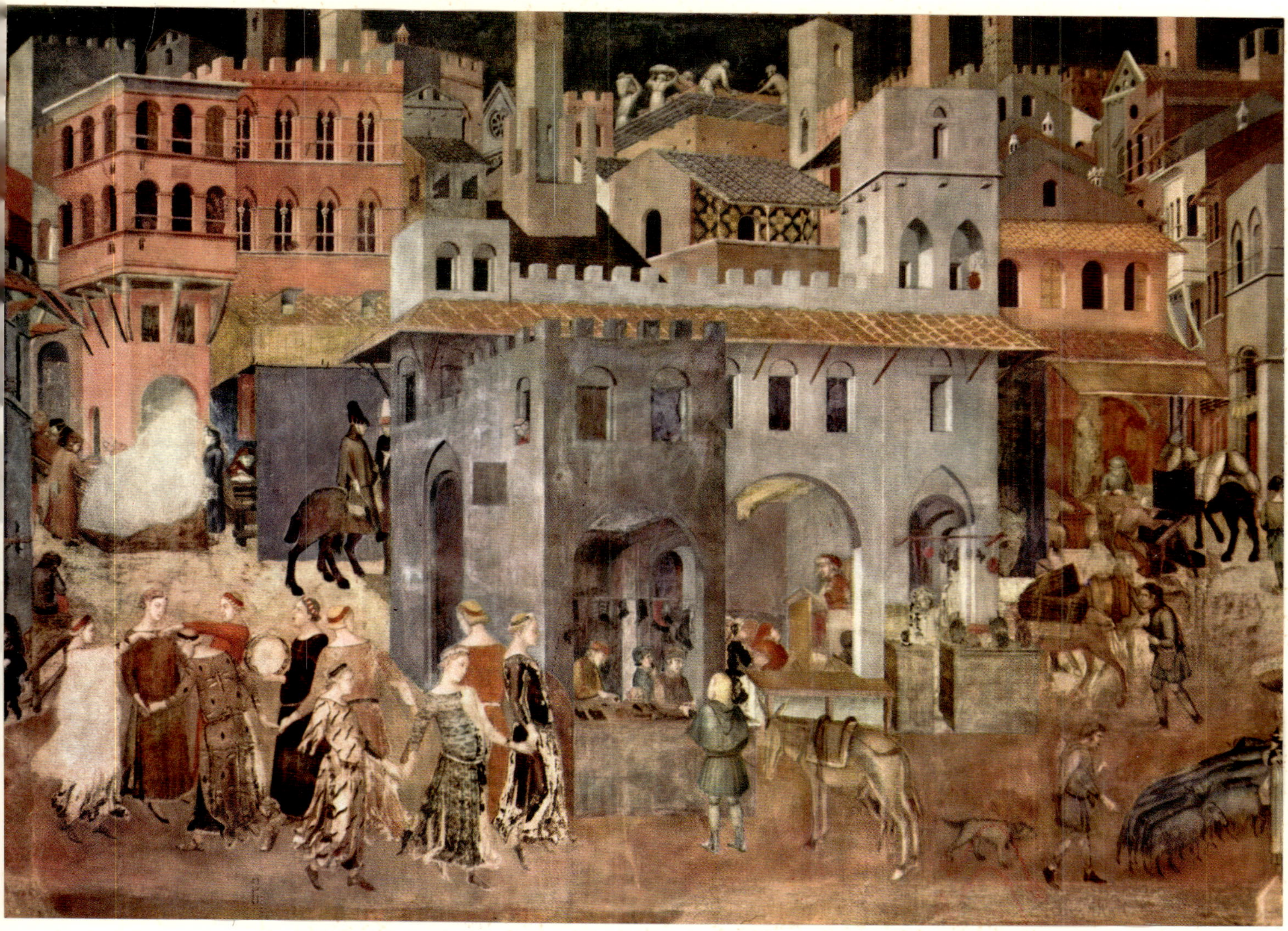

Ambrogio Lorenzetti: The Results of Good Government, detail. Town Hall, Siena

In the expanse of gold, in the clear colours, in the ornamentation of the saints who create a world of deep feeling round the ecstatic absorption of the Virgin, lost in the kiss which she is planting on the chubby face of the Child, Ambrogio's nervous yet controlled rhythm prevails and his vibrant vision of space carries us a long way from the calm ecstasies of Duccio and the sumptuous, regal elegance of Simone Martini. This same vision appears in his last works, such as the Presentation at the Temple, now in the Uffizi, where a new and direct contact with Pietro inspired a deeper spiritual feeling, almost a feeling of uneasines, which gives a hint of dramatic feeling to the calm serenity of his figures.

The sudden and unexpected deaths of Pietro and Ambrogio Lorenzetti brought to an end the most brilliant period of Sienese art, inaugurated a few years earlier by Duccio. Their many pupils had little if anything new to say, and were almost all fascinated by the arabesques of Simone Martini and the intensity of feeling in the Lorenzetti, developing their respective styles in an increasingly " Gothic " manner, with intricate decoration. Very occasionally a lively popular tone appeared to impart a new flash of life.

Among the delicate repetitions of Andrea Vanni, Luca di Tommè, Taddeo di Bartolo and others who fill in the period until the end of the fifteenth century, a special place is occupied by Barna, who painted the scenes from the Old and New Testaments

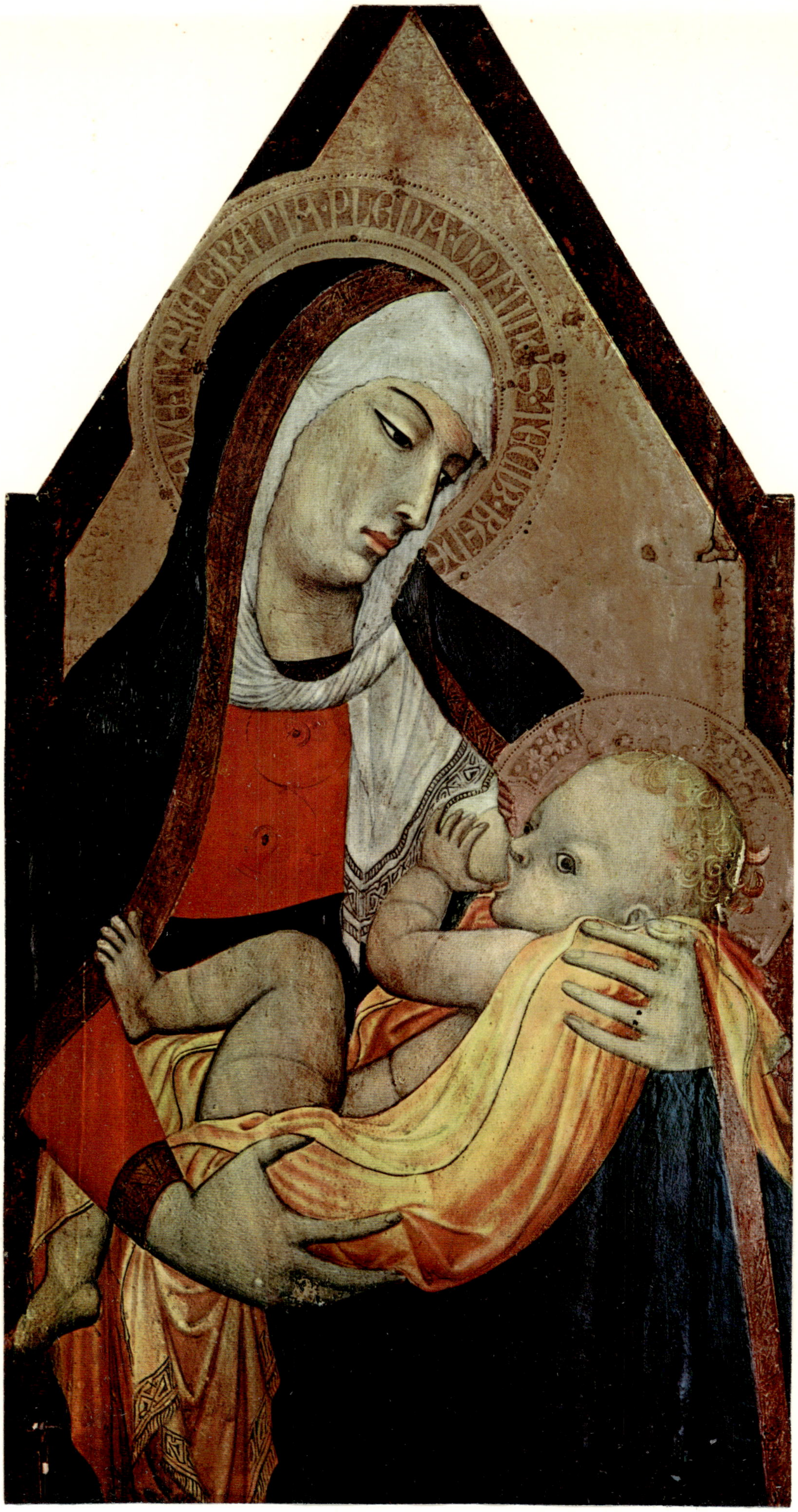

Ambrogio Lorenzetti: Madonna. Seminary of S. Francis, Siena

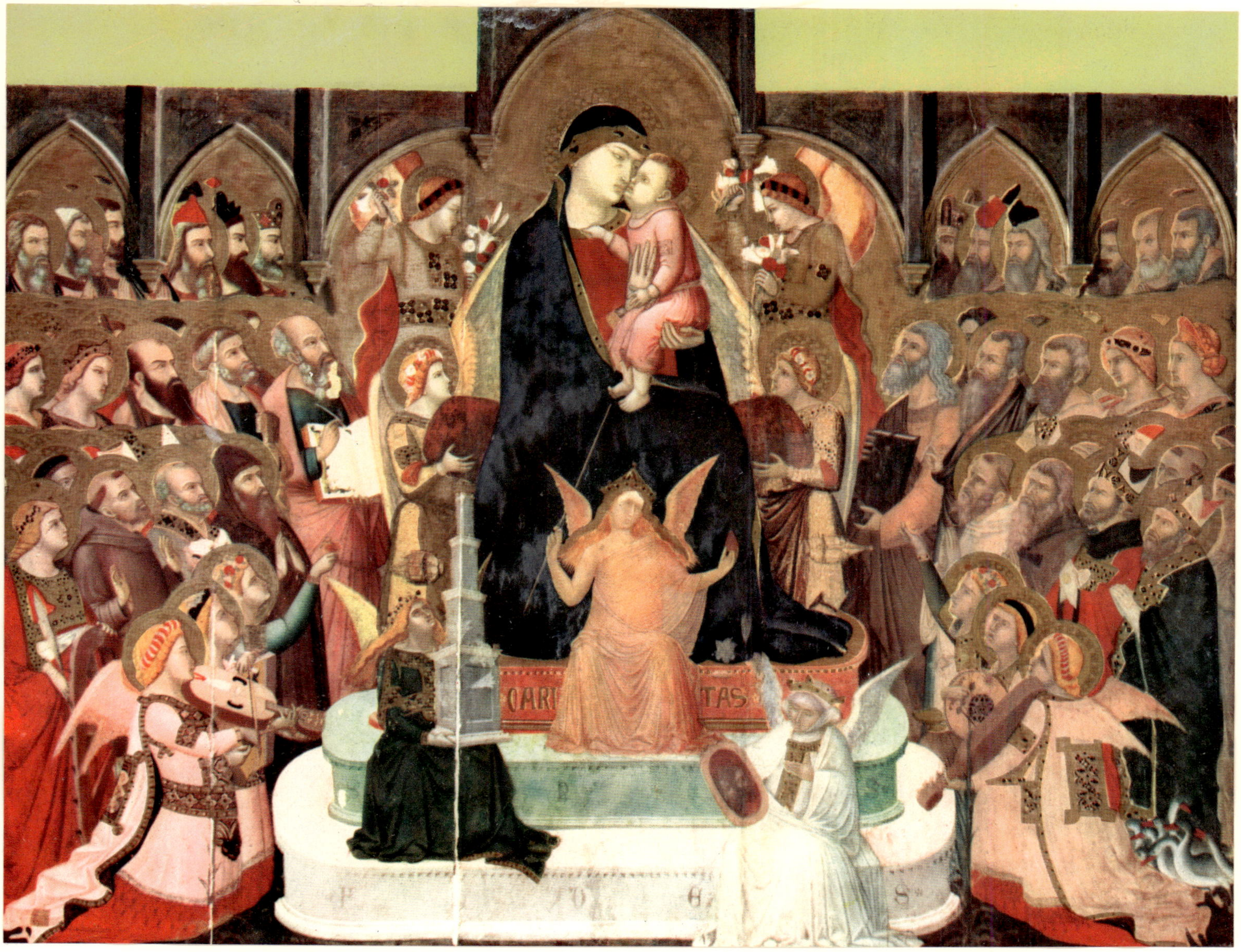

Ambrogio Lorenzetti: Maestà. Pinacoteca, Massa Marittima

in the Collegiata of S. Gimignano. The artist is unaffected by the work of the Lorenzetti, and shows himself to be a follower of Simone Martini, but although he composed his Passion of Christ rather in the manner of Duccio, he did not really belong to any school, and projected the horrifying tragedy which culminated in Golgotha on the faces of his characters in his own way. From the Betrayal to the Last Supper and the Road to Calvary, he painted a succession of sacred scenes full of colour and movement, crude and popular like the plays performed in country districts on the Feast Days of the Church.

After the death of Giotto a great variety of painters, problems and styles sprang up in Florence. The great artist had left a prodigious legacy, a world in which the mind and the imagination were renewed. He created the movement which marked the end of the Middle Ages and the beginning of the Modern World, a movement illustrated alike by a continuous improvement in the material things of life and a relaxing of moral constraints. Giotto, like Dante, belonged to the medieval world, with its rigid moral standards. His successors spoke a different, easier language, and they adopted only the simplest, most superficial and obvious elements in his style. Very few of them really understood him; certainly his contemporaries, such as the " Master of S. Cecilia ", who, with the subtle skill of a miniaturist translated his dramatic vision into a pleasing, almost gay narrative style, did not do so. Nor did Pacino di Buonaguida, a simple narrator who shows at times a childish ingenuousness. Nor did his followers of the first generation, whose names have been handed down by his earliest biographers, such as Filippo Villani, Ghiberti and Vasari: Buonamico Buffalmacco, Puccio Capanna, Pace da Faenza, Taddeo Gaddi and Bernardo Daddi.

Taddeo Gaddi (d. 1366) is the most famous and faithful disciple of Giotto, in whose studio he worked for 24 years. He is known through a number of panel paintings, but especially the scenes of the Virgin which he painted on the walls of S. Croce in Florence, in the Baroncelli chapel, between 1332 and 1338. His compositions are in the style of Giotto, but larger, more complicated and more decorative and obviously pleasing; he became a bourgeois narrative painter who translated the dramatic and exalted poetry of Giotto into prose. Occasionally, and especially in his panel-paintings, he reveals a contact with Sienese art in a warm, well-blended colouring which is combined with forms in the style of Giotto.

Personally, I would regard Bernardo Daddi (d. 1348) as more important. Although he was an inferior artist, he remained faithful to the solemn dramatic style of Giotto. His work can be seen on the walls of the Pulci Berardi chapel in S. Croce, where he painted, probably shortly after 1320, scenes of S. Lawrence and S. Stephen. The influence of Giotto's frescoes at Padua is obvious, but Daddi's gift for expression is much weaker, and Giotto's spatial depth becomes a vague atmosphere, where elaborate and fragile buildings form a background for elegant figures composed with a harmonious rhythm and touched with light, almost transparent, colours. Later Daddi fell under the influence of Sienese painting, particularly that of Ambrogio Lorenzetti, and he loosened the compactness of Giotto's compositions into something more delicate. In his later works Sienese gold is placed wherever possible as a background for exquisite Madonnas, and saints with flesh tints of mother-of-pearl, in materials and furnishings and backgrounds, which create the unforgettable brilliance of the altarpieces in Orsanmichele, S. Pancrazio and the Bigallo.

A group of anonymous artists at Assisi interpreted Giotto in a different, specialised manner, trying to keep strictly to his style. The " Master of the Magdalene Chapel " painted scenes of the Saint in the lower church, probably between 1314 and 1320, and developed the composition of the frescoes at Padua, making the figures softer and giving less importance to the part played by the landscape in the action. The painter of the scenes of S. Nicholas, and the painter (if they are not the same person) of the scenes of S. Francis have a dramatic intensity and at the same time a controlled depth of feeling.

The last and most famous artist of all is the " Master of the *Vele* ", who painted the vault of the crossing of the nave and transept, immediately above the tomb of the Saint. These allegories of the Franciscan virtues were long believed to be the work of Giotto himself, as were the scenes from the Childhood of Christ in the vault of the transept. But the rather stiff effect of the pictures contrasts with the lively directness of Giotto, and the thin, flat pictorial form differs greatly from his plastic style. The anonymous master substituted formal values — possibly through Sienese influence — and created a harmonious sequence of colours in delicate, iridescent tones against a shining golden background. His rich invention of new and pleasing figures in bright colours is seen particularly well in the scenes of Christ.

But above all it is Stefano, " Nature's ape ", and Maso, " the most delicate of them all ", who are praised by the original biographers. Together with Giottino they belong to the next generation, and constitute one of the most complicated and intricate problems in art criticism, and in our understanding of Giotto's influence.

Stefano was for a long time believed to be a mythical name like those of Puccio

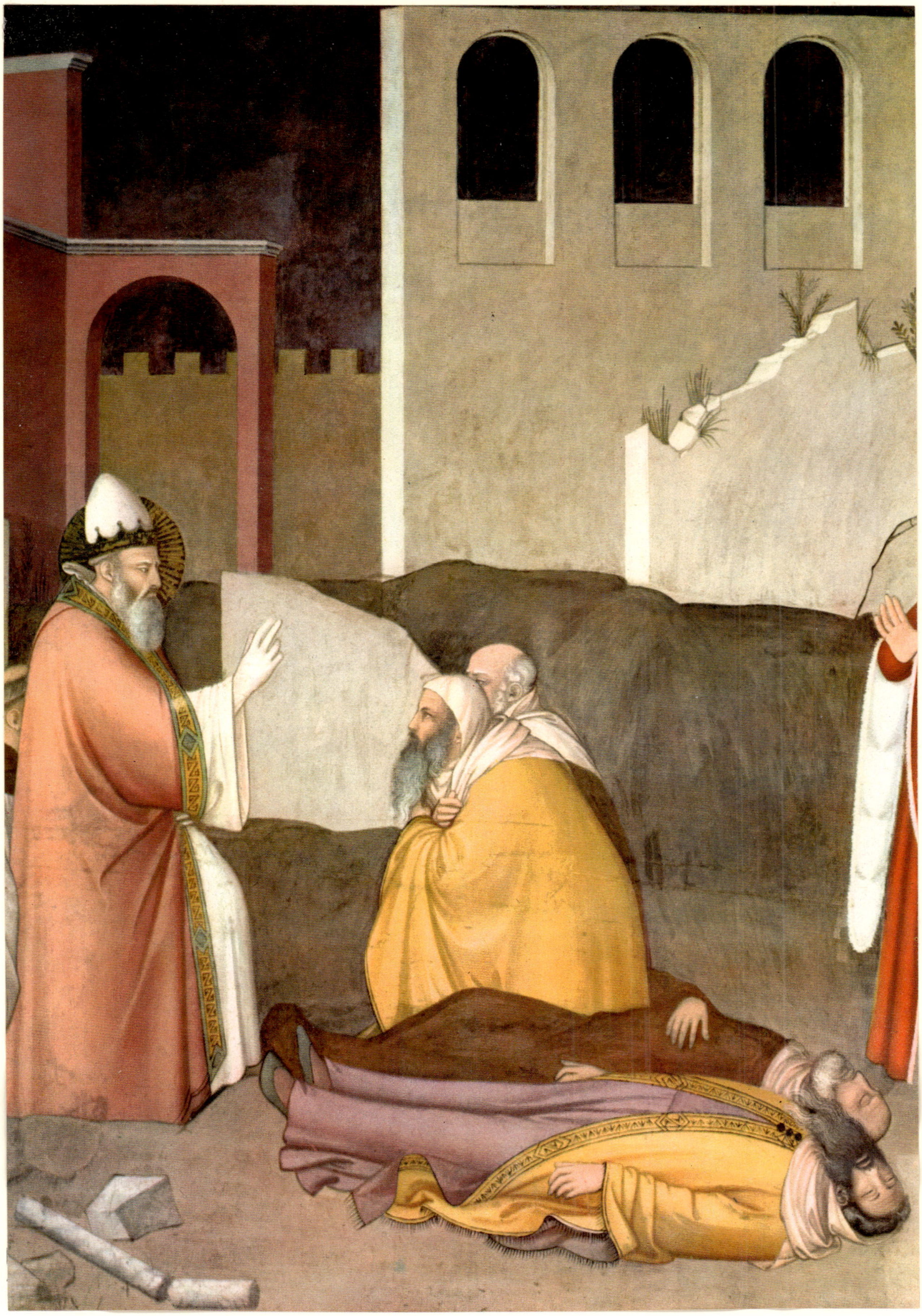

Maso di Banco: A Miracle of S. Sylvester, detail. S. Croce, Florence

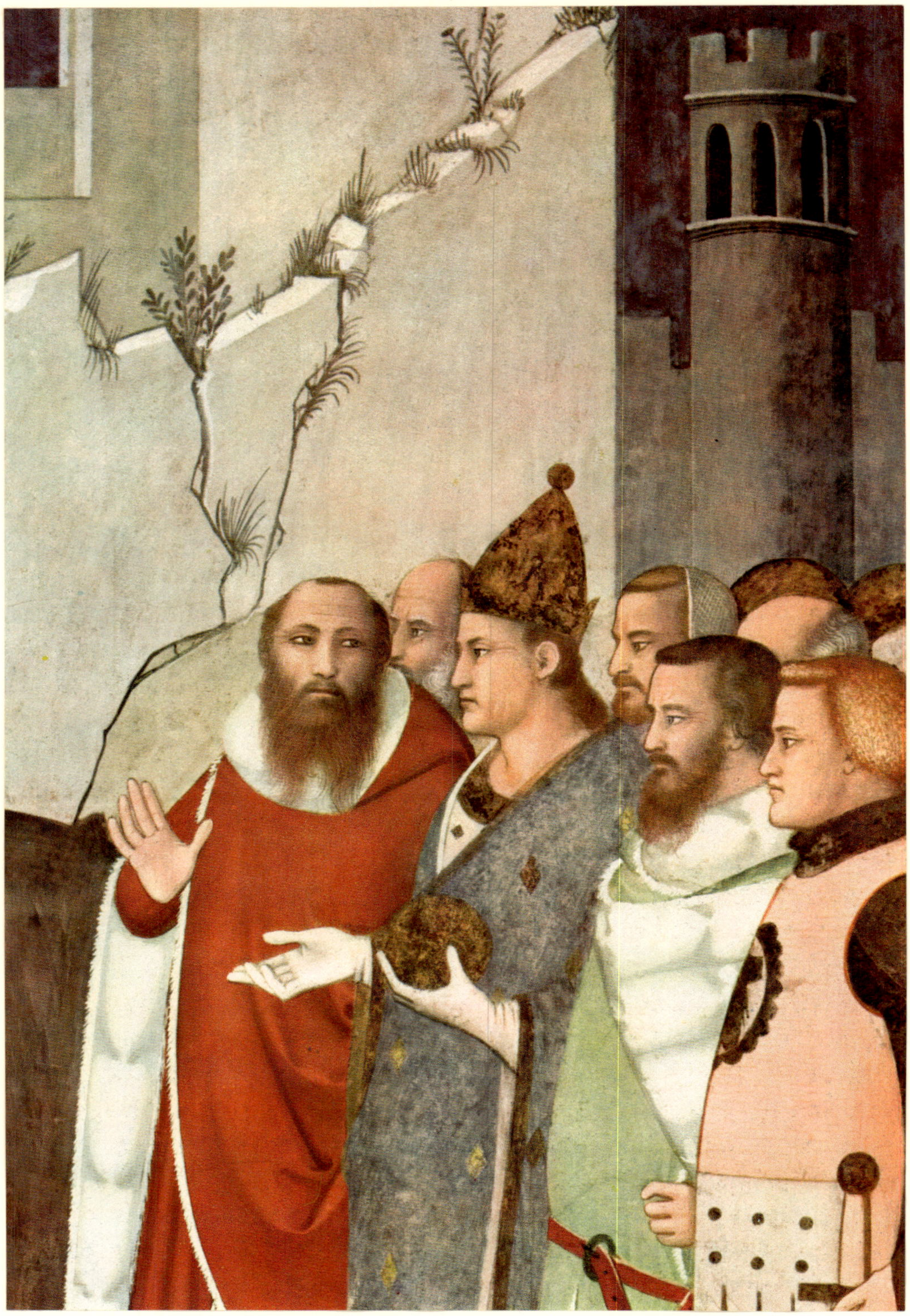

Maso di Banco: A Miracle of S. Sylvester, detail. S. Croce, Florence

Capanna and Buffalmacco; Maso and Giottino, as the result of a mistake by Vasari, were long considered to be the same person, known as " Maso ", who worked at Florence and at Assisi sometimes in a plastic and monumental style, and at others yielded to the attraction of bright colours, finally adopting a soft, loose style of modelling and colouring, mingling pale tones and delicate line work. Recently a number of distinguished art critics have attempted to unravel the problem, and have thrown some light on the names and work of the three painters, building up three separate and distinct personalities. They were certainly the most distinguished followers of Giotto, but they interpreted his work with great freedom of spirit and style, each one following his own ideas and inclinations, based on the models which Giotto had established.

Maso di Banco is perhaps the most important of them all. He breaks up Giotto's synthesis in his compositions in order to envelop his figures and landscapes in a continual and subtly sensual colour vibration. From the evidence it would seem that Maso was already working in 1340, and from time to time information is available about him until 1350, which may have been the year of his death. Some frescoes in a very bad state of preservation in the squinches of some windows in Castel Nuovo would seem to indicate that he probably followed Giotto to Naples. Very likely he was completing work by Giotto. This visit which was, as we shall see, of great importance in the history of Neapolitan painting, also constituted a new and helpful experience for Maso. Certainly the visit to Naples, and the halt at Rome which followed, enabled him to study classical and paleo-Christian painting closely and at length. In the same way a supposed stay at Milan, accompanying Giotto again, would explain why his taste in colour belongs so clearly to the Po valley and not to Florence. About 1340 Maso painted the scenes of S. Sylvester in the Bardi di Vernio chapel in S. Croce, which in themselves would prove his greatness. He certainly sought inspiration from Giotto's latest frescoes which, with all their grave beauty and spatial amplitude, were close beside him. His design is noble and classical, and while it lacks the dramatic quality of Giotto's thought and gesture, it is more solemn and imposing. Here for the first time we can see an example of the feeling which was to burst forth a century later on the walls of S. Francis at Arezzo, for this is the first breath of that adoration which Piero della Francesca was to embody in his wonderful paintings there. Maso's dignified characters seem to move in slow motion in an unreal, remote world where only the spatial depth of the landscapes, with their gloomy and barren ruins, is concrete. Deep, radiant colours, possibly based on Sienese or Po valley influence, vibrating with pinks, whites, blues and greens, bathe the strange walls and the rich clothing. The pale, transparent faces, deeply spiritual in expression, are touched with delicate passages of shading and highlights, which suggest the work of Fra Angelico. The undoubted authenticity of these paintings enables us to ascribe to Maso, on analogy, the shrine in the Via del Leone at Florence, a polyptych in S. Spirito, and, rather more doubtfully, a Coronation of the Virgin in the Museum of S. Croce.

The artist known as "Stefano" belongs to the same generation as Maso, and learned very largely from Giotto's frescoes in S. Croce, which are magnificent in their spatial feeling and colouring. Original sources praise Stefano for his "diligence" and for his skill in blending colours, and Ghiberti adds his aproval of Stefano's modern style and says that at Assisi "Stefano had worked well". Longhi has identified these ancient descriptions with an anonymous painter at Assisi who was responsible for scenes from the life of S. Stanislas in the lower Church, Crucifixions in the Franciscan chapter-house, in the churches of S. Clare and S. Joseph and in the Oratory of S. Rufinuccio. It is an attractive hypothesis, and even if this artist was not Stefano, he was certainly a painter of considerable importance in the fourteenth century. According to Longhi many original touches in his work anticipated future styles: the dignified, calm eloquence of Fra Angelico's saints; the delicate tenderness of pure Gothic sculpture; the soft, pale blended colouring of the Emilian school of Mannerists, which reached a peak with Correggio; and the brilliant colouring of the Venetians. Stefano's soft modelling with its airy lightness and its delicate pinkish tones, with shadows like pale pearl-coloured veils, is seen particularly well in the S. Stanislas cycle, which is given a new depth by these means. His dignified figures are no longer dramatic and taut like those of Giotto, but have a gentle gravity which the artist conveys in their calm gestures and expressions. Giotto's passion has been transformed into something still and even languid.

Thirdly there is Giottino, who may possibly have been Stefano's son, belonging in that case to the next generation. His work has affinities with that of the Lombard

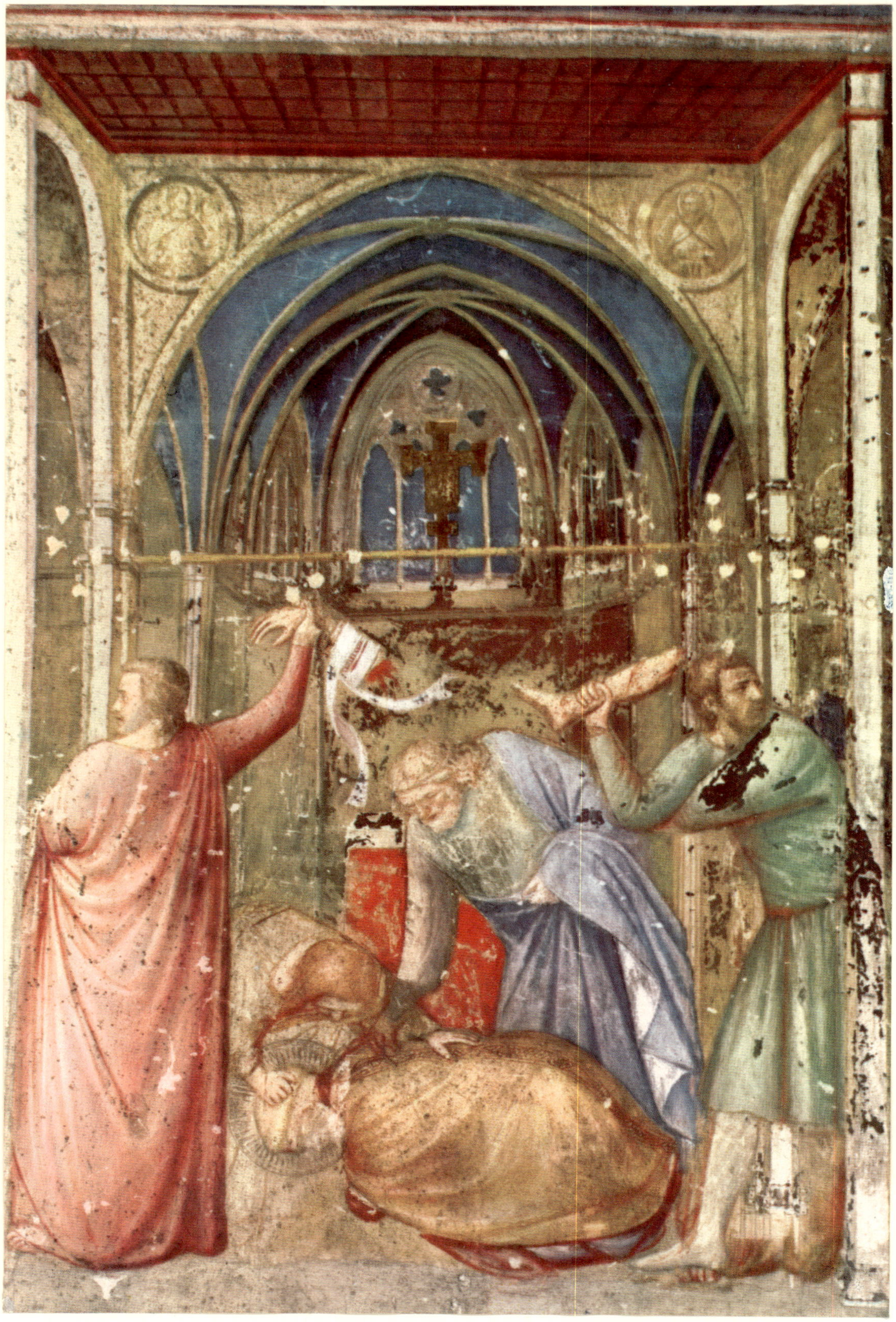

Stefano: The Martyrdom of S. Stanislas. S. Francis, Assisi

artist Giovanni da Milano, whom he resembled in feeling and training, and will be referred to again in that connection, but he is too closely connected with Stefano and Maso to be separated from the great enigma of which he forms the third important part. The reconstruction of Giottino's strong personality is quite recent. He is represented in the great Florentine school by a single work only, but it is one of the greatest works of the fourteenth century: the magnificent Pietà of S. Remigio, now in the Uffizi.

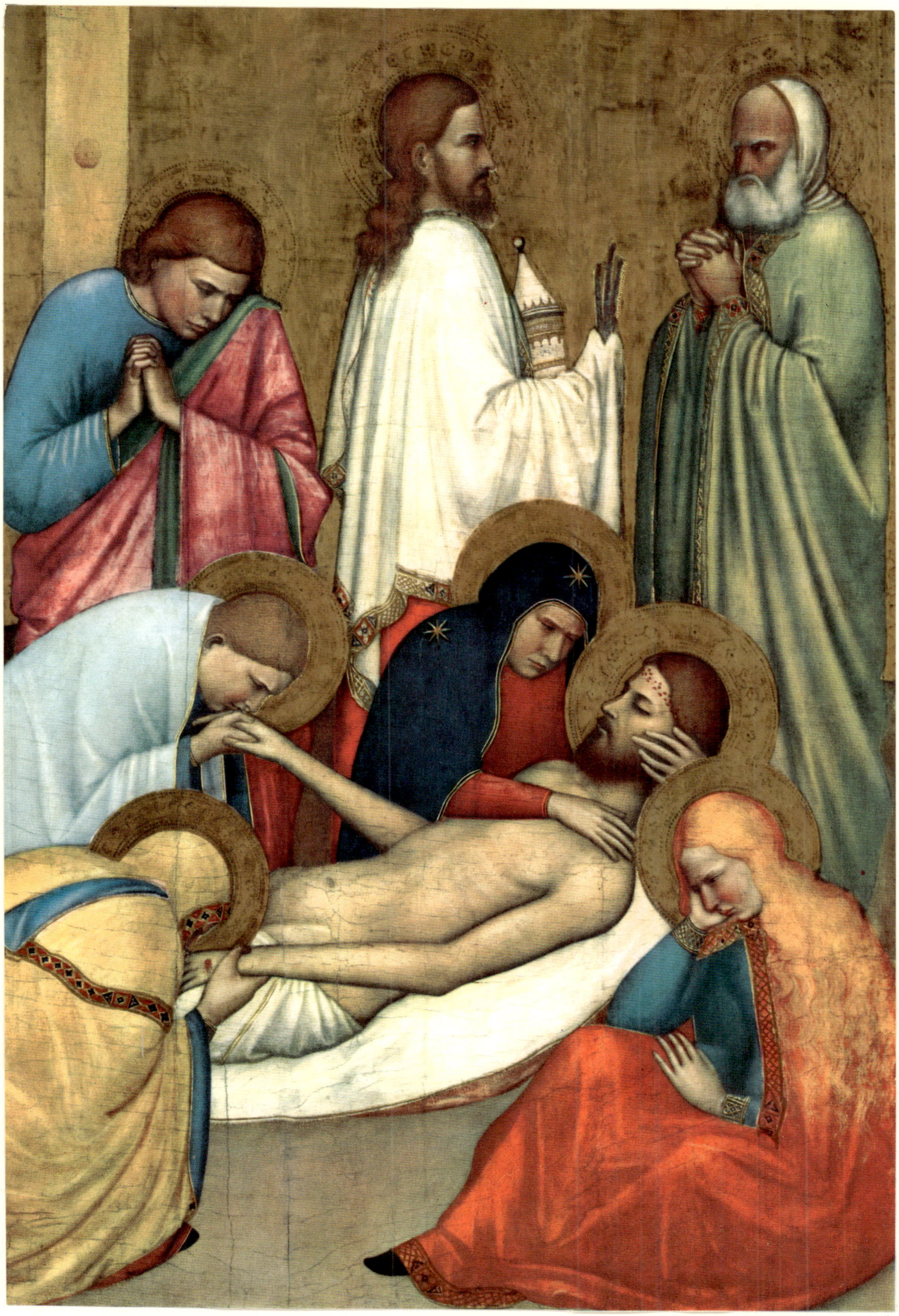

Giottino: Deposition, detail. Uffizi, Florence

Attempts have been made to reconstruct Giottino's life and development from the rather confused references in Vasari. Probably as a very young man he accompanied his father and Giotto to Lombardy, and as a result of Lombardic influence he transposed Giotto's solemnity into broader and also calmer rhythms. He acquired as well a knowledge of Northern art with its characteristic interest in costume, vivid colouring and heavy chiaroscuro. He then returned to Florence, where he probably painted the

Deposition of Christ which Vasari described as being " painted in tempera with so much care and love that there is nothing finer in wood ". This is a truly great work in which the arrangement of the figures and the plastic volume of the masses is wholly derived from Giotto, yet where everything is softened by a chiaroscuro and warm colouring which is obviously Northern in origin. The golden space is broken vertically by the great cross which dominates and embraces both the silent, solemn choir and the spectators of this final act in the drama of Christ. The body of Christ, now weightless, lies horizontally, and with the bent figure of John provides a connecting passage between the awed and silent figures of the mourners and bystanders, and the gaze of the sorrowing Mother at the transfigured face of her Divine Son. The painting is distinguished by its atmosphere of suspense, its harmonious arrangement of space, and by the choral effect of gestures entirely derived from Giotto. The drama unfolds in sorrow and silence, in the loving kiss which John places on Christ's hand, and in the figure of John himself, portrayed in the Lombardic Gothic manner in rich worldly costume, but wrapped in absorbed contemplation. The culminating point of the tragedy is to be found in the strong colouring which splashes the gold with violent red in the robe of the lonely, grief-stricken Magdalene, and in the strong blues, snowy whites, and browns.

As a result of contacts with the art of Giottino and Giovanni da Milano, Agnolo Gaddi, the son and pupil of Taddeo, transformed his style from the severity of Giotto to the Gothic images and delicate touches of the North. His delicate sensibility is seen to great advantage in the Scenes of the Passion in the great apse of S. Croce in Florence, where a slow, gentle linear pattern of graceful rhythm combines with clear, transparent colouring to create an effect which is visionary, gentle, and melancholy.

Another painter who is mentioned by Franco Sacchetti as working about this time, and who completes the picture of the great Florentine school of the fourteenth century, is Andrea Orcagna, painter, sculptor and architect. As leader of a group of artists, including the brothers Nardo and Iacopo, he occupied a special place in the artistic world of Florence and has now been taken up by critics who put him forward as a rival to Giotto, whom they relegate to the role of an archaic, academic practitioner in thirteenth-century styles. The importance of Andrea Orcagna was probably better understood by Lorenzo Ghiberti than by other critics, and in his Commentaries Ghiberti describes him as " a man of singular talent... a most distinguished master, unusually skilful in one medium and in the other... ". His attempts to reconcile plasticity and colour, volume and surface, suggest that his first efforts were directed towards copying Giotto. In the altarpiece of the Strozzi Chapel in S. Maria Novella, painted in 1357, which shows the vision of S. Thomas, he seems at times to be reverting to the Byzantine manner, but at others he develops a passionate contemplation which is hardly found anywhere else in Florentine art. This composition has a feeling of profound religious solemnity, and the strong colouring, which may be basically Sienese, is combined with a sculptural quality in the figures which for the most part are taut and harsh, and yet at times have an elegant linear quality which comes out particularly in the harmonious sweep of the gestures.

In addition to being influenced by Giotto, Orcagna was obviously affected by Sienese art. This can be seen in his decorative feeling for colour, and in his understanding of Andrea Pisano, who brought French Gothic style and flowing linear rhythm to Florentine sculpture. It seems likely that the Florentine background of those years about 1340 made a strong contribution to Orcagna's development. When the political independence of the Florentine Republic was interrupted, in 1342-43, by the rule of Walter of Brienne, Duke of Athens, a taste for French fashions and styles was brought into the city, which had been up to then a stronghold of Romanesque and Giottesque art. Andrea reflected this taste in sculpture as Orcagna did in painting, transforming it and modifying its worldly elements into a vision of "great religious solemnity, animated by an austere pathos". No doubt the transformation owed something to the religious fervour of the Dominicans and the denunciatory vigour of Fra Jacopo Passavanti. Orcagna's complex spirit and romantic emotional qualities are seen most clearly in the part of the great Crucifixion in S. Spirito, attributed to him by Ghiberti, who gives the clearest and most reliable account of his activity: "By the hand of Orcagna... is painted a refectory in a monastery of S. Augustine". Alongside the soft colouring of Nardo, with his gentle poetry and his way of reducing everything to light, we see in the magnificent horsemen the forcefulness of Andrea. It is strongly plastic and rich in a metallic brilliance which contrasts with the bright clothes and creates an extraordinary effect of volume. In this work Andrea anticipates the abstract play of forms which belongs to the fifteenth century: "groups not only of people but of helmets, shields, and armour which are outlined by strong lighting coming from a definite source...".

It is not possible to discuss in these pages the work of the less important followers of Giotto and Orcagna, such as Jacopo del Casentino or Niccolò di Pietro Gerini, who painted a number of pictures for Florentine churches about 1370, and also frescoes in the Bigallo in 1386. Andrea Buonaiuti of Florence was evidently influenced by Sienese gracefulness, especially that of Ambrogio Lorenzetti, but translated it into a cold, stiff style with very little poetry, which may be seen in the wall-paintings which he carried out in the Cappella degli Spagnoli in S. Maria Novella in 1365. Some twenty years later Spinello Aretino painted a considerable number of wall paintings at Florence, Arezzo, Pisa and Siena. He enlivened Giotto's manner of composition, and enriched it with fantasy, but his tone is humble and often peasant-like.

Gherardo Starnina has a special position. He was active during the last years of the fourteenth century, beginning in the same style as Agnolo Gaddi, with whom

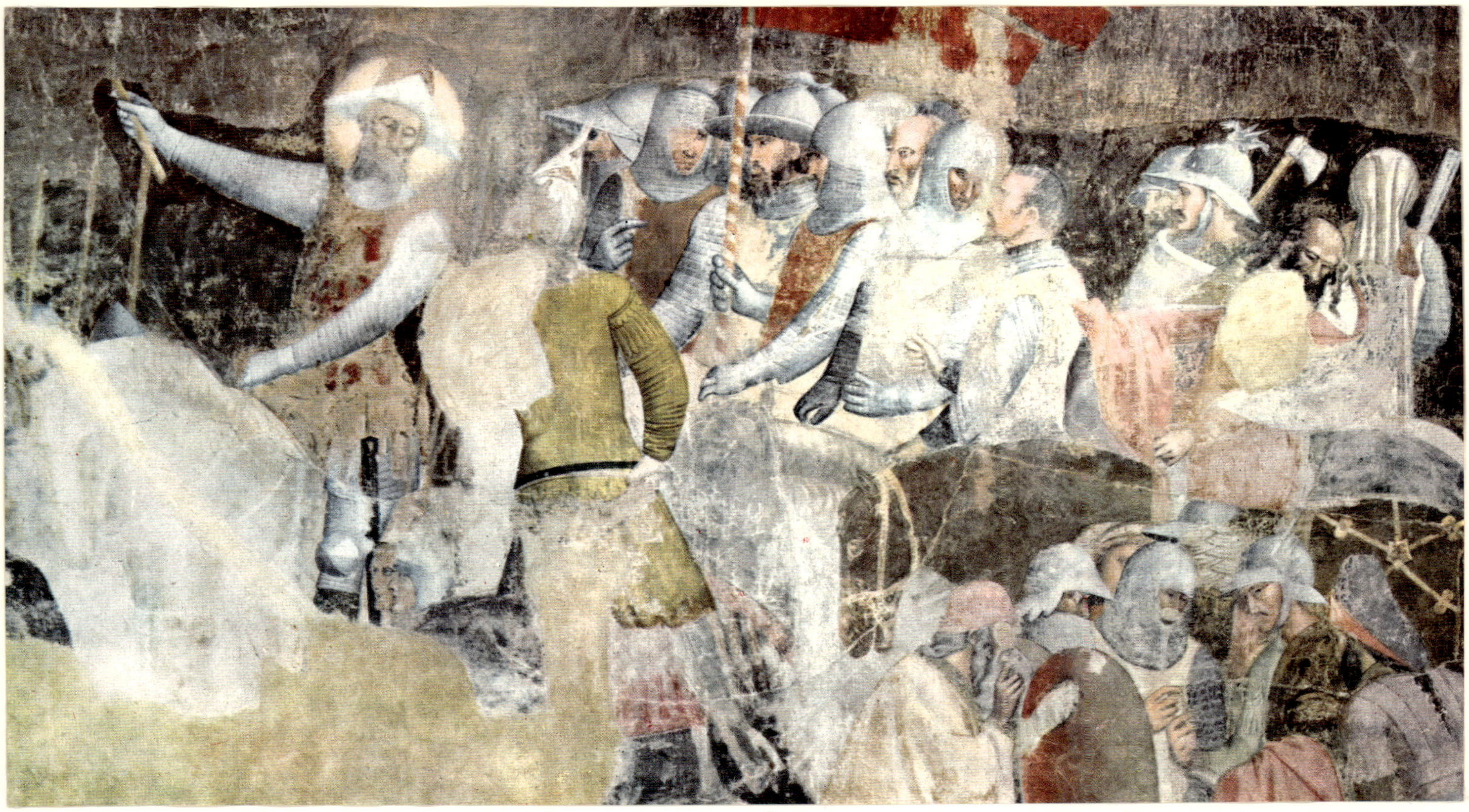

Andrea Orcagna: Crucifixion, detail. S. Spirito, Florence

he collaborated in S. Croce at Florence, and then creating in his Thebaid Desert his own non-realistic world, based on contemporary legends, with a stronger, more classical spirit reminiscent of Giotto. Along with Agnolo Gaddi and Spinello, Starnina initiated new tendencies which approached the full Florentine Gothic style, to be typified in the first twenty years of the fifteenth century by Lorenzo Monaco.

And so, with varying fortunes, painting flourished in Tuscany, always in the shadow of Giotto, but modified by the golden touch of Sienese art. The influence of these two clear, strong sources spread all over Italy, although less effectively in the South. In each region, however, there were local styles which were never wholly submerged.

Giotto's art even reached Naples, where he went himself to work for Robert of Anjou between 1332 and 1335. Simone Martini had already been to Naples, summoned by the same royal patron, who had also welcomed Petrarch. Neapolitan art never reached a very high standard in the fourteenth century, but even so its history is complex. Before the arrival of Simone Martini considerable changes had been brought about by Pietro Cavallini, who arrived in 1308, and had begun to decorate the church of S. Maria Donna Regina with wall-paintings which were continued and finished about 1318 by his many pupils. Until this time Neapolitan painters had wearily repeated established models in the thirteenth-century Benedictine manner, or in the style of the artists of S. Angelo in Formis, with strict geometrical patterns and a strong sense of balance. But now they began to develop Cavallini's rich colouring, and to absorb his deep religious feeling and his manner of creating form from colour. An example of this is in the mosaic of S. Maria del Principio, in S. Restituta, by a certain Lello " Ve de Urbe ", about 1322, in which the calligraphic style of his drapery resembles the pathetic manner. In 1317 Simone Martini arrived at the Angevin court to find an active cultural life under the influence of Gothic, especially French, art, which had been conveyed by means of miniatures and ivories. Simone plunged with enthusiasm into this cultured, sophisticated circle with which he had a natural sympathy, and it was there that he brought to maturity his elegant linear style, with the harmonious rhythms and colouring which had already produced such wonderful results at Siena. Further, he gave inspiration to Neapolitan painting. The very few existing works which belong to this period reveal their obvious derivation from his style. Among them is a Redeemer, formerly in the Monastery of S. Clare and now in the Vatican Gallery, which is sometimes attributed to Simone himself. Another example is the portrait of Bishop Montauro in the Archbishop's palace which recalls his early, plastic style, while another is a Madonna and Child in S. Restituta in Naples where the Sienese elegance becomes somewhat affected, and the emphasis is on pure colours, a foretaste of the brilliant colouring of the fifteenth-century Neapolitan school. Other painters studied Simone's work, but failed to catch his spirit and concentrated on his loving attention to detail, which in their hands was apt to become facile and frivolous, as for example in a Madonna in S. Lorenzo or that of the Umiltà in S. Domenico. Later the influence of Giotto was grafted on to the vestigial stump of Sienese influence in the lost wall-paintings in S. Clare, and those in the Incoronata. This is the most important monument of the Neapolitan school, whose artists adopted the dignified style of Giotto, which can be seen in his work at S. Croce. Their attribution has been discussed at length: they have been ascribed to a certain Paolo di Maestro Neri; to an unknown Sienese painter; even to Pietro Lorenzetti; to a non-existent Gennaro di Cola; and to Giotto himself. This last attribution can be discarded for chronological reasons, since it is known that Giotto died in 1337, whereas the church was not begun before 1352. The most likely hypothesis is that a number of artists combined in the work. This would explain the obvious connection with Florentine art in some scenes, which may even have been painted by a Florentine artist, whereas others are decidedly more

Sienese in style. At times there is a feeling for composition that stems from Giotto; at others a lively colour sense that is certainly Sienese. The " message " of Giotto is therefore undoubtedly present in the paintings in the Incoronata, and there is other important evidence of his work at Naples. An account book of 1329 states that the Florentine master appointed by the King, " Pictor familiaris et fidelis noster ", was commissioned by Robert of Anjou to decorate two chapels at Castelnuovo with wall-paintings. But nothing has survived of this important work, not one of the scenes from the Testaments which Giotto himself painted on the walls.

In the squinches of the windows some very beautiful human heads have survived, alternating with the arms of France and Jerusalem among large areas of rough plaster. The varying quality of these faces proves that they are the work of a number of assistants. Some are so good that they suggest Maso di Banco, and are like distant forerunners of the dignified figures which he painted in his mature period in S. Croce at Florence. They have the same quality of humanity, the same variety of poses, often with naturalistic touches, and are expressed in volume with soft colouring and warm tones. Others are weak and uncertain, and are evidently the work of less gifted assistants; probably local craftsmen of small talent who now began to adopt Giotto's style as a preparation, one might say, for the great work in the Incoronata. Possibly Roberto d'Odorisio, who shows a strong Giottesque influence modified by contemporary Sienese style, may have painted a Crucifixion in S. Francis at Eboli about the middle of the fourteenth century. Clearly there were a considerable number of variations on Tuscan themes at Naples, and an additional factor was the presence of the Sienese sculptor Tino di Camaino who was carving tombs for the Angevin princes in a style which united gently undulating rhythms and yielding masses in an idyllic vision. Later still, the Sienese artists Andrea Vanni and Paolo di Giovanni Fei also worked at Naples.

In Sicily the position was quite different. After the revolt of the Sicilian Vespers Sicily broke away and remained completely isolated and cut off from the cultural movements of Naples and the Continent. In any case the political confusion and the bloodshed resulting from feuds among the nobles, the conspiracies and quarrels between opposing factions, and between all factions and the sovereign, prevented the development of any interest in the arts. This more than anything else explains the way in which Sicilian art degenerated into an activity of artisans. Although Byzantine traditions continued — partly for nostalgic reasons — and the mosaics in the cathedral of Messina belong to the Byzantine world of the Paleologues, this artisan style, which is agreeable enough in its own way, began to spread, and imaginative craftsmen carved windows, doorways, and cornices, making use of popular themes which included Romanesque, Gothic and Arab elements. They also painted beams and ceilings, embellishing them freely with scenes of chivalry and charming decorations. Slightly before the middle of the fourteenth century, continental, and especially Tuscan, art reached Sicily through a series of pictures. The first, dated 1346, is that of the Madonna dell'Umiltà, which a certain " Magister Bartolomeus de Camulio ", who is identified with the Ligurian artist Bartolomeo da Camogli, painted for the church of S. Francis at Palermo. He used the Tuscan model of the Virgin seated humbly on the ground, and in the drapery, particularly in the hooded figures at her feet, his work has a Sienese quality, recalling the Lorenzetti. Other pictures followed, including Pisan work by Giovanni di Nicola, and Jacopo di Michele, known as Il Gera, who has a more decorative style and whose figures have a certain nobility. Later again came other works by Turino Vanni and the Sienese artist Taddeo di Bartolo; and so on up to 1388 when something different arrived in the shape of a picture painted by Antonio Veneziano for the Friars of S. Niccolò lo Reale now in the Diocesan

Museum of Palermo, which employs a new and limpid treatment of light in its portrayal of the Flagellation of Christ.

Thus the new influences in fourteenth-century art in western Sicily came principally from Pisa and were grafted on to local styles, so reinforcing early Sicilian art, of which only a few examples survive. They include some wall-paintings in the Badia Grande of Agrigento, the polyptych of the Confraternity of S. Michael Archangel now in the National Museum of Palermo, and another larger one in the Pepoli Museum at Trapani. In the East, however, at Syracuse and Messina, one may hear distant and muted echoes from Venice and even Byzantium, echoes of elegant styles and colouring against the golden backgrounds of Lorenzo and Paolo Veneziano. Many pictures from the city churches belonging to this period are now collected together in the Museum of the Palazzo Bellomo at Syracuse. Examples include the Madonna with flowers from the church of S. Lucia del Mela; a S. Agatha from Castroreale; and the fervid S. Placido from the Benedictine monastery of S. Placido at Calonerò. In the early years of the century ties with Siena were strengthened when Niccolò di Magio and Andrea Vanni moved from Naples to Sicily and exercised considerable influence on local art. On the threshold of the fifteenth century this melting pot of European styles was enriched by Spanish examples from Valencia, Barcelona and Seville.

Sardinia was reached by Tuscan art, especially from Siena and Florence, through Duccio and Bernardo Daddi. At the end of the century the island came under the rule of the Spaniards instead of the Pisans, but the Italian influence continued. The anonymous painter of a Polyptych in the church of Ottana, now in very bad state, reveals a close connection with Tuscan art in his dignified figure of the Virgin enthroned, while the Saints surrounding her are decidedly Sienese in their graceful decorative quality, and strongly resemble Duccio in his more archaic vein.

In Puglia the Byzantine tradition was modified by styles from central Italy. This can be seen in the votive paintings of S. Maria in Casale, where the influence may be direct or may have been transmitted through the art of the Neapolitan painter Roberto d'Odorisio. Further north, Roman artists continued to follow the great tradition of Pietro Cavallini and were comparatively unaffected by outside influences. Simone Martini must certainly have stayed in Rome on his journey to Naples, but no trace of his work is to be found there. A few traces survive of Giotto, but his influence seem to have been negligible. The same is true of the many Florentines, such as Giottino, Giovanni and Agnolo Gaddi, and Giovanni da Milano, who succeeded him and worked in Rome. Nothing remains of their work and we must rely on the evidence of biographers. Fourteenth-century Roman art (if indeed, apart from the work of Filippo Rosuti, it can really be called art) continued in the worn-out tradition of Cavallini, and it was only much later that the influence of Umbrian and Tuscan schools came to be felt.

On the boundaries of Rome lay Umbria and the Marches, regions as yet ill-defined, and here the influence of Tuscan art was felt in various ways. Umbria was rich in works by Cimabue and Giotto, by Simone Martini and Pietro and Ambrogio Lorenzetti, and in the memory of Pietro Cavallini, who may have worked at Assisi, and whose art is certainly reflected in the work of unknown artists who painted the scenes from the Old Testament in the Upper Church of S. Francis. Meo da Siena worked for a long time at Perugia. Having begun in the style of Duccio he broadened his forms, gave greater amplitude to his compositions and left a strong imprint on the Umbrian art of the period. In 1342 Guido Palmerucci began to decorate the chapel of the Palazzo dei Consoli at Gubbio with frescoes in the manner of Pietro Lorenzetti. And at Rimini, in the Marches, painters produced rich and graceful essays in the Tuscan, Sienese or Florentine styles. The unknown artist who painted frescoes near Fabriano worked in this style, but the painter of the scenes of the Passion, at S. Biagio in Caprile near Campodonico, was quite different. He seems to have been influenced by the great examples of Assisi, Florence and Siena, and in 1345 carried out his great Crucifixion in a hesitant, simple style with sensitive, luminous colouring. The vigorous strength of his figures and the deep intensity of his effects show him to be a direct descendant of Giotto. Allegretto Nuzi di Fabriano also belongs to the school of Giotto, but is more closely connected with Maso, Nardo di Cione and Daddi. In 1346 he belonged to the Company of Painters at Florence, and his works always showed a strong Florentine imprint, recalling either the imposing style of Maso or the softer, gentler manner of Nardo. At Orvieto, on the other hand, Sienese influence predominated from the time of Simone Martini. Ugolino di Prete Ilario based his work on the accomplished productions of Bartolo di Fredi and Luca di Tommè, and between 1270 and 1380 painted frescoes in the chapel of the Corporale in the Cathedral. Pietro di Puccio, who, among other things, decorated the Camposanto at Pisa in 1390-01 with frescoes of scenes from Genesis, introduced naturalistic touches, without however co-ordinating them in the Gothic manner of the day.

Meanwhile, beyond the Apennines, artists at Rimini were studying the art of central Italy, and in the fourteenth century their town itself became an active centre. As Rimini was of secondary importance both politically and economically, its artistic development is something of a mystery. It may have been partly due to the presence of superb Byzantine mosaics in the neighbouring town of Ravenna, and partly to the influence of the graceful Sienese artists, particularly Duccio, which reached Rimini through Umbria. Finally there was the distant memory of Pietro Cavallini, and the shadow of Giotto, who worked at Rimini about 1312 for the Malatesta in the church of S. Francis (Riccobaldo). The magnificent Crucifix in the Tempio Malatestiano is now ascribed by many critics to Giotto himself, and it certainly belongs to his school in feeling and style, resembling that in S. Maria Novella in Florence. The dramatic feeling of Giotto is however transformed by a subtle use of chiaroscuro and rich transparent colouring into something more emotional and fugitive, " like a distant vision ". The school of Rimini is something quite on its own, and the way in which it developed quite suddenly and unexpectedly at the beginning of the fourteenth century and faded away silently and swiftly some fifty years later presents a fascinating self-contained problem for modern critics. It is a school in which the splendour of Byzantine art is found in delicate motifs, and in which the power of Giotto is translated into something softer and more emotional. The Rimini school derived something from both these sources and also possesses a feeling of its own, archaic, poetical, and delightful. If an artist of strong personality had emerged among this group of painters he would undoubtedly have been a true original. In fact, however, Rimini produced no really important figures among its lively talents. At the beginning of the fourteenth century, before Giotto's innovations, a modest miniature painter, Neri da Rimini, produced closely-knit designs which sometimes show a Byzantine influence and sometimes that of the new Tuscan school. Later, Giuliano da Rimini and Giovanni Baronzio began by illuminating the elongated figures in their pictures with golden rays and graffito work, later adopting a style nearer to Giotto. About 1330 Pietro da Rimini, the strongest personality of the group, painted a Crucifix in the Church of the Dead at Urbania, and wall-paintings of S. Augustine in his own town. He was attracted sometimes by the Sienese influence of Pietro Lorenzetti and sometimes by the powerful dramatic quality of Giotto at Padua, which he revived to some extent, but into which he introduced an element at once polished and lyrical. Recently the magnificent wall-paintings in the refectory of the Abbey of Pomposa have been ascribed to him. In these there is a continuous linear movement in the design, in the supremely fine brush work, in an astonishing range of clear, brilliant colours which recall the magnificence of the Ravenna mosaics. The frescoes in S. Clare at Ravenna can be attributed to him with a good deal of certainty. They represent the Passion, and although a dramatic quality is present it is never overdone. These, in brief, are the most important painters of the Rimini school which, before it degenerated into lifeless repetitions, had a good deal of influence in Emilia, the Marches, the Veneto, at Milan, in Cadore and even in the more distant Trentino.

In the neighbouring city of Bologna, on the other hand, there flourished until the end of the thirteenth century a school of manuscript illumination which was closely connected with France and Tuscany. Painting on the full scale began to flourish from the beginning of the fourteenth century. For many years Bologna was neglected and despised as the most inferior school of fourteenth-century Italian painting. Certainly the inferior work has a coarseness which reveals the lack of any distinguished artistic tradition, but gradually, by discarding the poorest examples, a clearer and truer picture of this school is emerging. A rich imaginative feeling is skilfully expressed, although it occasionally falls into popular dialect. The first definite personality of the Bologna school is Vitale degli Equi, sometimes called "da Bologna" or "delle Madonne", and his work is typical. During Vitale's youth, roughly between 1325-30, art in the Po valley showed very few decided trends. The splendid legacy of Romanesque sculpture was flourishing, revived on the one hand by the Byzantine influence of gold and colour from Venice, and on the other by the capricious, sophisticated and intricate styles of western court art, especially from Paris and Avignon, while Oderisi da Gubbio taught Franco Bolognese the secret of the splendid miniatures which played so important a part in the figurative art of Emilia. Meanwhile a great polyptych in the style of Giotto reached Bologna, to join the Virgin by Cimabue in the Church of the Servites, and to reinforce the new, stern note of Florentine art. But the enlivening influence of Giotto is scarcely found in the Bologna school, as though the Apennines constituted a barrier even more impassable than the Alps for Tuscan artists. This is certainly remarkable if Giotto himself spent some time in Rimini and Ferrara, as his earlier biographers say he did. It is even more strange since no other part of Italy, with the exception of Venice, isolated in its lagoon, remained unaffected by Giotto's influence. Sienese influence on the other hand is obvious in Vitale's style, possibly acquired through the Marches and Umbria, and combined with that of Rimini it gave life and polish to his altarpieces with their brilliant golden backgrounds, and the rather affected grace of his smiling young Madonnas. Vitale's work, then, was based on many different traditions and tendencies. "Abstract and illusive... as lyrical as the most lyrical troubadour", he is the first and last major figure in a school which deteriorated into vulgarity and by the end of the fifteenth century consisted almost entirely of caricatures.

Vitale is known by a small number of signed paintings. There is a record of him in 1334 and again in 1338, 1343, 1347, and 1359. In 1345 he signed a Madonna, and in 1353 the great polyptych in S. Salvatore. He was in Udine in 1349. As a very young man he may have visited Tuscany, and been fascinated by Sienese life and art. This is indicated by the golden backgrounds with their delicate graffito work in his Madonnas, by the sinuous lines of his curtains, less Gothic than those of Simone Martini, and substituting for his delightful, slow, gliding rhythm one that is brusque, restless and headlong. Sienese influence is also to be seen in his gentle, delicate, and lively figure of the Madonna, with which he established a poetical note in the art of the Po valley. His happy imagination develops more freely in themes which were not bound up with age-old tradition like altarpieces; and he fills the scenes of S. Anthony Abbot "with his caprices". This work is now in the Museum

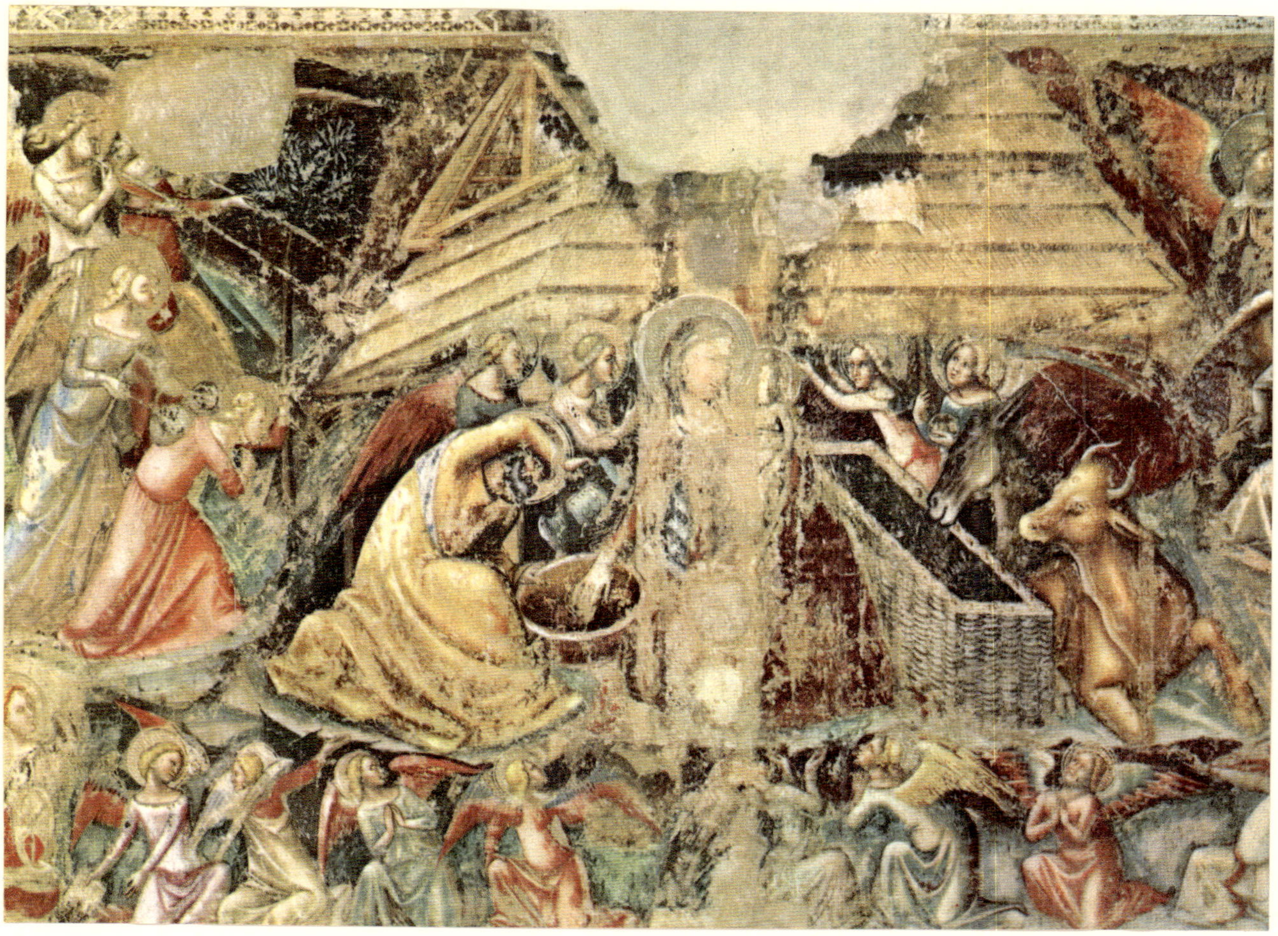

Vitale da Bologna: Birth of Christ, detail. Pinacoteca, Bologna

of S. Stefano at Bologna, and the impressive paintings of the Nativity, which were originally in Mezzaratta, have now been removed and are to be seen in the Pinacoteca in the same town. They form part of the cycle mentioned by the oldest written sources as being carried out by a group of craftsmen working about 1345, under the leadership of Vitale. In the Birth of Christ, which was attributed to Vitale at the end of the seventeenth century by Malvasia, we find a wholly new quality. There is no spatial depth, and the action takes place on a single plane, " where the figures, plants and other things are all on the surface like words on a page ". The centre of the picture is the impressive figure of the Virgin, who has an almost Oriental detachment and lack of concern, and who, without turning round, tests the water in the bath which S. Joseph is pouring with a sweeping gesture that is more than merely human. With this gesture Vitale creates a vortex of movement, which sets in motion the angels and other images. A delicate effect of light and shade suffuses the whole with gentle colouring. In 1349 Vitale completed the cycle of wall-paintings in the Abbey of Pomposa, in which dramatic scenes from both Testaments and even more violent scenes from the Apocalypse become simple, fluent, almost ingenuous stories. He then left his native city to work in the chapel of the Blessed Bertrand in the cathedral at Udine. In Friuli he left behind him seeds which later bore fruit, and returned to Bologna, where in 1353 he painted his last work, the polyptych with the Virgin enthroned, in the church of S. Salvatore. His style had now become more traditional, for he had abandoned his more extravagant and violent fantasies and imposed a Tuscan discipline on his art, as though he had been inspired by the sight of Giotto's work at Padua.

A flourishing local school grew up round Vitale. Many names have survived, but very few ever rose above mediocrity. Simone dei Crocefissi, a master painter in 1355 who was still alive in 1390, began to work in the style of Vitale, painting in very bright colours. The hypothetical Dalmasio, who spent a long time at Pistoia and Florence, where he may have painted the chapel of S. Gregory in S. Maria Novella, came into direct contact with Giotto's influence and achieved an intensely dramatic expression. Finally Jacopino dei Bavosi, who was active between 1350 and 1360, was strongly influenced by the school of Rimini, and developed a violent, imaginative quality which might be tragic, as in the battles of Clavijio in Mezzaratta, or else concentrated on exact psychological feeling as in a portrait, but always with a deep feeling for the poetry of fourteenth-century life. He transformed Vitale's force into a calmer realism, as in S. Naborre in the Pinacoteca at Bologna, although in this presentation of a knight *sans peur et sans reproche* (rather realistically treated) he expresses in the flashing eyes and dark colouring a strong dramatic feeling probably derived from Vitale. After this date painting in Bologna either deteriorated into an anonymous popular style or else moved towards the polished graces of international Gothic. An important example of this style at Bologna in S. Petronio, founded in 1390 and designed by the sculptor Antonio di Vicenzo.

There are obvious links with the Bologna school in the Triumph of Death and other frescoes in the Camposanto at Pisa, although they are usually attributed to Francesco Traini, a Pisan painter who united the Florentine strength of design with the imaginative colouring of Siena. This great decorative scheme was carried out between 1355 and 1360 in a simple popular style, either by an unknown painter from Bologna, or else by Traini, with a decided Emilian influence. This work, which was almost entirely destroyed in the last war, included a group of beggars and cripples, similar to the work by Orcagna in S. Croce in Florence, but otherwise the artist showed the cheerful, robust spirit which was characteristic of the Bologna school at this period. Since this popular style had great influence in Tuscany, particularly at Pisa, possibly through the wall-paintings in S. Maria Novella or the works of Dalmasio at Pistoia, it is natural to suppose that it continued to attract well-known artists in Bologna and the surrounding countryside, especially at Modena. Barnaba, who left his native land very early to work in regions as far distant as Liguria and Piedmont, where he remained probably from 1367-1383, was outside the orbit of the new trends which were now spreading through the Po valley. He worked in a nostalgic Byzantine world, painting many icon-like Madonnas, with sad, somewhat dull expressions, framed in brilliant light. His old-fashioned style, in which the linear Gothic feeling of Siena blended with the splendours of Venetian colouring, spread as a result of his enormous output as far as Sicily, and even further to the churches of Murcia in Spain.

The temperament of Tommaso da Modena was wholly different. He was fully aware of all the new developments which were going on round about him in the neighbouring city of Bologna, in Rimini, and beyond the Apennines. The son of a humble painter, Barisino Barisini, he was born in 1325 or 1326. He probably received his early training from his father, and then studied with the school of miniaturists who were working at Bologna, especially Niccolò di Giacomo, traces of whose work are to be seen in his style. With the exception of a few works which are attributed to him, especially a small, very delicate Madonna in the Pinacoteca of Modena, it is probable that nothing remains of his early work in Emilia. In 1352, when Tommaso's style was fully formed and he was already well-known, he worked on the wall-paintings of the chapterhouse of S. Domenico at Treviso. He painted portraits of famous Dominicans, the first examples of living, naturalistic portraits in Italian painting. Each figure, enclosed in his cell, with a chair and a bookcase in

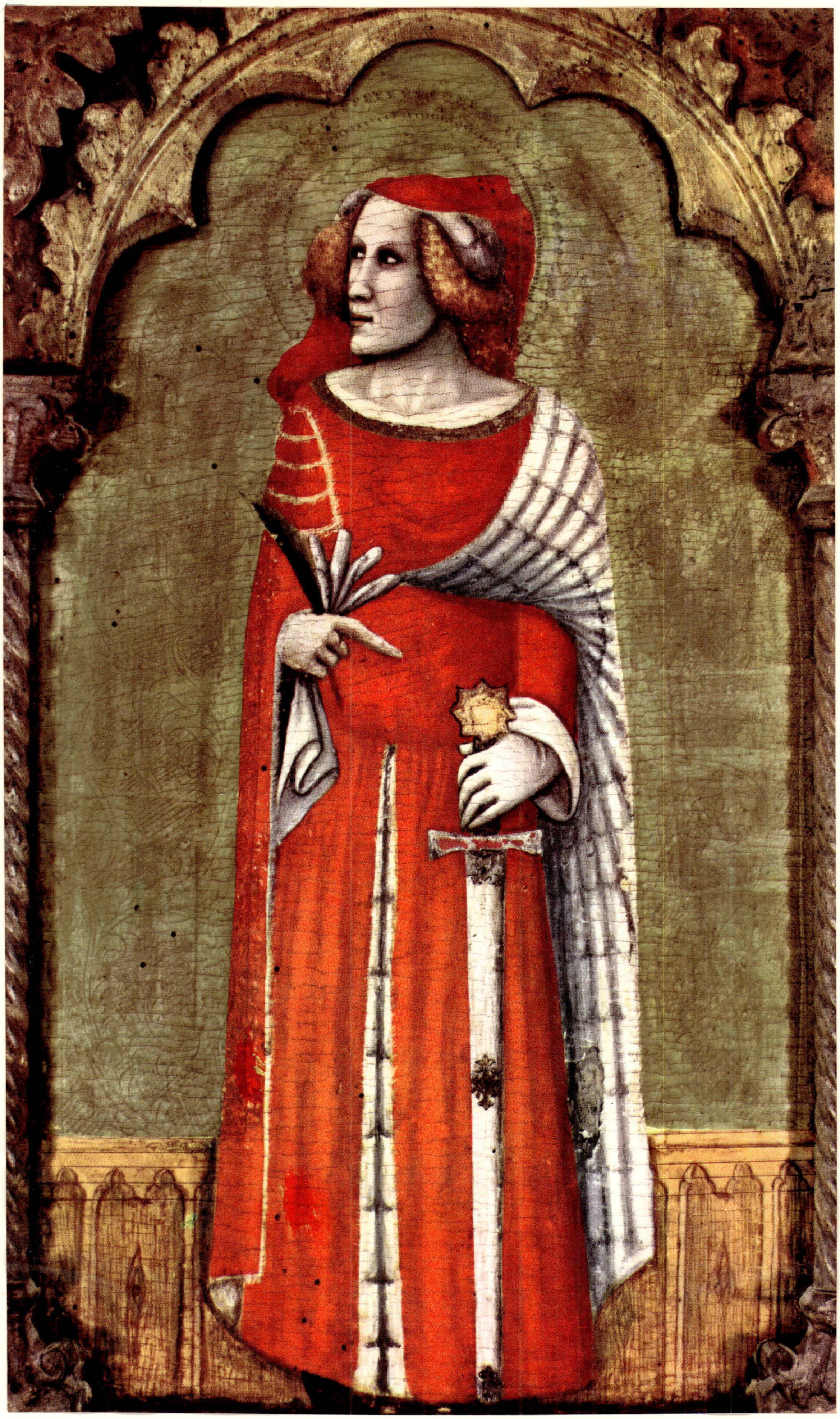

Jacopino dei Bavosi: Polyptych of S. Naborre, detail. Pinacoteca, Bologna

perspective, spends his day in contemplation, study, silent communion with himself, reading, writing or meditating. There is a directness in the gestures (occasionally rather clumsy), and the faces are realistically portrayed with lively expressions and all their physical defects; large nostrils, square determined chins, eyes that are short-sighted or bovine, and all with a pleasing and easy humour.

These pictures are displayed along the walls within frames, which are not drawn so much as sealed in their firmness, with warm, mellow colouring, rather muted and wonderfully harmonised; from pomegranate red to brown, from olive green to leaden blue. But when Tommaso portrays feminine figures his brush becomes lighter, and caresses the soft, graceful forms in a way that recalls the Gothic grace of Simone Martini. This is seen in his last work, the legend of S. Ursula, which was probably painted shortly before his death in 1379; it was formerly in the church of S. Margherita, and is now in the Civic Museum at Treviso. As a narrator he appears in a happy vein in the scenes from the life of the Saint, which have no iconographical ties with preceding styles. There is spontaneity and realism, anti-chivalrous and anti-heroic, in his descriptions of the costumes, the court, and the journeys. He emphasises the faces and their expressions, now concentrated, now inattentive, ready to listen to the gossip of courtiers and the chattering of the Saint's attendants, as she takes leave of her family. He gives the same importance to a large group of figures as to a single gesture or pose or smile. If, as is highly probable, Tommaso had seen works by Giotto at Padua, he would have seized on the vital, realistic element in his art; but he fails to achieve either Giotto's powerful dramatic quality, or his economy in selecting essentials. Tommaso incorporates every detail from the simplest feelings and most commonplace objects in a way that anticipates *genre* painting, where attention is centred on people and their surroundings. He did not understand Giotto's portrayal of space and perspective, nor yet his feeling for landscape: his feeling of depth is always uncertain and he is content with architectural backgrounds, ignoring landscapes.

In some mysterious way he was influenced by the art of Siena, which spread with prolific results through his own work into the Veneto and even further into Bohemia. When, at the invitation of King Charles IV, who built the castle of Karlstein, Tommaso sent his paintings to this remote country, they revived the primitive static art of Theodoric of Prague. Among other works he sent two signed triptychs, with the Madonna and two saints, which were painted between 1354 and 1365. Both have a strong Sienese strain, and considerable elegance. Like Simone Martini a few years earlier he thus became instrumental in spreading Italian art outside Italy.

Tommaso had great influence over Altichiero and Avanzo, who a few years later were working at Padua, and who acquired from him the Northern habit of emphasising costume, surroundings and characters, and also a taste for architecture which, as in Tommaso's own work, dominated their compositions to the detriment of landscape. Before this date however artists belonging to two different schools had worked at Padua, where the Scrovegni Chapel with its Giotto frescoes stands as one of the milestones of Italian art. One school was Venetian, and reached Padua through Guariento; the other can be traced back to the origins of painting in the hinterland, origins based on Tuscan and Lombardic styles, at times improved by touches of Venetian or pure Romanesque, and is found in the austere, even simple idiom of Giusto dei Menabuoi.

The Venetian basis of Guariento's style involves some mention of the artistic position along the lagoon. Venice was more subject to influences brought by sea than by land, and was strongly influenced by Byzantine art from the East, the great example of this influence being of course the series of beautiful mosaics in S. Mark's. Then the Venetians built, as a magnificent crown to their basilica, the brilliant golden cupolas, bearing the weight of all that golden splendour which kept the eastern tradition always before their eyes. This taste for colour on gold backgrounds was constantly reinforced by the arrival of icons from Candia. But even so new ideas seeped in from the mainland. A glance outside the immediate neighbourhood of the lagoon was enough — a slight acquaintance with the work of Giotto in the Scrovegni chapel, or later with the work of Giusto and Tommaso, especially as the political authority of the Republic gradually reached Treviso and Friuli. Various influences are to be found in the later mosaics of S. Mark's which obviously have some connection with the Romanesque wall-paintings of Aquileia. The art of mosaic was gradually dying, and by the end of the twelfth century had finally lost its beauty and *raison d'être* in the West. In Venice, following long-term plans, it was continued in the great Basilica. But from now onwards Venetian mosaic tended to become more like painting, painting in a rich style which at times recalls the grace of Siena and at others the harsh outlines of the primitive Florentine painters before Giotto. Great polyptychs are composed of frontal icons of the Virgin with small pictures, and such polyptychs were to remain characteristic of Venice even in the fifteenth century, when, with the Vivarini and Giovanni d'Alemagna, they became more elaborate. This Italian system of dividing the work into compartments, so that a story is told in different scenes, is very different from the hieratic spirit of Byzantine art. And while the manufacture of *Madonneri*, which originated in Candia, continued on the Rialto almost until modern times, a new trend developed in the early part of the fourteenth century. This was an impetus from the West, as yet timid and humble, which tried to inject new life

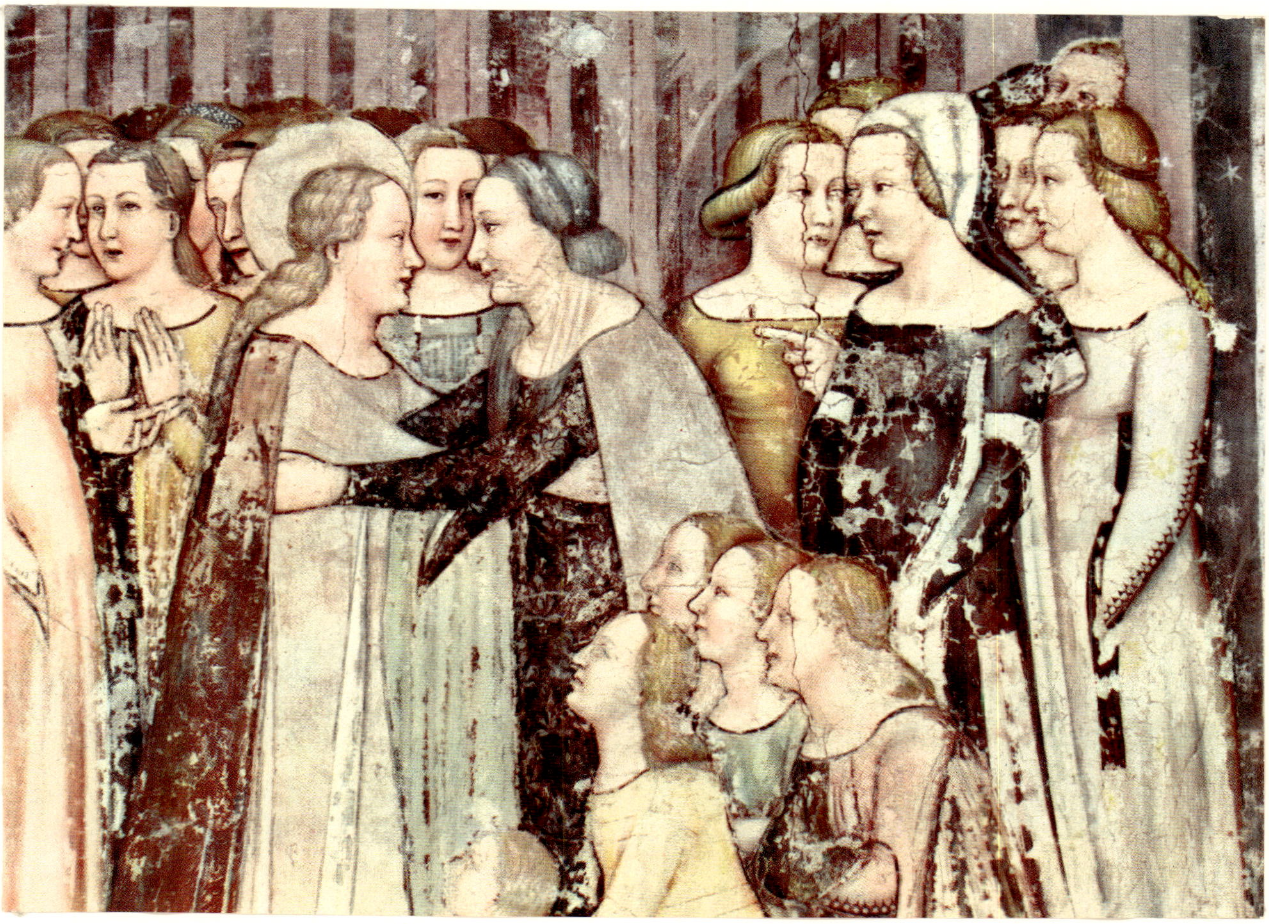

Tommaso da Modena: The Departure of S. Ursula. Civic Museum, Treviso

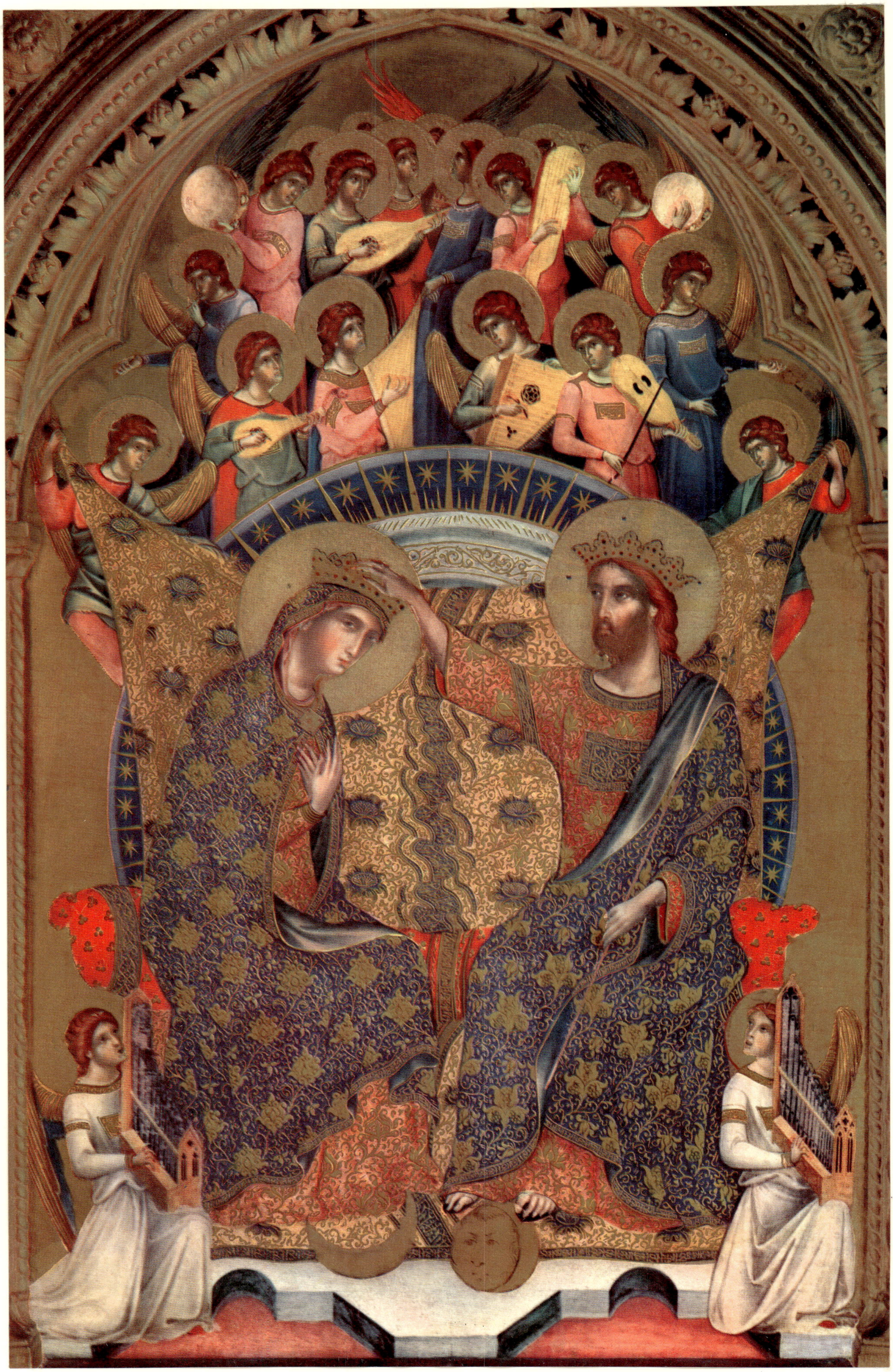

Paolo Veneziano: Coronation of the Virgin. Accademia Gallery, Venice

into the old Byzantine tradition. The Venetians showed an unconscious awareness of this impetus in the magnificent style of their new palaces, and they also began to elaborate their pictures by incorporating textiles, chairs, and so forth, into their gold backgrounds.

Looking at the works of Master Paolo, Lorenzo, and Stefano, the priest of S. Agnes, one wonders whether they were really living in the same Italy as Giotto and Simone Martini. Although they were highly skilled, loved magnificent materials, and were " aristocratic craftsmen who seemed to compose their pictures in tortoiseshell, lizard skin and gold ", they have very little talent for human expression or feeling for the more delicate poetical values.

The first and most important of these artists is Master Paolo. Many of his signed and dated works have survived and something is known about his life. Trained in Byzantine art, he reveals in his pictures an effort to bring new life into Venetian painting — a tendency to create space and impart some dramatic quality which is wholly Italian. His delicate colouring was based on the brilliant Byzantine schemes, but his faces are dark, while strong shadows and a greenish tinge in his flesh tints gives his figures the appearance of bronzes. There are traces of Florence and more frequently of Siena in his work, as in the Coronation of the Virgin in the Accademia of Venice, where the subdued treatment of light resembles Duccio. But there is also something of Giotto's ability to convey volume, and the angel musicians seated at the foot of the throne, with their swirling Gothic drapery, seem to be inspired by Sienese art.

Coletti and Fiocco assume, possibly correctly, that Paolo travelled to Siena, Assisi, and the Romagna, and they imagine him studying the work of Giotto's earliest follower, the Master of S. Cecilia. But sometimes he unexpectedly returns to the ecstatic Byzantine world, to the eastern linear idiom of pure light and colour, and he plunges once more into magnificent golden splendour, as in the altarpiece for the church of S. Francis at Vicenza in 1333. This is so like the work of Cretan painters that Fiocco assumes he must have travelled to Byzantium.

Other works, both early and late, are attributed to him, all containing the same mixture of Byzantine and Gothic elements, sometimes harmonising and sometimes contrasting among themselves. Examples may be seen in the polyptych of Dignano, in the Coronation in the Frick collection, in the lunettes of the Frari at Venice, and so on until his death, which probably occured about 1362. He was succeeded by his younger brother Lorenzo, who was working until about 1372 and signed two works in 1357 and 1359. A humble admirer of Byzantine splendour, he imitated it, using deep, enamel-like colouring and occasionally strong chiaroscuro, and (probably through the influence of Tommaso da Modena and other Emilian artists) weaving Gothic influences into Byzantine styles even more than Paolo did. Stefano resembled him very closely, although Stefano's designs are even more fluid.

Finally, mention must be made of Donato and Caterino, who signed a Coronation of the Virgin in 1359. This picture is now in the Querini Stampalia collection in Venice, and in it a gorgeous display of reds and blues blends with the gold in exquisite gradations of colour. Antonio Veneziano, who worked in a very different style, is said by Vasari to have painted frescoes in the Ducal Palace at Venice, but these have now disappeared. Because he was too much influenced by the styles of central Italy he was not liked or understood in his own country, and he worked almost exclusively in Tuscany. Between 1369 and 1370 he was at Siena, but nothing has survived of this period: between 1384 and 1386 he painted three scenes from the life of S. Ranieri in the Camposanto at Pisa which were almost entirely destroyed in the last war. In these he showed a strong feeling for colour, " with a very soft chiaroscuro which vibrates and harmonises like music ", which he owed to his Venetian inheritance, but which he had invigorated through contacts with Giottino, Maso and Stefano. His affectionate interest in naturalistic detail was derived from the traditions of the Po valley, and reveals the link with Giovanni da Milano. But his style was too new, too naturalistic and altogether too far removed from the accomplished, magnificent Byzantine manner to please the public in Venice. When the Signori of the Republic realised that the art of their city had become old-fashioned and was technically poor, they turned to the Paduan artist Guariento, finding in his work developments without extremism, and in 1365 he was commissioned to paint frescoes of Paradise in the Grand Council room in the Ducal Palace. This work, which was first mentioned by Michele Savonarola in 1445, was covered up by Tintoretto's great Coronation of the Virgin and only reappeared, greatly damaged, in 1903.

Guariento, recorded as a master painter in 1338, lived until 1370. He combined a number of different elements in his style: a Byzantine quality derived from Master Paolo, and something of Giotto, probably learnt from the wall-paintings in the Arena chapel. It can truly be said of his work that " it bridged the gap between the irresistible impetus of Giotto and the tenacious resistance of Byzantine art ", and evidence is provided by the only work which can be attributed to him with certainty after the war-time destruction of his later frescoes in the Eremitani. This cycle of pictures, with the heavenly army, the Virgin and Evangelists, formed part of the decoration of the Capitano chapel at Padua and was carried out about 1350. The series of angels, both in single figures and in groups, had a repetitive rhythmical movement continued with a grace which revealed the artist's great mastery of design, and were painted with a skilful use of shadows in the clear, cold colouring and with a goldsmith's care in the modelling of each detail. The linear Gothic rhythm of the figures and drapery eliminated almost all plastic feeling, and was Byzantine in its regularity; naturalistic feeling in the figures gave way to ceremonial abstraction.

During this period another Venetian, Nicoletto Semitecolo, worked at Padua. His work shows a strong influence of Tommaso da Modena and possesses a delightful, lively narrative quality with extensive detail.

Shortly afterwards Giusto dei Menabuoi also worked at Padua. An unusual character, Giusto was Florentine by birth and Paduan by choice, and created his own style. Nothing remains of his work at Florence, and the earliest record of it dates from 1363, when he signed a Madonna which is now in the Schiff-Giorgini collection at Montignoso di Massa. From then on there are many dates and records of his work at Padua. In 1367 he signed a triptych of the Coronation of the Virgin now in the National Gallery in London; in 1370 he was appointed " pictore cum privilegio magni et potentiss. D.D. Francisci de Carraria ", and was the favourite painter of Fina Buzzacarina, governor of the city. He painted the Baptistery with frescoes, completing the work in 1376. From 1382-83 he worked on the wall-paintings of the chapel of Beato Luca Belludi in the Santo which was built by the Conti brothers, he probably died about 1393. Possibly a slightly younger contemporary of Giotto, he belonged to the most distinguished group of Giotto's followers, the " dissidents ". His particular style of colouring shows that the chief influence on his work was probably Stefano, from whom he inherited delicate, velvety tones, with gentle shading, which was apt to turn into white in Giusto's work. He resembled Giovanni da Milano in style and education, and it is probable that they met in Lombardy, where, if some frescoes at Viboldone are in fact by him as critics are now inclined to believe, Giusto spent a fruitful period in his youth. The most noteworthy of the frescoes are a Madonna, enthroned between saints and a Christ as Judge, which date from about 1349. The move from Lombardy to Padua was an easy one, and the differences between

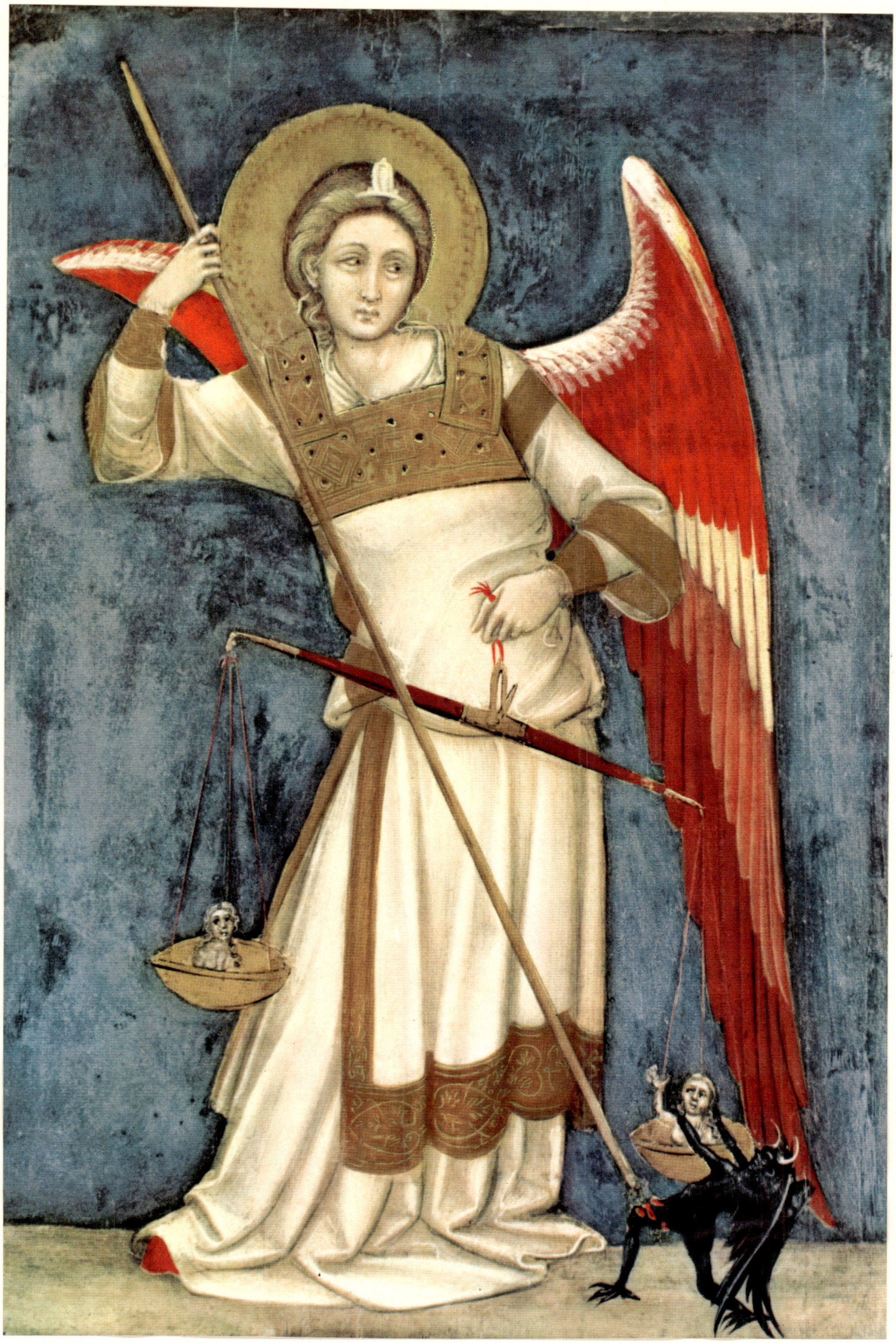

Guariento: S. Michael. Civic Museum, Padua

Giusto's work and the pleasing, free, narrative style of the northern artists are increased. He became almost Romanesque, perhaps as a result of studying the sculpture of the magnificent doorway of S. Giustina at Padua, as well as the ivories, mosaics and cupolas of the great basilica at Venice, sparkling in the clear sky against the shimmering waters of the lagoon. The spirit of the Venetian and Graeco-Byzantine artists who had created the golden miracle of the mosaics in S. Mark's lived again in the tremendous task of decorating the whole of the Baptistery at Padua which Giusto began in 1370. Here his interest lay in non-humanistic values which were most naturally expressed in the Byzantine idiom. The decoration of the Baptistery is the finest example of his work, and the magnificent cupola establishes an unusual feeling of a world in which there is no room for scenes of court life, or for grace and elegance in gesture or costume. It is like a great rainbow in which the myriad concentric circles of Angels, Saints, Patriarchs and the Blessed, move slowly round, suffused with warm delicate shades, with occasional contrasts in the strong blue of the mantles. This movement seems to go on for ever, spreading in endless ripples from the great figure of Christ at its centre. This wheeling circle of colour, descended through mysterious Venetian routes from the eastern Pantocrators, only comes to a halt in front of the white, motionless, brilliantly lit and Byzantine Orans Virgin. The delicate fascination of the shining paradise extends to scenes from the Old and New Testaments. Altichiero also worked at Padua about this time, and collaborated with Avanzo in the frescoes in the chapel of S. James, and that of the Oratory of S. George, which he began about 1369 shortly after his arrival in the city, when he was already a well-known painter in his native city of Verona.

The artistic traditions of Verona are remarkable. Since the beginning of the fourteenth century the city had been ruled by the Scaligeri, and Cangrande in particular gave encouragement to Verona, opening his doors to Italian artists and welcoming the exiled Dante and possibly Giotto as well. He also introduced a sophisticated type of court life which was unknown in the more puritanical cities of central Italy, especially in Florence, which at that time was governed by the citizens as a democratic republic. As a result painting began to acquire a delightful, luxurious spirit, with romantic, picturesque colouring which readily inspired beauty, grace and serenity. This courtly world ended gloriously about the middle of the fifteenth century with the magnificent work of Pisanello.

In any case the geographical situation of Verona was peculiar. Situated near the northern frontiers of Italy, it was open to new ideas from the North, especially from France, whose influence was ubiquitous. While Giotto was concerned with giving mass and weight to his figures, and creating volume beneath the heavy effects of his robes, the Veronese painters adopted the Northern Gothic style, and concentrated on caressing lines, flowing curves, and a gentle, charming rhythm. But Giotto's influence was now universally accepted in Italy, and this tended to curb exaggerations; Master Cicogna and the anonymous artists of S. Zeno are examples of this style. So was Turone, who came immediately before Altichiero and had already signed and dated a work, the polyptych of the Coronation of the Virgin in 1360, now in the city Museum. Turone's robust and naturalistic style reveals a knowledge of Giotto, but he also shows links with the style of the Po valley. He has something of the harmonious elegance of Vitale and Guariento, and the clear, transparent colour of Lorenzo Veneziano and the great Tommaso. Indeed he was known as Tommaso's " poor relation ".

Giotto's measured style and plastic strength had great influence on Altichiero, the first and most important of a long series of painters in Verona. Neither the date of his birth nor any details about his education are known, and the frescoes which

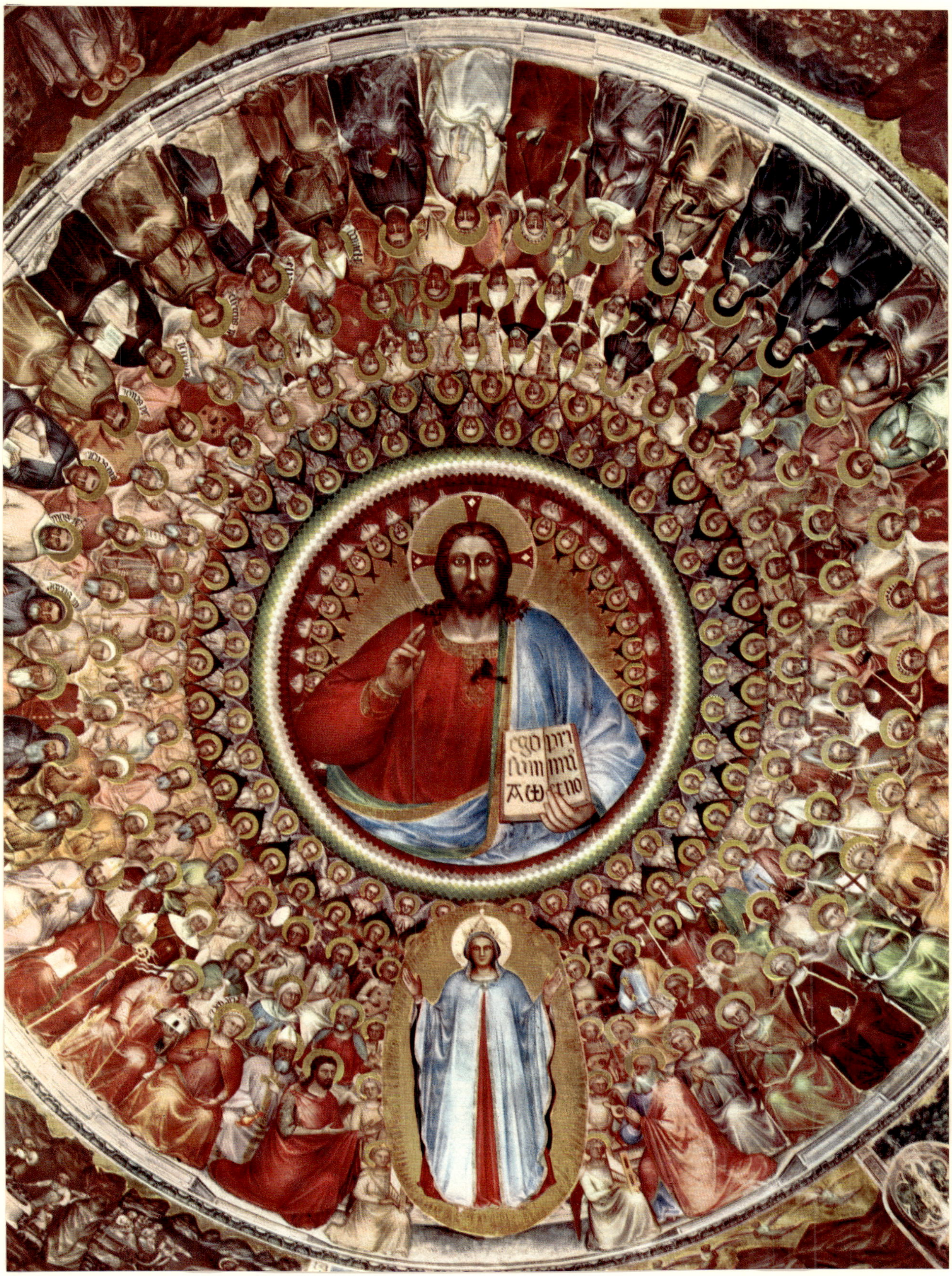

Giusto dei Menabuoi: Fresco in the cupola. Baptistery, Padua

he did for Cangrande have not survived. He is first recorded as working at Padua, in the Basilica del Santo, when he must already have been a famous painter whose reputation reached beyond his city boundaries, since Bonifacio Lupi had commissioned him, a foreigner, to work in the chapel. He was steeped in the traditions of his own city, and he had learnt something of Giotto's fundamental rules about space, construction,

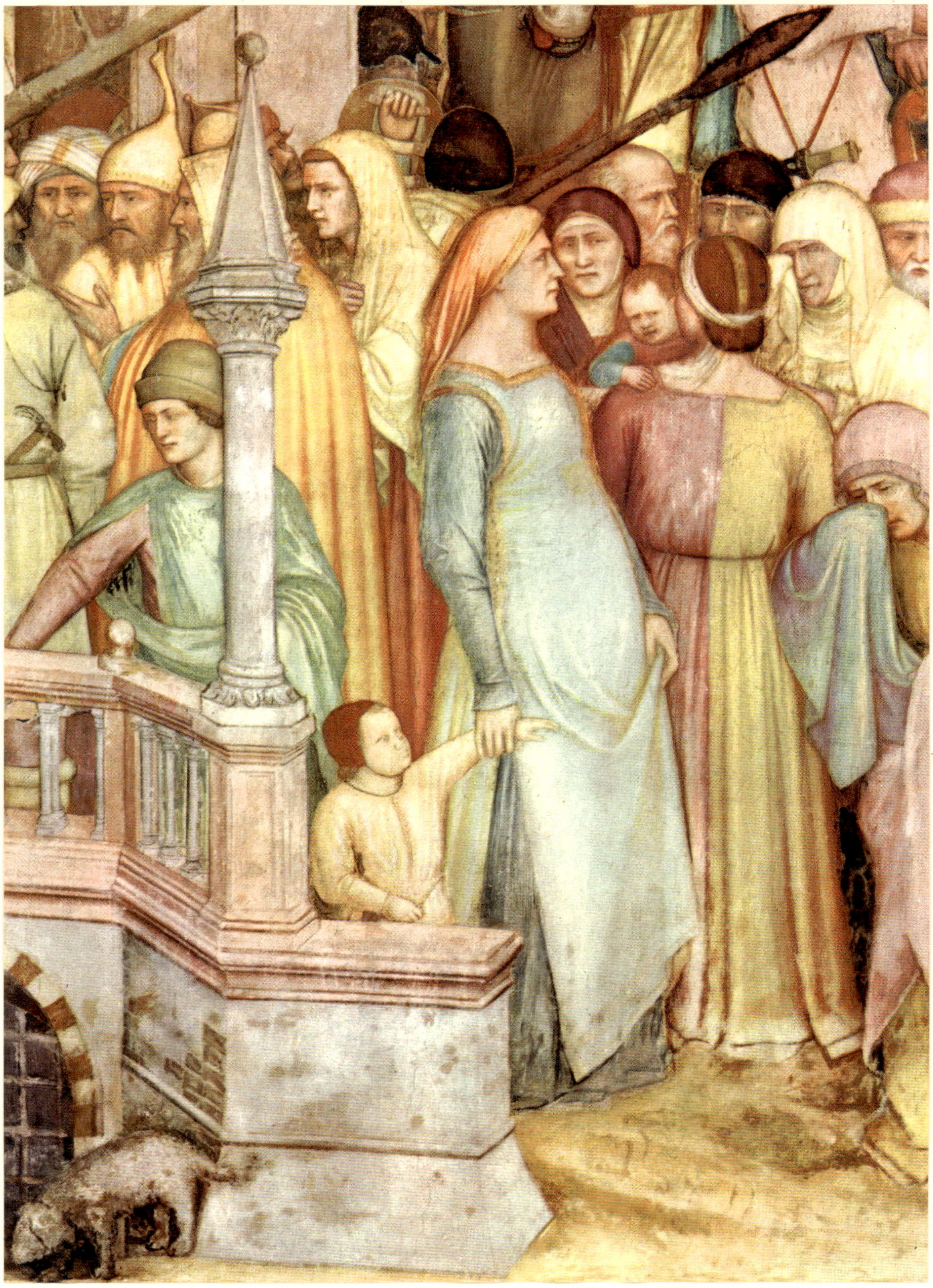

Altichiero: Crucifixion, detail. Chapel of S. James in the Santo, Padua

and emotional expression. He had also assimilated something from Tommaso da Modena's naturalistic treatment of faces and objects. It is not far from Verona to Treviso, and the distance was covered easily enough by a young artist in search of new ideas. So with a great deal of experience already behind him Altichiero went there, and between 1372 and 1379 worked on the frescoes in the chapel of S. James, which together with the frescoes of S. George constitute one of the most puzzling problems of attribution in the fourteenth century. He collaborated with another painter, Avanzo, of whom nothing is known except that he came from the North, possibly from Bologna. The two artists are mentioned together by Savonarola (1440) and by Marc'Aurelio Michiel (1530), and modern critics are undecided as to which

Voyagers of the light
Blooming from the seed of light
Blown into the space of
eternal dawn…
O let us move on
Like a wind
Blowing through the sun!

ॐ

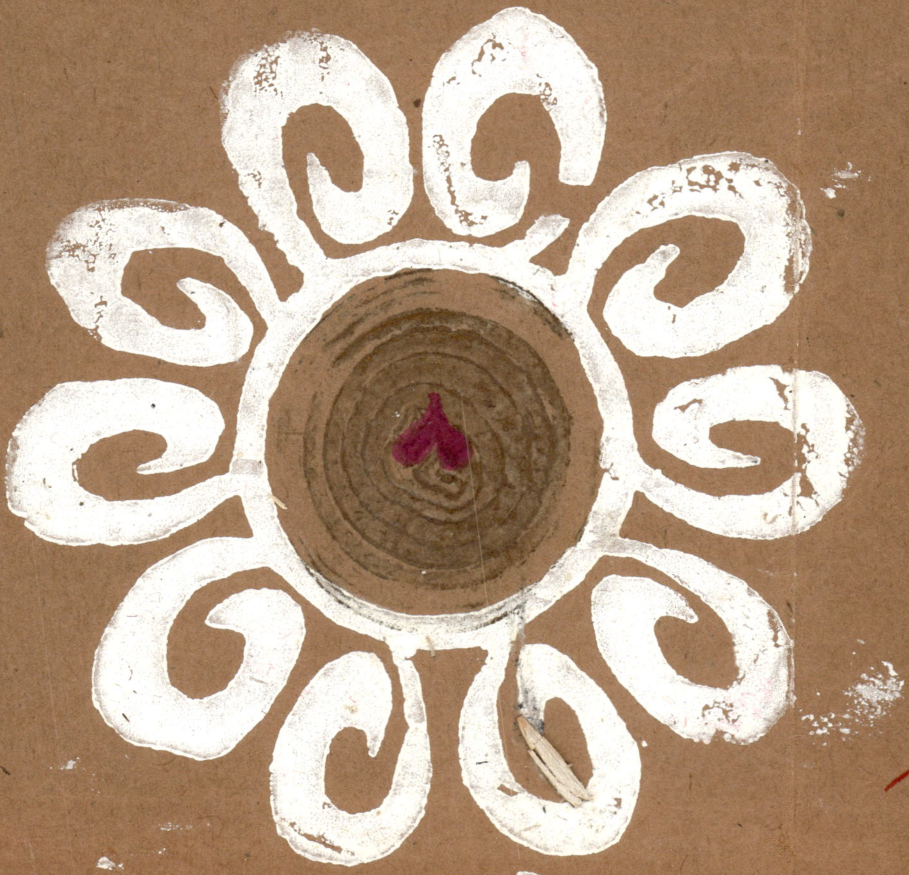

A sun flower seed
inside of it is a sunflower
inside of it a sunflower,
inside of it is a sunflo
forever, beyond forever, fo

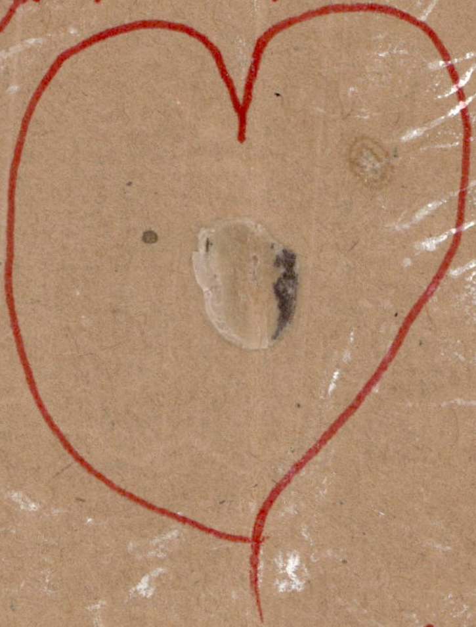

sow it, eat it, feed it to a b
and let it grow!

Happy Love day! Will, Peggy
Ananda

St. Luke, 8:5-15
Son Sean is in Jam

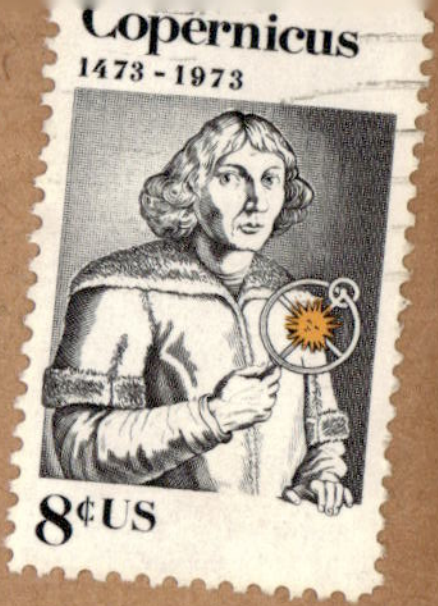

The Bacons

2117 Locust St.

Phila. Pa.

19103

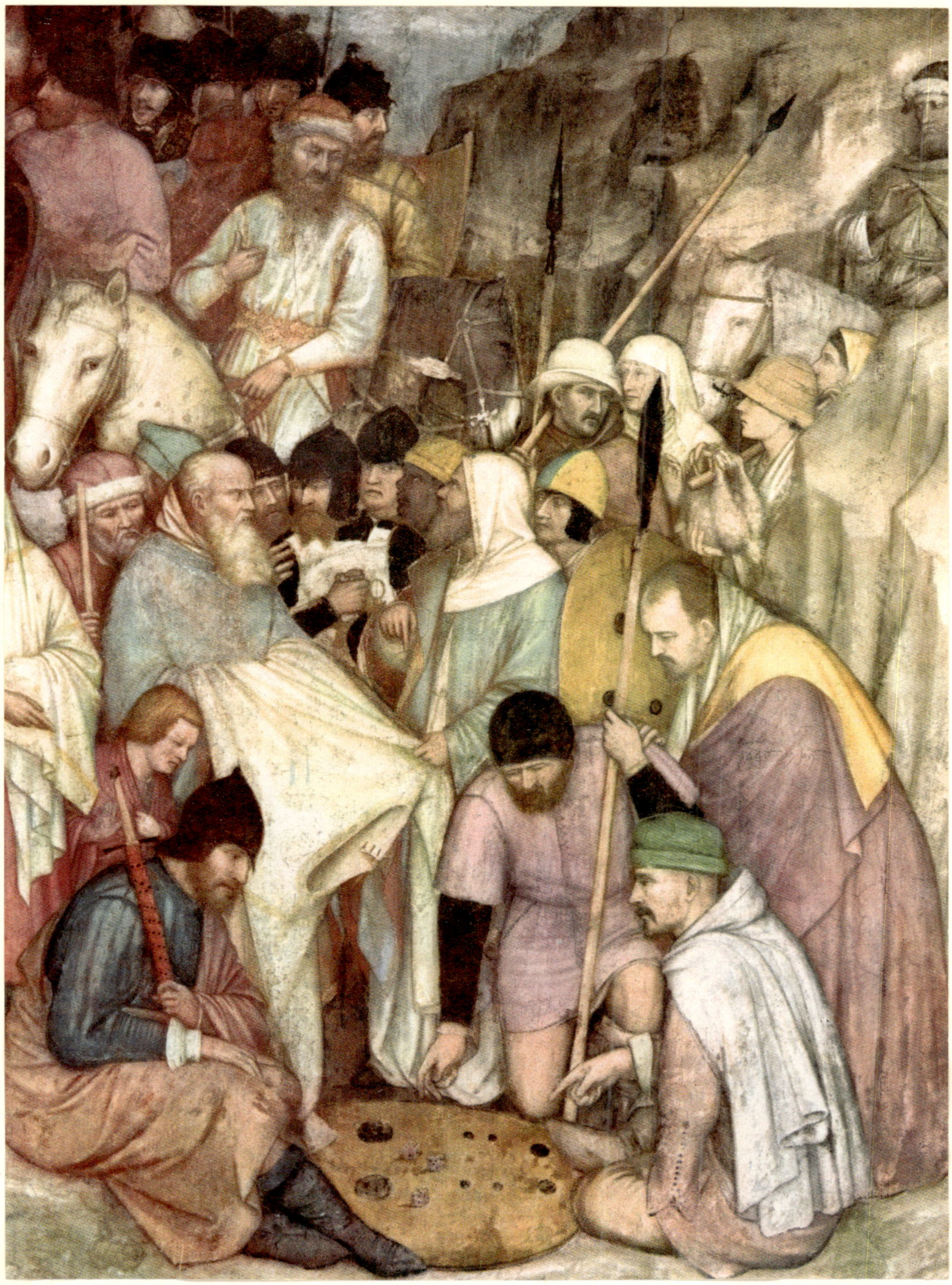

Altichiero: Crucifixion, detail. Chapel of S. James in the Santo, Padua

of them was the more important. It may be that Altichiero is responsible for those parts which show a greater effect of dignity, and even a certain stiffness, whereas Avanzo is more interested in the detailed observation of his characters with their defects and their good qualities. Possibly influenced by contacts with the good-natured, popular style of the early painters of Bologna, he catches individual likenesses and draws realistic portraits of the serious, wealthy burghers, who appear almost like casual spectators at, for example, the Martyrdom of S. Lucia in the oratory of S. George. It is impossible in this brief essay to attempt to distinguish clearly between the work of these two artists, and since Altichiero is generally accepted as being the more important in these frescoes, we shall devote our attention to those works which are

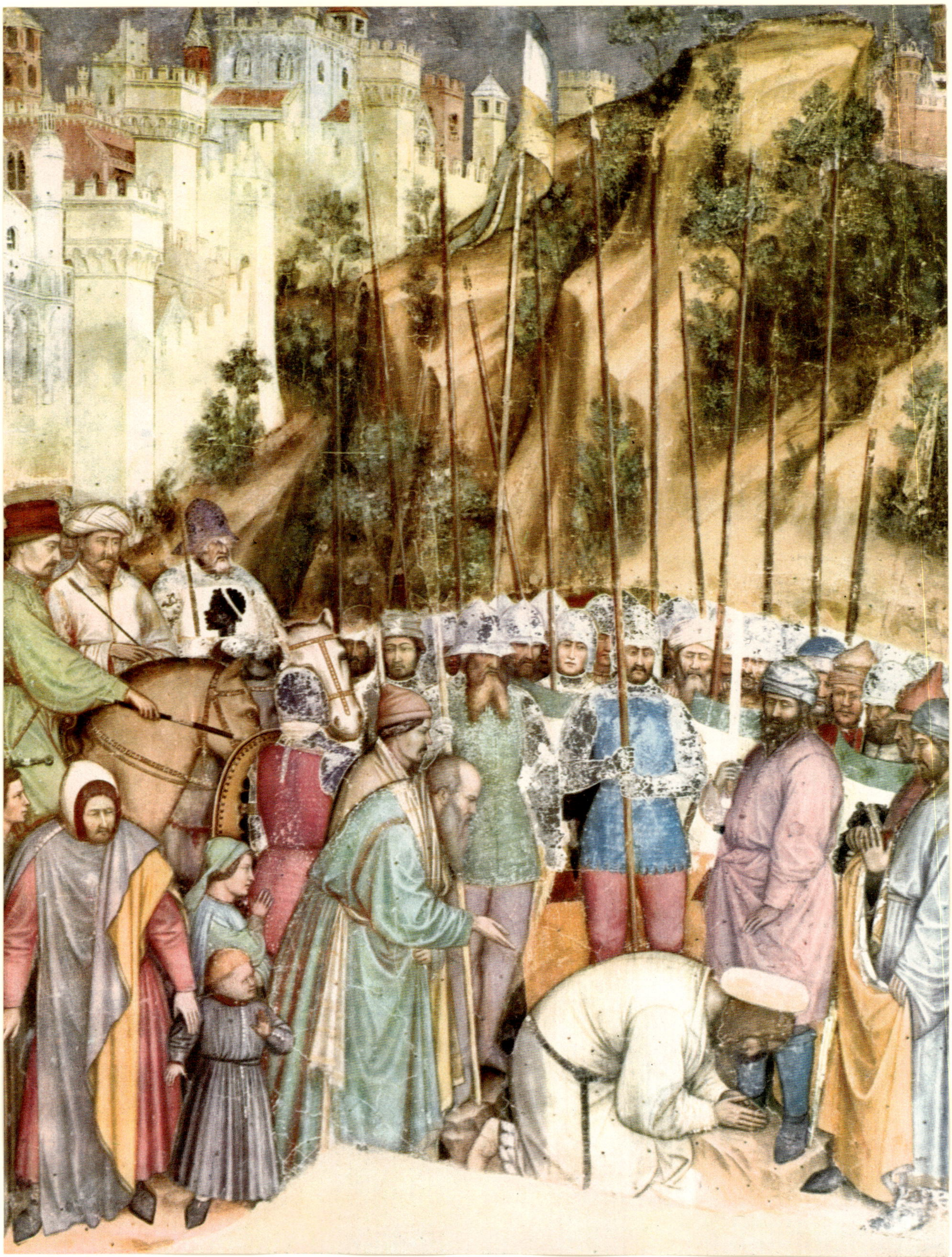

Altichiero: The Martyrdom of S. George. Oratory of S. George

most probably by him. In the chapels of S. James and S. George there are traces of both Florentine and Sienese styles, welded together to produce something new. In that straightforward bourgeois atmosphere of Northern Italy, he was free from the serious formal preoccupations of Tuscan artists, and was content with his achievements in the way of likeness, elegance and naturalism. The great Crucifixion is certainly by Altichiero, and places him immediately after Giotto and immediately before the Renaissance. He carries on the strong spirit of the Florentines by enlarging his compositions and giving to his scenes a choral value which is more extensive than the closely-knit schemes of Giotto, who expressed himself in a few essentials and a controlled, tense drama. Scenery and surroundings become larger and more varied as new scenes are added, and at times the descriptive style of the northern painters is lost. Emphasis is placed on the inquisitive women, on the executioners with their long ladders who are leaving Calvary; on the varied collection of squires and horsemen; on the head-dresses and outlandish costumes which are like a foretaste of the sumptuous knights of Pisanello and Gentile da Fabriano, who seem more fitted for tournaments and tilting than for battles. As in Giotto the central drama still revolves round the gentle crucified Christ, but he is also concerned with the detail of the sorrowing Virgin supported by the holy women, and with the excitement of the gamblers, playing for the robe of the Son of Man. The background no longer consists, as in Giotto, of a heavy sky. Instead there is a crystal clear, imaginary city of Jerusalem, which removes every trace of harshness from Golgotha. The colour changes continuously, with an enormous range of alabaster, pink and violet shades, and deeper tones of yellow and green, creating a brilliant shimmering effect. Altichiero's style was never again to be so pure and complete; certainly not in the scenes in S. James (where the harder style of a third master is also to be seen), but perhaps it may be glimpsed in the great battle of Clavijio, with its perspective, its amplitude and skilful colouring. Nor in the oratory of S. George, painted about 1384 for Raimondo Lupi, the brother of Bonifacio, where the personalities of the two artists are mingled together. The Martyrdom of S. George is nevertheless a work of high quality, in which the dignified figures of the soldiers in their closely packed rows, are arranged in a wide semicircle and form a strong wall in front of which is the kneeling figure of the Saint. With their long lances they measure, as it were, the enormous depth of space. Insensitive and motionless, they form a contrast to the sublime patience of the martyr, to the agitated movement of the priest on the left, to the executioner ready to strike, and to the hurried retreat of the horrified spectator leading a reluctant child. In the background there is once again a turretted city, and also a steep rock with a few scattered trees. The warm harmony of colours is here again with a succession of pink, pale blue, whites, and yellow. The quality which remains high in all the scenes by Altichiero and his companion, at times recalls the dignity of Giotto and at others (as shown in the pleasing detail of costumes, faces and architecture) the gay, airy quality of northern Gothic. An example is the Adoration of the Magi where the influence of Giotto is strong in the forbidding rocks, and where the perspective of the stable echoes the scene painted by Giotto in the Arena chapel.

Altichiero probably returned to Verona in the last years of his life, but only one work, his last, has survived there. It is a wall-painting with singularly beautiful colouring, in S. Anastasia, and was commissioned by the Cavalli family. The Virgin, angels, saints and knights, dressed in the fashion of the day, have a lively individuality which Altichiero expresses in his most accomplished style; they suggest that he had renewed his contacts with northern art during his stay at Verona.

He had many pupils and followers, most of them unknown, who gradually altered his style and built up a polished and sophisticated world of fantasy, which was reflected in the art of Trento and Bolzano. Painting had not developed to any great extent in these regions by the fourteenth century, but it was Italian in style, in the ample, dignified manner of Giotto, modified by variations from the Po valley, particularly in wall-paintings. At the same time northern influences could be observed, especially in altarpieces.

The remains of wall-paintings in the church of the Dominicans contain obvious traces of the style of Pietro da Rimini and Tommaso da Modena, especially in the soft, blond figure of S. Catherine, which resembles to some extent the saints of Tommaso at Treviso. And the altarpieces in the Abbey of Novacella and in the Austrunk chapel in the charterhouse of Senale, which are now in the museum of Bolzano, show an obvious affinity with fourteenth-century northern art, especially with the schools of South Germany.

Altichiero's style was carried by his followers beyond Bolzano, up the narrow valleys of the Adige, the Isarco and the Rienza, to the remote castles of the Alps, finally reaching the Tyrol, Austria and Bohemia.

The court art, a kind of forerunner of Flamboyant Gothic, which we glimpsed in Verona is, with slight variations, much like the style which flourished at this period in the neighbouring region of Lombardy, and generally speaking developments in Lombardy have a great deal in common with those which took place in Verona.

Milan was ruled by an absolute prince, Azzone Visconti, who, once he had established his authority, enriched the city with churches and palaces and summoned artists from France and other countries north of the Alps to beautify his own palace which was being built between the Broletto district and the new cathedral. The historian Galvano Fiamma praises the chapel, which seemed to him to be decorated entirely in gold and ultramarine blue, shining with beautiful glass windows and with occasional splashes of white from precious French ivories. Of all this graceful magnificence nothing remains except the truncated campanile of S. Gottardo, still carrying on its summit the angel and viper badge of the Visconti, and the name of Azzone. But the work of all these artists, Italian and foreign, was still not enough. Like Cangrande, Visconti was not contented, and extended his patronage to Giotto, who worked in the palace between 1333 and 1336. Nothing has survived of this work, although according to tradition Giotto painted frescoes representing Vainglory surrounded by pagan heroes from Aeneas to Attila, and others which included Charlemagne and Azzone Visconti himself.

There is no doubt at all that Tuscan influence spread over this region. It was not of course a sudden phenomenon, as though Giotto's arrival had conjured a miraculous crop. It is more likely, especially in the early years of the fourteenth century, that there was some local activity which can be distinguished even today from the work of Giotto and those followers who came with him from Florence: Stefano, Maso and possibly Giottino. Like Verona, Milan had its own artists who worked in their own style, which still had some connection with Byzantine art, but was also influence by northern Gothic. This same atmosphere is to be found at Como in the wall-painting in the apse of S. Abbondio, and is found in the miniatures of the codices produced in this region. In these the connection with the North seems still more evident, since it is easy to make comparisons with the great number of French illuminated manuscripts which have been preserved through the centuries. This particular feeling is to be found, for example, in the Liber Pantheon of Godfrey da Viterbo, a very important codex, written by the notary Giovanni de Nuxigia, and illuminated in 1331. Sometimes there are obvious connections with contemporary Emilian illumination, but as a rule the style is different, being rapid and, so to speak, impressionistic. The colours are very bright, with strong reds, blues, greens and yellows. Skilful, spirited compositions are found on every page, with the same vine tendrils and elaborate decorations that are to be found in contemporary French works by Master Honoré and Jean Pucelle. The figures are full of life, with a naturalistic and sometimes amusing way of moving, against simple backgrounds of rocks and architecture with a rudimentary perspective. There was moreover a logical connection

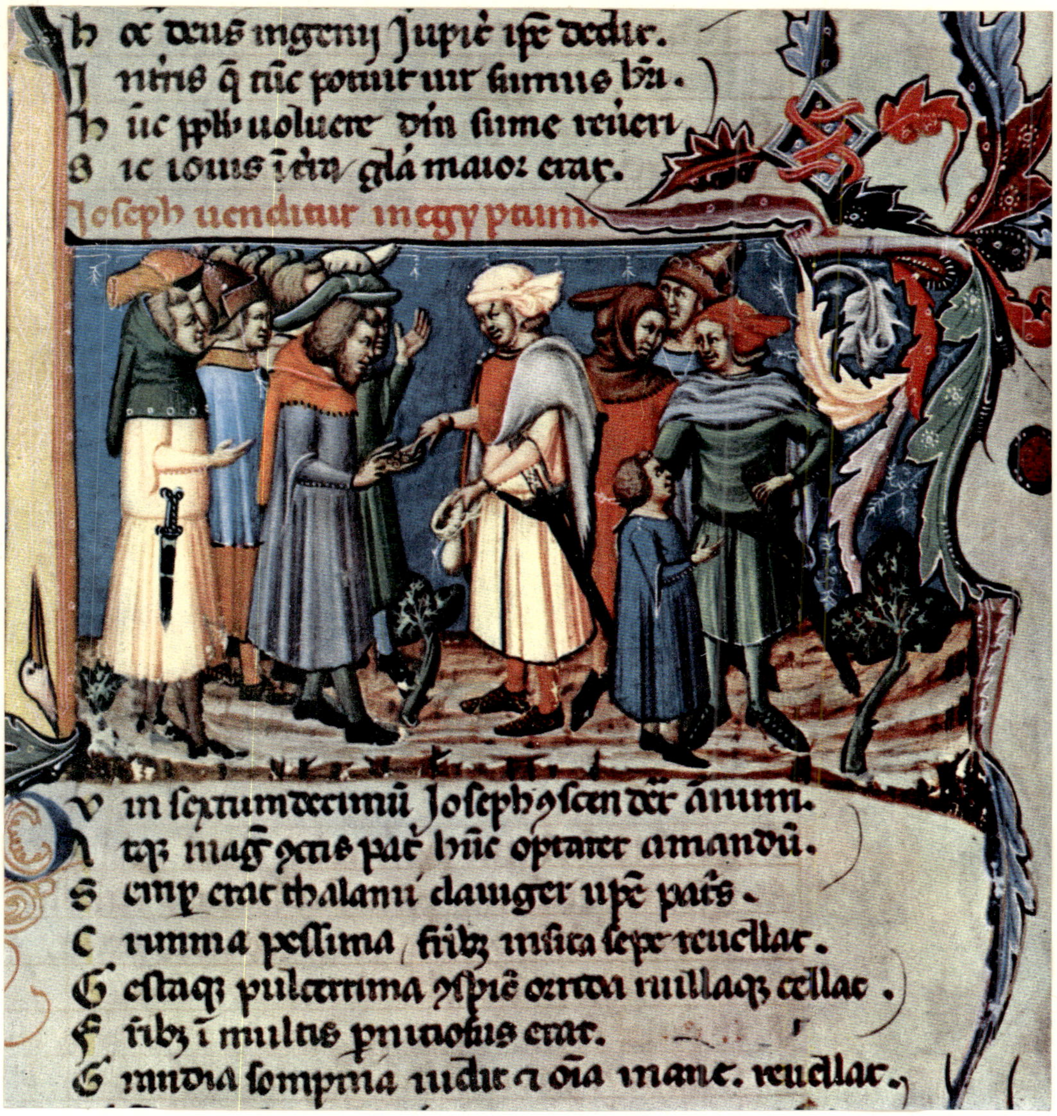

Godfrey da Viterbo: Liber Pantheon. Bibliothèque Nationale, Paris

between the Lombardy of Azzone Visconti and the world beyond the Alps. Political factors played an important part, not least the marriage between Visconti and a French princess, Catherine of Savoy. There were other connections too with the neighbouring state of Piedmont, which remained under French artistic influence at least until the end of the fourteenth century. This is about the date of the wall-paintings in the Abbey of Vezzolano and in the Val di Susa, and of those (slightly later) in the Castles of Fenis and Manta, with their flat colouring and contorted figures so like the delicate images which French miniaturists produced in Books of Hours for their princes. The grandeur of Giotto certainly made a strong impression on local artists (although at this particular period Giotto's austerity had been modified by a lengthy contact with Sienese art), and from now on the influence of his style was to be found all over Milan. Through his own work, which has now vanished, and through the work of his more important followers, Giotto gave to the charming school of Lombardy some of his nobility and his comprehension of human values.

This new style, combining the grandeur of Tuscan composition and the colouring of Lombardy, is first seen in the anonymous frescoes of the Abbey of Viboldone, dated 1349, which are attributed by some authorities to the Florentine artist Giusto dei Menabuoi, and in the frescoes in the Archbishop's palace in Milan, which, judging by the few surviving fragments, were Tuscan in style.

The new style is seen above all in the work of Giovanni da Milano, the greatest Lombard painter of the fourteenth century. Giovanni first arrived in Florence about 1345, and fell under the influence of Stefano and Giottino, who had returned from their visit to Lombardy. At this date the artist was already expert in the style of his native city, and must have been aware of Sienese art, which reached Milan by a number of different routes: through Sienese artists working in northern Italy, from Avignon, and especially through the miniatures of Emilia, which had acquired many Sienese characteristics by way of Rimini. It is obvious too that when he was a young man, Giovanni had seen Giotto and other Florentines working in Lombardy. He was influenced by the so-called " opposition ", consisting of Maso and Stefano who stood apart from the undistinguished imitators of Giotto, and he did not feel at home among all Giotto's pupils in Florence. He was not in sympathy with Taddeo Gaddi or Bernardo Daddi, but rather with Orcagna, and especially with the gentle Nardo, and more influenced by the grace and intense colouring which came at that time from Siena. The result was that with his brilliant range of colours he always remained the " Lombard " in the midst of the formal splendours of Florentine painting; this range included reds, blues, deep greens and yellows, and a gentle touch of pink barely noticeable in his subtle flesh tints. A " Lombard ", and up to the time of his arrival in Florence a charming storyteller and illustrator of daily life, of houses, animals and events; the creator of unforgettable human faces, where the skin becomes a subtle impasto of mother-of-pearl. In the end this careful naturalism of Lombardy and the Po valley became with Giovanni a gently austere vision where the simplest human events were invested with liturgical significance. This noble synthesis could only have occurred in Florence, and his polyptychs were in fact commissioned by Florentine patrons.

Indeed all Giovanni's known work between 1365 and 1369 was carried out in Tuscany. The polyptych of Prato gives a foretaste of the lyrical manner that was to come. That of Ognissanti, now in the Uffizi, shows the influence of Giotto modified by detailed attention to individuals and costumes, and gives him a place in the list of great Italian artists. In this work his delicate female saints, with their worldly costumes and attitudes, are the sisters of those who were soon to figure in the scenes in the Rinuccini chapel. Later, at the end of the century and beginning of the next one, they would appear once again in work of Giovannino de' Grassi, and on the walls of Casa Borromeo in Milan.

In 1365 Giovanni signed the Pietà, now in the Accademia in Florence. This in one of his best works, in his mature formal style, very sensitive to shades of feeling, particularly of human suffering. He arranges his mourners in a northern fashion, against a pale golden background with a pattern of haloes. They form a unitary mass of suffering humanity round the beautiful figure of Christ, who seems to groan in his agony, abandoning himself to the last embrace of his Mother.

The colour emphasises this feeling of deep suffering; the pallor of the wan faces and the ashen body of Christ graduates through gentle passages of light and shade into the stronger colouring of the Virgin, and shines in the bright golden hair of the Magdalene. The most distinguished works by Giovanni da Milano are undoubtedly the frescoes which he carried out in the Rinuccini chapel in S. Croce, portraying scenes from the lives of the Virgin and Mary Magdalene. He narrates events from the Bible with the imagination of a poet, although he transfers them to more familiar surroundings, creating at times a perfect accord between liturgical seriousness and homely intimacy.

Giotto's dramatic quality is not to be found in the scenes from the life of S. Joachim; instead there is a peaceful narrative quality. This is seen in the expulsion of the old priest from the Temple, where the artist is more concerned with depicting the holy objects than with the action. The majestic procession bearing offerings can be seen in the long arcades of the temple, as though the figures were in the wings of a great polyptych. The solemn choral effect of this hymn is skilfully blended by Giovanni with the cheerful rhythms of wordly song. On the left a tightly packed group of men stand against the brown and grey background; on the right there is a harmony of softly blended pink, violet and grey in the faces of the women as they move towards the centre. They are magnificent figures, dressed in the rich fashion of the day, with their tight-fitting aristocratic dresses in shades of white, yellow and pink, with splashes of bright colour accentuating the delicate flesh tints of their soft, handsome shoulders. The other scenes have the same spatial quality, derived from

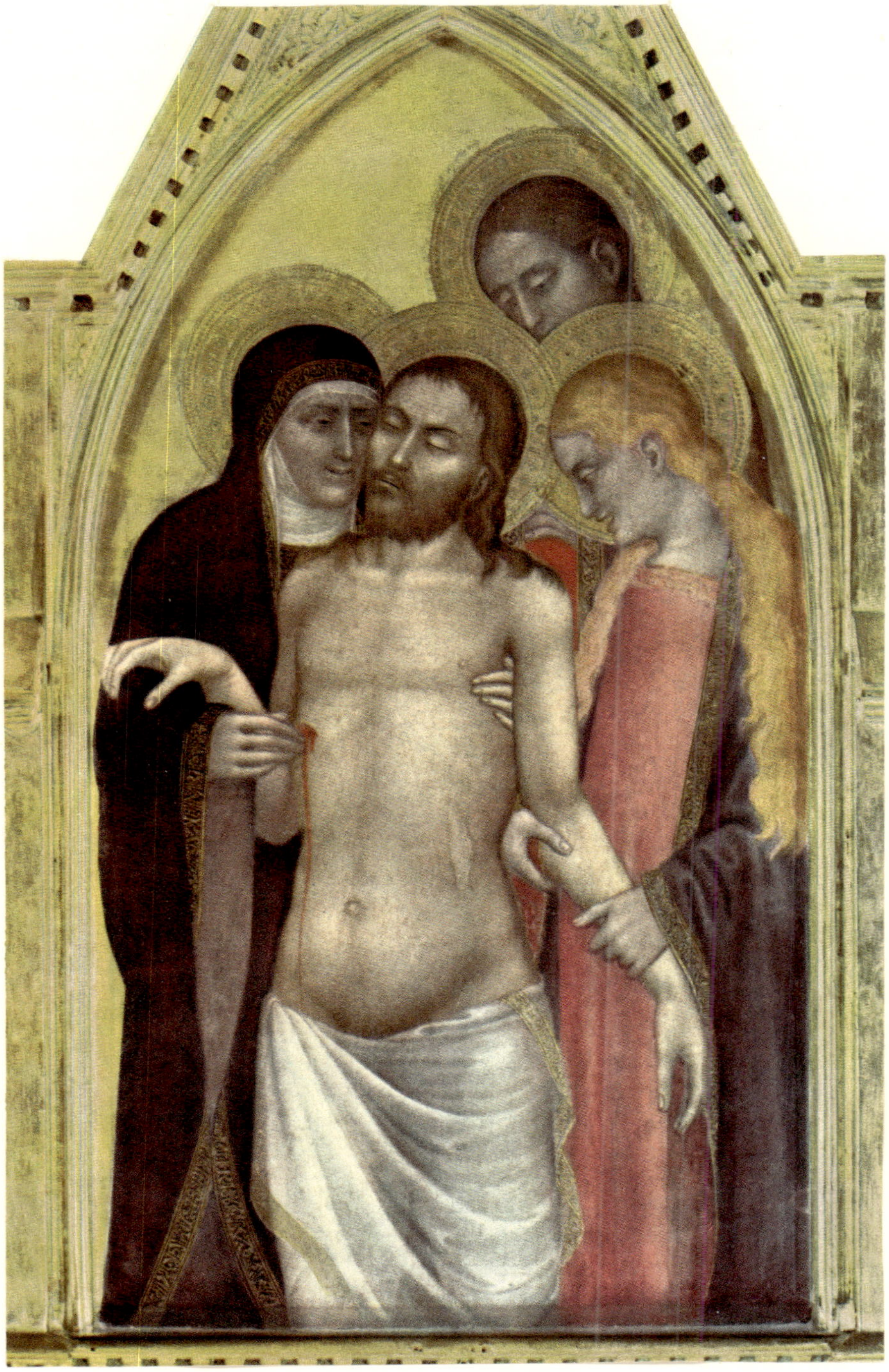

Giovanni da Milano: Deposition. Accademia Gallery, Florence

Giotto, and a continuous pattern of charming gestures, graceful women and rich costumes. Leaving his work unfinished, Giovanni left for Rome in 1369, and according to Vasari when he returned he " did a great deal of work in tempera and fresco " in Lombardy. Of this nothing has survived. But the legacy of Giovanni's lovely style remained. It was based on strong composition and design, obviously derived from Giotto, and combined with infinite grace and magnificent colour, and a taste for everything that is beautiful and true in the daily life of mankind.

This heritage is found in Lombardic paintings in the second half of the fourteenth century. There must have been a large number of these in the more important cities, but none of them has survived. Other fine examples also existed in scattered country chapels. The few surviving examples are at Solaro, near Saronno, where an unknown artist painted scenes from the life of the Virgin; at S. Biagio in Bellinzona; and again at Viboldone where the sleeping virgins wear costumes and head-dresses in the style of Giovanni da Milano. Lombardic art continued to develop in the latter part of the fourteenth century, as can be seen in the frescoes at Chiaravalle, at Vertemate, and especially at Mocchirolo, in Brianza, where in a small chapel in the fields a painter of considerable talent carried out a series of frescoes commissioned by the Porro family, who were local landowners. With delicate colouring, an accomplished design, and

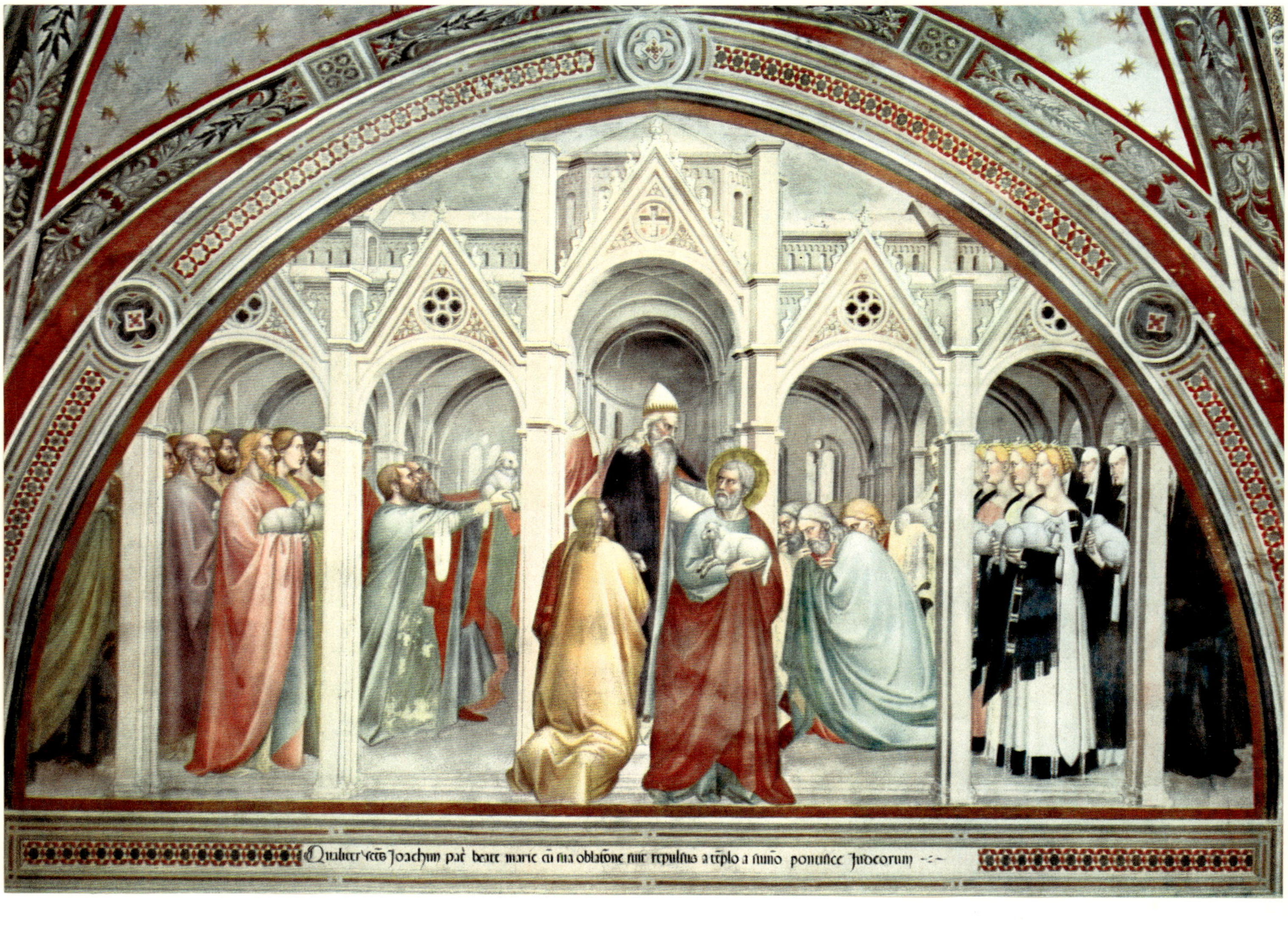

Giovanni da Milano: S. Joachim expelled from the Temple, S. Croce, Florence

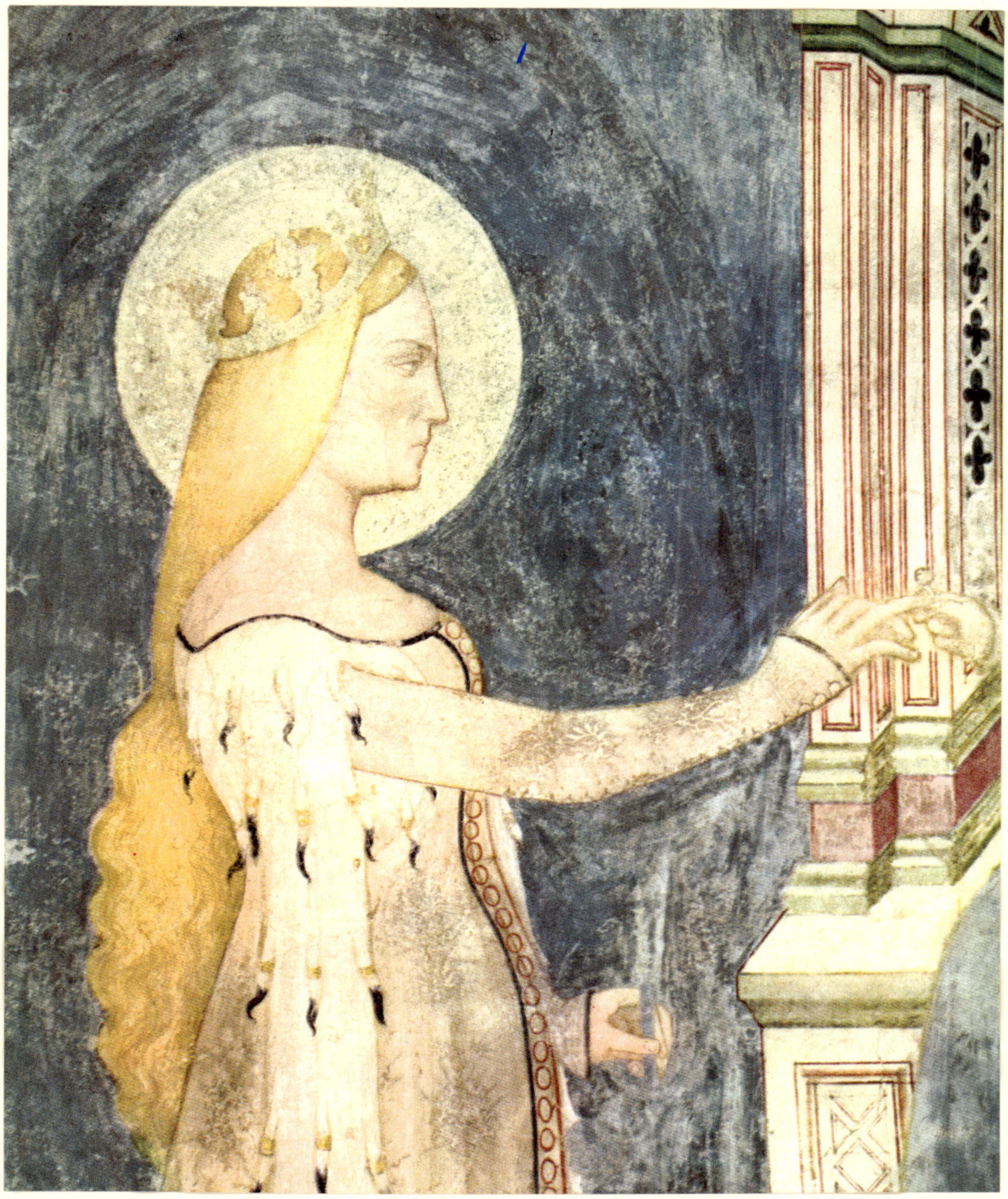

Unknown Lombard Artist: The Mystic Marriage of S. Catherine, detail.

Brera Gallery, Milan

acute psychological observation in an arrangement of simple scenes, this artist painted the Crucifixion, the Blessed Redeemer, S. Ambrogio, and the homage offered by his patrons to the Virgin. The exquisite feeling of the painter is seen to great advantage in the Mystic Marriage of S. Catherine, where he shows great sweetness both in conception and execution, particularly in the pale, regal figure of the saint, which is one of the happiest exaltations of feminine beauty, a theme dear to all Lombardic artists. She is an unforgettable vision, and there is great delicacy in the pale blue tone of her rich robe, in the pale pink shading of her face in profile with its barely perceptible lights and shades. Possibly the unknown painter of Mocchirolo, who was formerly confused with Giovanni da Milano, was the originator of a new style in Lombardic painting, characterised by an interest in direct impressions of external beauty and at times enriched by a more profound note of drama and a careful obser-

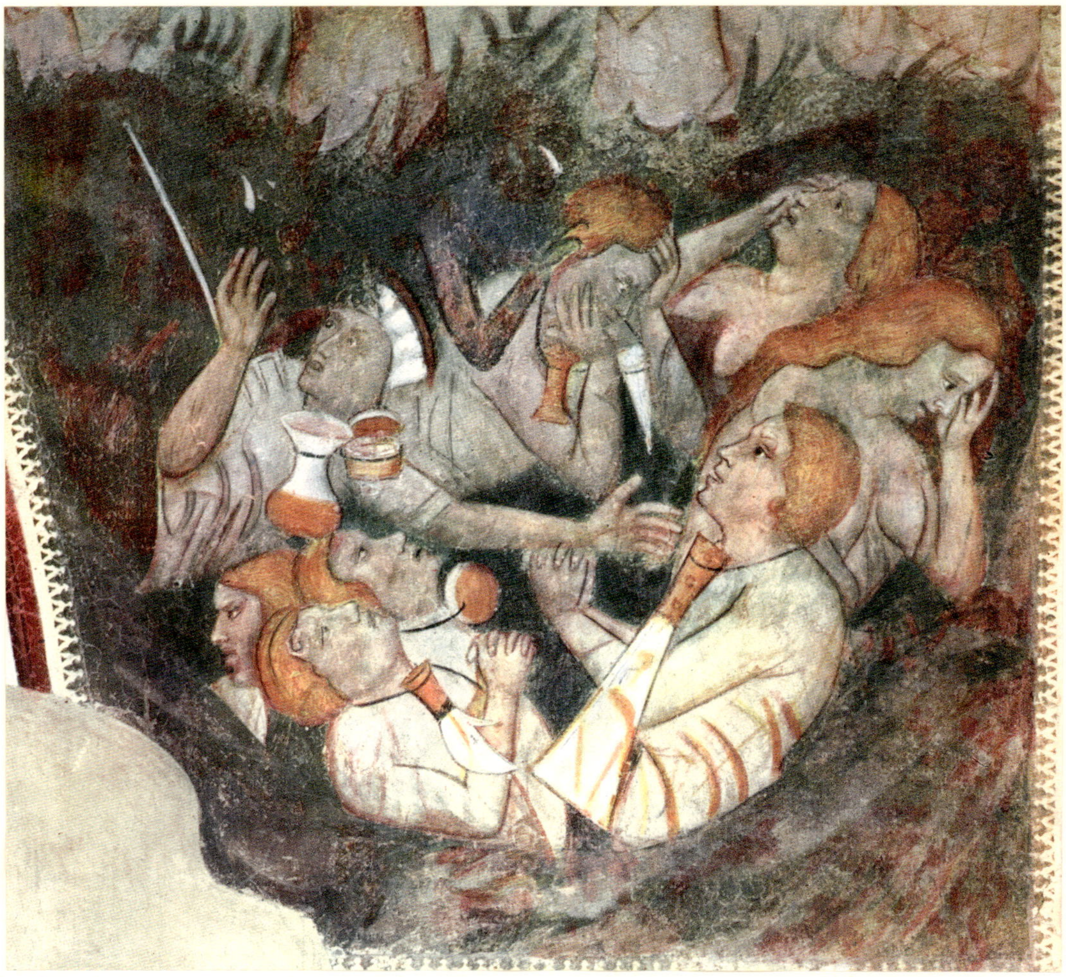

Unknown Lombard Artist: The Last Judgment, detail. Oratory, Lentate

vation of both the details and the delicacy of the features. An example is in the Oratory of Lentate, where another member of the Porro family commissioned an unknown artist whose work is in a minor key but who shows the same graceful quality of court art, in the fair-haired children rising up in the Last Judgement. They are delicate shadow-like images, although their young bodies are solid and their profiles clear cut.

This change in the style of Lombardic art was brought about by a number of factors, including the proximity of France, and the fact that northern workmen as well as Italians were employed on the construction of Milan cathedral. There was a lively interest in culture of all kinds; and the Visconti family, for example, built up a large collection of illuminated manuscripts in their castle at Pavia, including northern romances of chivalry as well as sacred books and scientific treatises. In these romances the miniaturists felt free to include landscapes, interiors, soldiers and children, interwoven in intricate linear patterns and brilliant colours. A Lombardic artist used delicate shading and architectural backgrounds, slightly tinged with gold, in the romance of Guiron le Courtois, for example, and his work has a happy idealistic quality, with bright colours and a design of exquisite fineness. He drew his inspiration from knight errantry and the lively court life of his time.

The fourteenth century in Italy is identified with the greatness of Giotto, with the Sienese painters, and with all the artists who bestowed an unmistakable character upon Italian art. This character may be seen in innumerable masterpieces; in the altarpieces, and the wall-paintings which reveal all the variety of the period, the anti-Gothic, pre-Renaissance style of Giotto, the polished Sienese manner, rich in gold and graceful linear patterns and their development and transformation according to local tastes in the various regions of northern Italy. Great churches and chapels were built with wonderful mural decorations whose purpose was to teach scripture to the faithful.

In France, where the characteristic arts were architecture and sculpture, the situation was quite different. Perhaps the great Gothic buildings had killed the mural painting which had been so important in the Romanesque period. Characteristic wall-paintings with bright colours on a blue background were scattered over Burgundy, Auvergne and Savoy, and there are examples based on Italian and Byzantine-Hellenistic models in the Cluniac abbey of Berzé-la-Ville, in S. Germain d'Auxerre, S. Julien

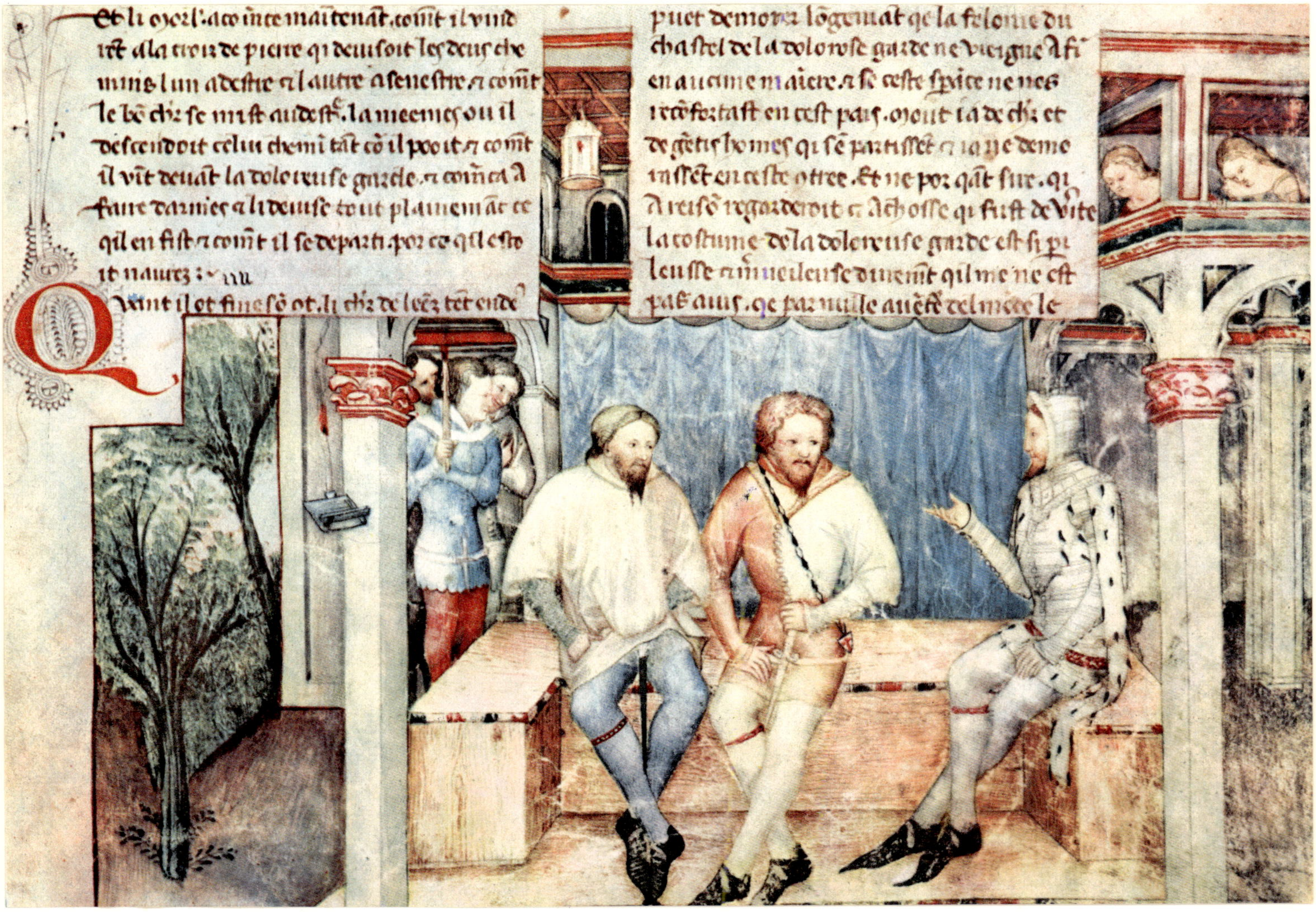

Unknown Lombard Artist: Fragment from the Romance of Guiron le Courtois

Bibliothèque Nationale, Paris

de Brinde, and the cathedral of Puy. A more popular style of wall-painting, which may have had its origins in Spain, grew up in Touraine and Poitou. The whole population contributed, crusader-like, to the great cathedrals which were being built in every city. But the high arches with their elaborate carving and the broad high windows with their vast rose tracery left no room for wall-paintings. Painting was thus forced to transfer to glass, which became a magnificent carpet of colours, a feast of light, a visionary decoration. Enthusiasm for stained glass ran so high as to exclude all other media, and once painting had been transferred to those transparent surfaces it had virtually no other purpose than to dazzle the beholder. French artists lost themselves in the delights of an art which became increasingly important in architecture, until windows were made larger than ever for their benefit. During a vogue for everything that was airy, light and impalpable, no style of painting could compete with the windows which seemed themselves to be sources of light. Even the theologians helped this wonderful flowering of brilliant light, suggesting new and simplified iconographical formulae. The only mural decorations which have survived are those in the archways of the Sainte-Chapelle at Paris, in a few country churches, and in the castle of Vaudreuil, but they are only small fragments consisting of ornamental designs which tell us very little about the dates and styles of the period. It is only at Avignon that a number of frescoes have been carefully preserved, a last remnant of the great enterprise which was begun by Simone Martini when he was summoned to the papal court in 1339. Avignon had become the seat of the pontificate in 1309, and a papal palace had been built there. It was begun during the reign of Benedict XII (1334-42) and enlarged immediately afterwards by Clement VI (1342-52); all the decorations were by Italian artists and were carried out in accordance with the taste and traditions of their country. Details of this work are known from the surviving frescoes and from many documents, which also refer to the presence of French and Catalan craftsmen. Simone Martini is mentioned, as are Francesco and Niccolò da Firenze, Rigo d'Arezzo, Giovanni Luca da Siena, and Pietro da Viterbo. Most important of all was Matteo Giovannetti da Viterbo, who, with the help of two assistants, painted, amongst other things, the wardrobe, the consistorial chamber, and " the servants' hall ".

Judging by the frescoes which have survived in the Papal apartments, Matteo seems to have resembled Simone Martini, but he probably had some knowledge of Franco-Flemish art, which is known to us only through illumination. His prophets and sibyls, with their elongated figures, slow graceful gestures, and ample robes, are modelled with great delicacy, in bright colours which are apt to be warmer than Simone's, yet betray his style, transformed and adapted to different tastes. A guide to these tastes would probably be found in the lost frescoes in French castles, and in the work of the many local painters who are known to us only by name. Northern Gothic influence is less noticeable in the other frescoes in the chapel of S. John; the modelling is more plastic and the perspective more in evidence, suggesting a renewed contact with Italy. Matteo's male and female saints are refined in outline, composition and treatment of light, and stand in flowery meadows, instead of against starry skies. In their luminous quality they recall, although they do not equal, the figures of Simone.

Other Italian artists painted frescoes in the church of Villeneuve-les-Avignon and the Salle du Cerf in the papal palace at Avignon. All these frescoes have come to be considered as part of primitive French art, but, being so obviously Italian, they are hardly representative. In any case there was a constant coming and going between France and Italy, and soon afterwards French painting developed along the lines of Giotto and the Sienese artists in the direction of naturalism.

The names of other Italian painters who worked in France have survived; they include the Sienese artists Giovanni di Nuccio, Michele Mignani, Nicola Cheloardi di

Lucca and Raimondo Pellegrino who worked at Montpellier, while there is an unconfirmed tradition that many years earlier Philip the Fair had brought Roman artists with him from Italy. It may have been these painters who left traces of their work, in the style of Cavallini, in the ruined frescoes in the chapel of S. Etienne in the church of S. Nazaire at Béziers. So that when all the evidence is taken together it is obvious that Italian infiltration was one of the most important influences in the artistic life of France.

The origins of French painting can be traced back to the reign of Philip the Fair. Many documents refer to painters and their works commissioned by the King and the French nobles. The first of these painters was Etienne d'Auxerre; then came Evrard d'Orléans, who belonged to a dynasty of artists and was already working in Paris in 1292. In 1304 he was appointed Court Painter to King John the Good. It is known that he was also in the service of Philip of Valois, and that he worked both as sculptor and architect for Mahaut d'Artois, Countess of Flanders. The name of his son, Girard, is also known and there is a record of his career in the King's service as valet de chambre. Documents and royal inventories speak at some length of these painters and their works. These consisted of pictures, bed backs, chair backs, chess men, wooden figures, and chairs. Nothing has survived of all this work except the portrait of John the Good, now in the Bibliothèque Nationale of Paris, which dates from about 1360. It is a half-length portrait of the King in profile, with a golden background. The unknown artist, who is thought by some critics to have been Girard d'Orléans, worked in the naturalistic Italian style, and has painted a faithful likeness of an unattractive, ugly man. His skilful design recalls the grace of Sienese art, modified by the cold style of Andrea da Firenze. A few years later, probably during the reign of Charles V, another unknown French artist at Narbonne painted the Passion of Christ in ink on white silk, which is now in the Louvre. The exaggerated gestures and expression belong to the North, but the balanced composition, some of the poses, and the elegant drapery of the figures, reveal a Sienese derivation. When all this evidence has been compared it is clear that there was no definite style of painting, still less a school.

Only in contemporary illumination, which was the highest form of art in fourteenth-century France, could a French school be said to exist. Illumination had never ceased to be practised by the monks all over Europe and in the thirteenth century a new style had begun to develop, possibly inspired by sculpture and stained glass. Designs had become softer and more polished, and fourteenth-century miniaturists, tired of the arid Benedictine styles, and dazzled by the magnificent colours of Gothic windows, had tried to achieve the same splendour by using very clear colours: red and blue against the shining gold which formed a background, as light did for stained glass. Soon this form of art, which until now had been a monastic accomplishment *par excellence*, entered upon a new phase. French literature also began to develop and knights and their ladies began to listen to legends, to *chansons de geste*, and to the amorous intrigues of the romances of chivalry. More illustrated manuscripts were called for, and now became, as Poussin called them, " toys ". Obviously there was no question of monks illustrating these new, profane books; they were in any case busy with their work of glorifying the Creator. So a school of lay miniaturists grew up, with their workshop in Paris, where the university and the court furnished a breeding ground of culture. There was an increasing demand for miniaturists to work on encyclopaedias, chronicles, romances and legends, and they even became open competitors of the religious artists in the decoration of Bibles, Breviaries, and Psalters. At the beginning they remained faithful to the stylised forms of their predecessors, even though some of the most archaic styles were soon discarded. By the late thirteenth century, however, pictures had already become freer, with that kind of lively grace which may be seen in the sketchbooks of Villard d'Honnecourt, or in the Psalter of S. Louis where smiling faces resemble some of the sculptures at Rheims and Chartres. The miniaturists seem to copy the sculptors in their interest in daily life, and perhaps they absorbed something of Italian naturalism. Gold, which up till now had formed the background of every composition, was only used occasionally, and soon it was discarded altogether as an architectural background, and attempts were made to convey a natural perspective. Throughout the fourteenth century this movement towards naturalism was accelerated, and completed the revolution which had begun when illumination was transferred from pen-and-ink artists into the hands of the humble craftsmen who used brushes. Very few names have survived; the first one is that of a certain "Henri" who illustrated a manuscript in 1285: next we hear of a group who worked near the university in the rue de la Boutebrie, and whose most important members were Honoré, who had a studio and, as assistants, his son-in-law Richard de Verdun and Tomassin, his valet; and another artist called Nicholas who was helped by his mother. There were others too, scattered over Paris, some of whose names have survived: Raoul, Thomas, Grégoire, Badouin.

It is probably right to recognise Honoré as the leader of a school, and the Breviary of Philip the Fair is attributed to him. In this work we can see the hesitant beginnings of marginal decoration, an art which was to have a considerable future. France was now beginning to increase in political importance; her kings were patrons of the arts, and appointed court painters. In particular they were patrons of illumination, which remained the main form of French painting. A rivalry developed between the sovereign and his nobles to see who could secure the most beautiful Psalters, Bibles, romances and chronicles, with the richest and most beautiful decorations. The king, his brothers, and most of the great nobles, became patrons.

During the reign of John the Good (1350-64), the Legend of S. Denis was produced by an unknown artist. It contains miniatures which are exceptionally beautiful, even if they are a trifle monotonous, and are of great importance for the study of Parisian costume of the day. The superb work of Jean Pucelle also belongs to this period. The name of Jean Pucelle was only re-discovered in the nineteenth century by L. Delisle, who noticed at the end of an illuminated Bible (which is probably the one written by Robert Billyng) three lines of microscopic letters which read: "Jehan Pucelle, Anciau de Cens, Jacquet Maci, il hont enluminé ce livre ci. Ceste lingne de vermeillon que vous vées fu escrite l'an de grace M.CCC et XXVII en un jeudi darrenier jour d'avril, vieille de mai, Vto. die".

Pucelle's miniatures belong in some ways to an earlier period, but, possibly influenced by Italian art, he sought to give his figures some feeling of volume. His name appears again in the later Breviary of Belleville in 1342, which is certainly his most important work, and which shows him to be closely connected with Honoré, who was probably his master. Their styles have something in common, but Pucelle's imaginative quality is more exuberant, his colours are brighter, and his designs elegant and precise. He possesses a quality at once delicate and capricious, as seen in his naturalistic butterflies and birds, vine tendrils and flowers, monkeys, pheasants, and dragon-flies. The seeds of this style had been sown by Honoré — if Honoré was in fact the author of the Breviary of Philip the Fair — and it was to remain an important legacy of Jean Pucelle until the period of Jacquemart de Hesdin and the Limbourg brothers at the end of the fifteenth century. Pucelle was therefore one of the most important artists of the fourteenth century in France, an artist who, by adopting Italian ideas, carried out a considerable revolution in the art of illumination. In his actual scenes he introduced a modified from of Tuscan perspective, in contrast to his

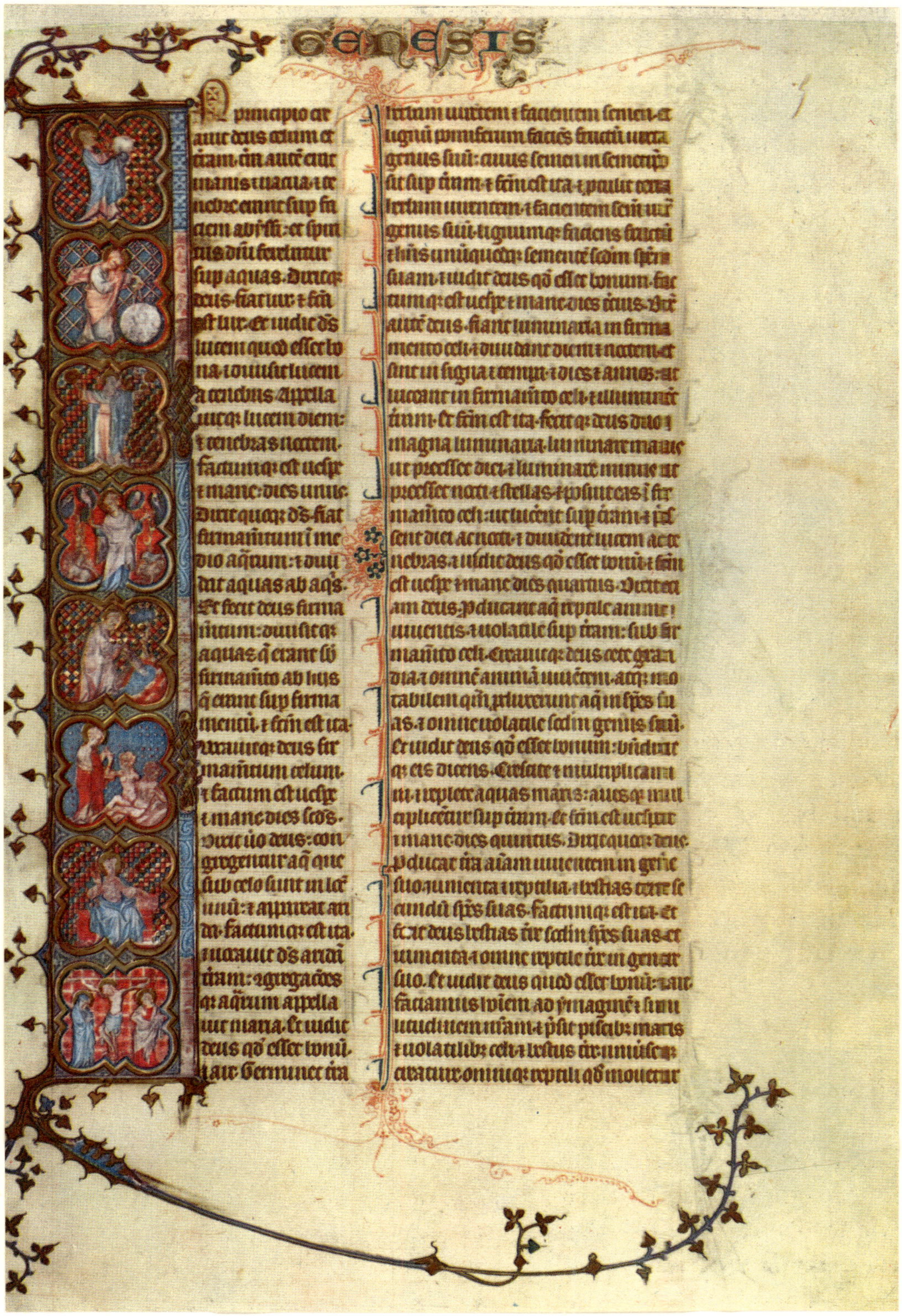

Jean Pucelle: The Billyng Bible. Bibliothèque Nationale, Paris

figures, which lacked the plastic quality of his Italian contemporaries. His rich naturalistic decoration, with its easy elegance and accomplished design, was wholly new in French painting.

Other names belonging to the period of John the Good have survived: Jan de Montmartre, who worked on an unidentified Bible between 1349 and 1353; Jan de Wirmes who illustrated a book of Mottetti for the king about 1349; Jan Luzanne, who was helped by his daughter Bourgot, and was perhaps the most distinguished of all. The work of these artists represents the finest examples of the Paris style.

Other centres of illumination were at Tours, Dijon, and Toulouse, but this provincial work was greatly inferior to the products of Paris. Illumination was also being done in the North, in Picardy, Artois, and Flanders, which although it was an independent earldom, was associated for political and artistic reasons with Paris. Although the school of Jean Pucelle continued to flourish other styles grew up which were less precise although more expressive. The poses became more lively, and the artists attempted to portray naturalistic scenes from contemporary court life, as for example in the series by an unknown artist of the great Chronicles of France. Naturalism in figures is followed by naturalism in surroundings, with accurate, detailed pictures of architectural interiors, and landscapes in a delightful perspective, as though the artist were leading us by the hand and introducing us into his scenes.

The reign of Charles V of Valois (1364-80) marks the re-establishment of French power after the final struggle against England, the great enemy of France, which had burst out once again at the end of the reign of John the Good. Charles's reign is more happily remembered as a period of generous patronage of the arts, especially illumination, which had now become a great tradition. Towards the end of the reign of John there had been an influx of new painters to Paris. Their numbers continued to increase and a number of Flemish painters settled there permanently, giving rise to a fusion of French and Flemish styles. Travelling artists were to be found at the courts of all the French princes who, following the king's example, became patrons. During this period they are to be found at Paris, Poitiers, Bruges, Dijon, Brussels, Ghent and even at Milan.

The most important artists of this period were Jean Bondol, sometimes described as being " of Bruges ", André Beauneveu and Jacquemart de Hesdin. Together they laid the foundations of the French school of painting, and of the great development of international Gothic. Jean Bondol of Bruges was active between 1368-81, and was probably responsible for illustrating the first Bible in French, translated by Jean de Sy and commissioned by John the Good.

This work in itself testifies to the greatness of the Flemish artist, who handles the beautiful figures in an accomplished linear style, grouping them in landscapes which are barely sketched but which herald the development of a more naturalistic manner, just as his carefully observed animals herald the wonderful animals of the international, especially the Italian, Gothic style. The solemn Biblical scenes are delicately harmonious in their subdued colouring. Henri Martin is doubtful about ascribing this Bible to Jean de Bruges, and on the basis of this work prefers to create an anonymous personality known as the " Master of the Bouqueteaux ", to whom he also attributes, on analogy, the Bible of Charles VI which formerly belonged to Charles V, a manuscript containing poems by Guillaume de Machaut and the great Chronicles of France dated 1379.

Commissioned by the king's brother, the Duc d'Anjou, Jean Bondol designed the cartoons for the magnificent series of tapestries, representing scenes from the Apocalypse, in the cathedral of Angers. With a firm and free imagination he translated images which are probably from a contemporary manuscript, and possibly from the Apocalypse belonging to the library of Cambrai, now in the Bibliothèque Nationale. He enriched the visions of John the Evangelist with fantastic Gothic architecture, a non-realistic perspective, and graceful figures which are so naturalistic that they recall the images in the Bible of Sy.

The greatest artist of his day was André Beauneveu, who was already working in 1360 for Yolande of Flanders, and who died in 1402. In addition to being a miniaturist he was an architect, sculptor, and painter, and was active in Valenciennes, his native city, in 1365, when he carved the tombs of Philip VI of Valois and King John and his Queen at S. Denis. In 1378 he carved a Madonna at Cambrai; then he returned to Valenciennes to work for the Count of Flanders and finally for the Duc de Berry, for whom he painted a series of twenty-four austere figures of prophets and saints in a Psalter. These are genuine pictures, which in their firm design, decisive composition, advanced perspective, and judicious colouring, distinguish the painter from his contemporaries and establish him among the greatest artists of the fourteenth century. This is the only known work by André Beauneveu, and judging by his style he does not seem to be connected with any earlier school. Probably, like all great artists, he broke away from his training and created a style that was personal and independent.

Not so Jacquemart de Hesdin, who was working for the Duc de Berry about 1384 and who, although he belonged to the next generation, may be regarded as the direct successor of Jean Pucelle, especially in the matter of marginal decoration. Nothing could be more skilful and delicate than the architectural frames of his compositions, in which beautiful flowers and wild creatures, especially birds, are portrayed with an exquisite naturalism.

This brings us to the luxurious world of the Limbourg brothers, and the manuscript of the " Très riches Heures du Duc de Berry ", the greatest example of Franco-Flemish art. But before considering this magnificent work, which dates from 1416, we must conclude our rapid survey of fourteenth-century illumination, the greatest mani-

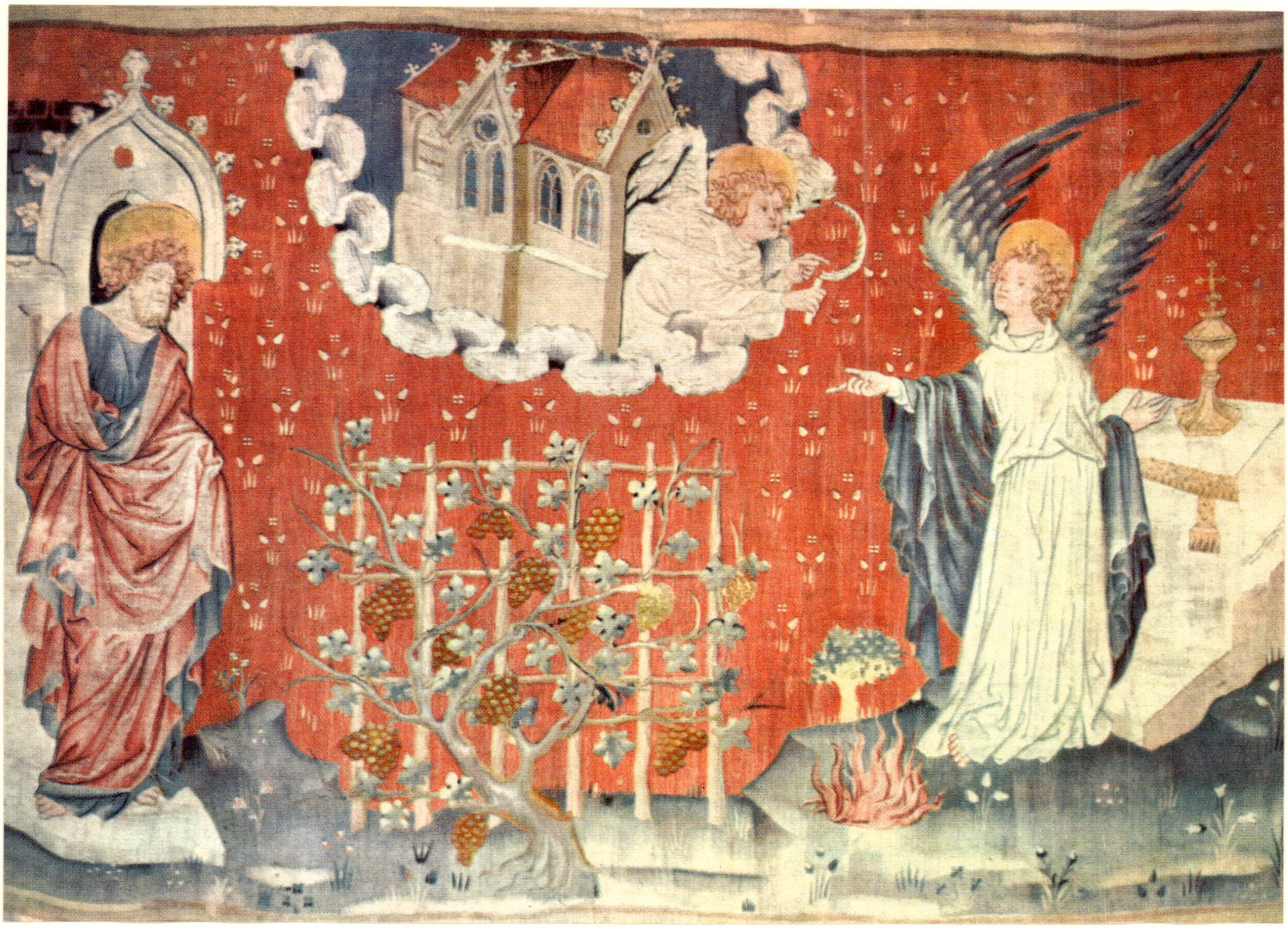

Jean Bondol: Scene from the Apocalypse, tapestry. Cathedral of Angers

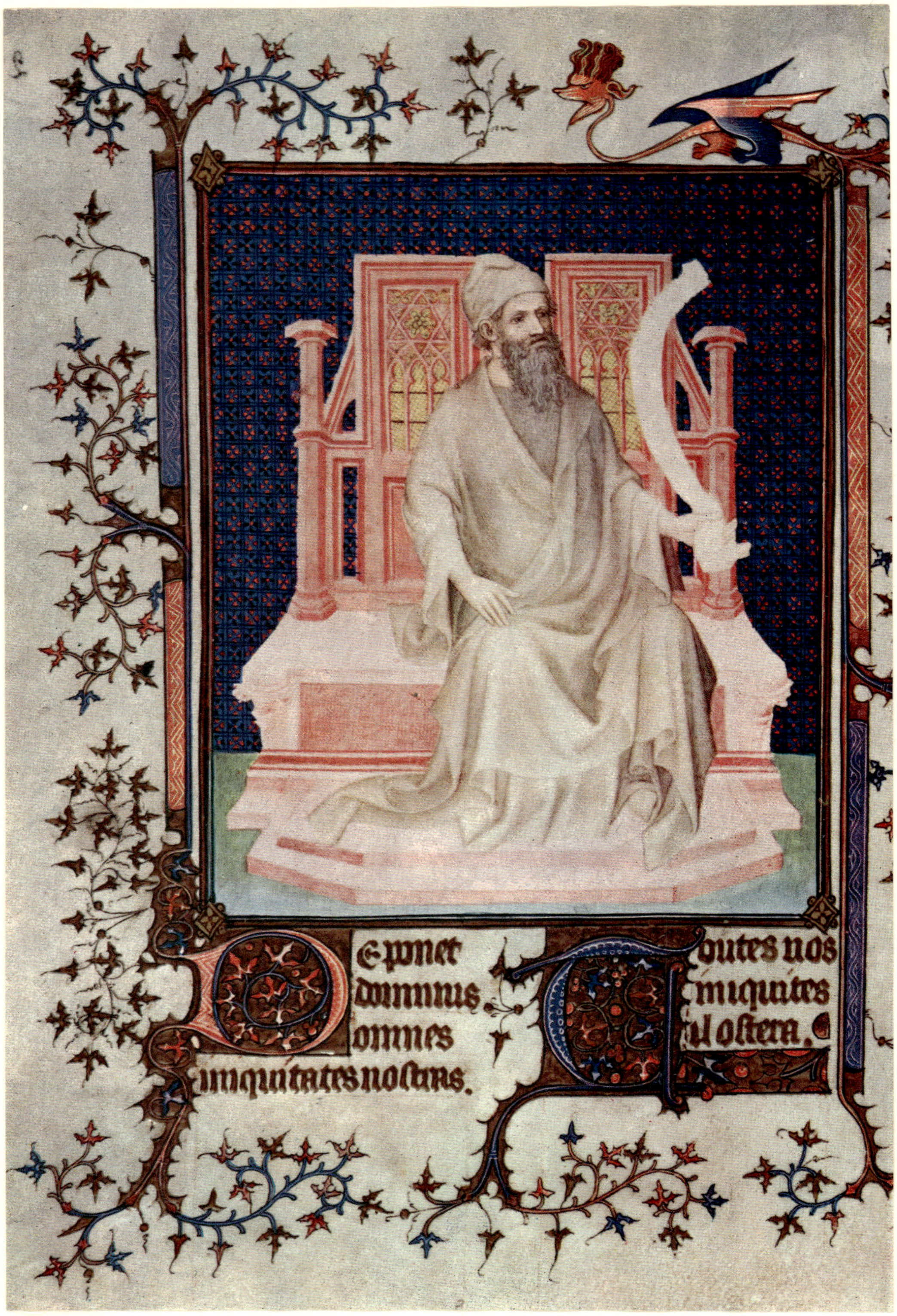

André Beauneveu: Psalter of the Duc de Berry. Bibliothèque Nationale, Paris

festation of French painting. From now until the fifteenth century the painters working in France were almost all Flemish, and panel paintings as well as illuminated manuscripts, Psalters, and illustrated chronicles became increasingly numerous. In Burgundy Philip the Bold became a patron of Flemish artists living in France, especially Jan de Hasset and Jan de Baumetz, while Jan Malouel and Henri Bellechose painted their early works at the court of Philip the Good. At the end of the fourteenth century another Fleming, Melchior Broederlam of Ypres, painted four scenes from the life of the Virgin for the Abbey of Champmol, where Philip and later John the Fearless were buried. These scenes formed part of a triptych carved by Jacques de Baerze, and are preserved in the Museum of Dijon. Broederlam, the greatest Flemish painter before the van Eycks, was deeply interested in spatial problems, and in these scenes he arranged his elegant figures among imaginary buildings, distantly Italian in style. His landscapes were intended to be naturalistic, but in reality were still visionary, although there are naturalistic details, such as the burden of the weary S. Joseph in the Flight into Egypt, and his clumsy peasant boots made of cloth. As in the works of Malouel and Bellechose, there are extremely successful details resulting from delicate observation. But the pale colouring and the too frequent use of gold prevent a really naturalistic effect, which is not to be found until a later period.

Broederlam's work brings us to the fifteenth century, during which in the works of the Master of Flemalle, Nicholas Froment, and Jean Fouquet, a happy fusion of Italian and northern art was soon to take place. So as the fourteenth century drew to its close we already see foreshadowed the great period of Flemish art.

Our discussion of French art ended with the work of miniaturists and Flemish painters immediately before the somewhat unexpected advent of Hubert and Jan van Eyck. The similarity between French and Flemish styles has already been seen in the work of Melchior Broederlam, André Beauneveu, and Jacquemart de Hesdin. In Paris there was a vast output of illuminated manuscripts, codices, Psalters, and Flemish Bibles. Both the King of France and the Flemish nobles, notably the Dukes of Burgundy, were patrons of art and letters, and towards the end of the century, the luxurious, almost Baroque, art of Burgundy brought new blood to Paris, where a mingling of artistic trends from the Netherlands, Avignon, Lombardy and Burgundy made it the chief centre for the development of the future international Gothic style. The same artists, who were mainly Flemish, travelled between France and Belgium, strengthening the links between the two countries, and some of them left France to enlarge their circle of activity. Among these was Jean Coën, who worked on the construction of the great cathedral of Milan in the early years of the fifteenth century. Between Flanders and Holland the community of interest was even more marked. They were not as yet two separate countries, and their art and culture formed a single unit. Flemish painting, which did not become established as a separate school until the fifteenth century, should perhaps be regarded as an appendix of French art. As in France, so in the Netherlands, practically nothing has been preserved of fourteenth-century painting.

It is known that Flemish painters in the fourteenth century produced vast murals, and made timid attempts at panel painting, but very little remains of the frescoes which covered the walls of their churches, rooms and monasteries. The damp climate and salt air of the region have been responsible for a good deal of damage, but even more, especially in Holland, is due to the iconoclastic fury of the sixteenth-century Calvinists. The few works which have survived reveal a primitive simplicity. They often show timid leanings towards naturalism, although at the same time they were remarkably faithful to contemporary French sculpture. This is seen in the angels of the chapel of the Holy Sacrament in the College of SS. Peter and Guidon at Anderlecht, and above all in the considerable group of frescoes at Ghent, among which the most beautiful are those in the Abbey of Biloke, representing the Last Supper, the Virgin, SS. John the Baptist and Christopher probably all dating from the first half

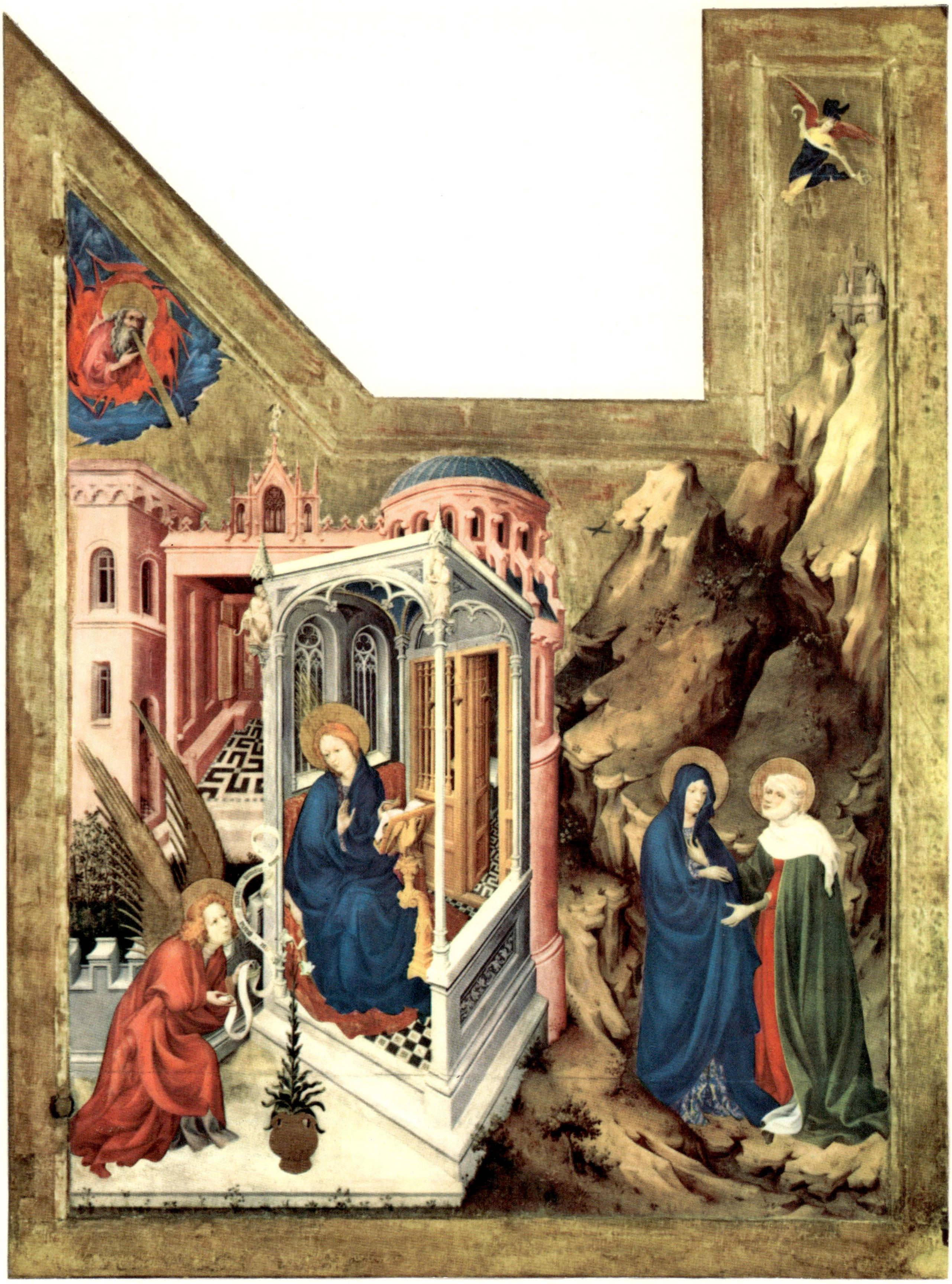

Melchior Broederlam: The Annunciation and the Visitation. Dijon Museum

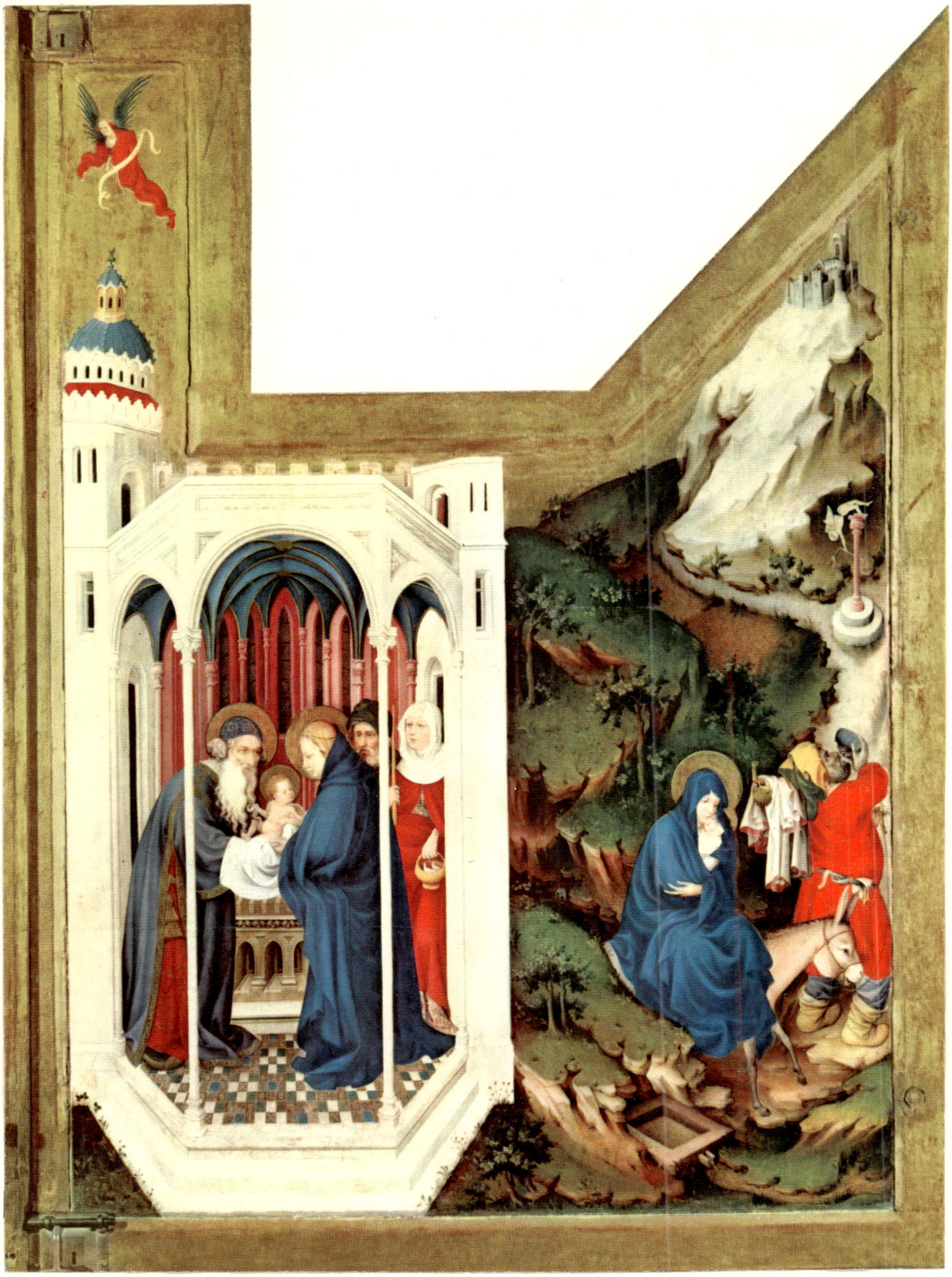

Melchior Broederlam: Presentation at the Temple and the Flight into Egypt.

Dijon Museum

of the fourteenth century. In the series of portraits of the Counts of Flanders in the Church of Notre Dame de Courtrai an unknown Flemish artist may have tried to paint an imposing procession, but from the few fragments which remain the result appears to have been simply a series of frontal figures, carried out in monotonous linear patterns, and devoid of any expression. It is only in their colouring that these northern artists give some indication of the superb colourists who were soon to follow them, such as the van Eyck brothers, and after them Roger van der Weyden and Hugo van der Goes.

The same awkwardness and timidity can be seen in their few surviving panel paintings, such as that from the church of S. Odile, with the four dead governors of Montfort being presented to the Virgin by S. George, which an unknown painter, possibly Dutch, painted towards the end of the fourteenth century. In this work there is something of a new note in the costume of the frail-looking saint, but on the whole the design, in its repetition of the four kneeling figures, enclosed as it were between the two living brackets formed by the enthroned Virgin and the standing figure of S. George, is hard and monotonous.

There is some indication of a new, more lively and polished style in later works, which, although they lack perspective, belong to the international Gothic style now becoming more firmly established in France. Illumination remained the principal art form. Throughout the thirteenth century this medium had been the prerogative of the monasteries of S. Lawrence at Liège and S. Remarcle at Stavelot, where an accomplished style, based on French and English influences, had been developed. But from the beginning of the fourteenth century French influence predominated and Flemish illumination becomes indistinguishable from French. In a Flemish Bible copied by Jacques de Maerlant in 1332, an artist named Michel van der Borch painted a series of miniatures in which French influence is very strong, both in the elegance of the outline and in the clear colouring; it differs from contemporary French miniatures however in its dramatic expressiveness. Later on Jacquemart de Hesdin, a Fleming by birth, became the most faithful follower, although many years later, of the French artist Jean Pucelle.

From now on the chief interest of miniaturists in the Netherlands was in the creation of external beauty.

And so our rapid survey of fourteenth-century art in the Netherlands closes, as it opened, with emphasis on the close connection with French art and illumination, and we end just before the glorious advent of the two Limbourg brothers, who were followed by the supreme manifestation of Flemish genius in the art of the van Eycks.

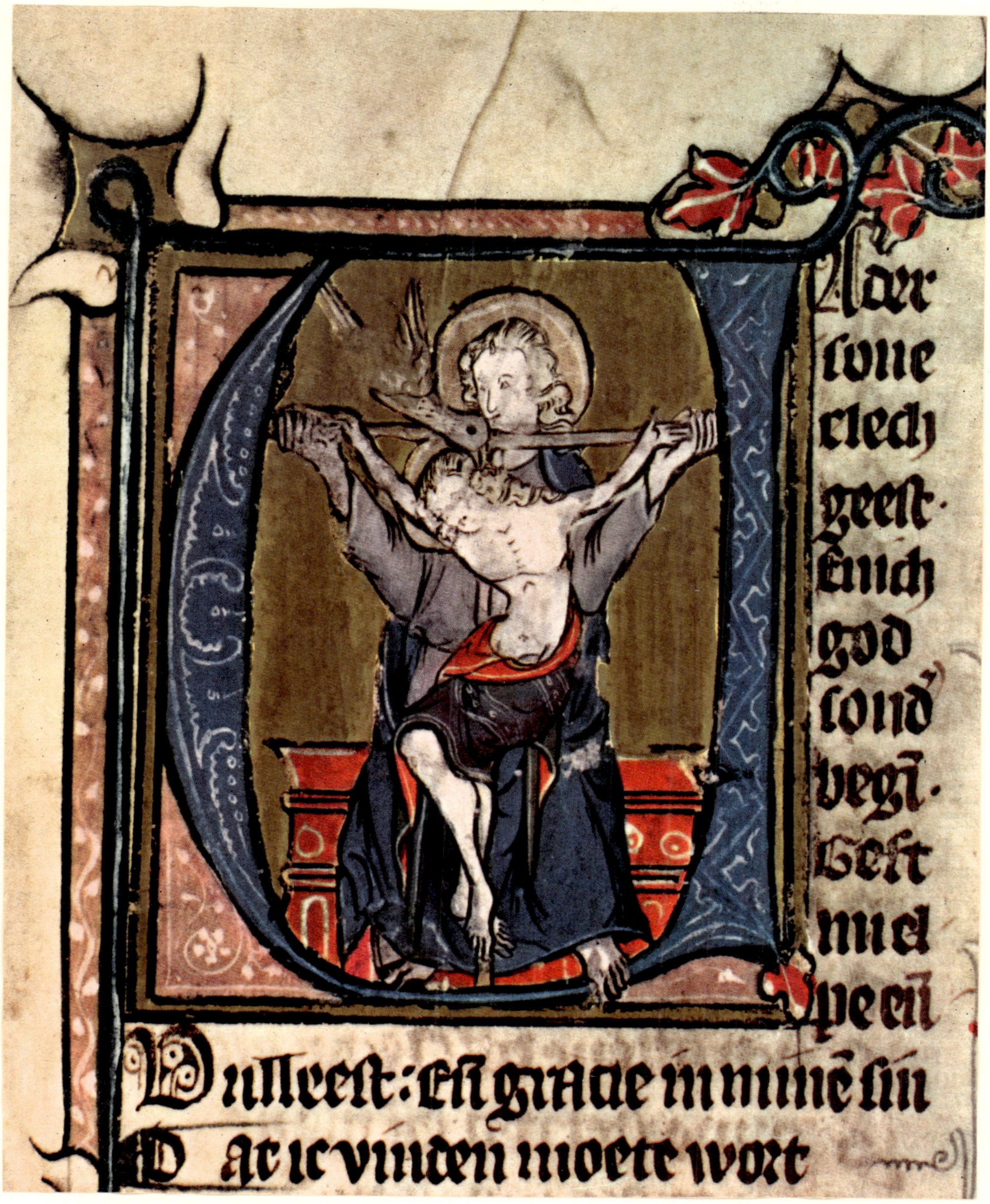

Michel Van Der Borch: Bible in Flemish. Royal Library, The Hague

Painting in the countries of western Europe seems to have endured a common fate, for in England as elsewhere very few works have survived from the fourteenth century, and most of them are fragmentary and by unknown artists. Probably the dispersal of the artistic heritage of fourteenth-century England is due, as it is in Holland, to the Reformation and the sequestration of religious benefices, followed by the iconoclastic destructiveness of the seventeenth-cenury Puritans. Since the production of pictures at this period was almost entirely limited to the churches, the religious communities and commissions by private citizens, both noble and bourgeois, this destruction was extremely serious.

On the other hand French Gothic architecture was rapidly adopted in England, and the churches of Salisbury, Canterbury and Westminster arose at the same time as the great French cathedrals. The enormously high arches of the French style were modified by a horizontal development, but the architects used the same elaborate ribbed vaulting, carvings, mouldings and friezes which, combined with the vast windows rhythmically arranged, resulted in a lack of large areas for mural painting. It is known that from the end of the twelfth century, painting was widely practised in England, especially in the Romanesque churches such as Peterborough. Unknown painters composed cycles of frescoes representing a variety of subjects such as the mystic Lamb, SS. Peter and Paul, King Edward the Martyr, and Edward the Confessor. Examples of this period may be seen at Kempley and at Patcham in Sussex.

With the accession to the throne of Henry III in 1216 it is known that artistic activity in England greatly increased, and the names of some of the painters of the day, together with information about the great frescoes in the Palace and the Abbey of Westminster, have survived. This activity continued in the reign of Henry's successor, Edward I (1272-1307), and during the reign of his son Edward II. In the reign of Edward III (1327-77) painting once more took on an official tone, when Thomas, son of Master Walter, was commissioned by the King to restore and paint the chapel of the Palace of Westminster. It is known from documents that John Athelard was commissioned to carry out further frescoes at the same time, while in 1363 William of Walsingham recruited workmen to help him in the great task of decorating the chapel of S. Stephen with frescoes. But of these paintings nothing now remains except the records and copies made in 1800 when the originals were discovered behind some panelling. They were then covered up again and were finally destroyed in the fire of 1834.

So far as can be judged from the somewhat inferior reproductions, the frescoes, which were done about 1356, must have presented a wonderful display of royal costumes, and were probably executed in a polished French style, but with definite independent characteristics. The description of the rich robe of the Queen " blue with golden stars, trimmed with ermine ", indicates that the colouring was very fine. All that remain are a few poor fragments with scenes of Job and Tobias, which another unknown artist produced in the same period for the same chapel. They had delicate designs and colouring which were once pleasing and even in their present state reveal a pleasant personality, and gift of observation, implying considerable maturity of style among English painters in the fourteenth century.

From the end of the thirteenth century there is a noticeable change in illumination which was losing its Romanesque strength, and moving towards an elegance which indicated the imminence of the Gothic age. Colours became paler, and the background decoration became freer, although traces of the far-off Byzantine style still lingered on. Probably the influence of French illumination had already reached England, and the difference between the two schools diminished, until in the early years of the fourteenth century they became indistinguishable. An example is the Psalter of Queen Mary which has a great many miniatures by unknown artists (thought by some critics to have been Frenchmen working in England) of small scenes with delicate designs, and light touches of green, brown or violet, and lively figures which move with an inimitable grace and harmony. This simplicity was later replaced by greater pomp. The brilliant golden background was extended throughout the whole composition, and the warm, deep colours stood out in contrasts which were at times violent. The subjects portrayed increased in number and variety, and included hunting scenes, tournaments, caricatures, and various games. The same expressive ability, and equal facility in design, is to be found in miniatures in a French Apocalypse. This was the favourite English subject for illustration at the time, and this example like the Psalter of Queen Mary, is preserved in the British Museum.

In England during the fourteenth century psalters were the most characteristic products of the scriptoria. There was a flourishing school in East Anglia, whose style is less fluid and less elegant than that of the Psalter of Queen Mary, but is distinguished by great decorative richness in the surroundings of the principal scenes. Flowers, leaves, birds and grotesque figures are sometimes displayed all over the page rather in the French manner. The most beautiful example is possibly the Psalter of Robert of Ormesby, in which the decorations were begun in a stylised manner unknown in contemporary French work, and gradually transformed into a naturalistic style, especially in the case of flowers and fruit. Shortly afterwards, between 1347 and 1364, the Psalter of Sir William was produced, and in this there are pleasing elements of landscape, carefully observed and executed with a great freshness of expression, which heralds the imminent naturalistic style. This style continued with very little variation until the reign of Richard II, although few examples of it have survived. Between 1350 and 1370 there is a gap in the production of English illuminated manuscripts. When Richard came to the throne in 1377 a new style began to appear, possibly inspired by continental influences. In the great Bible and the mutilated Missal executed for the King, and in the Missal which Nicolas Lytlington illuminated for the Abbey of Westminster between 1383-84, there is a tremendous advance in naturalism, with sensitive, polished modelling, after the new style which was now to be found all over Europe. The best English example is the magnificent Book of Hours composed for John, Duke of Bedford. It may be that the artists who painted some of these miniatures were French, but there is no doubt that the English soon became apt pupils and the two styles blended harmoniously: the signature of an English Dominican, John Siferwas, is contained in the Sherborne Missal of the Duke of Northumberland. Painting was developing along similar lines, and the first panel paintings now began to make their appearance in a style that was polished and elegant. A rather languid Madonna surrounded by a band of angels is attributed by some critics to an unknown French artist, thus confirming once again the similarity of style between the two countries. A portrait of Richard II, which has, however, been considerably restored, in the presbytery of Westminster Abbey, reveals a somewhat rigid sweetness. His crown, his elegant costume and the delicate, ornate throne recall the noble knights and saints who populated the pictures of northern Europe and Italy at the end of the fourteenth and beginning of the fifteenth centuries.

It may be said that the autonomous development of German art began with the establishment of a national state immediately after the disruption of the Carolingian empire. But the continuous disturbances and upheavals which went on during the formation of the German empire have prevented the survival of many works of art from the early periods, and this is true even of Romanesque art which kept the same primitive characteristics over a long period, even in the regions which bordered on France. From the beginning of the thirteenth century onwards, two streams can be distinguished in German painting; the one a search for monumental dignity stemming from the Byzantine tradition, and the other a search for greater expressiveness through swirling, almost baroque, drapery. In any case it must not be forgotten that the many races united in the Holy Roman Empire gave to each region of Germany its own individual character. They were also affected by external influences: the eastern Byzantine style, and the styles of western and southern Europe. After the middle of the thirteenth century the influence of French

Gothic became more insistent. To begin with, only some architectural details were affected, but with the establishment of the Universal Church, German art underwent a complete transformation and the influence of western Gothic was brought to bear on art of all kinds. The supremacy of this new and more mature style lasted throughout the whole of the fourteenth century, until in the early years of the fifteenth century long-submerged local traditions began to revive, and a new style evolved: German Gothic.

Painting began in Germany in the fourteenth century, during that period when European art is characterised by the interest in naturalism which began in Italy with Giotto. It is difficult to establish the precise characteristics of German art at the period of initial contact with France. Figures, especially in the West and the North, were harsher and more robust than in France, while gestures and expressions were more direct. Outlines were more severe, more nervous and awkward, and the general effect was sharp and incisive, with disconnected whirls and zig-zags. The colouring was usually crude, sometimes modified by shadows which represented a timid attempt at chiaroscuro, although this was an unfamiliar idea to these anonymous German artists. Germany differed from France in that neither mural painting nor stained glass ever became very important there. Panel painting developed considerably, and many examples have survived, some of which are very important. The preachers who travelled all over Germany such as Eckhart, Tauler and Suso, contributed burning enthusiasm, a factor of special importance in the Rhineland. The first important school of German painting grew up at Cologne, near the French border and Cologne cathedral was begun at the end of the thirteenth century, modelled on the great French cathedrals. The least German of all Gothic buildings in Germany, it contains a cycle of fourteenth-century pictures which, in view of the scarcity of works of this kind, are important as evidence of the local style. A cycle of scenes from the lives of SS. Peter and Sylvester and the legend of the Three Kings, were painted on the wall above the stalls of the magnificent choir, which was the oldest part of the building, consecrated in 1322. These paintings are by an unknown German artist, and probably date from the first twenty years of the fourteenth century. Presumably these artists were fairly well known, since the building of the cathedral was of great importance to the citizens of Cologne, and only the best architects, sculptors and painters were entrusted with commissions. At any rate, despite obvious French influences, especially in the elegant architectural borders, the origins of the German style are to be seen in this work particularly in the compact, reddish figures and in the rather dark, heavy colouring.

These pictures, together with an outstanding series of panel paintings, make Cologne one of the most important artistic centres in Germany and it may be regarded as the capital of the school of north-west Germany. In the work of the Cologne artists we may see both French influence and a religious mysticism decidedly Gothic in its effects; but there are also signs of the future German expressionistic style, especially in a series of polyptychs preserved in the Wallraf-Richartz museum.

Judging from the large number of works which have survived, as for instance the beautiful Crucifixion in the Von Hirsch collection, which probably dates from about 1350, the school of Frankfurt probably had the same characteristics. In addition to the usual French influence revealed in the calligraphic linear patterns, there is a trace of Pietro, and even more of Ambrogio Lorenzetti, in the foreshortening and breadth of form. Italian influence was also felt in other regions, for example in Thuringia in central Germany, where a number of panel paintings contain rudimentary attempts at perspective, obviously derived from early fourteenth-century Italian art. The delicate, elongated architecture resembles the "Master of S. Cecilia", and some poses and expressions are reminiscent of Lorenzetti's Assisi period. There is also a strong hint of the frescoes of the Sienese artist Barna, in the Collegiata of S. Gimignano. Probably these unknown artists were drawn to Italy by the fame of Italian art.

Meanwhile, in Hesse in western Germany, and in the North, new links were being forged with French art in a polished stylisation that can be seen in the altar of Hofgeismar, and in the lovely miniatures of the " Troubadours ", who were the German literary movement equivalent to the Italian *Dolce Stil Nuovo*. There are examples in the very fine Codex of Heidelberg.

In the South, and especially in Austria and Bohemia, relations with Italy are more obvious. Contacts between Austria and Italy were facilitated by the valleys of the Adige and the Isarco and have already been referred to in connection with painting in Bolzano. Italian influence reached Bohemia chiefly through the patronage of the kings and nobility. Gothic architecture came to Austria in the thirteenth century, as for example the magnificent choir of the Abbey of Heiligenkreuz, and the Church of the Augustines in Vienna, and was finally established with the construction of S. Stephen's about 1304. At this point it is possible to make a comparison between the construction of the Viennese cathedral and that of Milan. For many years both constituted the focal point of city and artistic life, and both resulted in an influx of artists and ideas from abroad. In Vienna and Milan alike craftsmen from Germany, France, Hungary, Flanders and Bohemia worked together, and it is probable that Italians travelled to Vienna through the Alpine valleys, taking with them a detailed knowledge of Italian art. This knowledge had indeed already penetrated into Austria during the preceding centuries, by way of illumination; Salzburg had an important scriptorium in which Italian influence was very strong. No doubt Austrian painters travelled into Italy by the same routes and studied Italian art from Giotto to Tommaso da Modena.

In fact the Master of the altarpiece of Klosterneuburg produced a Gothic version of Giotto's work at Padua, in four scenes representing the Life of Christ and the Virgin which he painted in 1329, on the back of the altarpiece in enamels done by Nicholas de Verdun in 1189. Both perspective and decoration are inspired by Italian art and each scene can be traced back to Italian examples, through Giotto and Duccio, and possibly even to Byzantium by way of Siena. The Austrian and Bohemian schools became closely identified and moved towards international Gothic, especially with the work of Johann Sachs, who painted aristocratic, accomplished altarpieces with softly modelled, graceful figures.

It was during this period that the artistic importance of Bohemia was established. In the middle of the thirteenth century the Kings of Bohemia promoted the cultural development of the country, built many castles, and formed important collections of illuminated manuscripts.

In 1310 the Luxembourg dynasty ascended the throne in the person of John I, supplanting the Premyslide dynasty founded by Boleslav I in the last years of the tenth century. At the same time John IV became Bishop of Prague. These two events marked the beginning of definite contacts between Bohemia and the western world, particularly France. The new bishop came from the papal court at Avignon, where he had spent some time, and on returning to his own country he founded churches and monasteries, and built bishops' palaces, all modelled on the French style. In 1333 he summoned from France celebrated architects such as William of Avignon to complete his work. Charles of Luxembourg, at that period the heir to the throne, had been educated at the French court and had frequently visited Italy. When he succeeded in 1346 he introduced the polished, western ideas which had become part of his life.

Following the example of the enlightened bishop he summoned the French architect, Mattieu d'Arras, to his capital to build the cathedral of S. Vitus and lay the foundations of the great new city of Prague. The court art of Bohemia followed the example of architecture, and adopted the Gothic style, while retaining a simple, naturalistic feeling which resulted in an individual pleasing local style.

Yet the Byzantine substratum in Bohemian art is very obvious. It continued even later than in Italy, and contributed a gentle, luminous quality to the style. About the middle of the fourteenth century the Gothic style was widely developed through French, German and Italian influences. This can be seen in the polyptych of Hohenfurt, the work of a distinguished unknown artist, who was obviously also acquainted with both Giotto and the Sienese artists. Florentine forms and iconography derived from Nardo and Jacopo di Cione continue to appear in the various Madonnas painted during this period, as for example that of Wyscherad; while the graceful figures of Bernardo Daddi inspired other works such as the Morgan diptych with the Adoration of the Magi and the Death of the Virgin.

As Italian influence became stronger, it is clear that Italian artists and pictures must have been present at the court of Prague. In the reign of Charles IV Bohemia enjoyed a period of peace and consolidation and played an important part in the politics of central Europe. The rebirth of culture in central Europe owed a special debt to John of Neumarkt, the humanist bishop and chancellor, who was instrumental in spreading Italian Humanism. Probably western painters, especially Italians, were summoned by the king, but there is no record of their names, nor have many works survived to give evidence of their presence in the Bohemian capital and the royal castles. An exception is, of course, the castle of Karlstein, built by Charles IV, to which Tommaso da Modena sent paintings, including two signed triptychs now in the State Museum in Prague. Even if Tommaso himself never went to the court of Bohemia, as he is traditionally believed to have done, his work introduced a natural and lively style. This was interpreted in a special way by an unknown artist in the monastery of Vyssi Brod, who painted a cycle of frescoes which represent a departure from the primitive style of placing motionless figures against a gold background. In this Italianate work the figures move with easy gestures and have lively expressions. It is perhaps the first example of the style which the Germans have named the " weicher Stil ", the gentle style, and which, with soft folds in the drapery, an attempt at naturalism, and a trace of both northern Italian and French influence in the figures and expressions, resembles international Gothic.

The culmination of this style is represented by the Master of Wittingau's scenes from the Passion, now in the Gallery of Prague, which date from about 1380. They are a development of the style of the Master of Hohenfurt, imbued with a gentle Italianate expression in the soft, flexible figures, and with backgrounds which gradually begin to include landscapes, even if this is limited to a bush, as in the *Noli Me Tangere,* or a rock in the Resurrection. Theodoric of Prague painted a cycle of frescoes in the castle of Karlstein at the end of the century in this style, which may be regarded as international. In a remarkable way he combined western refinements with north Italian naturalism, adding an ingenuous primitive note, a feat which was due both to his profound conception of art and to his great technical ability. In some of the paintings representing bishops in meditation or prayer there is a strong resemblance to Tommaso da Modena, in that the figures of the prelates are placed between desks and bookcases, with a simple attempt at foreshortening, recalling the Dominican saints which Tommaso painted at Treviso.

And finally, the cycle of the Passion by the Master of Trébon, which dates from about 1380, is a striking example of naturalism, which had now supplanted local styles

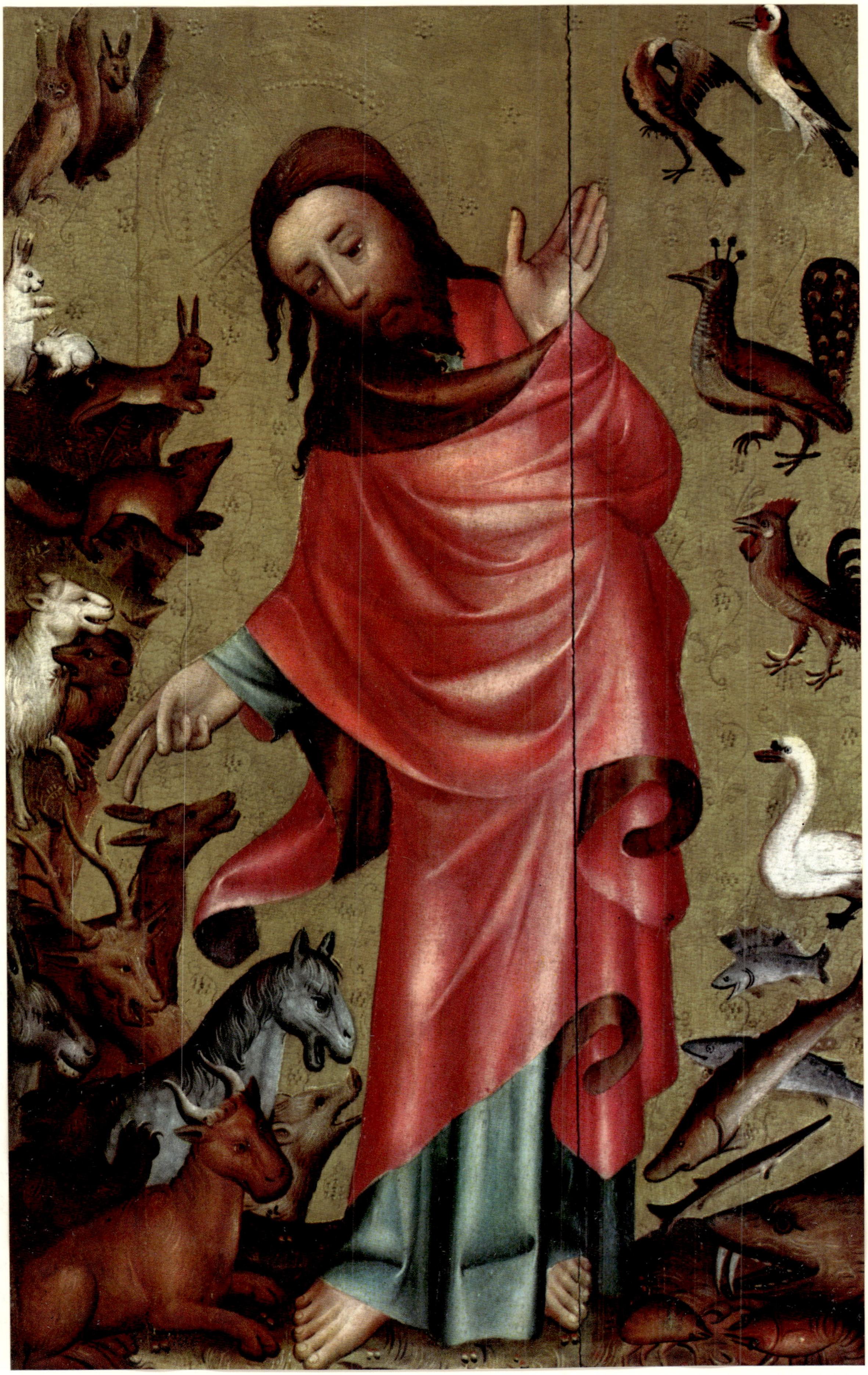

Master Bertram: Altarpiece from the Cathedral of S. Peter. Kunsthalle, Hamburg

and brought Bohemian art into the international Gothic movement. The polished tradition of Cologne continued, though tending to fall into decadence, while in the north the naturalistic trend produced the harsh, rough works of Master Bertram, for example the altarpiece in the church of S. Peter, now in the Kunsthalle of Hamburg, painted probably about 1380. This work seems to be connected, through the famous Evangeliary of Troppau, with Bohemian illumination, although it has the clear colouring of the north-west, as opposed to the softer colouring of the Austro-Bohemian school.

These are the final expressions of the German Gothic style in some of its many aspects, which in the continued repetition of the Deposition, the Flagellation and the Madonna, had a direct impact on the minds of the Faithful. It was this concentration of aim which, as in Italy from Giotto onwards, determined the individual nature of works of art. This development is the dominating feature of German painting in the transitional period between French Gothic and the Italian Renaissance.

The situation in eastern Europe and the Balkans was quite different. Throughout the fourteenth century Russia remained completely cut off from western Europe and was wholly under the influence of Byzantine art. It was only at the end of the century that a number of local schools grew up, which however had no connection with the international Gothic movement. Some remarkable figures emerged, such as Dionisus and Andrew Rubliev, the leaders of the new Russian school. This school represents the ultimate development and local variant of the style known as the " Paleologue Renaissance ", which took place in the Byzantine Empire during the fourteenth century, and whose causes are still obscure. Western influence did undoubtedly penetrate eastern regions at the end of the thirteenth century, and attempts have been made to trace the course of events. This has proved extremely difficult, but it seems that the strongest influence was French. At any rate this infiltration of Gothic style is connected with the last Crusades, with sea trade, which was increasing in volume between the East and the West, and with the many marriages on the one hand between western princes and Paleologue princesses and on the other between daughters of the great Italian families like the Malatesta, the Savoy, and the Monferrato, with eastern kings and nobles.

Balkan art in the fourteenth century remains unique as compared with the style which had been adopted generally throughout western Europe, although some change in style is noticeable from about 1320, the date of the earliest wall-paintings at Gracanica in Yugoslavia. From the time of the Macedonian and Comnenian emperors all painting, even miniatures, had been solemn and imposing, with a monumental style and composition similar to the grandeur of an apsidal mosaic or fresco. In the Paleologue era however, and particularly during the fourteenth century, both frescoes and icons, which were the most important productions of the time, were more like enlargements of illuminated miniatures. They possess a narrative feeling and precise detail, and they were carried out with the same technique as miniatures. The decline of mosaic art dates from this time, and was replaced by the less costly technique of fresco.

In the fourteenth century, Kahrieh Djami, in the monastery of Chora at Constantinople, is the only example of rich mosaics with a gold background, which is broken by slight traces of architecture showing some attempt at perspective. These mosaics represent scenes from the lives of Christ and the Virgin taken from the Apocrypha. The elongated figures are arranged in expressive attitudes and move in a world which is realistic down to the smallest details — a world which is, indeed, almost humanistic. The colouring has the same delicate profusion of pinks, blues, greys and greens that is found in the classical examples at Ravenna and Salonika. The arrangement of decorative motifs reveals a new level of delicacy.

The same feeling is found in the frescoes of Aphentico and Peribleptos, the churches of Mistra in Greece built by the despotic princes of the Morea, along with the later one at Pantanassa, although they have a somewhat more archaic quality. So that this region, which was already rich in the traditions of ancient civilisation, remained the least affected by the new French and Italian influences. In the early years of the century frescoes were painted at Aphentico which in their delightful narrative quality, their magnificent colouring, their gracefully complex design and their perfect technique, recall the elegant polished style of the Kahrieh Djami. The same lively design, splendid colouring and profound thought is also found in the frescoes of the great cycles from the Gospels at Peribleptos. These works all resemble one another in their accomplished form and technique, and seem almost like the continuation of the same story in a series of illuminated pages. The models most commonly used by these talented eastern painters and mosaicists were manuscripts, evangeliaries, and theological treatises, with their brilliant miniatures. Like icons and portable paintings, these were still being produced in enormous quantities in the Balkans at the end of the fourteenth century.

The execution and development of painting in Spain was peculiar to itself, and it may be said that from the very beginning Spanish painting possessed qualities wholly different from those of any other European school. This may be due to the Moorish element in Spanish history, while Spain's geographical situation at the extreme end of the European continent was also of some importance. Western ideas, especially from France and Italy, reached Spain across the Pyrenees and by way of the Mediterranean, and these influences mingled to some extent with Mohammedan culture. Spain, therefore, was always subject to two wholly different influences, which often contrasted with each other and which had arrived in completely different ways. The older, Moorish influence had been imposed during long periods of political domination; the other, the western influence, had as it were seeped in, by means of miniatures and ivories and probably later through the visits of foreign artists to Spain, and Spanish, especially Catalan artists visiting France, possibly Avignon, after 1300. Another even easier means of penetration were the pilgrimages to the tomb of S. James of Compostella, which drew pilgrims to Spain from all over Europe. Some of these pilgrims were undoubtedly Italians steeped in the religious fervour which swept over Italy in the thirteenth century.

From this rich variety of cultures the Spaniards made a happy selection of the finest elements. From the Moslems they adopted the rich decoration, the great variety of ornaments, the ingenuous and skilful fantasy, the display of vivid contrasting colours, which stood out against backgrounds as dark as an eastern night. From the West they took an impressionist manner, elegant line drawing, and an intense interest in gestures and faces. Yet from the earliest periods Spanish art always kept its innate characteristics, which were strengthened by the simplicity of the general effect, by the unaffected poses and surroundings, and above all by a severe asceticism. This separated it from Flemish realism and from the lively and even pagan feeling of the Italian Renaissance, especially at the end of the fourteenth and beginning of the fifteenth centuries. These qualities are seen from the time of the unknown artists at Tahull and Llussanes, with their simple, direct, wide-eyed figures, representing a simplified, ingenuous version of Byzantine hieratic art, which had probably reached Spain in a number of ways. The colouring was intense and brilliant, only to be equalled in later periods by the fifteenth-century Flemish colourists.

In Spain, as elsewhere, each region had its own style, brought into being by the temperament of the people and by the foreign influences which played on them. Those regions which managed to free themselves of Mohammedan influence at an early date sought, at times successfully, to align themselves with western civilisation and to share the same intellectual and artistic aspirations. They also at various times received something from France, Italy and the Netherlands, and these influences were variously used by the great Spanish artists.

Illumination, for example, strongly resembled the French school, but kept a more lively, earthy quality akin to the popular Mohammedan chronicles, and gave an effective, detailed picture of daily life.

Painting was also affected by the developments of independent kingdoms freed from Mohammedan rule, by the increasing power of the Church, especially of the great religious orders, and finally by the necessity of coming to terms with the new architectural forms. The cities became centres of commerce, of politics, and of craftsmen; the kingdoms became stronger and the courts more luxurious. Christianity triumphed over Mohammedanism, and built magnificent new churches where painters at last had a free hand. Later, when the Gothic style was adopted in Spain, altarpieces, polyptychs, the so-called " retablos ", very largely supplanted frescoes. This was a particular feature at the end of the thirteenth and the beginning of the fourteenth centuries, when Spain (now composed of Aragon and Castile) began to erect the vast Gothic cathedrals of Burgos, Valencia, and Palma di Majorca with ogives, triforia, pinnacles, towers and spires. Mural surfaces became more restricted as carving and stained glass became more important, although these media never achieved the eminence that they did in France. From the fourteenth century onwards artists became more individual, with definite, even aggressive and dominating, personalities, and Spanish painting developed without any particular connecting links, except those which joined one painter of genius to another.

Outside influences, even the influence of the great Italian artists, were for the Spaniards merely a point of departure for the development of their own original style. This dignified and highly distinguished art placed Spain in a special and independent position in the field of European culture as early as the fourteenth century.

Generally speaking the anonymous highly-skilled craftsman disappeared in Spain and Italy from the fourteenth century onwards, and the names of individual artists, who were often members of a Guild, begin to be mentioned.

At the very beginning of the fourteenth century André Sanchez of Segovia painted exquisite figures of saints in a simple narrative style in a chapel of the old cathedral of Salamanca. Schools of painting grew up in Catalonia and Valencia which were very influential in Spain and commanded attention in Europe. There was a tremendous output in these two regions, particularly Catalonia, and the work was carried on from father to son, so that dynasties of artists, such as the Emfos and the Crou, were founded.

The most important Catalan artist of the fourteenth century, however, is Ferrer Bassà, who suddenly appears with the magnificent wall-paintings in the monastery of Pedralbes. This work was brought to light in 1909 by M. Sampere y Miquel. It is known from the contract, which is still in existence, that the work was begun on Easter Day 1345, and finished on the 23rd November 1346, and it is the only known work of Ferrer Bassà, who was probably a contemporary of Simone Martini. He must have been a figure of importance, since he worked at the court of Pedro IV of Aragon, from whom he obtained many commissions and favours. In 1316 he painted some altarpieces for the chapel of Lerida; in 1324 he painted pictures for the two chapels at Sitges, and in 1332 and 1342 two altarpieces for Saragozza, one for the chapel of the castle of Perpignan and another for the royal palace in Barcelona. These works, which would have enabled us to follow the development of his style, have all perished. There were probably a large number of French works of art in Spain at this period, and the first examples of Italian art may have arrived by way of the papal court at Avignon. The wall-paintings at Pedralbes may be regarded as a late work of Ferrer Bassà, probably in his final style. By then he had studied Italian art, especially that of Siena, and possibly that of Bologna and of the Po valley as well.

These wall-paintings were adapted to the narrow space of a small square room, and are painted with a little-known oil technique, which was highly effective, since the magnificent colours and the elegant shapes of his visionary figures have been preserved almost intact. They appear today in all their graceful freshness and immediacy, radiant with colours which are either transparent or so brilliant that they resemble miniatures.

On the three principal walls Bassà painted seven scenes from the life of the Virgin, from the Annunciation to her Triumph. Each one is a separate, self-contained picture and has a legendary, nostalgic feeling. For example, the rocky landscape of the Nativity has no real perspective or atmosphere, but is placed in a void in which a series of brilliantly lit angels are flying headlong, carrying the news to an astonished shepherd. The blonde Virgin is praying in a mystical rapture and neither she nor the sleeping figure of S. Joseph really belong to the scene at all. Only the ox and the ass are watching the Child, in the background of the silent cave. The story continues, and ends with the women at the Sepulchre, where a shining white angel points a peremptory finger, and the Virgin and the Magdalene are transfigured by their grief. The empty tomb is portrayed with a bold foreshortening which heralds the Renaissance. The sharp, pearl-coloured faces, with their nun's head-dresses, are staring at the face of the youthful messenger from Heaven, which has a faint suggestion of a smile. The features and the gestures are economical, precise, and measured, as for example in the clasp of a hand, or the decisive gesture of the pointing finger. This feeling of poetry and nostalgia disappears in the more realistic, living figures of the saints, including S. Clare and S. Francis, austere and dignified, lightened only by touches of bright colour in the brilliant green background, in the red of S. Clare's book and in the wound of S. Francis.

The complexity of these frescoes places Ferrer Bassà in the front rank of artists and lends great interest to the study of his personality. It is obvious that he was acquainted with Giotto and the Sienese school, probably in the work of Simone Martini, who was living at Avignon during this period. It may be that the papal court was again responsible for transmitting a knowledge of Italian art. A visit to Siena, Florence or some other town in Italy would explain many things — the Sienese style of his faces, the elegance of some of his drapery, the somewhat disjointed and legendary nature of his narrative, and the Giottesque directness of his style. Ferrer Bassà selected his details and gave them an original, impressionistic form, a happy synthesis of expression and content. Obviously influenced by Italian art, he used his knowledge in such a way that it is his own talent and feeling which predominate, and he created a masterpiece, probably the culmination of his earlier works, which have been lost.

After the death of the Master of Pedralbes, Ramon Destorens of Barcelona became court painter. Recently two panels from a large polyptych in the cathedral of Palma, both showing strong Sienese influence, have been attributed to him. Spanish and Italian influences both reached Majorca, while variations of Ferrer Bassà's style are to be found as far afield as Barcelona.

Exchanges with Avignon were now very frequent, and in the second half of the century Italian influence also reached Spain from Sardinia. The island was now under Spanish rule and was later to develop a Catalan style of painting. The works of Italian artists were often sent to Spain, for example the mellow, golden, hieratic, Madonnas of Barnaba da Modena.

The golden backgrounds and elegant figures of Sienese art also began to appear in Spanish polyptychs. This new trend merged with local styles, a combination which produced some of the finest examples of Spanish art in the following century. The brothers Jaime and Pedro Serra, who were active from the beginning of the fifteenth century, subordinated the mystic realism of Spanish art to Sienese grace and the lively simplicity of the Po valley. But their work became monotonous, uniform, and over-precise, emphasising trivialities. Even at its best their colouring lacked the vigour of Ferrer Bassà; compared with their precise and lively designs it seems over-delicate. Luis Borrassà, who belongs to the middle of the fifteenth century and the international Gothic style, kept a quality of realism and poetical ingenuousness. He evolved a gentle style of Catalan art, showing Italian influence, and also possessed the good nature that is found in all Spanish primitives. This quality conveys a deeply felt sympathy for human beings and for nature, and makes even the most austere religious subjects appear familiar and accessible.

Meanwhile, at the end of the century, which was the best period of Catalan art, another tendency can be found which was to have great importance in future developments of Spanish painting. This was the school of Valencia. Contacts with Italian art were particularly strong at the close of the century, owing to the presence in Valencia of a Florentine painter, Gherardo Starnina, who paid two visits to Spain and went as far as Toledo. He seems to have introduced new ideas of perspective and naturalism in the fifteenth-century Florentine manner. Filtering these new trends through the simple poetry of his art, he gives his pictures a remarkable appearance, in which Giottesque plasticity is combined with an imaginative quality stemming from international Gothic, and bringing to life a world which has an unexpected, robust vigour. Lorenzo Saragozza was strongly influenced by Starnina, as is shown in the four pictures of scenes from the life of S. Luke which he painted, almost certainly between 1370 and 1380. There was too an anonymous painter who composed a very fine polyptych for the charterhouse of Portacoeli during the last years of the fourteenth century. This work is now in the Don Carlos Museum in Valencia, and is attributed by some critics to Starnina himself. It possesses qualities which are entirely Florentine in their simplicity and strength, and are combined with linear elegance and Sienese colouring. We may take it that from now on exchanges between the two countries became very frequent and complicated. Germans as well as French and Italians now came to Spain.

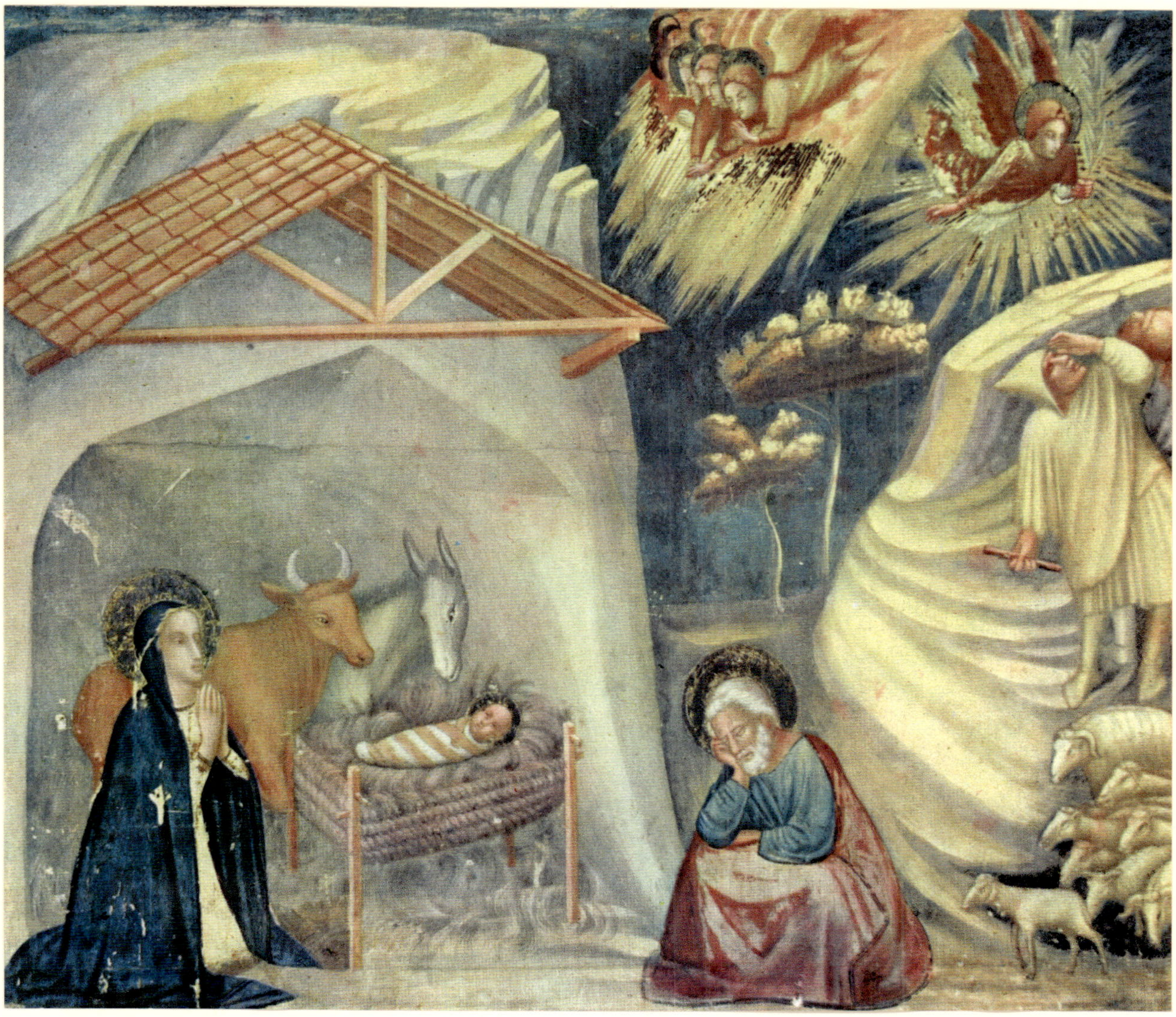

Ferrer Bassà: The Nativity. Monastery of Pedralbes

In Portugal painting did not begin until the fifteenth century, when artists were greatly influenced by the Flemish style, which, for political reasons, reached Spain in a pure form where it combined with Italian trends and, like all foreign styles, was transformed into the lively, individual, personal manner of the Spaniards. The south of Italy was now ruled by the Kings of Aragon, who had supplanted the Angevins, and Spanish painters travelled in Campania and Sicily, bringing their strong colouring, lively fantasies, and naturalistic and realistic qualities with them. At times Italian painting in these regions was frankly Catalan in its decorative fantasy.

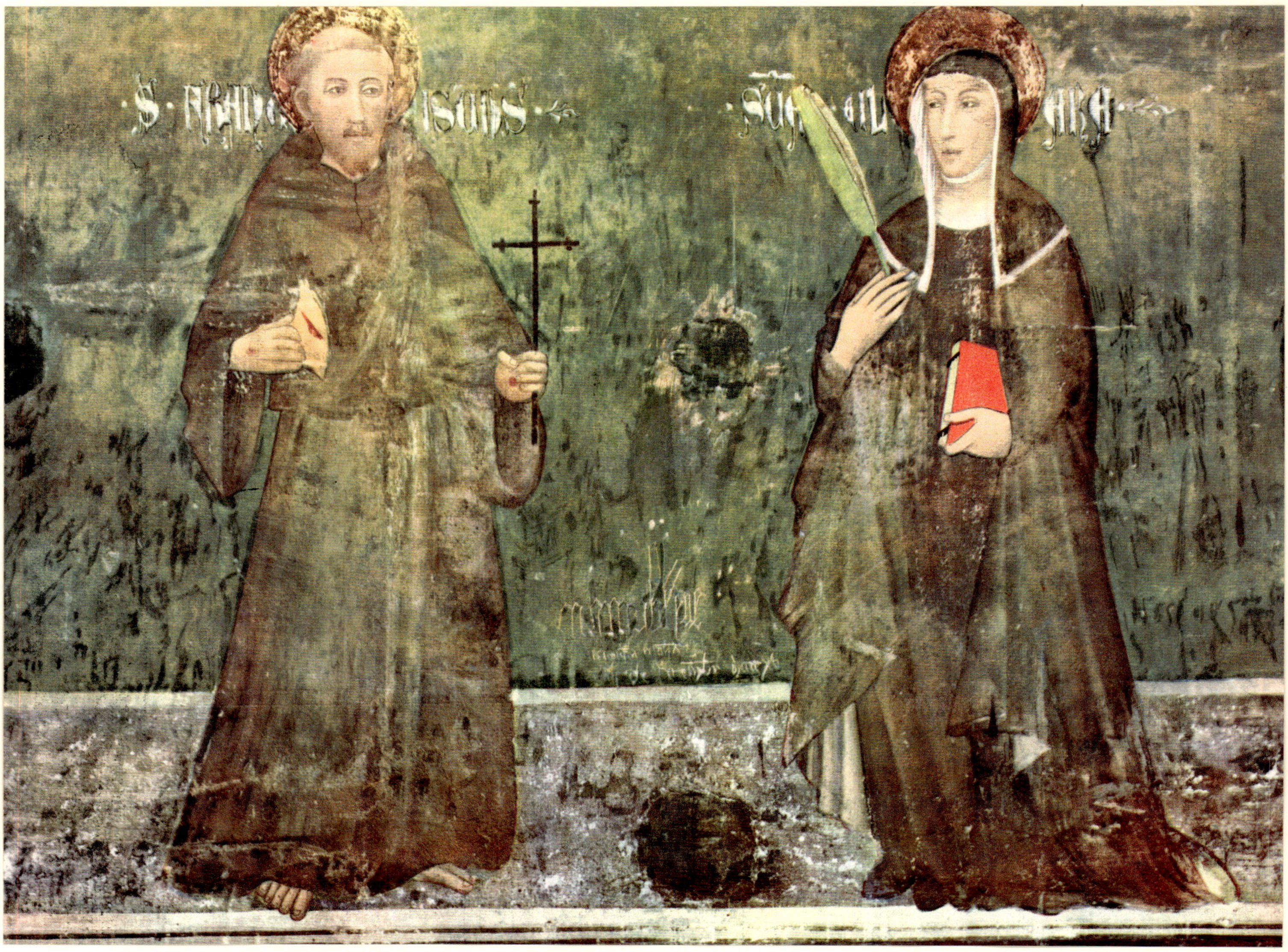

Ferrer Bassà: S. Clare and S. Francis. Monastery of Pedralbes

Italy was undoubtedly the dominating influence in European art in the fourteenth century, especially in the first half. This was due partly to her ancient civilisation, but even more to the wonderful flowering of genius which made her the cultural centre of Europe, and this is true not only of painting but of every artistic and literary form. No other country has great poets so closely bound up with modern thought through the centuries as were Dante, Petrarch and Boccaccio. No other artist, whether architect, sculptor or painter, has the same continuity in style and thought with later artistic developments as Arnolfo and Simone Martini, Nicola and Giovanni Pisano. But the outstanding figure is Giotto, whose rule was undisputed throughout the century, the symbol of its painting, with his volume, his strength and his space which he handed on in all their splendour to Masaccio, and Piero della Francesca in the next century, after an interval bridged by Maso and " Stefano ", Giotto's two most important followers. The new Gothic style, created in Paris, spread in greater or lesser degree all over Europe, with common characteristics consisting of rich and enamel-like colouring, light, delicate forms and an emphasis on detail which together inspired international Gothic. But in Italy, with a very few exceptions (admirable in themselves), painting set out in the fifteenth century to reconquer Giotto's strength. This became almost a classical tradition which supplanted Gothic mannerism, and was the chief foundation of the Italian Renaissance and the consequent development of the great European schools.

E. M.

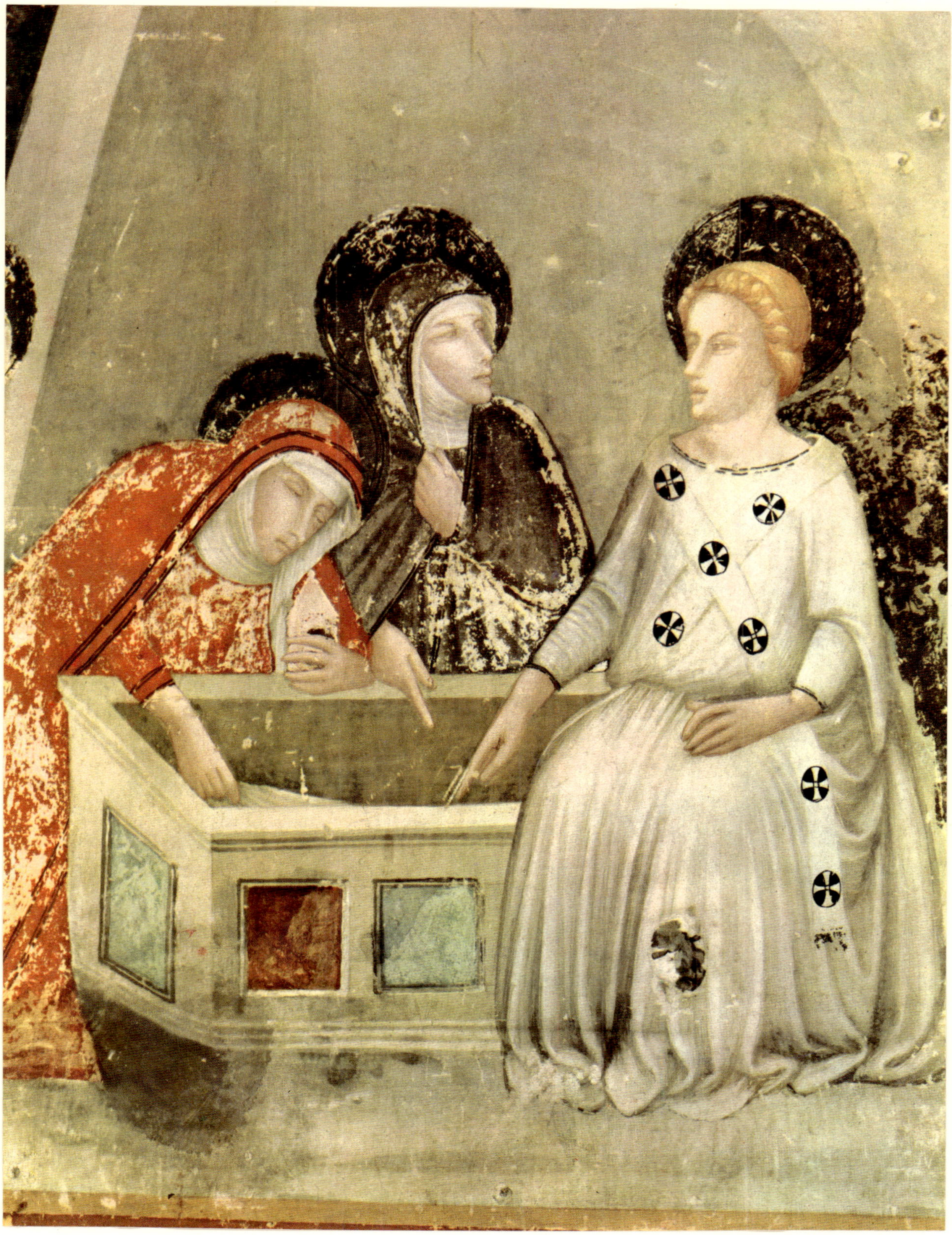

Ferrer Bassà: The Holy Women at the Sepulchre. Monastery of Pedralbes

INDEXES

ESSENTIAL BIBLIOGRAPHY

D. Passavant - *Die Christliche Kunst in Spanien*, Leipzig, 1953

J.A. Crowe, G.B. Cavalcaselle - *A New History of Painting in Italy*, vols. I - II, London, 1864 - 66

J.A. Crowe, G.B. Cavalcaselle - *Storia dell'antica pittura fiamminga*, Florence, 1899

Ch. Blanc - *Histoire des peintres* - Ecole Espagnole, Paris, 1886

A. Michel - *Histoire de l'art*, vols. I - II, III, 1, Paris, 1905-7

A. Venturi - *Storia dell'arte*, vol. V, Milan, 1907

G. Vitzhum - *Die Pariser Miniaturmalerei von der Zeit des hl. Ludwig bis zu Philipp von Valois und ihr Verhältnis zur Malerei in Nordwesteuropa*, Leipzig, 1907

L. Venturi - *Le origini della pittura veneziana*, Venice, 1907

L. Testi - *Storia della pittura veneziana*, Bergamo, 1909

Ch. Diehl - *Manuel d'art byzantine*, Paris, 1910 (2nd ed., vols. I - II, 1925-6)

O.M. Dalton - *Byzantine Art and Archaeology*, Oxford, 1911

P. Toesca - *La pittura e la miniatura in Lombardia*, Milan, 1912

F. Burger - *Im Handbuch der Kunstwissenschaft*, Berlin, 1913

A.L. Mayer - *Geschichte der spanischer Malerei*, Leipzig, 1913

C. Wulff - *Altchristliche und byzantinische Kunst*, Berlin, 1914

G. Millet - *Recherches sur l'iconographie de l'Evangile*, Paris, 1916

P. Clemen - *Die romanische Monumentalmalerei in dem Rheinlande*, Düsseldorf, 1916

E.H. Zimmermann - *Vorcarolingische Miniaturen*, Berlin, 1916-18

J. Strzygowski - *Die bildende Kunst des Ostens*, Leipzig, 1918

W. Neuss - *Die Katalanische Bibelillustration, um die Wenden des ersten Jahrtausends und die altspanische Buchmalerei*, Bonn Leipzig, 1922

R. van Marle - *The Development of the Italian Schools of Painting*, vols. I-IV, The Hague, 1923-5

O.M. Dalton - *East Christian Art*, Oxford, 1921

E. Sandberg-Vavala - *La pittura veronese del Trecento e del primo Quattrocento*, Verona, 1926

P. Toesca - *Storia dell'arte italiana*. Il Medioevo, vol. I, Turin, 1927

P. Muratov - *La pittura bizantina*, Milan, 1928

E. Male - *L'art religieux du XII siècle en France*, Paris, 1928

O. E. Saunders - *English Illumination*, Florence - Paris, 1928

E. Cecchi - *Trecentisti senesi*, Milan, 1928 (2nd ed., 1948)

R. Longhi - *Frammenti di Giusto di Padova*, in *Pinacoteca*, 1928

E. Sandberg-Vavala - *La Croce dipinta italiana*, Verona, 1929

E. Sandberg-Vavala - *Vitale delle Madonne*, in *Rivista d'Arte*, 1929-30

Ch. R. Post - *History of Spanish Painting*, Harvard, 1930

C.H. Weigelt - *Sienese Painting of the Trecento*, New York, 1930

J. Baum - *Malarei und Plastik des Mittelalters*, vol. II, *Deutschland, Frankreich, und Britannien, im Handbuch der Kunstwissenschaft*, Potsdam, 1930

L. Mercier - *Les Primitifs français. La peinture clunysienne à l'époque romane*, Paris, 1931

E. Male - *L'art religieux de la fin du Moyen-Age*, Paris, 1931

H. Glaser - *Peintres primitifs allemands du milieu du XIV siècle à la fin du XV*, Paris, 1931

A. Nicholson - *Cimabue*, Princeton, 1932

L. Coletti - *L'arte di Tommaso da Modena*, Bologna, 1933

G. Sinibaldi - *I Lorenzetti*, Siena, 1933

A. Duran y Sanpere - *La peinture catalane à la fin du Moyen-Age*, Paris, 1933

H. Stange - *Deutsche Malerei der Gotik*, Berlin, 1934

R. Longhi - *Momenti della pittura bolognese*, Bologna, 1935

M. Salmi - *L'Abbazia di Pomposa*, Roma, 1935

C. Brandi - *Catalogo della Mostra dei pittori riminesi*, Rimini, 1935

M. Trens - *Ferrer Bassà y las pinturas de Pedralbes*, Barcelona, 1936

G. Haseloff - *Die Psalterillustration im 13 Jahrhundert*, Kiel, 1938

G.L. Micheli - *L'enluminure du haut Moyen-Age et les influences irlandaises*, Brussels, 1939

L. Coletti - *I Primitivi, vols. I-III*, Novara, 1941-7

L. Coletti - *Contributi al problema Maso-Giottino*, in *Emporium*, 1942

C.R. Morey - *Early Christian Art*, Princeton, 1953

S. Bettini - *Giusto dei Menabuoi*, Padua, 1944

R. Longhi - *Viatico per cinque secoli di pittura veneziana*, Florence, 1946

O. Morisani - *La pittura del Trecento a Napoli*, Naples, 1947

G.P. Bognetti, G. Chierici - *A. De Capitani d'Arzago, Santa Maria di Castelseprio*, Milan, 1948

R. Longhi - *Giudizio sul Duecento*, in *Proporzioni*, II, 1948

V. Lazareff - *Storia della pittura bizantina* (in Russian), vols. I-II, Moscow, 1948

O. Demus - *The Mosaics of Norman Sicily*, London, 1949

R. Blum - *Jean Pucelle et la miniature du XIV siècle*, in *Scriptorium III*, 1949

E.B. Garrison - *Italian Romanesque Panel Paintings. An illustrated index*, Florence, 1949

W. Oakeshott - *The Sequence of English Medieval Art*, London, 1950

R. Longhi - *La pittura bolognese del Trecento*, in *Paragone*, 5, 1950

P. Toesca - *Il Trecento*, Turin, 1951

K. Weitzmann - *Greek Mythology in Byzantine Art*, Princeton, 1951

P. Deschamps, M. Thibout - *La peinture murale en France. Le haut Moyen-Age et l'époque romane*, Paris, 1951

C. Brandi - *Duccio*, Florence, 1951 (1st ed. 1941)

T.S.R. Boase - *English Romanesque Illumination*, Oxford (Bodleian), 1951

R. Longhi - *Stefano fiorentino*, in *Paragone*, 13, 1951

C. Volpe - *Ambrogio e Pietro Lorenzetti,* in *Paragone,* 13, 23, 1951
A. Boeckeler - *Deutsche Buchmalerei vorgotischer Zeit,* Königstein, 1952
J. Lassaigne - *La peinture espagnole,* Geneva, 1952
A. Grabar - *La peinture byzantine,* Geneva, 1953
T.S.R. Boase - *English Art 1100-1216,* Oxford, 1953
G. Galassi - *Roma o Bizanzio,* Rome, 1953
E.B. Garrison, *Studies in The History of Mediaeval Italian Painting,* Florence, 1953
M. Rickert - *Painting in Britain. The Middle Ages,* London, 1954
S. Bottari - *La pittura del Quattrocento in Sicilia,* Messina, 1954
G. Paccagnini - *Simone Martini,* Milan, 1955
E. Carli - *La pittura senese,* Milan, 1955
Catalogo della Mostra d'arte lombarda dai Visconti agli Sforza, Milan, 1958
E. Sindona - *Pietro Cavallini,* Milan, 1958 (note bibliography)
G. Rowley - *Ambrogio Lorenzetti,* Princeton, 1958
C. Brandi - *Pietro Lorenzetti,* Rome, 1958 (note bibliography)
G. Gnudi - *Giotto,* Milan, 1959 (note bibliography)

PLACE INDEX

INDEX OF ARTISTS

INDEX OF ILLUSTRATIONS

The Colour Plates are Photographs of the original works and have been supplied by: Photo Giraudon, Paris; Hans Hinz, Basle; Foto MAS, Barcelona; Laboratorio Fotografico, SCALA, Florence; Studio dell'Illustrazione di Federico Arborio Mella, Milan; Studio Editoriale Fotografico, Turin